One of a Kind

One of a Kind

*The Relationship between Old and
New Covenants as the Hermeneutical Key
for Christian Theology of Religions*

ADAM SPARKS

Foreword by Gavin D'Costa

⌒PICKWICK *Publications* · Eugene, Oregon

ONE OF A KIND
The Relationship between Old and New Covenants as the Hermeneutical Key for Christian Theology of Religions

Copyright © 2010 Adam Sparks. All rights reserved. Except for brief quotations in critical publications or reviews, no part of this book may be reproduced in any manner without prior written permission from the publisher. Write: Permissions, Wipf and Stock Publishers, 199 W. 8th Ave., Suite 3, Eugene, OR 97401.

Pickwick Publications
An Imprint of Wipf and Stock Publishers
199 W. 8th Ave., Suite 3
Eugene, OR 97401

www.wipfandstock.com

ISBN 13: 978-1-60608-345-1

Cataloging-in-Publication data:

Sparks, Adam.

One of a kind : the relationship between Old and New Testaments as the hermeneutical key for Christian theology of religions / Adam Sparks with a Foreword by Gavin D'Costa.

ISBN 13: 978-1-60608-345-1

xxvi + 310 p. ; 23 cm. —Includes bibliographical references and index.

1. Christianity and other religions. 2. Bible. N.T.—Relation to the Old Testament. I. D'Costa, Gavin. II. Title.

BT83.85 S61 2010

Manufactured in the U.S.A.

To my parents, Brian and Anne Sparks

CONTENTS

Foreword by Gavin D'Costa | ix
Preface | xiii
Acknowledgments | xv
Introduction | xvii
Abbreviations | xxv

Part I Israel in a Christian Theology of Religions

1 An Introduction to the Israel Analogy and Fulfilment Theology | 3
 - 1.1. Defining the "Theology of Religions" | 3
 - 1.2. Towards a Definition of Fulfilment Theology | 10
 - 1.3. Early Church Sources Used to Support Fulfilment Theology | 13

2 Recent and Contemporary Use of the Israel Analogy and Fulfilment Theology | 19
 - 2.1. Roman Catholic Use of the Israel Analogy and Fulfilment Theology | 20
 - 2.2. Mainline Protestant Use of the Israel Analogy and Fulfilment Theology | 51
 - 2.3. Evangelical Use of the Israel Analogy and Fulfilment Theology | 60
 - 2.4. Summary | 69

Part II Israel and the Church

3 Why Israel Matters for Christian Theology | 73

4 An Outline and Critique of Supersessionism (Replacement Theology) | 82
 - 4.1. The Jewish People Are Still in a Covenant Relationship with God | 85
 - 4.2. God's Purposes for Israel Will Be Fulfilled. Israel Still Serves a Purpose | 90

5 An Outline and Critique of the "New Majority Views" | 93
 - 5.1a. The Dual- or Two-Covenant Paradigm | 95
 - 5.1b. The Single-Covenant Paradigm | 98

- 5.2. The Gospel Is for the Jews | 101
- 5.3. There Is No Special Way of Salvation for Israel | 105
- 5.4. The Israel-Church Relationship and the Implications for a Christian Theology of Religions | 111
- 5.5. Summary | 115

Part III Critique of the Israel Analogy and Fulfilment Model

6 Salvation History 1: Continuity and Unity | 121
- 6.1. An Introduction to Salvation History | 121
- 6.2. Two Testaments—One Salvation History | 130
- 6.3. The Structure of Salvation History | 133
- 6.4. The Christological and Eschatological Orientation of Salvation History | 138
- 6.5. Summary | 140

7 Salvation History 2: Chronology and Crisis | 142
- 7.1. Christ the Midpoint of Salvation History | 142
- 7.2. The Impossibility of Being Pre-Messianic in Post-Messianic Times | 157
- 7.3. Summary | 176

8 Covenant Confusion | 177
- 8.1. Introduction | 177
- 8.2. An Introduction to Covenant Theology | 177
- 8.3. Covenant Confusion: A Reformed Covenantal Critique of the Israel Analogy and Fulfilment Model | 203
- 8.4. Summary | 221

9 A Biblical, Historical, and Theological Critique of the Fulfilment Model | 223
- 9.1. Biblical Arguments Outlined and Assessed | 224
- 9.2. The Early Church Fathers and Fulfilment Theology | 238
- 9.3. Biblical and Extra-Biblical Fulfilment | 257
- 9.4. Summary | 283

10 Conclusions and Recommendations | 285

Bibliography | 289

Index | 311

FOREWORD

I had the pleasure of working with Adam Sparks as his PhD supervisor. I also had the shock of finding myself having to rethink many of my inherited theological assumptions in the light of Sparks's own work. This is clearly what a supervisor should find, but it is rare and especially valuable in this case. Most significantly, I commend Sparks's book as a thoroughgoing critique of one of the main pillars of the increasingly popular position of "inclusivism" in the theology of religions. The debate in this area had revolved around three positions up until recent times. For the sake of argument, let me summarize these three positions and show why Sparks's critique and constructive alternative are so helpful.

Exclusivism holds that salvation comes through *Christ* alone (and for some, also through Christ's *Church*) and other religions are finally erroneous. Within this group there is a spectrum of valuations on other religions, ranging from entirely negative (other religions are from the devil) to carefully qualified positive appreciation, which sees other religions as *preparatio evangelica*, preparations for the gospel, at best. Inclusivism holds that while salvation comes through Christ (and for some, through his Church), classical inclusivists also hold that salvation may be found in imperfect but meaningful ways within other religions. Karl Rahner, the German Jesuit, developed this position with astute rigor, arguing that other religions might be understood on the analogy of Old Testament Israel, as positive means of grace, and thus of salvation, until such time as the non-Christian was confronted by the gospel historically and existentially. If the religion of Old Testament Israel was lawful before the coming of Christ, Rahner asked: might other religions be analogically 'lawful'? Further, if the non-Christian rejected Christianity, their religion could not be considered 'lawful' for them any longer, for they would have willfully turned their back on the fullness of truth to which their religion was, in its best form, a preparation.

Rahner's position gained great acceptance for it seemed to hold together a tension that was tearing the theological world apart. On the one hand, Christians must hold to the traditional claims found in the gospel and developed in the tradition (*sola Christus* or/and *extra ecclesiam nulla salus*), while at the same time, do justice to and show respect for the religions of the world. Rahner seemed to facilitate both, avoiding the seemingly closed minded 'exclusivist' and the overly-open minded 'pluralist' who seemed so intent on showing respect to others that they abandoned traditional claims.

Let me outline the pluralist position in this group to complete the picture before returning to Sparks. Pluralists hold that all religions, at their best, are paths to the divine. Exclusive claims by any religion display a parochialism that is unpardonable in contemporary society. Pluralists urge Christians to stand fast in their own tradition, but interpret exclusive claims as poetic or mythological and to thereby move into a new era of interreligious ecumenism.

Sparks creates sparks in showing how so many theologians, from very different Christian denominations, base their inclusivist approach on decidedly shaky and combustible foundations laid deep and apparently secure by Rahner. With unshakeable focus and rigour, Sparks dismantles the central argument provided by a wide range of inclusivists: if the religion of Old Testament Israel might have been a lawful religion, then analogically, so might other religions. He argues that the *sui generis* relation of Old Testament Israel to Christianity disallows any such analogy. Interestingly, Rahner actually acknowledged this *sui generis* relation, but then continued to build upon it. Sparks shows what is at stake. If one pushes the analogy, one flattens the shape of revelatory history with its specificity and key theme and practice of 'covenant'. If one respects the *sui generis* relation, one respects the shape of revelation and most importantly, the universal transformation of the entire cosmos wrought in Christ's atoning death and resurrection. Sparks works his way through all aspects of this powerful analogy, systematically calling it into question and thus providing an alternative narrative of the theology of religions that might be described as exclusivist, but uniquely exclusive and inclusive in relation to Old Testament Israel.

Inevitably Sparks has to address the debate about the role of Judaism/Israel in relation to Christianity by dealing with the inclusivist linking. In this respect, you get a double theological helping for your

Foreword

money. Not only does Sparks make an original and decisive contribution to the deconstruction of the inclusivist paradigm, Sparks also makes a decisive contribution to the debate in Jewish-Christian theology in chapters 5 and 8 of this book. Sparks throws much light on this profoundly complex area and develops a path within Reformed theology, from out of which he writes, to address the question of Judaism. One of the intellectual thrills of this book is seeing how Sparks is constantly faithful to his roots and open to all sorts of possibilities before judiciously choosing one and accounting for these decisions with rigorous biblical and theological reasoning. Sparks shows both the strength of his tradition of Reformed theology and its increasingly incisive engagement with the theology of religions. His work indicates how this tradition is able to deeply engage with other denominational assumptions and to call them into question and propose a challenging alternative. Sparks ignites a fire that burns bright and illuminates afresh a field that looked too settled. We are indebted to his work.

Gavin D'Costa
Professor of Catholic Theology, University of Bristol

PREFACE

A fundamental requirement in an inclusivist understanding of the relationship between Christianity and other religions is evidence of God's salvific activity outside of any knowledge of Christ. This is commonly identified in the religion of Old Testament Israel. On this basis an analogy (hereafter, the "Israel analogy") is drawn between the Old Covenant and contemporary non-Christian religions. Closely related is the parallel argument that as Christ has fulfilled the Old covenant he can also be seen as the fulfillment of other religious traditions and/or their scriptures.

This thesis outlines the use of the Israel analogy and fulfillment model, and subjects these concepts to a biblical and theological critique revealing that the exegetical and patristic data are misconstrued in support of these concepts. Furthermore, these concepts undermine the *sui generis* relationship between the Old and New covenants and fail to respect the organic, progressive nature of salvation-history. They also misconstrue the Old covenant and the nature of its fulfillment in the New covenant.

The Israel analogy and fulfillment model rely on a correspondence between the chronologically pre-messianic (Israel) and the epistemologically pre-messianic (other religions), and in so doing consider the "BC condition" to continue today. In so doing, they undermine the significance of the Christ-event by failing to appreciate the decisive effect of this event on history and the nature of existence. It marks a radical turn in salvation history, a crisis point, rendering the BC period complete and fulfilled. Therefore, the concept of a continuing "pre-messianic" condition or state is seriously flawed, as are the Israel analogy and fulfillment model. Thus, the inclusivist paradigm which is reliant in large part on these defective concepts is also problematic and proponents of this paradigm need to reconsider its basis.

ACKNOWLEDGMENTS

This publication was conceived during my PhD research, and I am very grateful for the patient and supportive supervision provided by Professor Gavin D'Costa. I am also grateful to my examiners, Oliver Crisp and Robert Letham, for their constructive criticism.

Many scholars (too many to list) were gracious enough to discuss aspects of this research with me via e-mail. Their willingness to interact in this way is greatly appreciated. I particularly want to thank Dr. Dominic Veliath, who entered a lengthy e-mail exchange with me regarding Jean Daniélou's theology of religions.

Daniel Strange kindly read a draft of this work, and provided very useful feedback, for which I am very grateful.

I appreciate the editorial staff at Wipf and Stock Publishers for accepting this work for publication, and for their attention to detail.

Earlier versions of sections of this work have previously been published in the following journals, and I appreciate their publishers granting permission to include this material here:

"Salvation History, Chronology, and Crisis: A Problem with Inclusivist Theology of Religions, Parts 1 and 2," *Themelios* 33.2 (September 2008) 7–18; and 33.3 (December 2008) 48–62.

"The Fulfilment Theology of Jean Daniélou, Karl Rahner and Jacques Dupuis," *New Blackfriars* 89 [1024] (November 2009) 634–57.

"Was Justin Martyr A Proto-Inclusivist?" *Journal of Ecumenical Studies* 43.4 (Fall 2008) 495–510.

Finally I owe my wife, Cynthia, and the children a debt of gratitude for putting up with my being locked away in "the shed" for so long.

INTRODUCTION

The focus of this study lies within the theological subdiscipline known as the "theology of religions." It is the area of theology which deals with such issues as the question of truth and revelation in non-Christian religions, the relationship between Christianity and other religions, the "fate of the unevangelized," and issues of interreligious dialogue. It is the discipline that "attempts to account theologically for the meaning and value of other religions" and "to think theologically about what it means for Christians to live with people of other faiths and about the relationship of Christianity to other religions."[1] Theology of religions is one of the most contentious issues in the disciplines of theology and religious studies. The diversity of religion is nothing new. However, the Church is poorly equipped to meet the contemporary challenges this presents. There is a pressing need for a comprehensive theology of religions. The Church's affirmation of the finality of Christ does not relieve

---

1. Kärkkäinen, *Introduction to the Theology of Religions*, 20. Among the recent book-length works in this field are Anderson, *Christianity and World Religions*; Corduan, *Tapestry of Faiths: The Common Threads between Christianity & World Religions*; Crockett and Sigountos, *Through No Fault of Their Own? The Fate of Those Who Have Never Heard*; D'Costa, *Theology and Religious Pluralism*; D'Costa, *The Meeting of Religions and the Trinity*; Dupuis, *Toward a Christian Theology of Religious Pluralism*; Heim, *The Depth of Riches: A Trinitarian Theology of Religious Ends*; Heim, *Salvations: Truth and Difference in Religion*; Hick, *An Interpretation of Religion*; Hick, *A Rainbow of Faiths*; Kärkkäinen, *Trinity and Religious Pluralism*; McDermott, *Can Evangelicals Learn from World Religions?*; Netland, *Dissonant Voices: Religious Pluralism and the Question of Truth*; Netland, *Encountering Religious Pluralism*; Newbigin, *The Gospel in a Pluralist Society*; Knitter, *No Other Name? A Critical Survey of Christian Attitudes Towards the World Religions*; Knitter, *Introducing Theologies of Religions*; Pinnock, *A Wideness in God's Mercy: The Finality of Jesus Christ in a World of Religions*; Race, *Christians and Religious Pluralism*; Sanders, *No Other Name*; Sanders, *What About Those Who Have Never Heard?*; Strange, *The Possibility of Salvation among the Unevangelized*; Stackhouse, *No Other Gods before Me?*; Sullivan, *Salvation Outside the Church?*; Tiessen, *Who Can Be Saved? Reassessing Salvation in Christ and World Religions*; Yong, *Beyond the Impasse: Toward a Pneumatological Theology of Religions*.

Introduction

it of its responsibility to explain the relationship between Christianity and other religions.[2]

The theology of religions, when considered as a separate subdiscipline, is a relatively new focus for theology; however, the issues with which it grapples are perennial.[3] I will argue that these issues are best considered in close connection with other theological loci, and indeed must be treated in this way to avoid mishandling the exegetical and theological data and distorting crucial tenets of the resulting theology of religions. This is necessarily so due to the organic nature of doctrine. As Millard Erickson states, "Doctrine is organic, so that the position taken on one doctrine influences conclusions in other areas as well. Even when this is not done, and a doctrinal scheme is internally inconsistent, sooner or later the matter of logic prevails, producing a modification of other beliefs."[4]

As I shall show, the Israel analogy and fulfillment model cannot be adopted without also requiring or presupposing certain (mis)understandings of central Christian doctrines, such as those relating to covenant, revelation, and atonement.

Much recent theology of religions has been concerned largely with soteriological matters and in particular the vexing question of the "fate of the unevangelized." Issues relating to the relationship between other religions and Christianity have received less attention. The focus of this study is not on soteriological issues but rather is on the question of whether the relationship between the Old and New covenants can be considered to be analogous to the relationship between

---

2. While the number of publications in this field is increasing rapidly (as evidenced by the above examples), the focus of many of these studies is on soteriological concerns and on the uniqueness of Christ with reference to salvation. However, as Harvie Conn has stated, "Affirming the finality of Christ does not relieve us of the responsibility to explain the relationship between Christianity and other religions" (Conn, "Do Other Religions Save?" 207).

3. Kärkkäinen suggests the subdiscipline of theology of religions started with Vatican II, and then accelerated in the late 1980s until present time (Kärkkäinen, *Introduction to the Theology of Religions*, 22). While there is some truth to this claim, I suggest it is more accurate to see the contemporary origins of a theology of religions in the 1910 Edinburgh World Missionary Conference, and with its associated missiologists and theologians such as Hendrik Kraemer.

4. Erickson, "The Fate of Those Who Never Hear," 3.

Introduction

other religions and Christianity, as is commonly suggested in inclusivist methodologies.[5]

The current study is original in the field of the theology of religions as it is the first full critique of the Israel analogy.[6] The approach here adopted also sets this work apart from other works in the field as it approaches the question of the relationship between other religions and Christianity by first setting out the relationship between Israel and the Church and between Old and New covenants. Throughout the study, I shall maintain that this prior relationship must be established before the relationship of other religions to Christianity is considered.

Two matters require clarification before proceeding. The first concerns the use of the concept of analogy. The term "analogy" is commonly employed in theological discourse in two main ways: one is the concept of "analogy of being" (*analogia entis*). In this context, analogies are used in order to address the problem of using finite language to describe the infinite (God).[7] The second usage of *analogy* is in the concept of "analogy of faith" (*analogia fidei*). Here it refers to a hermeneutical principle that maintains the clearer passages of Scripture should be used to interpret the less clear passages.[8] However, in this study "analogical"

---

5. The issue of soteriology in the context of inclusivism has recently received a substantial treatment in the study by Strange, *The Salvation of the Unevangelised*.

6. Strange's work referred to above touches on this subject, but not in a sustained manner.

7. Thomas Aquinas considered that no finite concepts are adequate for expressing the infinite essence of God. He argued, "It is impossible for anything to be predicated univocally of God and a creature: that is made plain as follows. Every effect of a univocal agent is adequate to the agent's power: and no creature being finite, can be adequate to the power of the first agent which is infinite" (Geisler and Corduan, *Philosophy of Religion*, 224–25, quoting Thomas Aquinas, *On the Power of God*, trans. The English Dominican Fathers, 3 bks. in 1 [Westminster: Newman, 1952], Q.7, A.7). Aquinas's solution is to employ analogical language about God: "For we can name God only from creatures. Thus whatever is said of God and creatures, is said according to the relation of a creature to God as its principle and cause, wherein all perfections of things pre-exist excellently. Now this mode of community of idea is a mean between pure equivocation and simple univocation. For in analogies the idea is not, as it is in univocals, one and the same, yet it is not totally diverse as in equivocals; but a term which is thus used in a multiple sense signifies various proportions to some one thing" (*Summa Theologica of St. Thomas Aquinas*, 1.13.5).

8. The expression is based on a development of the Pauline phrase "in proportion to his faith" (Rom 12:6). In addition to the general hermeneutical principle mentioned above, "analogy of faith" has also taken on other specific meanings in theological discourse. For Augustine, the analogy of faith requires that the interpretation

Introduction

is being used in neither of these ways; rather, it is used in a logical or rational sense. That is, it is used as a form of argumentation. Here in its broadest sense it "comprehends any mode of reasoning that depends on the suggestion or recognition of a relationship of similarity between two objects or sets of objects."⁹ The term is derived from the Greek *ana logon*, "according to a ratio," that is, to refer to proportionality. Analogical arguments are to be distinguished from deductive, inductive, and abductive arguments.¹⁰ As A. Juthe explains, the elements of an analogical argument are as follows:

> The *Target-Subject* (TS) is the object of comparison to which the conclusion of the argument by analogy assigns a new predicate. The *Analogue* (A) is the object which is compared with the Target-Subject in order to make the analogical inference to a new predicate about the Target-Subject. The Analogue is the source of the new predicate which is assigned and concluded about the Target-Subject. The *Assigned-Predicate* (AP) is the predicate of the Analogue which is assigned to the Target-Subject in virtue of the analogical relation between them. The Target-Subject and the Analogue are analogous with respect to the Assigned-Predicate if and only if each of the elements of the Analogue ($\varepsilon 1^*$ ... εn^*) which determines the Assigned-Predicate corresponds one-to-one with a counterpart element in the Target-Subject ($\varepsilon 1$ ... εn). It is by virtue of this that the Assigned-Predicate can be assigned to the Target-Subject. Since the Target-Subject has a counterpart of every element of the Analogue that determines the Assigned-Predicate, it means they are analogous and that the Target-Subject also has the Assigned-Predicate. Thus, the Assigned-Predicate can *mutatis mutandis* be concluded about the Target-Subject. A bad argument by analogy, then, is an argument which violates one of the conditions for a good argument by analogy; usually the projection of the Assigned-Predicate is based on an incorrect analogy. An incorrect analogy is an analogy where the elements that determine the Assigned-Predicate

---

of Scripture not violate the Church's summary of Christian faith (i.e., the Apostles' Creed). In Roman Catholicism, this idea is developed to insist that that the Bible must be interpreted in accordance with the body of tradition (Demerest, "Analogy of Faith," 43–44).

9. "Lloyd, "Analogy in Early Greek Thought," 1
10. Juthe, "Argument by Analogy," 2–3.

of the Analogue do not correspond one-to-one with a counterpart element in the Target-Subject.[11]

Thus in the Israel analogy the relationship between the Old and New covenants is the Analogue, and the relationship between other religions and Christianity the Target-Subject. The Assigned-Predicate is that the relationship between other religions and Christianity is analogous to the relationship between the Old and New covenants. In this usage of the concept of analogy, "similarity" or "likeness" is a key concept. Some proponents of the Israel analogy maintain there is greater similarity than others, but all see significant similarity in the relationships between the Old and New covenants and between other religions and Christianity.

The second issue requiring early clarification concerns the precise target of my investigation. Two related matters warrant substantiation here. First, while the Israel analogy and fulfillment model are important components of inclusivism, I am not seeking to critique inclusivism per se. Furthermore, I acknowledge that although there is often a strong link between the Israel analogy and the fulfillment model, the latter is not totally reliant on the former. Indeed, in principle, it is possible to hold the fulfillment model without also holding the Israel analogy.[12] The primary target of the work is an examination and critique of the Israel analogy, as this has received no major treatment to date. The second related subpoint needing clarification concerns the nature of the Israel analogy. In inclusivist theologies, analogies are sometimes made with Israel as a *religious system*, with the *faith* of the people of Old Testament Israel, and with people living during the time of Old Testament Israel, but who are not part of the covenant community, and yet, nevertheless, it is claimed, possessed saving faith, (i.e., the so-called holy pagans).[13] It is the first of these that is my precise target. I have selected this target due to the importance it plays in the inclusivist paradigm, and because of the extensive use made of this analogy in the theology of religions across the confessional spectrum.

---

11. Ibid., 2–3.

12. Such a fulfillment model could be proposed on the basis of concepts such as *Logos* theology and on the presence of truth in non-Christian religions. However, in the literature surveyed for this study, all those who adopt the fulfillment approach also adopt the Israel analogy.

13. See particularly Daniélou, *Holy Pagans of the Old Testament*.

Introduction

Throughout this work I use the terms "fulfillment concept," "fulfillment theology," and "fulfillment model" to refer to the theory that Christ can be considered the fulfillment of non-Christian religions. I shall argue that such usage of the term "fulfillment" is misguided. However, it should be noted from the outset that I consider the relationship between the Old and New covenants to be characterized by fulfillment of a *sui generis* nature, and so I will also use the term "fulfillment" in this context. The reader should bear in mind the context of the usage of the term, as this will indicate which meaning should be inferred.

A dominating theme throughout the book will be the theological concept of Israel. I use the term "Israel" (as in "Israel analogy") to refer primarily to the covenant community of the Old Testament. I am not referring to the current geographical territory or the political entity, and neither am I equating contemporary Judaism/s with the Old Testament Jewish faith; for from the perspective of Christian theology, there is significant discontinuity between these two forms of religion. While contemporary Judaism has its roots in the covenantal religion of the Old Testament and maintains the Tanak as part of its Scriptures, there are major discontinuities between these origins and the current Jewish religion.

Discontinuity has resulted from the loss of the temple and the land. Furthermore, the addition of extracanonical texts to the Jewish Scriptures, most notably the Pseudepigrapha and the Talmud,[14] has exerted a profound affect on how later Judaism has developed.[15] Importantly, for Orthodox Judaism it is the Talmud which interprets the Tanak.[16] From the perspective of Christian theology, the nonrecognition or rejection of the Messiah by the majority of the Jews has estab-

---

14. The Pseudepigrapha was compiled circa 200 BC and AD 200. The Talmud is composed of the Mishnah, which was completed circa 90–200 CE, and the Gemera circa. 200–500 CE (See Scott, *Jewish Backgrounds of the New Testament*, 30–33).

15. Later writings include the Midrashim, which were compiled in periods up to the eighth century AD (Ibid.). From a Protestant perspective, the Apocrypha (completed in the second century BC) could be added to this list of extracanonical sources considered to be authoritative by later Judaism.

16. Corduan, *Tapestry of Faiths*, 60. Corduan cautions against what he describes as the "Protestant Fallacy"—that is, viewing the Scriptures of other religions as Protestant Christians view their Bible. He highlights the flawed assumption that to understand Judaism one must study the "Old Testament" (59).

Introduction

lished a fundamental discontinuity between the Old Testament Jewish religion and the development of this religion from the era of Christ.

Not only do these major factors introduce significant discontinuities between the covenantal religion of the Old Testament and contemporary Judaism/s; further discontinuities must be recognized between other periods of Jewish history. In particular, intertestamental (Second Temple) Judaism should be distinguished from the preceding and following forms of Judaism. J. Julius Scott states, "Students of this historical period [the intertestamental period] have become increasingly aware of its distinctives, not only from the Old Testament but also from the form of Judaism which followed it."[17] Rabbinic Judaism arose after AD 70 from a branch of the Pharisees, and while the rabbinic writings in places reflect intertestamental Judaism, this first-century tradition is often intertwined with sources that reflect practices and conditions that arose after the intertestamental period.[18] Therefore it is deeply problematic to conflate the covenantal religion of the Old Testament, intertestamental Judaism, rabbinic Judaism, and contemporary Judaism/s under the one rubric "Judaism." A recognition of the distinctions highlighted above will play an important role in this work.

My theological approach can be described as "Reformed," that is, I place myself within the tradition represented by the magisterial Reformers, and which is later represented by the major Reformed confessional statements.[19] Among the aspects of Reformed theology that are particularly pertinent to the topic of this thesis are its covenantal

---

17. Scott, *Jewish Backgrounds to the New Testament*, 18.

18. Ibid., 33. "All too often the unique character of Intertestamental Judaism goes unrecognized. Students frequently have proceeded on the assumption that the background of the New Testament can be determined by supplementing the Old Testament with information from rabbinic writings . . . which, in their present form, actually came into being after the New Testament Era. The result has been to risk anachronistically reading into the New Testament setting conditions, practices, and ideas which arose or were modified after A.D. 70" (Scott, *Jewish Backgrounds to the New Testament*, 20).

19. Among the most important are, in date order, the Augsburg Confession (1530, Lutheran); the Gallican/French Confession (1559), the Heidelberg Catechism* (1563), the Belgic Confession* (1561), the Canons of Dordrecht* (1618–1619), the Thirty-Nine Articles (1571, Anglican), the Westminster Confession of Faith (1643–1646, Presbyterian), and the London Confession (1689, Baptist),* together known as the "Three Forms of Unity."

Introduction

framework and emphasis on the unity and continuity of salvation history theology.[20]

In part 1 of the book I shall introduce the key terminology encountered in the theology of religions and will provide an overview of the use of the Israel analogy and fulfillment model in contemporary theology of religions. In part 2 I shall outline the importance of a correct understanding of Israel and its relationship with the Church for a Christian theology of religions. In part 3 I will submit the Israel analogy and fulfillment model to a biblical and theological critique and will contend that these approaches are fundamentally flawed. Among the contributing factors of these flaws are, I shall argue, a misunderstanding of the relationship between the Old and New covenants, and an erroneous construal of the nature of the Old covenant itself. I shall maintain that the relationship between the Old and New covenants is *sui generis*. A key concept throughout the critique will be that of salvation history, and I will maintain that the Israel analogy and fulfillment model have failed to comprehend the organic, progressive nature of this salvation history. I will further demonstrate that the Israel analogy and fulfillment model undermine the significance of the Christ-event in salvation history by failing to appreciate the decisive effect of this event on history and the nature of existence.

I shall assert that as the inclusivist model is reliant on the Israel analogy and fulfillment model, this paradigm itself is substantially weakened and this therefore presents a challenge to inclusivists, who need to reexamine the basis of their approach to the relationship between other religions and Christianity.

---

20. These major strands of Reformed theology will be treated in chapters 8 and 6 respectively.

ABBREVIATIONS

AG	Declaration on the Church's Missionary Activity (*Ad Gentes Divinitus*)
AThR	*Anglican Theological Review*
CTJ	*Conservative Theological Journal*
ESV	*Holy Bible*. English Standard Version (London: Collins, 2002).
EQ	*Evangelical Quarterly*
HeyJ	*Heythrop Journal*
IBMR	*International Bulletin of Missionary Research*
JES	*Journal of Ecumenical Studies*
JETS	*Journal of the Evangelical Theological Society*
JPSSCB	"The Jewish People and Their Sacred Scriptures in the Christian Bible" (Pontifical Biblical Commission document)
KJV	*Holy Bible*, King James Version, (London: Collins, 1955).
LG	Dogmatic Constitution on the Church (*Lumen Gentium*)
NA	*Declaration on the Relationship of the Church to Non-Christian Religions* (*Nostra Aetate*)
NAC	New American Commentary
NIBCNT	New International Biblical Commentary on the New Testament
NICNT	New International Commentary on the New Testament
NIV	*Holy Bible*, New International Version (London: Hodder & Stoughton, 1984).
NPNF1	*Nicene and Post-Nicene Fathers*, Series 1.
NSBT	New Studies in Biblical Theology
OBT	Overtures to Biblical Theology
StPatr	Studia patristica
TNTC	Tyndale New Testament Commentaries

Abbreviations

TS	*Theological Studies*
WBC	Word Biblical Commentary
WTJ	*Westminster Theological Journal*

All references to the works of the ante-Nicene Church Fathers are from Alexander Roberts and James Donaldson, editors, *Ante-Nicene Fathers: Translations of the Writings of the Fathers down to A.D. 325* (Grand Rapids: Eerdmans, 1988).

Part I

Israel in a Christian Theology of Religions

1

AN INTRODUCTION TO THE ISRAEL ANALOGY AND FULFILMENT THEOLOGY

1.1. Defining the "Theology of Religions"

It is commonplace in the field of Christian theology of religions to delineate a number of prevailing paradigms for the relationship of Christianity to other religions. Until recently the threefold categorization of exclusivism, inclusivism, and pluralism has dominated the discussion.[1] Harold Netland, in *Dissonant Voices,* offers the following definitions for these models. His definitions represent a broad consensus of what has been understood by these three terms and I will therefore cite them in full: "*Exclusivism* maintains that the central claims of Christianity are true, and that where the claims of Christianity conflict with those of other religions, the latter are to be rejected as false. Christian exclusivists also characteristically hold that God has revealed himself definitively in the Bible and that Jesus Christ is the unique incarnation of God, the only Lord and Saviour. Salvation is not to be found in the structures of other religious traditions."[2]

> *Inclusivism*, like exclusivism, maintains that the central claims of Christian faith are true, but it adopts a much more positive view of other religions than does exclusivism. Although inclusivists hold that God has revealed himself definitively in Jesus Christ

1. Alan Race first adopted this typology in *Christians and Religious Pluralism*, 6.
2. Netland, *Dissonant Voices*, 9.

and that Jesus is somehow central to God's provision of salvation for humankind, they are willing to allow that God's salvation is available through non-Christian religions. Jesus is still held to be, in some sense, unique, normative, and definitive; but God is said to be revealing himself and providing salvation through other religious traditions as well. It is the attempt to strike the delicate balance between affirmation of God's unique revelation and salvation in Jesus Christ and openness to God's saving activity in other religions that distinguishes inclusivism.[3]

Pluralism parts company with both exclusivism and inclusivism by rejecting the premise that God has revealed himself in any unique or definitive sense in Jesus Christ. To the contrary, God is said to be actively revealing himself in all religious traditions. Nor is there anything unique or normative about the person of Jesus. He is simply one of many great religious leaders who have been used by God to provide salvation for humankind. Pluralism, then, goes beyond inclusivism in rejecting the idea that there is anything superior, normative, or definitive about Christianity. Christian faith is merely one of the many equally legitimate human responses to the same divine reality.[4]

More recently, as the debate has advanced it has been acknowledged that this three-fold typology is problematic. In Netland's more recent publication *Encountering Religious Pluralism* he writes: "I am increasingly unhappy with this taxonomy as it tends to obscure subtle, but significant, differences among positions and thinkers."[5] Nevertheless,

---

3. Ibid., 9–10. It should be noted at this point that Netland's definition of inclusivism would not be accepted by all inclusivists. Some would affirm God's salvific work outside Christianity but would stop short of affirming other religions *in themselves* as salvific structures. See the discussion below.

4. Ibid., 10.

5. Netland, *Encountering Religious Pluralism*, 47 Netland is not alone in his recognition of the problems with this typology. S. Mark Heim writes regarding exclusivism, inclusivism, and pluralism: "These distinctions serve some purposes, but seriously mislead us as the definitive map of our options. The typology is fully coherent only on the assumption that salvation is an unequivocal, single reality. Given that assumption, it distinguishes between the limitation of salvation to one group [exclusivism], its qualified availability to all [inclusivism] or its full achievement by parallel distinct paths [pluralism]. This a priori limitation of the religious possibilities is dubious, and the usefulness of the typology hinges on that limitation" (Heim, *Salvations*, 4). Instead Heim proposes a plurality of religious ends or salvations. Another challenge to the typology has also been made by D'Costa, who argues that rather than representing distinct paradigms, both pluralism and inclusivism are better considered as different forms of exclusivism. Pluralism "represents a tradition-specific approach that bears

An Introduction to the Israel Analogy and Fulfilment Theology

Netland does see some merit in adopting a basic typological approach to the discipline, suggesting "In very broad terms we can distinguish three basic paradigms for understanding the relation of Christianity to other religions."[6] With these qualifications in mind I will now discuss the typology referred to above, as this remains influential in the relevant literature.

The pluralist position can be eliminated from the discussion at this stage because this thesis is written with the presupposition that the work of Christ is our sole basis for salvation, and Christianity is unique

---

all the same features as exclusivism, except that it is western liberal modernity's exclusivism" (D'Costa, *Meeting of Religions*, 22). Inclusivism logically collapses into exclusivism in three ways: "First, inclusivists, like exclusivists, hold that their tradition finally contains the truth regarding ontological, epistemological, and ethical claims . . . Second, both inclusivists and exclusivists hold to the inseparability of ontology, epistemology, and ethics such that truth cannot be separated from the mediator: Christ and his church . . . Third, both inclusivists and exclusivists recognise the tradition-specific nature of their enquiry, such that they are committed to defend their position and engage with argument with rival or alternative traditions" (22–23; cf. Clark, *To Know and Love God*). Clark highlights a further important limitation of the threefold typology, namely, that different theologians use the continuum to answer two entirely different questions, and this leads to confusion about the meaning of the three categories. One usage concerns what he describes as "alethic questions" (from the Greek *aletheia*, "truth"), questions concerning the "ontological reference or descriptive truth of various religious teachings: Are the religious doctrines true?" (323). The other usage concerns "soteriological questions," the potential of each religion to help its adherents experience salvation (or liberation, enlightenment) (323–24). For a helpful survey of the development of the typology and its problems, see Perry, *Radical Difference: A Defence of Hendrik Kraemer's Theology of Religions*, 9–28, "Typological Issues."

6. Netland, *Encountering Religious Pluralism*, 47. Netland qualifies this assertion stating, "But we should not think of these as three clear-cut categories so much as three points on a broader continuum of perspectives, with both continuities and discontinuities on various issues across the paradigms, depending upon the particular question under consideration. Within each paradigm there is considerable diversity on subsidiary issues, and we must recognize that, as the discussion become increasingly sophisticated and nuanced, it is often quite difficult to locate particular thinkers in terms of the three categories" This difficulty is highlighted by Lesslie Newbigin who says of his own theology of religions: "The position which I have outlined is exclusivist in the sense that it affirms the unique truth of the revelation in Jesus Christ, but it is not exclusivist in the sense of denying the possibility of the salvation of the non-Christian. It is inclusivist in the sense that it refuses to limit the saving grace of God to the members of the Christian Church, but it rejects the inclusivism which regards the non-Christian religions as vehicles of salvation. It is pluralist in the sense of acknowledging the gracious work of God in the lives of all human beings, but it rejects a pluralism which denies the uniqueness and decisiveness of what God has done in Jesus Christ" (Newbigin, *Gospel in a Pluralist Society*, 182–83).

and normative. Furthermore, a pluralist theology of religions employs neither the Israel analogy or fulfilment concept (the topics of the thesis). However, the issues that form the heart of this thesis have direct relevance for the inclusivist model, and to a lesser extent also have some relevance to some varieties of exclusivism; therefore further elaboration of these models is necessary before proceeding.[7]

To begin my discussion of exclusivism, I refer the reader back to Netland's definition given above, which I believe is an accurate representation of this position. However, what this definition does not reveal is that within exclusivism there exists a spectrum of views, the extremes of which I shall refer to here as "soft exclusivism" and "hard exclusivism." The major variable that exists concerns the issue of the extent of salvation, or how restricted is the availability of salvation. While there is agreement that salvation is through Christ alone there is disagreement concerning whether this necessarily means salvation is only available to those who have concrete knowledge of Jesus Christ and conscious faith in him. The issue can be expressed thus: all exclusivists affirm the ontological necessity of Christ for salvation, but this is to be distinguished from the epistemological necessity of Christ for salvation—i.e. the necessity of knowledge of Christ.[8] At the heart of the issue is the question of the situation of those people who have not had the opportunity to hear the gospel of Jesus Christ—the unevangelized. "Hard exclusivists" would generally argue that salvation is not available to those who have not heard and responded to the gospel. This position has been called "restrictivism" by John Sanders[9]—because salvation is restricted to those who hear the gospel and believe in Jesus Christ. "Soft exclusivists" affirm (with careful qualification) that there are good grounds to maintain that salvation is available (through Christ) for those who have not had the opportunity to hear and respond to the gospel. This affirmation

---

7. This is particularly important as the terms *inclusivism* and *exclusivism* are used very differently by different theologians. It is also important as the terms are often used rather pejoratively. Perry suggests that "this typology tends to misrepresent non-pluralist approaches as theologically deficient and/or ethically insensitive" (Perry, *Radical Difference*, 11).

8. As will be shown subsequently, the distinction between the ontological necessity and epistemological necessity of Christ for salvation is also at the heart of the inclusivist position.

9. Sanders, *No Other Name*, 37. See chapter 2 of that work, "Restrictivism: All the Unevangelized Are Damned," 37–80.

An Introduction to the Israel Analogy and Fulfilment Theology

is often defended by employing the arguments relating to the salvation of Old Testament believers,[10] children dying in infancy and the mentally defective. Within Christian theology there is mainstream support for affirming salvation for these groups of people—none of whom had the opportunity to know Christ—and they extend this principle to the unevangelized today.[11] However, while affirming the accessibility of salvation outside of the knowledge of Christ, "soft exclusivists" stop short of affirming other religions as salvific structures, and they emphasize the discontinuity that exists between other religions and Christianity.

The basic premises of the inclusivist model are noted in Netland's definition above, which, with one qualification (see below), I believe represents an accurate summary of this position. Inclusivism is not the opposite of exclusivism as the terminology might suggest. With exclusivism it affirms the axiom of *solus Christus*. However, in variance to exclusivism it affirms that Christ who is the Truth includes all other truth wherever it is found. All goodness and truth come from God and therefore must also in some way be from and through Christ. Thus, any truth and goodness in other religions must be attributed to Christ who is somehow present and active in these religions, though in hidden ways.[12] Therefore, inclusivists emphasize continuity between other religions and Christianity, exclusivists emphasize discontinuity. Inclusivists have no difficulty in affirming God's salvific activity in other religions, although the precise nature of this activity is debated. Some argue that the religions *themselves* are vehicles of salvation, while others dispute this allowing only that Jesus Christ is somehow operative within the context of other religions.[13] The latter position is associated with the stance of Vatican II, the former with the work of Karl Rahner (see below, 2.1.v and 2.1.2). What is common to all inclusivists is the clear

---

10. These include both members of the covenant community (Israel) and some individuals from outside this community (Gentiles). Both are called upon to support this argument because the Scriptures clearly affirm these individuals had saving faith and yet, it is agued, could not have had faith in Christ.

11. While soteriology is not the focus of this study, I will argue in chapter 8 that there is substantial continuity between saving faith in the Old and New Testaments. For a detailed defense of the confession of Christ by Old Testament believers see Strange, *Possibility of Salvation among the Unevangelized*, esp. chapter 6, "The Covenant, Christ, and Confession of Christ."

12. Wright, *Thinking Clearly about the Uniqueness of Jesus*, 58.

13. The former type of inclusivism is labeled "normative inclusivism" and the latter type "constitutive inclusivism" by Clark, *To Know and to Love God*, 321–22.

affirmation of a distinction between the ontological necessity of Christ and the epistemological necessity of *knowing* Christ for salvation.

From the brief accounts of exclusivism and inclusivism offered so far, it is apparent that there is some overlap between aspects of the two models. Indeed, "soft" exclusivism is very near inclusivism in some aspects, and the various ways in which the terminology is employed can confuse. John Sanders includes what I have described as "soft exclusivism" in his account of inclusivism,[14] and Don Carson describes this "soft exclusivism" as "soft inclusivism."[15] However, he also argues that "soft inclusivism" is "barely distinguishable from exclusivism."[16] Chris Wright suggests that the variety of exclusivism which tentatively maintains the possibility of salvation for those who have not heard the gospel may be referred to as "non-restrictive" exclusivism or "soft exclusivism."[17] However, he adds that if this view is going to be called inclusivism it would be better qualified as "evangelical inclusivism" since it is a view held "by those who claim fundamental allegiance to the central evangelical affirmation of salvation through Christ alone and by faith alone."[18] Wright suggests the term "inclusivism" should be retained "for the view that sees some lesser or greater salvific value in *other religions as such*, even while asserting that ultimately all such salvation is somehow centred on, or normatively defined by, Christ."[19] This is a subtle but important distinction, and is one which I think is helpful.

In an effort to overcome some of the difficulties inherent in discussions of these terms, numerous scholars have proposed alternative typologies—none of which has become widely accepted. The evangelical theologian Terrance Tiessen has recently proposed a further typology,

14. Sanders, *No Other Name*, chapter 7: "Inclusivism: Universally Accessible Salvation apart from Evangelization," 215–80.

15. Carson's term, "soft inclusivism," is applied where a tentative affirmation of salvation outside of knowledge of Christ is held. He uses the term "hard inclusivism" when a definite affirmation of salvation outside of knowledge of Christ is held. See Carson, *Gagging of God*

16. Ibid.

17. Wright, *Uniqueness of Jesus*, 162 n. 121.

18. Ibid., 159–60 n. 113.

19. Ibid. Gavin D'Costa offers a similar definition for inclusivist theologies, suggesting they are theologies which claim that "the one revelation or religion is the only true and definitive one, but truth and therefore salvation can be found in various incomplete forms within other religions and their structures" (D'Costa, *Meeting of Religions*, 21).

which has five rather than three paradigms thus allowing for more careful delineation of the various positions.[20] In place of the term "exclusivism," Tiessen proposes two terms. The first is "ecclesiocentrism." This is the restrictive or "hard" exclusivism outlined above. This view is characterized by the belief that in the Christian dispensation only those who hear the gospel (at least in the case of competent adults) can be saved. Thus, the possibility of salvation is coextensive with the presence of the Church. The second term is "agnosticism." This is used for the position which, while maintaining the necessity of belief in Christ for salvation, does not think Scripture indicates clearly enough that none of the unevangelised is ever saved. Agnostics find the Bible silent on the fate of the unevangelized and are therefore unwilling to speculate on this matter.

Tiessen notes the confusion that exists regarding the term "inclusivism,"[21] and in order to try to avoid this he replaces this term with two others: "Accessibilism" and "Religious instrumentalism." [22]

"Accessibilism asserts that Jesus Christ is exclusively God's means of salvation and that the covenantal relationships God established with Israel and the church, in working out his saving program, are unique and unparalled. Accessibilists believe, however, that there is biblical reason to be *hopeful* (not simply agnostic) about the possibility of salvation for those who do not hear the gospel . . . God makes salvation *accessible* to people who do not receive the gospel. Although they grant that non-Christians can be saved, they do not regard the religions as God's instrument in their salvation."[23]

Religious instrumentalism goes further than this and regards other religions as God's instruments in the salvation of non-Christians, whilst at the same time holding Jesus Christ to be in some sense unique, normative and definitive. Finally, Tiessen uses the term "relativism" as the equivalent for pluralism.[24] From this brief survey of Tiessen's typology it can be seen that his category of "accessibilism" encompasses types of

---

20. Tiessen, *Who Can Be Saved?* 31–47.

21. Tiessen notes that the term "inclusivism" is "used differently from one book to another" (ibid., 32).

22. Tiessen acknowledges he has appropriated this term from Craig, "Politically Incorrect Salvation," 84. See Tiessen, *Who Can Be Saved?* 33 n. 36.

23. Tiessen, *Who Can Be Saved?* 33.

24. Ibid., 35. He does this to emphasize that what is meant here is not religious pluralism merely as a fact of history (pluralism de facto) but is rather pluralism in principle (pluralism de jure).

both exclusivism ("soft exclusivism") and inclusivism. The inclusivism it embraces is the cautious form that affirms God's saving action outside the Church—including within the context of other religions—but not *through* these religions.

This rather prolonged discussion of the major terminology and taxonomy encountered in the theology of religions has been necessary because these concepts will be met repeatedly throughout this thesis. It is now possible to proceed with an introduction to the primary topic of this thesis.

A fundamental requirement in any inclusivist or other accessibilist understanding of the relationship between Christianity and other religions is the evidence of God's salvific activity outside of any knowledge of Christ. Evidence for such redemptive activity is commonly identified in the people of Old Testament Israel. On this basis an analogy is drawn between these Old Testament believers and contemporary followers of other religions. This chapter will outline the application of the relationship between the Old and New covenants as an analogical basis for the relationship of other religions to Christianity.[25] This will be accomplished by a detailed exposition of the use of the Israel analogy and the fulfilment concept. The two are not the same, but are closely connected. The former, briefly stated, suggests this: Because God has clearly worked redemptively in the people of Old Testament Israel, who had no direct knowledge of Christ, we can analogically assume he is also at work redemptively in the people of other religions now who have no knowledge of Christ. If God's salvific activity was effective for those who lived chronologically BC (and it was), so it must analogically also apply to those who are epistemologically or informationally BC—i.e., followers of contemporary non-Christian religions.

1.2. Towards a Definition of Fulfilment Theology

A common definition or description of fulfilment theology is not found in the relevant literature. Paul Hedges notes that: "The question as to what fulfilment theology is immediately encounters a very great problem, namely, the vast range of thought that has been classified under

---

25. Later sections of the thesis will argue that this is a misuse in many ways, but this chapter will be limited to an exposition of the concepts.

this title."²⁶ Therefore, rather than offer a single definition, it is probably more accurate to note that the fulfilment concept, or fulfilment theology encompasses a range of positions. Frank Whaling suggests it takes three main forms, which can be described as follows:²⁷

1. Phenomenological fulfilment. This form is based on the problematic notion of a common essence in all religions. This common essence has been variously defined as moral imperative (Kant); the feeling of absolute dependence (Schleiermacher); the numinous sense of the holy (Otto); personal encounter with God (Farmer); and the sacred manifested through symbols and hierophanies (Eliade). It maintains that all religions partake in this essence, but the Christian tradition partakes in it more fully than other traditions. This common essence of religion is therefore fulfilled phenomenologically in Christ.

2. Fulfilment of other religious traditions. This form of fulfilment is based on the principle that as Christ fulfilled the Old covenant he can also be seen as the fulfilment of other religious traditions and their scriptures, as they also possess revelation and truth (albeit partially). Thus, they act as a preparation for the gospel (*praeparatio evangelica*) and Christ can be seen as the fulfilment of these other Scriptures and other faiths. *Logos* theology often plays an important role in this form of fulfilment.²⁸

3. Evolutionary fulfilment by the Cosmic Christ. This form of fulfilment is based on an evolutionary understanding of the whole cosmic process. Lower religions are fulfilled by higher religions. Christ the Omega Point is the ultimate fulfilment of all. Frank Whaling associates this approach with the work of R. C. Zaehner, who was strongly influenced by Pierre Teilhard de Chardin's evolutionary thought:

   > Zaehner took up Teilhard's notion of creative evolution whereby the world had evolved in stages punctuated by genetic leaps from the simple cell, to plant life, to animal life, and finally to human life. This creative evolution was continuing and had its focus in humanity. The mass of the human race was still evolving and its

---

26. Hedges, *Preparation and Fulfilment*, 26.

27. Based on the typology outlined by Frank Whaling in Whaling, *Christian Theology and World Religions*, 83–87. Whaling also makes the important point that fulfilment theology is not restricted to Christianity—some other faiths also have a version of it (87).

28. Logos theology is discussed in chapter 9 of this work.

> points of convergence, its goal of fulfilment, was Omega Point or the Cosmic Christ . . . Christ is no longer merely the static fulfilment of the world's religious traditions, He is the goal of the whole cosmic process, natural and human, religious and non-religious.[29]

The discussion in this thesis will focus on the second form of fulfilment, as it is within this form that the use of the relationship between Old and New covenants as an analogical basis for the relationship between other religions and Christianity is employed. It should be noted at this stage that the typology outlined by Whaling is a simplification of the whole spectrum of fulfilment approaches. Within the second form there is a continuum along which various sub-categories of this fulfilment concept exist. Towards one end of the continuum is a view that understands Christ to be the only answer to the longed-for but unrealized spiritual quest of all people. Within this definition a radical discontinuity between the prior worldview and Christianity is maintained. The various religions themselves play no part in the salvific process. All non-Christian religions are natural rather than supernatural. Here a very qualified use of the Israel analogy is employed in an attempt to preserve the *sui generis* relationship between Israel and the Church. At the other pole of the continuum is an understanding of fulfilment that emphasizes continuity between the prior religion and Christianity. Within this scheme non-Christian religions represent distinct interventions of God in salvation history. All religions play a positive, albeit preparatory role. In its most pronounced form this model tends to treat other religions/ their sacred texts as alternative "Old Testaments." Between the two poles are a variety of approaches, some giving more emphasis to one pole, and others giving more emphasis to the other. This chapter will compare and contrast the various nuances of the fulfilment paradigm and in doing so I will develop a more sophisticated fulfilment typology.

Fulfilment theology warrants a full analysis because of its continued prevalence in considerations of the relationship between Christianity and other religions, and particularly because of its key role in inclusivism. Indeed, in his *Introducing Theologies of Religions* (2002), Paul Knitter makes the bold claim that it is now the predominant view within the field of theology of religions "If the Replacement model . . . held sway over most of Christian history, the Fulfilment Model embod-

---

29. Whaling, *Christian Theology and World Religions*, 86–87.

An Introduction to the Israel Analogy and Fulfilment Theology

ies the majority opinion of present-day Christianity."[30] Knitter suggests that this is especially true for present day Roman Catholicism.[31]

Proponents of fulfilment theology offer a number of biblical texts in support of the theory. Prime among these is Matthew 5:17: "Do not think that I have come to abolish the Law or the Prophets; I have not come to abolish them but to fulfil them." Also key is the *Logos* theology of John's Prologue. Another text commonly cited is Galatians 3:24—"the law was put in charge to lead us to Christ" (NIV). This is interpreted in a broad sense to suggest that other scriptures and other traditions can also act as a pedagogy. This chapter will not include an analysis of the biblical arguments employed by fulfilment theologians, as this will be considered in chapter 9 of this work.

The focus of this chapter will be on recent and contemporary usage of fulfilment theology and the Israel analogy. I will not enter into a critique of the concepts at this stage as this will be reserved for later sections of the thesis (chapters 6–9). For the exposition of recent use of the Israel analogy and fulfilment theology, I will draw on examples from across the confessional spectrum to demonstrate that the analogical application of the relationship between Old and New covenants to the relationship between other religions and Christianity is widespread and influential within current theology of religions, especially inclusivism. Before proceeding with an exposition of contemporary sources I will briefly outline the historical evidence that is commonly employed by proponents to support their use of the concepts.[32]

1.3. Early Church Sources Used to Support Fulfilment Theology

Proponents of fulfilment theology argue that this theory is not new, but can be traced back to the Church's origins.[33] It is argued that the early Church had a much more positive assessment of other religions than has

---

30. Knitter, *Introducing Theologies of Religions*, 63.

31. Ibid., 64.

32. This will be more of a summary than a comprehensive account, as this has already been ably covered. See, for example, Dupuis, *Toward a Christian Theology of Religious Pluralism*, 53–58; Hedges, *Preparation and Fulfilment*; Sullivan, *Salvation Outside the Church?*

33. It should be noted at his stage, however, that the interpretation and use of these sources to support fulfilment theology is contested and we will take up this matter again in chapter 9 of this work.

generally been the case in the modern period. Indeed, exclusivism is a development that does not reflect either the Scriptures or early Church thought, according to Paul Knitter.[34] In *Toward a New Age in Christian Theology,* Richard Drummond presents this argument and suggests Augustine (354–430) and Fulgentius (468–533) are to blame for the introduction of a more exclusive view, which he calls "barbarism."[35] Jacques Dupuis suggests that "in the view of the Church Fathers, salvation history . . . extends beyond the Judeo-Christian dispensation to the surrounding cultures which they encountered—indeed, in some cases, to the ancient wisdom of the East of which they had but a scanty knowledge."[36] He refers to the early tradition's "remarkable opening toward other aspects of surrounding culture and tradition."[37] However, the concept of fulfilment has not been consistently accepted. Avery Dulles points out: "Since the age of the apostles, Christian theology has vacillated between looking on other religions as providential preparations for Christianity and as idolatrous perversions."[38]

Dupuis gives the subject extensive treatment in *Toward a Christian Theology of Religious Pluralism.* He argues that Justin Martyr (died c.165), Irenaeus (c.130–c.200) and Clement (c.150–c.215) shared a common general outlook on this matter, but with each offering different specific contributions.[39] According to Dupuis, Origen (c.185–c.254) and Augustine (354–430) were much more ambivalent towards other philosophies and religions but did nonetheless credit them with a preparatory function.[40] He suggests the Church Fathers considered the history of salvation not to be limited to a chosen people but extended to all humankind and human history.[41] The pre-Christian activity of the *Logos* was considered to be divine pedagogy. He cites Tertullian (c. 160–c. 220), who thought of this divine activity as "stepping stones" for Christian revelation, and Eusebius (c.263–c.340) who would later be the first to define this divine activity as *praeparatio evangelica* (prepa-

---

34. See, for example, Knitter, *Introducing Theologies of Religions,* 121–23.
35. Drummond, *Toward a New Age in Christian Theology,* 41–42.
36. Dupuis, *Toward a Christian Theology of Religious Pluralism,* 53.
37. Ibid., 54; cf. Whaling, *Christian Theology and World Religions,* 83.
38. Dulles, *Models of Revelation,* 174.
39. Dupuis, *Toward a Christian Theology of Religious Pluralism,* 56.
40. Ibid., 74.
41. Ibid., 33.

ration for the gospel).⁴² Dupuis develops his argument to suggest that after the Christ-event, the pedagogical quality of other philosophies and religions has not ended.

Justin Martyr is perhaps cited most often as early evidence of fulfilment theology. According to Dupuis, the cosmological function of the *Logos* is the foundation for Justin's theology of revelation. All divine manifestations of the Father are through the Son, and these manifestations are not limited to the Christian dispensation.⁴³ Everywhere there have been people who lived by the Word and deserve to be called Christian: "We have been taught that Christ is the first-begotten of God, and have previously testified that he is the Logos (*Logos*) of which every race of human partakes (*metechein*). Those who have lived in accordance with the Logos (*meta logou*) are Christians, even though they were called godless, such as, among the Greeks, Socrates and Heraclitus, and others like them."⁴⁴

Christianity exists beyond its visible boundaries and prior to its historical appearing. In this respect Justin compared Socrates and others to the Old Testament saints who had not known Jesus either, but lived in the light of the *Logos*. This idea has been taken up in recent *Logos* theology which forms an important element in much fulfilment theology. In his defense of Rahner (whose theory of the Anonymous Christian is a form of fulfilment theology—as will be seen later, in section 2.1.2), Eugene Hillman employs the argument that anonymous Christianity represents "an ancient belief of Christianity, and is clearly formulated as far back as Justin Martyr."⁴⁵

Hillman also suggests Irenaeus, Clement and Origen, were "associated with this sympathetic and optimistic application of St. John's Logos theology."⁴⁶ Jean Daniélou, in his discussion of resemblances between the "authentic religious values in the pagan tradition," the "teaching of philosophers" and those values found in the Old Testament, acknowledges that they could be "borrowed" from the Old Testament by the Greeks but he suggests "a more probable view was that they represented a revelation parallel to that in the Old Testament, a preparation for

---

42. Ibid., 131.
43. Ibid., 57; cf. 58–59.
44 Justin Martyr 1 *Apology* 46, cited in ibid., 58.
45. Hillman, *Wider Ecumenism*, 38. Hillman cites Justin Martyr 1 *Apology* 10.46.
46. Ibid., 39.

Christ on the pagan soul." [47] He continues: "That was the attitude of all the first Christian writers, called the Apologists. The first to expound it clearly was Justin. . . . In Justin's view this was not a matter of speculative knowledge arrived at by reason, but of total adhesion to the truth, conversion to the true God. That is why he does not hesitate to recognise as disciples of the Word and as saints the pagans who had given their adherence to that revelation and conformed their way of life to it."[48]

Irenaeus (c.130—c.200) is credited by Oscar Cullmann as the founder of the "theology of history" in which Christ stands at the centre of the Old Testament expectation and the New Testament hope for the coming of the kingdom.[49] According to Dupuis, Irenaeus explained the historical significance of the Mosaic and Christian dispensations, and integrated the pre-Mosaic dispensation in the history of salvation, thus accommodating the possibility of pre-Biblical religions being of salvific value.[50]

Dupuis suggests Irenaeus believed that the *Logos* reveals the Father progressively through the dispensations (the various administrations, economies or stages through which God accomplishes his purpose for the created order). In Himself the Father is and remains through all economies the unknown—but he is manifested in the Son.[51] His manifestation in creation is not just historical but cosmic. Irenaeus finds in the order of creation itself a historical and personal manifestation of the *Logos*. In his view, human knowledge of God is already a response to a personal divine initiative. The order of creation itself is part of God's historical and personal manifestation. Thus, to know God is to know him as a person on an existential level.[52] Kärkkäinen highlights Irenaeus' understanding of the universal revelation of the Father through the Son (*Logos*):

> According to Irenaeus 'through his Word [Logos], all learn that there is one sole God and Father who contains all things, who gives being to all things.' The Son has not only made known the Father, but 'moreover, the Word was made the dispenser of his

---

47. Daniélou, *Holy Pagans*, 18.
48. Ibid., 19.
49. Cullmann, *Christ and Time*, 56–57.
50. Dupuis, *Toward a Christian Theology of Religious Pluralism*, 60.
51. Ibid., 61.
52. Ibid., 62.

An Introduction to the Israel Analogy and Fulfilment Theology

Father's grace for the benefit of the people, for whose sake he carried out such great divine plans, showing God to people.' And, he adds, 'For if that manifestation of God which comes through the creation gives life to all who live on the earth, how much more does the manifestation of the Father which is performed by the Word give life to those who see God.'[53]

Thus, "natural knowledge of God" (through creation) and the personal knowledge of God on the basis of the revelation of the Word are not necessarily to be distinguished. They belong to one and the same category. What began in creation—the revelation of God through the *Logos*—was fulfilled in the revelation of the Father by the Son. The creation dispensation was followed by the Jewish and Christian dispensations. There is continuity and discontinuity between the coming of Christ and what preceded it: "What then did the Lord bring when he came? Know this, that he brought something completely new, for he brought himself." The incarnation of Christ is the newness brought by Christianity.[54] Irenaeus' theology of history allows him to speak in the following terms regarding those who had lived before the coming of Christ:

> Christ did not come only for those who lived at the time of the Emperor Tiberius, nor does the Father exercise his providence only for those who are living now. Rather, he has provided for all those who from the beginning have lived virtuously in their own generation and feared and loved God, and treated their neighbours with justice and kindness, and have longed to see Christ and to hear his voice.[55]

Francis Sullivan contends that the last phrase (longed to see Christ and to hear his voice) "obviously refers to the people of Israel who looked for the coming of the messiah."[56] However he extends this suggesting: "It can perhaps be taken also to refer to Gentiles who had come to believe in God as savior, and thus could be said to have longed implicitly for the coming of Christ."[57]

---

53. Kärkkäinen, *Introduction to the Theology of Religions*, quoting Irenaeus *Against Heresies* 4.20.6–7.

54. Ibid., 59, quoting Irenaeus *Against Heresies* 4.34.1.

55. Irenaeus *Against Heresies* 4.22.2, quoted by Sullivan, *Salvation Outside the Church?* 16.

56. Ibid.

57. Ibid.

There are many similarities between Clement's (c. 150–c. 215) thought and that of Justin and Irenaeus. Clement agrees that all manifestations of the Father are through the Son, but he distinguishes two distinct levels of revelation – a distinction not made by Justin or Irenaeus. The first is a common, elementary, natural knowledge of God, which can be acquired through the use of human reason and is accessible to all. At another level, the personal action of the *Logos* introduces people into God's secrets that are otherwise inaccessible. This is supernatural.[58] Dupuis argues that in making this distinction, which was unknown to his predecessors, Clement's theology is brought closer to our own theological categories.[59]

Clement suggests the influence of the *Logos* extends beyond the Judeo-Christian tradition. Philosophy is God-given and constitutes for the Greek world a divine economy, parallel, (but not equal) to the Jewish economy of the Law. Both were designed by God to lead people to Christ. "By reflection and direct vision, those among the Greeks who have philosophized accurately see God."[60] Greek Philosophy was viewed by Clement as a school-master or *paidagogos* directing the philosophers to Christ. It was a stepping stone, "given to the Greeks as their [Old] Testament."[61] Clement viewed the Old Testament and Greek philosophy as "two tributaries of one great river."[62]

This brief survey of some of the patristic sources that are commonly cited to support fullfilment theology,[63] suggests that there is an abundance of early Church support for the concept. As noted above, however, the interpretation and use of these sources to support fulfilment theology is contested. We will take up this matter again in a later section of the volume (chapter 9). Our focus now turns to recent and contemporary use of fulfilment theology and the Israel analogy.

---

58. Dupuis, *Toward a Christian Theology of Religious Pluralism*, 66.

59. Ibid. Dupuis does not actually use these terms at this point, but he is almost certainly referring to the commonly held distinction between general and special revelation.

60. Ibid., quoting, Clement *Stromata* I, 19.

61. Race, *Christians and Religious Pluralism*, 43. quoting Clement *Stromata* I, 5, 8.3.

62. Tiessen, *Who Can Be Saved?* 110. quoting *Stromata* 1.28–29; 4.67,117.

63. I recognize that the sources quoted do not necessarily speak explicitly in terms of "fulfilment theology," but I include them here because proponents of fulfilment theology use them to support their approach.

2

RECENT AND CONTEMPORARY USE OF THE ISRAEL ANALOGY AND FULFILMENT THEOLOGY

The following exposition will outline the use of the Israel analogy and fulfilment model by seven theologians from across the confessional spectrum.[1] I have selected these seven to illustrate the broad support the Israel analogy and fulfilment model receive in Christian theology.[2]

---

1. I shall restrict the period considered to the last one hundred years, for it is within this period that the subdiscipline of "theology of religions" has particularly developed. For further elaboration, see the introduction to this book, nn. 1 and 3.

2. I acknowledge that these seven theologians do not represent the entire confessional spectrum. Most notably, I have not included an example from the Orthodox Church. This is justified on the basis of an extensive literature review conducted for this study, which indicated that the "theology of religions" is a much less developed discipline among Orthodox theologians than it is among other branches of the Church. Furthermore, I have been unable to find any Orthodox theologians who employ the Israel analogy. These observations are confirmed by other theologians working in this field. For example, Alan Race suggests, "Because of the Orthodox stress on the apophatic method and their sense of the unknowability of God, it is difficult to discern anything which may be said to be definitive in the Christian theology of religions from that community" (Race, *Christians and Religious Pluralism*, 51). The apophatic method is "The dominant idea in the Eastern Church that we know God primarily through mystical contemplation rather than through positive propositions or intellectual activity. Indeed, we are to empty our minds of logical and intellectual categories and in ignorance engage in prayer" (Letham *Through Western Eyes*, 298). Harold Netland writes, "I simply cannot think of any particular [Eastern Orthodox] thinker or work that is significant here" (e-mail from Netland, "Eastern Orthodox Theology of Religions," July 8, 2007). Similarly, the Eastern Orthodox theologian George Papademetriou suggests, "Orthodox sources on the topic you mention [Eastern Orthodox theology of religions] are very scarce" (e-mail from George Papademetriou, "Eastern Orthodox Theology of Religions," July 8, 2007). The Orthodox priest Gregory Hallam writes, "What you have

Throughout the rest of the book, I will interact in varying degrees with these theologians, but I will not limit the subsequent discussion to these theologians.

2.1. Roman Catholic Use of the Israel Analogy and Fulfilment Theology

I will begin this chapter by focusing on the work of three Roman Catholic theologians, as it is within this tradition that these concepts have received their fullest treatment, and the fulfilment paradigm has been most influential. The three—Jean Daniélou, Karl Rahner and Jacques Dupuis—have been selected because each represents a different variety of the fulfilment approach. A comparison of their positions will follow the exposition.

2.1.1. JEAN DANIÉLOU (1905–1974)

My exposition of the relevant aspects of Jean Daniélou's theology of religions will be the most extensive of all the theologians here studied, as his position is complex and nuanced,[3] and it is here that we will

---

described [that is the Israel analogy] would be a non-starter in Orthodoxy. It presupposes an essential distinction and difference between the Old and New Covenant is based on a separate strand of revelation . . . as if OT revelation could simply be set alongside putative revelations in other faith as equivalent. We certainly do not believe that. The Old Covenant (or covenants) were predicated on the same basis as the New; namely that they were construed with an elected people and it is this SELF SAME PEOPLE that became the Church of the Messiah. St. Paul's treatment of those Jews who did not accept Christ in Romans 9–11 is apposite NOT because he assumes some sort of separate arrangement but because such communities and persons still belong to the Old Covenant dispensation which has not been abrogated. So, as a practical illustration of this principle, in the Orthodox Church (unlike ANY other church), all the Old Testament righteous are saints in our Calendar and have their own feasts. If what you were supposing were true (not just true "for us") then there would be a St. Gautama and St. Mohammed in there, which, of course, there isn't! Such equivalence does not work nor does it find any place in Christianity before the so-called Enlightenment in the west" (e-mail from Hallam, "Eastern Orthodox Theology of Religions," July 16, 2007, emphasis original). While it appears as though Eastern Orthodoxy is less concerned with "theology of religions" than other branches of the Church, it is likely that the Orthodox emphasis on the "cosmic Christ" and its rejection of the *filioque* clause would play significant roles in such a theology of religions.

3. Dominic Veliath, declares that Daniélou's theology of religions is "difficult to understand," and that he "never elaborated his views in any systematic manner" (Veliath, *Theological Approach and Understanding of Religions*, 5, 9).

Recent and Contemporary Use of the Israel Analogy and Fulfilment Theology

first encounter many of the concepts and arguments that we will meet again in the subsequent expositions. Daniélou holds a three-stage history of salvation, through which God has been revealing his purposes progressively. Salvation history begins with creation: "In the Christian tradition, the history of salvation begins, not with the choosing of Abraham, but with the creation of the world. St. Augustine constantly makes this point."[4]

The first stage[5] of salvation history is that of "cosmic religion"[6] representing the period of history anterior to Abraham. The next stage is that of the Jewish[7] religion, through which the holiness and faithfulness of God are manifested. In this second stage, God appeared as a living God who intervened directly in the life of people: "He did not merely make signs from a distance, as he does to the pagans."[8] The final phase is that of Christianity, in which the mystery of the Trinity is revealed.[9] Daniélou refers to the religion of the first phase as "pagan religion." He uses the term "pagan" to refer to all religious peoples that are "strangers to the covenants of Abraham and Jesus"[10]—that is, all those religions

---

4. Daniélou, *Lord of History*, 28. Cf. Veliath, *Theological Approach and Understanding of Religions*, 35. Veliath argues that Daniélou views salvation history as extending between two cosmic events—the creation and the transfiguration.

5. Daniélou sometimes calls these successive stages "missions." See, for example, Daniélou, *Salvation of the Nations*, 16.

6. See, for example, Daniélou, *Holy Pagans*, 3.

7. Daniélou uses this term, by which he means the Old Testament Israelite religion.

8. Daniélou, *Salvation of the Nations*, 24.

9. Ibid., 27. Here, Daniélou calls this third phase or mission "the real one." 26. Jacques Dupuis contends that in Daniélou's three-stage scheme, "Salvation history proper is . . . limited to the Judeo-Christian tradition: it starts with God's personal revelation to Israel through Abraham and Moses, runs through the history of the chosen people, and culminates in Jesus Christ . . . Whatever came before God's personal manifestation in history, even though already inscribed in God's unique plan for humankind, can at best be called 'prehistory' of salvation. The same term would apply to whatever religious experience may be found today, outside the Judeo-Christian tradition, within the religions of the world" (Dupuis, *Toward a Christian Theology of Religious Pluralism*, 134). It should be noted that Daniélou does not use the term "prehistory" in any of the publications consulted by the current writer (see the bibliography for details). It may therefore be a term Dupuis imports. This cannot be verified, for Dupuis does not cite his source here. However, Veliath's doctoral study on Daniélou (and Raimundo Panikkar) does not use the term, and in correspondence with the current writer Veliath suggests Daniélou would *not* use this term (e-mail from Dominic Veliath, January 13, 2005).

10. Daniélou, *Holy Pagans*, 2.

which are beyond the context of historical revelation.[11] He does not include the non-religious world in the term "pagan."[12] The cosmic covenant, between God and Noah extends, according to Daniélou, to all humanity.[13] He suggests Hans Urs von Balthasar's concept of "cosmic liturgy" is the most appropriate term to "designate the period of sacred history anterior to the covenant with Abraham and to include at the same time whatever there is of truth in the non-biblical religions."[14] This principle continues to apply today, to those people who are beyond the reach of the gospel.[15] Daniélou suggests these religions have a certain knowledge of God from the cosmic covenant while "ignoring the fact of his intervention in the historical process—as to which there is no witness before Abraham."[16] Daniélou argues that the pagan saints were unacquainted with the positive revelation which begins with Abraham.[17] Nevertheless, he affirms the holiness of many "pagans."

Daniélou maintains that the Noahic covenant marks a turn in salvation history from the period of preservation to that of redemption —"from a heart-burning for primeval innocence to the first steps towards final restoration of it."[18] This covenant is the first manifestation of redemptive love, whilst the former divine economy showed only creative love:[19]

"The [Noahic] covenant thus marks a turning point in the history of salvation, the passage from a vision directed to a past that is to be maintained despite the destructive action of time, to a vision turned

---

11. Daniélou, "Christianity and Non-Christian Religions," 86.

12. Ibid., 87.

13. Dulles, *Models of Revelation*, 179.

14. Daniélou, *Holy Pagans*, 3. Daniélou does not cite the source of the term "cosmic liturgy."

15. Dupuis, *Toward*, 134. I have been unable to find explicit affirmation of this in the primary Daniélou texts (see the bibliography for list), and Dupuis does not cite his source. However, this assertion does seem to be implied by the available Daniélou sources.

16. Daniélou, *Lord of History*, 137. The meaning of Daniélou's reference to "intervention in the historical process" is not clear, for surely the flood was "intervention"— and this precedes Abraham.

17. Daniélou, *Holy Pagans*, 3.

18. Ibid., 82.

19. Ibid., 83.

Recent and Contemporary Use of the Israel Analogy and Fulfilment Theology

upon a future that is to be prepared for by the constructive action of time. With the covenant nature becomes history."[20]

Daniélou distinguishes between natural and supernatural religion. Dupuis asserts that in Daniélou's approach "Non-Christian religions belong to the order of natural reason, the Judeo-Christian revelation to the order of supernatural faith. Both constitute different orders."[21] The current writer agrees with Dupuis that this distinction is made by Daniélou. However, it should be noted there are isolated references in Daniélou's work that seem to be at odds with this distinction. For example, in *Holy Pagans*, Daniélou writes "the cosmic covenant is itself a supernatural covenant. It is not of a different order from that of the Mosaic or the Christian covenant."[22]

There is therefore an apparent ambiguity regarding this matter. However, Daniélou's overall framework certainly seems to rely on a natural—supernatural dichotomy, and this assessment is confirmed by other evaluations of Daniélou. Veliath writes "[For Daniélou] religions belong to the realm of nature, whereas Christian revelation belongs to the supernatural realm. There is a radical distinction between the order of nature and the order of grace."[23]

---

20. Ibid., 82.

21. Dupuis, *Toward a Christian Theology of Religious Pluralism*, 134.

22. Daniélou, *Holy Pagans*, 23. In the same publication, he states: "The cosmic religion is not natural religion, in the sense that the latter means something outside the effective and concrete supernatural order. That is the reason we avoid the expression. It is not natural except in the sense that it is through His action in the cosmos and His call to the conscience that the one God is known. The cosmic covenant is also a covenant of Grace, but it is still imperfect, in the sense that God reveals himself therein only through the cosmos, and it is very difficult to grasp by reason of the fact that it is addressed to an already weakened humanity" (Daniélou, *Holy Pagans*, 20). Daniélou prefers to use the term "cosmic religion" rather than "natural religion," because of the latter term's incorrect implication of meaning "apart from grace" (Daniélou, *Holy Pagans*, 3). Veliath notes that "in his earlier books and articles, Daniélou used the qualification 'natural' to designate these religions [i.e., pagan religions]. Subsequently, however, he preferred the terms 'pagan' or 'cosmic'" (Veliath, *Theological Approach to Understanding Religions*, 44).

23. E-mail from Veliath, 17 January 2005. Chrys Saldanha's assessment of Daniélou reaches the same conclusion. Saldanha argues that Daniélou "attempted to draw a distinction between Christianity and the religions on the lines of supernatural versus natural, or grace versus nature" (Saldanha, *Divine Pedagogy*, 154).

The cosmic covenant is a covenant of grace, however it has been superseded by a "new and better covenant."[24] The Judeo-Christian faith is quite different to religious faith in general. It is testimony to an event—an event that constitutes sacred history. "The object of revelation is a unique event, designated as *hapax* in the Epistle to the Hebrews. If this event is unique, revelation must necessarily be unique."[25] Thus, Daniélou distinguishes sharply between religion and revelation:

> The religions are a gesture of man towards God; revelation is the witness of a gesture of God towards man . . . The religions are creations of human genius; they witness to the values of exalted religious personalities, such as Buddha, Zoroaster, Orpheus. But they also have the defects of what is human. Revelation is the work of God alone . . . Religion expresses man's desire for God. Revelation witnesses that God has responded to that desire. Religion does not save. Jesus Christ grants salvation.[26]

For Daniélou biblical revelation is "radically different" from the content of the other religions.[27] However, this distinction is not absolute, for Daniélou does not deny fallen humanity all possibility of knowledge of God.[28] Daniélou affirms the "genuine spiritual worth" of other religions, but the "unique transcendence" of Christianity.[29] The "nature-religions" represent an authentic manifestation of true religion—the representation of God through the regular procession of cosmic events.[30] There is thus a "portion of truth" in every religion. "Paganism does not enjoy the immense benefits of Revelation in its search for truth" but it does contain a certain natural knowledge of God.[31] Nevertheless, the religion of nature is invariably found, in the forms known to us, in a more or less corrupt condition.[32] Daniélou also makes a sharp distinction between knowledge of God and saving faith. Other religions are

---

24. Daniélou, *Lord of History*, 119.
25. Daniélou, "Christianity and Non-Christian Religions," 92.
26. Daniélou, "Christianisme et Religions Non-Chrétiennes" *Etudes* 321 (1964), 327, quoted in Sullivan, *Salvation Outside the Church?* 187.
27. Daniélou, *Lord of History*, 119.
28. Barnes, *Christian Identity*, 47.
29. Daniélou, *Lord of History*, 107–8.
30. Ibid., 119.
31. Daniélou, *Salvation of the Nations*, 6, 23.
32. Daniélou, *Lord of History*, 119.

human expressions of a real knowledge of God available through the proper use of natural reason. This natural knowledge of God, however should not be confused with supernatural faith which comes only from God's active intervention in the unfolding history of salvation (beginning with Abraham and culminating in Christ).[33] Between the cosmic and historical covenants there is some continuity as the first serves as the necessary substratum for God's personal revelation in history. But God's personal intervention initiates a new order which commands a greater discontinuity.[34]

Veliath states that influential in Daniélou's scheme are Patristic sources, particularly Irenaeus.[35] Drawing on the thought of Irenaeus, Daniélou proposes that the Old and New Testaments belong to the same scheme of things, but mark two successive stages in the development of history. For Daniélou these are the second and third stages of his scheme. This succession is a system of pedagogy: "Everything that belongs to the temporal order must be imperfect at first . . . Before granting the plenitude of revelation to his people, he began by familiarizing them gradually with his ways, that is, by educating them."[36]

Daniélou makes an important distinction between non-Christian *religions themselves* and *adherents* of these other religions. In *The Salvation of the Nations*, Daniélou writes "true religion" (which he defines as the Catholic religion) is "the religion in which God's grace has made answer to man's cry. In other religions grace is not present, nor is Christ, nor is the gift of God."[37] However, in the same publication he contends

---

33. Daniélou, *Salvation of the Nations*, 6–8.

34. Dupuis, *Toward a Christian Theology of Religious Pluralism*, 135.

35. Veliath, *Theological Approach and Understanding of Religions*, 59.

36. Daniélou, *Lord of History*, referring to Irenaeus, *Against Heresies*, 4:11,2 and 4:9,1. Veliath summarizes Daniélou's understanding of the progressive nature of salvation history as follows: "This includes in the first place, the unity of the plan of God which also presents a great diversity. It implies progress in different stages, within each of which there is growth. This is seen as a pedagogy on the part of God who adapts his blessings to man's conditions as a temporal being. The plan of God is to recapitulate all things in Christ. The pagan religions form the first stage of this education; to be followed by Judaism; and then by Christianity. Hence, on the one hand there is continuity between the religions, Judaism and Christianity; and on the other hand, discontinuity, since Christianity is a nouveauté totale" (Veliath, *Theological Approach and Understanding of Religions*, 63). Note that "nouveauté totale" is Daniélou's term. Veliath is quoting it from *Le Mystère de l'Avent* (Paris, 1948), 13.

37. Daniélou, *Salvation of the Nations*, 8.

that "No man is a stranger to the grace coming from Christ,"[38] and elsewhere he states that "pagan saints" were not strangers to grace.[39] The terms "pagan saints" or "holy pagans" are used by Daniélou to describe all those people, who were not part of the Old Testament covenant community but nevertheless attained a right relationship with God. Daniélou is here asserting that grace is available to all, but is not mediated by non-Christian religions. There is no salvation but through Christ. Those who are saved without knowledge of Christ (whether BC or AD) are not saved by their religions—only Christ saves. And if they were saved it was because they, in a sense, already belonged to the Church, for there is no salvation outside the Church: "This obliges us therefore to accept the conclusion that the domain of Christ and of the Church extends beyond the limits of the explicit revelation of Christ and of the visible expansion of the Church. In every age and in every land there have been men who believed in Christ without knowing Him and who have belonged invisibly to the visible Church."[40]

He finds support for this assertion in the Thomistic principle of Baptism of Desire.[41] Thus, the Church includes all who like Abel, express in their lives the supernatural quality of faith in the provident God: "They [Holy Pagans] are the intercessors for that immense body of pagan humanity, existing both before and after Christ, which has known Him, not in the fullness of His actual presence nor in the certitude of prophecy, but in that rectitude of desire which theology recognises as a form of Baptism.[42]

---

38. Ibid., 20.
39. Daniélou, *Holy Pagans*, 4.
40. Ibid., 9.

41. Saint Thomas writes: "The sacrament of baptism may be wanting to someone in two ways. First, both in reality and in desire (*et re et voto*), as is the case with those who neither are baptized, nor wish to be baptised: which clearly indicates contempt of the sacrament, in regard to those who have the use of free will. Consequently those to whom baptism is wanting thus, cannot obtain salvation . . . Secondly, the sacrament of baptism may be wanting to someone in reality but not in desire: for instance, when someone is overtaken by death before receiving baptism. Such a person can obtain salvation without being actually baptized, on account of the person's desire for baptism, which is the outcome of faith that works through charity, whereby God, whose power is not tied to visible sacraments, sanctifies a person inwardly" (*Summa Theologiae* III, q.68, a.1).

42. Daniélou, *Holy Pagans*, 4–5.

All religions apart from the three monotheistic faiths (Judaism, Christianity and Islam[43]) are classed by Daniélou as cosmic religions. According to Veliath, Daniélou maintains that these three are "not on the level of religious sentiment but positive revelation."[44] In contrast, the cosmic religions are just human elaborations of a knowledge of God through nature: "As such they [cosmic religions] were unable in the past, and remain unable today, to lead to the saving faith which can only come from God's gracious intervention in the lives of people."[45] Nevertheless, people living under this regime of the cosmic covenant can exhibit a proper faith—as shown by the "Holy Pagans." They are "saints of the first covenant. They represent the initial stages of that divine educating of mankind which the history of salvation portrays. But by this very fact they exemplify the initial stages of that divine educating which the history of every man portrays."[46]

However, it is important to note that although Daniélou considers it possible for an individual outside the visible Church to be saved, he considers this a "limit-situation (that is an exception[47]) which cannot constitute the basis for a theological approach regarding the salvific validity of non-Christian religions."[48]

Daniélou argues that the Old Testament envisages cosmic revelation only in the generations before Abraham.[49] After Abraham the Gentiles are considered as "knowing not God."[50] However, with the Advent of Christ this changes. The message of Christ is addressed to all. "The universal call to salvation makes its appearance."[51] Daniélou points out that this raises questions regarding the position of pagans who preceded Christ (but lived after the call of Abraham). He suggests

---

43. Islam constitutes a singular exception and will be considered below.
44. Veliath, *Theological Approach and Understanding of Religions*, 61.
45. Dupuis, *Toward a Christian Theology of Religious Pluralism*, 135.
46. Daniélou, *Holy Pagans*, 6–7.
47. This understanding of the term "limit-situation" is confirmed by Veliath. (e-mail from Veliath, 4 June 2007).
48. Veliath, *Theological Approach and Understanding of Religions*, 60. Veliath cites Daniélou, "La Participation Active des Séminaristes à la Recherche Théologique" in *Seminarium* NS 8 (April–June 1968), 254, as his basis for this observation.
49. Daniélou, *Holy Pagans*, 14.
50. Ibid.
51. Ibid.

the answer is to be found in St. Paul's affirmation of a continuous revelation of God "made by way of the cosmos and directed to all mankind . . . To this exterior revelation there is conjoined the interior revelation of the conscience."[52] Daniélou finds further support for his argument in his assertion that the apostle Paul likens the case of pagans in his own day to those of primitive humanity prior to Abraham.[53]

Salvation history reaches its apex in Christ. Christ's resurrection is the decisive event for all history which nothing can surpass. Christ's saving presence within time is now continued by the Church. Christ "inaugurates the stage that will not pass away. So there is nothing beyond Christianity."[54] Pre-Christian religions (he mentions Judaism and Buddhism as examples) are not so much false as *old*—survivals of ancient civilizations.[55] Daniélou judges therefore that "the error of the Jews is strictly an anachronism, because they would arrest the development of God's plan, and perpetuate an obsolete pattern of reality. Origen, following Melito of Sardis, described the Old Testament as a preliminary sketch—something indispensable at one stage, but of no further use once the work is finished."[56]

Daniélou considers all religions[57] other than Judaism and Christianity to be "doubly anachronistic"—superseded by Judaism and then by Christianity. Christianity, in contrast, is the "eternal youth of the

52. Ibid.

53. Ibid., 15. Daniélou does not cite the Pauline text/s he is referring to here. While there may be an apparent inconsistency in Daniélou's argument here, the continuation of cosmic revelation does seem to be consistent with Daniélou's overall framework. Dupuis interprets Daniélou as affirming this. Dupuis writes: "Whatever came before God's personal manifestation in history, even though already inscribed in God's unique plan for humankind, can at best be called 'prehistory' of salvation. *The same term would apply to whatever religious experience may be found today*, outside the Judeo-Christian tradition, within the religions of the world" (Dupuis, *Toward a Theology of Religious Pluralism*, 134; italics added). This is also Eugene Hillman's understanding of Daniélou. Hillman writes: "If St. Paul could 'liken the case of the pagans of his own day to those of primitive humanity previous to Abraham,' as Daniélou has pointed out, then we may say also that the unevangelized peoples of our time are still under the irrevocable and salutary cosmic covenant. The rainbow still appears in the sky" (Hillman, *Wider Ecumenism*, 75. quoting Daniélou, *Holy Pagans*, 14–15).

54. Daniélou, *Lord of History*, 7. In the same book Daniélou describes the "Absolute finality" of Christ's work. (191).

55. Daniélou, *Advent of Salvation*, 18, quoted in Barnes, *Christian Identity*, 62 n. 63.

56. Daniélou, *Lord of History*, 5.

57. Islam excepted—see next paragraph

world."⁵⁸ "The covenant with Noah was the true religion of mankind until the covenant with Abraham was made; but from that moment it was superseded. From the time of the Gospel it has been doubly obsolete; it is anachronistic twice over. What is wrong with the heathen religions is that they have not made room for revelation."⁵⁹

Anomalies such as Islam are "regressions."⁶⁰ Islam is a special case due to its Jewish and Christian borrowings.⁶¹

Daniélou's paradigm considers the primary relationship between other religions and Christianity, to be one of fulfilment. In *The Lord of History*, Daniélou suggests the Christian mission is ultimately about engaging in the fulfilment of history.⁶² Paul Knitter suggests Daniélou's fulfilment model views other religions as "imperfect" or "negative" preparations for Christ.⁶³ For Daniélou, fulfilment encompasses both a perfecting and a replacing of the former religion. Pagan religions are "divine pedagogy."⁶⁴ Revelation "purifies paganism."⁶⁵ The Church "does not despise pagan teaching, but sets it free, fulfils and crowns it."⁶⁶ To become a Christian is not to change one's religion but to move from the plane of religion to that of truth.⁶⁷ "Religions are one of creation's most remarkable aspects and contribute to its splendour. How, then, could Christianity destroy these religions? Christianity with its mission not to destroy but to fulfill, to save what has been created?"⁶⁸

---

58. Daniélou, *Advent of Salvation*, 18, quoted in Barnes, *Christian Identity*, 62 n. 3.

59. Daniélou, *Lord of History*, 19.

60. Daniélou, *Advent of Salvation*, 18, quoted in Barnes, *Christian Identity*, 62 n. 63.

61. "[Islam] is a very particular case, for Islam appeared after the beginning of the Christian era and, on the whole, it was grafted on the Jewish trunk. It is an extension of Jewish monotheism and at the same time it contains certain elements derived from Christian heretics" (Daniélou, *Salvation of the Nations*, 37). Cf. Daniélou, "Christianity and Non-Christian Religions," 86.

62. Daniélou, *Lord of History*. This is a theme throughout the book.

63. Knitter, *Towards a Protestant Theology of Religions*, 212 n. 2.

64. Daniélou, *Salvation of the Nations*, 28.

65. Daniélou, "Christianity and Non-Christian Religions," 94.

66. Daniélou, *Lord of History*, 121. Daniélou is here paraphrasing a quote from Pope Pius XII in *Divini praecones* (full reference not given).

67. Daniélou, "Christianity and Non-Christian Religions," 89–90.

68. Ibid., 89. However, Veliath maintains that in Daniélou's fulfilment theology there is also an element of destruction: "Christianity presents a double relationship to religion, historical and dramatic. By *historical*, Daniélou means that between Christianity and religions there is a chronological relationship inasmuch as Christianity

Daniélou's understanding of the relationship of other religions to Christianity employs (and is arguably dependent on) the analogy made between the Old covenant and other religions. More precisely, he utilizes a dual analogy here. The first is the analogy made between those he considers to be outside the Old covenant[69] and people beyond the reach of the gospel today. The second is the analogy drawn between the religion of the Old covenant (that is the Old Testament Jewish faith) and non-Christian religions today.

Regarding the first analogy, Daniélou considers the Noahic covenant to be valid for all people in all places today outside the Judaeo-Christian tradition: "They [Holy Pagans] are the intercessors for that immense body of pagan humanity, *existing both before and after Christ*, which has known Him, not in the fullness of His actual presence nor in the certitude of prophecy, but in that rectitude of desire which theology recognises as a form of Baptism."[70] They are "saints of the first covenant. They represent the initial stages of that divine educating of mankind which the history of salvation portrays. But by this very fact *they exemplify the initial stages of that divine educating which the history of every man portrays*."[71]

Daniélou's scheme permits this analogy because of the way he divides the pre-Christian history of salvation into the cosmic covenant (pre-Abraham) and historical covenant (after Abraham). I will later argue that the entire Old Testament era is part of one and the same overall covenant, and that this analogy is therefore problematic.[72] Of

---

represents that to which all the others lead; but at the same time "dramatic": While it is true that Christianity fulfils the religions, it is also true that Christianity destroys them. Consequently, once they have found their fulfilment in Christianity, the religions have to die to make room for Christianity (Veliath, *Theological Approach and Understanding Religions*, 67–68).

69. That is, in Daniélou's scheme, all those living prior to Abraham, and all those living after Abraham (but prior to Christ) who are not part of the covenant community, but who nevertheless have saving faith.

70. Daniélou, *Holy Pagans*, 4–5 (italics added).

71. Ibid., 6–7 (italics added).

72. There are also other grounds for questioning whether the pagan saints were really "pagan." I concur with Strange (*Salvation among the Unevangelized*, 167–68), who argues that the epithet "holy pagan" is a contradiction either because they (the so-called 'holy pagans') were pagans who *became* saints by virtue of being ingrafted into Israel, or they were never "pagans" but were recipients of a special revelation and so cannot be counted as pagans.

more direct relevance for the current thesis is the analogy Daniélou draws between the Old Testament Jewish religion and other religions: The following quotations show how Daniélou uses this analogy:

> It was for Him, for Christ, the centre of the world, the centre of history, not only that the Jewish people had been prepared, but that all these pagan civilizations—the conquests of Alexander, the thinking of Socrates and Aristotle—had also been prepared.[73]

> Just as the convert Jews rightly saw in Christianity not the destruction but the fulfilment of their faith, so likewise would these pagans be conscious that in their adherence to Christ, far from denying what was best in themselves, they were on the contrary finding its completion.[74]

With regard to the "authentic religious values in the pagan tradition . . . they represented a revelation parallel to that in the Old Testament, a preparation for Christ in the pagan soul."[75] Daniélou quotes from Augustine to support his position here: "It is necessary to include within the Church all the holy people who lived before the coming of Christ and believed that he would come just as we believe He has come."[76] He then immediately extends this principle beyond Israel:

> It is important to note that this preparing for Christ is not confined to Israel. The authors concerned always make it clear that it is a question of the preparation for Christ as related in the Old Testament; but in the Old Testament Israel does not come into the picture until the eleventh chapter of Genesis. All the preceding chapters are devoted to recounting the religious history of mankind before Israel . . . To be exact, therefore, it should be said that the Old Testament describes the preparation for Christ first of all in the cosmic covenant, illustrated by the early chapters in regard to pagan humanity, and after that in the Mosaic covenant.[77]

However, it is important to recognize that Augustine was *not* referring to pagan religions here, but was referring to the covenantal

---

73. Daniélou, *Salvation of the Nations*, 35.
74. Daniélou, *Holy Pagans*, 18.
75. Ibid. 18–19.
76. Ibid., 10. quoting Augustine *De catech. rud.*, 3.
77. Ibid., 10–11.

people of the Old Testament. It is *vital* to maintain this distinction, but this is something the fulfilment model and use of the Israel analogy fail to do.

Daniélou considers the concept of covenant to be key in understanding salvation history.[78] The current writer also affirms this. However, there appears to be a certain lack of clarity in Daniélou's scheme regarding the nature and progression of the biblical covenants. In some of his writing he suggests that the first covenant is that made with Noah.[79] Indeed, he calls the pagan saints "saints of the first covenant,"[80] but elsewhere he suggests the first covenant is that made with Abraham: "God intervenes in history to accomplish a certain plan. We first glimpse this plan when He makes the first covenant with Abraham and thereby founds what is to become the Judaeo-Christian religion."[81]

I will show later (in chapter 8) that a lack of clarity with regard to the covenantal development of salvation history has important implications for one's theology of religions.

To conclude this exposition, I will summarize the key characteristics of Daniélou's scheme and offer a classification for it. On the continuum outlined in section 1.2, Daniélou's fulfilment approach is located toward the "discontinuity" pole. He emphasizes the distinction between religion and revelation, natural and supernatural, nature and grace, knowledge of God and saving faith.[82] Within Daniélou's three-stage understanding of salvation history, non-biblical religions[83] are natural, and are relegated to the prehistory of salvation, they have no abiding value. Judaism has been superseded, and is therefore now an anachronism. Grace and salvation are not mediated by non-Christian religions. However, no one is a stranger to grace, and salvation is available to adherents of non-Christian religions, reaching them as the divine response to the universal religious aspiration. Although he

78. Veliath, *Theological Approach and Understanding of Religions*, 57.

79. See, for example, Daniélou, *Holy Pagans*: "The notion of the *berith* [covenant] characteristic of the biblical God, does not appear for the first time with the Mosaic covenant but in the covenant made with Noe [Noah]" (12).

80. Ibid.

81. Daniélou, *Salvation of the Nations*, 7.

82. I recognize that Daniélou qualifies these distinctions (see above). However, for the purposes of this summary, I am merely stating the prevailing strands to his theology.

83. See above for discussion of Islam.

uses the terms "preparation" and "pedagogy," Daniélou, does not see non-Christian religions *themselves* as playing any part in salvation, and they are not providential instruments raised up by God. Rather, they represent natural responses to the revelation of God made known in the cosmos and the conscience. They contain some truth, but are inevitably vitiated and corrupt. Henceforth, I shall refer to this approach as "Fulfilment 1" or "F1."

2.1.2. Karl Rahner (1904–1984)

Karl Rahner's theology of religions is based on the dual axioms of God's universal salvific will and the necessity of *Christian* faith, which Rahner holds in tension. He insists salvation is *solus Christus,* but at the same time maintains there are those who are saved who have *not* responded to the Christian message because they have not had the opportunity to respond, through no fault of their own.[84] His theological anthropology maintains that humankind is created by God and is destined to union with God. Humans carry more than just a passive potency for self-transcendence in God. That which Rahner calls the "supernatural existential" is built into us by God's free initiative of grace. This spurs our intentional activity toward him—an activity that is destined to become historically concrete in the categorical or thematic order, that is through religions.[85]

His theology of religions is given extensive treatment in various essays in his *Theological Investigations*.[86] In one such essay he outlines this in a four-stage thesis—the first three of which are of particular import to our study. In his first thesis, Rahner proposes that the fact Christianity understands itself as the absolute religion and demands adherence, must be balanced by the difficulties in discerning "when the existentially real demand is made by the absolute religion in its historically tangible form."[87] Rahner wants to leave open the question of when in time "the absolute obligation of the Christian religion has in fact come into effect for every man and culture."[88] Thus those who lived before Christ, and those who live after Christ but have never

---

84. Rahner, "Observations on the Problem of the Anonymous Christian," 282–83.
85. Rahner, "Christianity and the Non-Christian Religions," 127–29.
86. See "Rahner" in the bibliography for details.
87. Rahner, "Christianity and the Non-Christian Religions," 119.
88. Ibid., 120.

encountered the gospel through no fault of their own, are not excluded from salvation. The universal demand of the gospel cannot be seen in isolation from the historical and existential situation. D'Costa suggests this avoids the difficult exclusivist claim that all religions are rendered invalid at the moment of the incarnation.[89]

His second thesis states that until the moment when the gospel really enters the historical situation of an individual, a non-Christian religion, even one outside the Mosaic covenant may be lawful. Salvation history is coextensive with world history—it is not limited to the period of the Old and the New Testaments. In history each person experiences God's free offer of grace. This is not necessarily thematically apprehended in Christianity, but is always concretely and existentially in Jesus Christ.[90] It is therefore a priori quite possible to suppose that there are supernatural grace-filled elements in non-Christian religions. The religions of pre-Christian humanity must not be regarded as simply illegitimate from the very start but be seem as quite capable of having a positive significance. They can, in short be "lawful religions."[91] Lawful religions can contain errors, as did the Old covenant.[92] However, the Old covenant remained lawful until the time of the gospel, and according to many Christians, was then grafted onto and fulfilled by the New covenant. Thus non-Christian religions can be lawful up until the time when Christianity becomes a historically real factor for their adherents. They can be "a positive means of gaining the right relationship to God and thus for the attaining of salvation, a means which is therefore *positively included in God's plan of salvation.*"[93] Rahner defends this assertion by appeal to the Old Testament Israelites, who were saved without possessing any explicit knowledge of Christ. Rahner accepts that "This thesis is not meant to imply that the lawfulness of the Old Testament religion was of exactly the same kind as that which we are prepared to grant in a certain measure to the extra-Christian religions."[94] He acknowledges

---

89. D'Costa, *Theology and Religious Pluralism*, 84. The relationship between an individual's encounter with the gospel and the universal significance of the Christ-event will be considered in chapter 7.

90. Rahner, *Foundations of the Christian Faith*, 144–47.

91. Rahner, "Christianity and the Non-Christian Religions," 121.

92. Ibid., 126.

93. Ibid., 125 (italics added).

94. Ibid., 130.

Recent and Contemporary Use of the Israel Analogy and Fulfilment Theology

that "the main difference between such a salvation-history and that of the Old Testament will presumably lie in the fact that the historical, factual nature of the New Testament has *its* immediate pre-history in the *Old Testament*. Hence, the New Testament unveils *this* short span of salvation-history distinguishing its divinely willed elements and those which are contrary to God's will. It does this by a distinction which we cannot make in the same way in the history of any other religion."[95]

However, the thrust of his argument is clear, as D'Costa explains: "The important point to note is that the Old covenant facilitated and provided the concrete means by which many attained salvation. Rahner then suggests that these theological considerations may be applied, at least in principle, to other non-Christian religions."[96]

Rahner's third thesis follows the second. Because grace is mediated through religions, not despite them, adherents of other religions should not be viewed as totally devoid of truth and salvific grace. They may already have accepted God's grace as it is made known to them. However, God's grace and salvation cannot be divorced from Jesus Christ—thus these believers can be considered as "anonymous Christians."[97] This anonymity can only be lifted by communicating the explicit message of the gospel. On this basis, Rahner proposes degrees of membership of the Church from full membership descending into a "non-official and anonymous Christianity, which can and should yet be called Christianity in a meaningful sense, even though it would not describe itself as such."[98]

From this brief overview of Rahner's theology of religions it is evident that his assessment of other religions is far more positive than Daniélou's. While both maintain it is possible for non-Christians to be saved, Rahner (contrary to Daniélou) proposes that the religions are instruments of salvation (but always related to Christ and the Church). There are supernatural elements in other religions arising out of grace.[99]

---

95. Ibid., 130–31. Rahner contends that the Old Testament salvation-history is "insignificantly brief in comparison with the general salvation-history which counts perhaps a million years—for the former can be known with any certainty only from the time of Abraham or Moses" (131).

96. D'Costa, *Theology and Religious Pluralism*, 86.

97. Rahner, "Christianity and the Non-Christian Religions," 131–33.

98. Rahner, "Anonymous Christians," 391.

99. Rahner, "Christianity and the Non-Christian Religions," 121, 130.

Rahner maintains other religions are "lawful," but this lawfulness is only provisional—it is valid only up until the occasion of historical and existential encounter with Christianity. Rahner employs the Israel analogy, and although he acknowledges the unique relationship between Old and New covenants, this acknowledgement seems to be undermined by his overall position. Rahner makes less distinction between natural and supernatural, religion and revelation, than Daniélou does. He perceives a greater (but not full) continuity between other religions and Christianity.[100] Salvation history is coextensive with world history and other religions are positively included in God's plan of salvation. On the fulfilment continuum already referred to, Rahner's approach is located between the discontinuity and continuity poles—being perhaps slightly closer to the latter. I shall refer to this Rahnerian form of fulfilment as "F2."

2.1.3. Jacques Dupuis (1923–2004)

The aim of Jacques Dupuis in his magnum opus *Toward a Christian Theology of Religious Pluralism* is to work towards a genuinely *Christian* theology of religious pluralism.[101] He builds on his earlier approach of "theocentric Christocentrism" which sought to "open up a theological perspective which, while holding fast to faith in Jesus Christ as traditionally understood by mainstream Christianity and church tradition, would at the same time, integrate in their differences, the religious experiences of the living religious traditions and assign to those traditions a positive role and significance in the overall plan of God for humankind, as it unfolds through salvation history."[102]

Dupuis argues that salvation history operates as an "important hermeneutical key for Christianity's self-understanding as well as the way in which it situates itself in relation to world history in general and to the history of religion in particular."[103] However, it is not "exempt of theological problems" and Dupuis believes "the Christian view of salvation history allows for a more positive appraisal of other religious

---

100. The approaches of Rahner and Daniélou (and Dupuis) are compared further in section 2.1.4.

101 Dupuis, *Toward a Christian Theology of Religious Pluralism*, 1.

102. Ibid.

103. Ibid., 121.

traditions than has often been held."[104] He questions whether it is right to see other religions as transient. Instead, Dupuis suggests they could have "a lasting role and a specific meaning in the overall mystery" of the relationship between God and humanity.[105] His Trinitarian model allows for the abiding validity of other religions by stressing "the universal presence and activity of the Word of God and of the Spirit of God throughout human history as the mediums of God's personal dealings with human beings independently of their concrete situation in history."[106] Therefore, for Dupuis, the idea that salvation history began with Abraham must be dismissed: "Every attempt to situate the beginning of salvation history in the vocation of Abraham, and thereby to reduce its extension to 'sacred history', must be firmly resisted. Such an attempt, wherever it is made, always betrays an a priori tendency to discount any personal engagement of God with humankind prior to and outside the tradition that issues from the call of the biblical patriarch."[107]

Instead, Dupuis suggests salvation history coincides and is coextensive with the history of the world.[108] He maintains that the Noahic covenant is cosmic or universal and this is a fundamental assumption in his thesis. "The covenant with Noah constitutes the lasting foundation for the salvation of every human person."[109] He distinguishes between general salvation history (which is universal) and special salvation history (which is particular). In the latter, "God's revelation-salvation becomes 'thematized' and categorical."[110] Dupuis recognizes the concept of special salvation history is, of course, clearly realized in the Jewish and Christian traditions but states that it need not be reduced to these traditions:

> For other religious traditions too may contain prophetic words interpreting historical happenings as divine interventions in the history of peoples. In fact, the Judeo-Christian revelation itself testifies to saving acts performed by God on behalf of other

104. Ibid.
105. Ibid.
106. Ibid., 212.
107. Ibid., 215–16.
108. Ibid., 217.
109. Ibid., 226.
110. Ibid., 218.

peoples. Such historically tangible saving deeds of God are analogous to those performed by God in favor of Israel according to the Old Testament record—notwithstanding the fact that the Christian tradition ascribes to the history of Israel the singular distinctive character of being the immediate historical prologue to God's decisive saving intervention in the Christ-event.[111]

In his effort to account positively for the value of other religions in the economy of salvation, Dupuis draws on the relationship between the Old and New covenants as an analogical basis for the relationship between other religions and Christianity. Dupuis acknowledges the unique bond between Israel and the Church, and that between the Old and New Testaments, and notes that "such a scheme readily lends to the idea that in the advent of special revelation history and, specifically, of the Christ event, pre-Christian religions belonging to the 'general' history of salvation are run past and ousted, having become obsolete or even 'illegitimate.'"[112]

Nevertheless, he believes the question must be asked "whether the history of other peoples cannot play for them, in the order of salvation, a role 'analogous' to that played for the Hebrew people by the history of Israel, as comprising historical events whose divine salvific significance is guaranteed by a prophetic word . . . Israel and Christianity obviously represent a singular case, owing to the unique relationship existing between the two religions; however . . . it may furnish, *mutatis mutandis*, an emblematic model for the relationship between Christianity and other religions."[113]

For Dupuis the relationship between Judaism and Christianity serves "as a catalyst for the reorientation of the relationship between Christianity and the other religions."[114] His position here is similar to Rahner—an attempt is made to acknowledge the *sui generis* nature of the relationship between Old and New covenants, but as I will argue later, his theology of religions fails to do so adequately.

The direction of Dupuis' latest theology of religions is described by him as "inclusive pluralism."[115] This, as the name suggests, tries to

111. Ibid., 219.

112. Ibid.

113. Ibid., 219–20, 229.

114. Ibid., 233.

115. Dupuis, *Christianity and the Religions: From Confrontation to Dialogue*; see especially 87–95.

combine inclusivism and pluralism: "It represents a qualified pluralism allied with a broad inclusivism. It thus offers the key for a theology capable of accounting at once for the Christian faith in Jesus Christ universal Saviour and a positive role of the religions of the world in God's plan for humankind."[116]

This is a "qualified pluralism" because he insists that the ultimate reality towards which all religion tends is the Triune God.[117] The "Christian Trinitarian God represents the Ultimate Reality *an sich*."[118] Within this developing paradigm Dupuis is proposing a dynamic, complementary fulfilment:

> The complementarity intended here is not a mere simple complementarity, understood as a 'one way traffic'. Such a one-way complementarity would mean that, while it is true that the other religions must find their 'complement' in Christianity, the reverse is in no way true, as these have nothing to contribute to Christianity. To hold such unilateral complementarity would amount to going back to the 'fulfilment theory' in the theology of religions, according to which all other religions represent but different expressions, in the various cultures of the world, of the universal aspiration of human beings for union with the Divine Mystery. All would then be merely 'natural' religions, destined to find the fulfilment of their aspirations in the only 'supernatural' religion, which is Christianity. It is easy to see that this theory, largely abandoned today by theologians, makes true interreligious dialogue inconceivable. Christianity has nothing to receive but only to give, nothing to learn but only to teach. There can be no dialogue between religions, but only a Christian monologue directed to the others.[119]

Dupuis suggests here that the type of fulfilment theology which sees Christianity and Jesus Christ as the fulfilment of other religions is "largely abandoned today." However, as will be seen below, fulfilment theology still represents a major theme in Catholic theology of religions, and is far from abandoned in official Church teaching.

On the fulfilment continuum already established, Dupuis' approach is located at the continuity pole, for his approach maintains greater

---

116. Dupuis, "Inclusivist Pluralism as a Paradigm for the Theology of Religions," 4.
117. Dupuis, *Toward a Christian Theology of Religious Pluralism*, 237.
118. Ibid., 259.
119. Dupuis, "Renewal of Christianity through Interreligious Dialogue," 7.

continuity between other religions and Christianity than Rahner's (and far more so than Daniélou's). Dupuis avoids the distinctions between natural and supernatural, religion and revelation. Grace is mediated through other religions, which are salvific. They have abiding value and are not invalidated by encounter with Christianity. Salvation history is coextensive with world history. Other religions are providential, having been raised up as preparations for Christianity. The fulfilment of these in Christianity however, is not to be seen as unidirectional, for Christianity is also complemented by its encounter with the Other. I will refer to this position as "F3."

2.1.4. Daniélou, Rahner, and Dupuis Compared

There are many similarities between Rahner's, Daniélou's, and Dupuis' approaches. All three suggest that the relationship between the Old and New covenants has some analogical application to the relationship between other religions and Christianity, and all believe that Christ or Christianity is in some sense a fulfilment of prior revelation found in other religions (not just Judaism). However, there are also important differences between the three, and highlighting them will emphasize the various nuances of the fulfilment theory.[120]

According to Hedges, there are two main areas of variation in fulfilment theology, and each may be seen as bipolar, having two extremes (a "weak" and a "strong" form), between which a range of options exists. The first variable is the assessment made of the teachings and experiences of non-Christian religions: "There is thus graduation of differences from those who regard the teachings of the non-Christian religions as essentially negative, but redeemed either through some recognition of the need for God, or due to some primal revelation [the 'weak' form], through to those who are ready to speak of the religious experience of Hinduism and Buddhism as being on a par with Judaism, and who see the non-Christian saints as being comparable to the Christian saints [the 'strong' form]."[121]

The second variable involves the assessment made of the origins of other religions:

---

120. To avoid extensive repetition, I refer readers back to the relevant sections above for elaboration of points raised in this comparison and for associated sources.

121. Hedges, *Preparation and Fulfilment*, 41.

> [A] bipolarity appears between those who believe that the non-Christian religions have been created through the Providence of God, and represent part of His divine plan, and believe that they actively point, therefore, towards Jesus [the 'strong' form]. The other extreme consists of those who would suggest that, while the non-Christian religions may have similarities to Christianity, and provide points of contact, these similarities are due only to the fact that there is a common religious instinct in man, and that God has not actually prepared the non-Christian religions as teachers for other nations. However, this does not mean that they cannot be seen, or used, as 'preparations' for Christianity, in that their teachings may be used as pointers to Christianity, but merely makes a statement about their ontological status [this is the weak form].[122]

I suggest that in terms of these variables, Daniélou, Rahner, and Dupuis, represent progressively "stronger" versions of fulfilment. This should be clear from the brief expositions given above, but I will now draw attention to some particularly pertinent points.

In his treatment of "preparation" and "fulfilment" Dupuis suggests these two concepts are "opposite"[123] positions. He suggests the fulfilment theory views all other religions as natural—"varied expressions of *homo naturaliter religiosus*."[124] Only Christianity is the divine response to God, that is, supernatural. Salvation reaches the members of other religions as the divine response to the human religious aspiration but the prior worldview plays no part in their salvation. He suggests Daniélou's approach is an example of this fulfilment category.[125] In direct contrast with fulfilment is preparation, which Dupuis calls the "theory of the presence of Christ in the religions" or the theory of "Christ's inclusive presence."[126] The various religions are ordained by God in salvation history—but to the decisive event in Jesus Christ. The preparation theory refuses to separate nature from grace, it attempts to transcend the dichotomies between the human search for self-transcendence and "God's stooping down to meet us."[127] Members of other religions

---

122. Ibid., 41–42.

123. Dupuis, *Toward a Christian Theology of Religious Pluralism*, 132.

124. Ibid.

125. He also includes John Farquhar, Henri de Lubac, and Hans Urs von Balthasar here. See Dupuis, Ibid., 137–42.

126. Ibid., 132. See also, his exposition of this approach, 143–45.

127. Ibid., 143.

are saved by Christ not *in spite* of their religion but through that religion.[128] No religion is purely natural. They play a positive role before the Christ-event as *praeparatio evangelica,* and they keep "even today a positive value in the order of salvation."[129] Dupuis offers an exposition of Rahner's theology of religions as an example of this category.[130]

Dupuis is correct to recognize the differences between fulfilment and preparation, but I see little reason why such an absolute dichotomy is needed. As I have argued above, I consider it more accurate to identify a continuum characterized by various bipolarities, between which there is a range of intervening positions. For example, Dupuis describes Daniélou as being representative of the "fulfilment" approach, but as I have shown, Daniélou also incorporates elements of "preparation" in his scheme. I concur with Hedges, who asserts that although "it would be possible to use the term 'fulfilment' without reference to 'preparation' . . . it is, to say the least, normative within fulfilment theology for the two to go together."[131] With this qualification in mind, I maintain that Daniélou, Rahner, and Dupuis place increasing emphasis on the "preparation" pole.[132] All three hold a progressive theology of revelation within history in which Christ forms the apex and in this respect they share a common fulfilment perspective. In contrast to Daniélou though, Rahner and Dupuis make a less strict distinction between the natural and supernatural orders, than Daniélou. All agree that humans are never complete strangers to divine grace, but for Rahner and Dupuis this grace is always at work in humans *in concrete ways*—that is through religions. On the contrary, Daniélou maintains this grace is operative apart from these non-Christian religions.[133] Because of this conviction

128. Ibid.

129. Ibid., 132. It is important to note that within this approach there are divergent views concerning the precise nature of the continuing validity of non-Christian religions, after historical and existential encounter with Christianity. This matter will be taken up below.

130. Ibid., 143–45. He also groups Raimondo Panikkar, Hans Küng, and Gustave Thils here.

131. Hedges, *Preparation and Fulfilment*, 29, 33.

132. The subject of "preparation" will be discussed in section 9.3.2 of this volume: "Continuity, Discontinuity, Preparation, and Points of Contact."

133. Veliath notes that Daniélou expressed his satisfaction that the final draft of *Nostra Aetate* eliminated a phrase included in earlier versions, a phrase that Daniélou found "ambiguous." The eliminated phrase described non-Christian religions as "economies of salvation." Veliath, *Theological Approach and Understanding of Religions*, 70.

Rahner and Dupuis come to a very different assessment than Daniélou, of the role and meaning of non-Christian religions. Rahner states: "In view of the social nature of man . . . it is quite unthinkable that man, being what he is, could actually achieve this relationship to God . . . in an absolutely private interior reality and this outside of the actual religious bodies which offer themselves to him in the environment in which he lives."[134]

In a similar vein, Dupuis contends that Daniélou is "unduly restrictive" in his appraisal of the extent of salvation history. For although Daniélou affirms that the "cosmic religion" that preceded the Abrahamic covenant already belongs to the "concrete historical supernatural order" this is not in the sense that God would have manifested himself personally through it. According to Daniélou, under the cosmic covenant, God's self-revelation is only through the cosmos—and is thus only the "prehistory" of salvation based on a natural knowledge which God gives through the creation.[135] Thus, for Rahner and Dupuis, non-Christian religions cannot be seen as merely natural expressions of human wisdom and aspiration as with Daniélou. It follows also that Christianity cannot claim to be the only supernaturally revealed religion.[136] Other religions mediate supernatural grace to those who follow them. They are not merely preparation, they are supernatural acts of God that make saving grace available. Neither can they be relegated to the "prehistory" of salvation as Daniélou does.

Dupuis argues for a continuing role for other religions, even after the Christ-event: "They [other religions] keep, even today, a positive value in the order of salvation by virtue of the operative presence within them, and in some way through them, of the saving mystery of Jesus

---

134. Rahner, "Christianity and the Non-Christian Religions," 128. James Fredericks argues that for Rahner "the notions of a natural and supernatural order are merely 'remainder concepts': although they may be helpful as conceptual clarifications, they refer to a 'Holy Mystery' in which the human and the divine are already incomprehensibly and profoundly interrelated" (Fredericks, "Catholic Church and the Other Religious Paths," 230, referring to Rahner, "Concerning the Relationship between Nature and Grace" in *Theological Investigations*, 1:297–317, esp. 302). Barnes suggests, "Rahner presents us with an important alternative to the fulfilment theory of Daniélou by allowing for the sacramental presence of the Holy Spirit within the religions" (Barnes, *Christian Identity* 60).

135. Dupuis, *Toward a Christian Theology of Religious Pluralism*, 216.

136. Rahner, "Christianity and the Non-Christian Religions," 122.

Christ."[137] In contrast, Rahner suggests that other religions have only provisional value. Non-Christian religions before Christ "in principle were positively willed by God as legitimate ways of salvation,"[138] though they were overtaken and rendered obsolete by the coming of Christ and his death and resurrection.[139] However, we cannot define the precise moment at which that obsolescence takes place in the experience of any individual.[140] It happens only when "Christianity in its explicit and ecclesiastical form becomes an effective reality."[141] Dupuis considers Rahner's view that religions remain "lawful" only up to a point in time as a "weak expression which continues to suppose their provisional and transitory character."[142] Daniélou also maintains that other religions have only provisional value, as was seen above, but for Daniélou their provisional nature is emphasized even more strongly—they are superseded by both Judaism and Christianity. They are "doubly anachronistic."

2.1.5. Vatican II and Post-Conciliar Fulfilment Theology

In order to demonstrate the continued importance of the fulfilment approach in Roman Catholic thought particularly, I here offer a brief analysis of the influence of this view in the teaching of the Second Vatican Council and subsequently. The achievement of the Second Vatican Council has been hailed a "watershed" by Knitter.[143] Its "Declaration on the Relationship of the Church to Non-Christian Religions" (*Nostra Aetate*), approved in 1965, "represents the first time in its history that the Roman Catholic Church has faced this question [the relationship of Christianity to other religions] in such an official way."[144] According to Alan Race, it signaled a change "from exclusivism to inclusivism in the approach to other faiths at a fundamental theological level."[145] The concepts of preparation and fulfilment are evident in the theology of a number of the Council documents. The "Declaration on the

---

137. Dupuis, *Toward a Christian Theology of Religious Pluralism*, 132
138. Rahner, "Church, Churches and Religions," 46.
139. Ibid.
140. Ibid., 48.
141. Ibid., 47.
142. Dupuis, *Toward a Christian Theology of Religious Pluralism*, 314.
143. Knitter, *No Other Name?* 121, 125.
144. Wright, "Watershed of Vatican II," 206.
145. Race, *Christians and Religious Pluralism*, 45.

Church's Missionary Activity" *(Ad Gentes Divinitus)* contains several references to the non-Christian religions. Sullivan notes that the first of these "seems to reflect the view that such religions represent purely human endeavours to reach out to God. However, even such human initiatives fall under the sway of divine providence, and can serve as 'preparation for the gospel.'"[146] He points out that other passages of this decree go further in their evaluation of non-Christian religions and suggest that there are elements in the non-Christian religions which are not the fruit of merely human initiative, but have been sown there by the Holy Spirit.[147]

The notion of preparation is also clearly seen in the document "Dogmatic Constitution on the Church" (*Lumen Gentium*):

> Those also can attain to everlasting salvation who through no fault of their own do not know the Gospel of Christ or his Church, yet sincerely seek God, and moved by grace, strive by their deeds to do His will as it is known to them through the dictates of their conscience. Nor does divine Providence deny the help necessary for salvation to those who, without blame on their part, have not yet arrived at an explicit knowledge of God, but who strive to live a good life, thanks to His grace. *Whatever truth or goodness is found among them is looked upon by the Church as a preparation for the gospel.* She regards such qualities as given by Him who enlightens all men so that they may finally have life.[148]

Nevertheless, the same document also clearly retains an exclusivist dimension. *LG* 16 continues: "But rather often men, deceived by the Evil One, have become caught up in futile reasoning and have exchanged the truth of God for a lie, serving the creature rather than the Creator . . . Or some there are who, living and dying in a world without God, are subject to utter hopelessness. Consequently, to promote the glory of God and procure the salvation of all such men, and mindful of the

---

146. Sullivan, *Salvation Outside the Church?* 165.

147. Ibid. Sullivan refers to *Ad Gentes* 3, 9 and 11. *Ad Gentes* 3 states: "These initiatives [religious endeavors] need to be enlightened and purified, even though, through the kindly workings of Divine Providence, they may sometimes serve as pedagogy toward the triune God, or as a preparation for the gospel." *Ad Gentes* 9 includes, "Whatever elements of truth and grace are to be found among the nations " are describes as "a sort of secret presence of God." *Ad Gentes* 11 refers to "seeds of the Word which lie hidden in other traditions."

148. *Lumen Gentium*, 16 in Ibid., 153–55 (italics added).

command of the Lord, 'Preach the gospel to every creature,' the Church painstakingly fosters her missionary work."[149]

This tension between a certain openness to other religions and yet an insistence that salvation is always in and through Christ and the Church, is characteristic of the Conciliar documents.

We turn now to a brief assessment of how the fulfilment approaches of Daniélou, Rahner, and Dupuis compare to Vatican II and post-Conciliar fulfilment theology. Though the Second Vatican Council represents a major development in the official teaching of the Church, the new assessment of the relationship of Christianity to the non-Christian religions was not unprepared for. David Wright argues that "If any one theologian paved the way for its declaration on non-Christian religions, it was Karl Rahner."[150] Race suggests Rahner has also been the "major architect of the post-Conciliar Catholic contribution to the subject."[151] According to Dupuis, "The fulfilment theory proposed by Daniélou exercises a profound influence . . . The 'Daniélou tendency' has had a significant impact on the magisterium of the church, and it is still found in some post–Vatican II documents."[152] Similarly Michael Barnes asserts that it could be argued that the theology of Vatican II "is simply a reaffirmation of the ancient perspective outlined by Daniélou."[153] Daniélou and Rahner were *Periti* (special advisors) at the Council.[154]

Although the Conciliar documents clearly affirm the possibility of salvation for those outside the Church,[155] they do not submit a detailed theory of the relationship between Christianity and other faiths.

---

149. Vatican Council II, "Dogmatic Constitution of the Church (*Lumen Gentium*), 16. This exclusivist dimension is even more apparent in *Lumen Gentium* 14: "This Sacred Council wishes to turn its attention firstly to the Catholic faithful. Basing itself upon Sacred Scripture and Tradition, it teaches that the Church, now sojourning on earth as an exile, is necessary for salvation. Christ, present to us in His Body, which is the Church, is the one Mediator and the unique way of salvation. In explicit terms He Himself affirmed the necessity of faith and baptism and thereby affirmed also the necessity of the Church, for through baptism as through a door men enter the Church. Whosoever, therefore, knowing that the Catholic Church was made necessary by Christ, would refuse to enter or to remain in it, could not be saved."

150. Wright, "One God, One Lord," 217.

151. Race, *Christians and Religious Pluralism*, 45.

152. Dupuis, *Christianity and the Religions*, 50.

153. Barnes, *Christian Identity*, 51.

154. Vance, "Daniélou, Jean," 147, and Masson, "Rahner, Karl," 427.

155. *Lumen Gentium* 16 is unequivocal in its affirmation of this. See above.

Recent and Contemporary Use of the Israel Analogy and Fulfilment Theology

"In regard to the way in which such people are saved, the Council maintains a studied ambiguity and restraint."[156] Because of this they have been interpreted variously, and this is a matter of controversy.[157] Knitter acknowledges that the Council does not explicitly state that the religions are ways of salvation, but he maintains that "The majority of Catholic thinkers interpret the Conciliar statements to affirm, *implicitly but clearly*, that the religions *are ways of salvation*."[158] Others such as D'Costa dispute this assertion. D'Costa contends that "it is difficult to read the Conciliar documents as giving a positive answer to the question: can other religions, *per se*, in their structures be mediators of supernatural revelation and salvific grace?"[159] He also notes that they are also restrained in their assessment of revelation outside the Judaeo-Christian tradition. In *Nostra Aetate* the term "revelation" is used exclusively of the Old Testament, and D'Costa observes: "This is highly significant, for the term 'revelation' is not used in any of the sections dealing with other religions. This also highlights the *sui generis* relationship with Judaism."[160] Of importance here is the recognition that although Rahner's fulfilment approach does, as had been shown above, propose other religions to be salvific structures, he acknowledges the Council documents are silent on this point.[161]

The position of Vatican II on this matter is therefore closer to that of Daniélou than Rahner. According to Veliath, Daniélou "accepted the orientations of the Council,"[162] but "had some reservations towards what he considered some of the unilateral interpretations of the Conciliar de-

---

156. Fredericks, "Catholic Church and the Other Religious Paths," 227.

157. See, for example, Dupuis, *Toward a Christian Theology of Religious Pluralism*; Sullivan, *Salvation Outside the Church?* 168–81; D'Costa, *Meeting of the Religions*, 101–9. For a comprehensive study, see Ruokanen, *The Catholic Doctrine of Non-Christian Religions according to the Second Vatican Council*.

158. D'Costa, *Meeting of the Religions*, 105, quoting Knitter, "Roman Catholic Approaches to Other Religions: Developments and Tensions." *International Bulletin of Missionary Research* 8 (1984) 50 (italics D'Costa's).

159. Ibid. Cf. Ruokanen's study, which concludes by stating, "This study has shown that the common interpretation of the Council documents as recognizing non-Christian religions to be capable of specific mediation of God's saving grace is invalid" (115).

160. D'Costa, *Meeting of the Religions*, 102–3.

161. Rahner, "On the Importance of the Non-Christian Religions for Salvation," 290–91.

162. Veliath, *Theological Approach and Understanding of Religions*, 9.

crees which characterized the subsequent period."[163] Since the Council, the focus of discussion has shifted from whether those who follow other religions can be saved, to the role of other religions in their salvation. Space prohibits an inclusion of the complex discussion here.[164] However, one document is particularly relevant. In 2000 the Congregation for the Doctrine of the Faith issued a Declaration entitled *Dominus Iesus* (*DI*).[165] The purpose of the document was to address "the growing presence of confused or erroneous ideas and opinions, both within the Church generally and in certain theological circles, regarding . . . the salvific event of Jesus Christ . . . and the necessity of the Church for salvation."[166] Much controversy followed. Indeed, Peter Stravinskas, writes "Aside from *Humanae Vitae* in 1968, I cannot recall any other ecclesiastical text to raise such a brouhaha."[167] According to James Fredericks, *Dominus Iesus* offers an assessment of the Council's teaching regarding the salvation of other religious believers that "is cautious and . . . accurate."[168]

163. Ibid. In correspondence Veliath suggests that with regard to *Nostra Aetate*, Daniélou "felt that too much credit was being given to the role religions played in the salvation of their adherents. But, on the other hand, as a Catholic, he had to accept the doctrine of NA (and he did so, albeit, I suspect reluctantly). If you were to go through the articles written by him at the time of Vatican II, you will observe this hesitancy" (e-mail from Dominic Veliath, 13 January 2005).

164. See the discussion in Sullivan, *Salvation Outside the Church?* 162–98. Sullivan argues that Pope Paul VI preferred to follow the direction of Daniélou and not that taken by Karl Rahner and others. Sullivan's discussion of the position of Pope John Paul II highlights some documents where the pope's theology is closer to Daniélou's, but others where he is closer to Rahner. Gavin D'Costa notes that "While the Pope acknowledges, as with the Council, much that is good, true and holy in non-Christian religions, he is clear in keeping the Council's silence intact regarding non-Christian religions as salvific structures *per se* . . . It is also clear that the grace encountered in non-Christian religions is viewed as a *preparatio evangelica*, though *not* in terms of a division between the grace of creation and the grace of salvation, or natural and supernatural grace, but only because within the historical church is this grace finally properly ordered toward its eschatological fulfilment" (D'Costa, *Meeting of the Religions*, 108–9).

165. Congregation for the Doctrine of the Faith, *Dominus Iesus*. The official status of this declaration is confirmed by the inclusion of the following statement: "The Sovereign Pontiff John Paul II, at the Audience of June 16, 2000, granted to the undersigned Cardinal Prefect [Joseph Cardinal Ratzinger] of the Congregation for the Doctrine of the Faith, with sure knowledge and by his apostolic authority, ratified and confirmed this Declaration, adopted in Plenary Session and ordered its publication."

166. Covering letter by Joseph Cardinal Ratzinger, quoted in Fredericks, "Catholic Church and the Other Religious Paths," 225.

167. Stravinskas, *Salvation Outside the Church?* 126.

168. Fredericks, "Catholic Church and the Other Religious Paths," 233.

Recent and Contemporary Use of the Israel Analogy and Fulfilment Theology

For example, *DI* 21 states that although "some prayers and rituals of the other religions may assume a role of preparation for the Gospel,"[169] these do not have "a divine origin or an *ex opere operato* salvific efficacy, which is proper to the Christian sacraments."[170] *DI* 7 makes a clear distinction between what it calls "belief" as found in other religions and "theological faith" as found in Christianity, and warns that this distinction must be "firmly held."[171] It continues to state that other religions can only provide "religious experience still in search of the absolute truth and still lacking assent to God who reveals himself."[172] Fredericks concludes that: "For the most part, *Dominus Iesus* is more comfortable with Daniélou's approach to religious diversity than with Rahner's,"[173] and this is a judgment with which I concur.

However, this matter is not completely clear and some internal tension exists. For example, although *DI* suggests a "Daniélou preference," there are also Rahnerian characteristics here. For instance, *DI* 8 finishes by quoting from Pope John Paul II, in a way that, according to Fredericks, "does not seem entirely compatible with the strict distinction just asserted between faith and belief. Quoting *Redemptoris missio* no. 55, a text with affinities with Rahner's theology of religions, *Dominus Iesus* acknowledges that God 'does not fail to make himself present in many ways, not only to individuals, but also to entire peoples through their spiritual riches, of which their religions are the main and essential expression.'"[174]

Last, reference must be made to another recent document. In 2001 the Vatican Congregation for the Doctrine of the Faith issued a "Notification" on Dupuis' *Toward a Christian Theology of Religious Pluralism*. Drawing heavily on *DI*, the Notification found "notable ambiguities and difficulties on important doctrinal points, which could lead a reader to erroneous or harmful opinions. These points concerned the interpretation of the sole and universal salvific mediation of Christ, the unicity and completeness of Christ's revelation, the universal salvific

---

169. Congregation for the Doctrine of the Faith, *Dominus Iesus*, 21
170. Ibid.
171. Ibid., 7.
172. Ibid., 7.
173. Fredericks, "Catholic Church and the Other Religious Paths," 231.
174. Ibid., 232.

action of the Holy Spirit, the orientation of all people to the Church, and the value and significance of the salvific function of other religions."[175]

Elsewhere the document states: "The historical revelation of Jesus Christ offers everything necessary for man's salvation and has no need of completion by other religions."[176] Showing clear affinity with parts of *Lumen Gentium* and *Ad Gentes,* the notification continues: "The fact that the elements of truth and goodness present in the various world religions may prepare peoples and cultures to receive the salvific event of Jesus Christ does not imply that the sacred texts of these religions can be considered as complementary to the Old Testament, which is the immediate preparation for the Christ event."[177]

Such statements were almost certainly prompted by Dupuis' suggestion in *Toward A Christian Theology of Religious Pluralism*, that there is such an element of complimentarity: "The sacred scriptures of the nations, along with the Old and New Testaments, represent various manners and forms in which God addresses human beings throughout the continuous process of the divine self-revelation to them." "Revelation is progressive and differentiated. It may even be said that between revelation inside and outside the Judeo-Christian tradition there exists a true complementarity—without prejudice to the decisiveness of the Christ-event. And, equivalently, it may even be said that between the sacred books of the religious traditions and the biblical corpus a similar complementarity may be found."[178]

From the preceding overview it can be seen that the Vatican II and post-Conciliar approach does not proceed as far as Dupuis. D'Costa notes that "While Dupuis's position is extremely nuanced, it still falls short of retaining this delicate Conciliar balance by removing some of the terms of the relations (Church), rather than by fruitfully engaging with them as necessary parameters."[179]

---

175. Congregation for the Doctrine of the Faith, "Notification on the Book *Toward a Christian Theology of Religious Pluralism*," Preface.

176. Ibid., sec. 3.

177. Ibid., sec. 8.

178. Dupuis, *Toward a Christian Theology of Religious Pluralism*, 250, 252.

179. D'Costa, *Meeting of the Religions*, 110. Brad Harper's assessment of the theology of Dupuis and of recent Catholic statements is one with which I concur: "Dupuis' theology of the universal saving revelation of the Logos, not simply *ensarkos*, but especially *asarkos*, leads him to go beyond the 'fulfilment theory' typical of Vatican II which says that God's revelation in Jesus Christ fulfils what is lacking in the inad-

To locate the Conciliar and post-Conciliar fulfilment approach on the fulfilment continuum I have established, I would suggest it lies between "F1" (Daniélou) and "F2" (Rahner). Whether it is closer to F1 or F2 is subject to debate, but I would suggest that on balance it has more affinity with the former.

2.2. Mainline Protestant Use of the Israel Analogy and Fulfilment Theology[180]

As noted above, fulfilment theology is less prominent in Protestant thought than in Roman Catholicism. However, it does form an important strand in some contemporary Protestant approaches. The recent doctoral study by the Indian Protestant Ivan Satyavrata, which focused on the fulfilment approach of Krishna Mohan Banerjea (1813–1885) and Sadhu Sundar Singh (1889–1929) proposes a recovery of the fulfilment approach as a viable way of understanding the relationship between Christianity and other religions. Satyavrata believes the "potential of fulfilment theology has yet to be realised fully."[181] "The experience of Indian converts affords significant evidence to confirm the fulfilment claim that there are elements in the Hindu tradition that can serve as a 'pedagogy' to Christ. It offers empirical verification of a Trinitarian scheme of progressive, differentiated and complementary divine revelation for affirming revelational continuity between Christianity and Hinduism."[182]

---

equate paradigms of other religions—thus, other religions are not technically a way of salvation—but salvation is gained by God's gracious revelation of himself in Christ in spite of the errors of that religion. Moving beyond fulfilment, Dupuis reasons, 'It is legitimate therefore, to point to a convergence between the religious traditions and the mystery of Jesus Christ, as representing various, though not equal, paths along which, through history, God has sought and continues to seek human beings in his Word and his Spirit'" (Harper, "Recent Roman Catholic Statements on the Relationship of the Church to Other Religions," 14 n. 47.) Harper refers to Dupuis, *Toward a Christian Theology of Religious Pluralism*, 37–52.

180. I am using the term "Protestant" in its broadest sense to include "The whole movement within Christianity that originated in the sixteenth century Reformation and later focused in the main traditions of Reformed church life—Lutheran, Reformed (Calvinist/Presbyterian), and Anglican-Episcopalian" (Wright, "Protestantism," 888).

181. Satyavrata, "God Has Not Left Himself without Witness," 317–19, 325.

182. Ibid., i.

Elements of the fulfilment approach and Israel analogy are evident in the 1984 Anglican report *Towards a Theology for Interfaith Dialogue*. In its exposition of inclusivism the report states:

> The relationship between Christianity and other religions is ... analogous to the traditional judgement on its own heritage. As Judaism became interpreted as a preparation for the greater light of the Gospel, so the other religions are seen as forerunners of the Gospel. Some inclusivists would wish to underline more strongly than others the special place of Judaism among the forerunners of the Gospel as witnessing to a special divine disclosure and redemptive activity. The revelation of God in Christ is the concrete, historical form of what remains hidden in the depths of other religions ... *Inclusivist theory stresses how Christianity does in fact complete other forms of religion. As the New Testament writers searched the Jewish Scriptures (what we have come to call the Old Testament), for signs of Christ before his incarnation in the person of Jesus, so the same can be done in relation to other religions.* They too have their teachers, prophets, holy people and scriptures.[183]

We turn now to an exposition of two Protestant theologians who have employed the Israel analogy and fulfilment model in their theology of religions.[184]

2.2.1. John Farquhar (1861–1929)

It has been suggested that in missiological thought (particularly Protestant missiology) in the late nineteenth and early twentieth centuries the fulfilment paradigm was the primary paradigm for understanding the relationship between Christianity and other religions.[185] Its influence can be seen in the proceedings of the Edinburgh World Missionary Conference (1910). Here, a survey of about two hundred missionaries on their view of the relationship between Christianity and other religions revealed that most understood the relationship to be

---

183. Church of England General Synod Board for Mission and Unity, *Towards a Theology for Inter-Faith Dialogue.*, 8–9 (italics added). I accept that the report does not advocate such a view explicitly. However, it offers no critique of the view set forth, thus implying that the analogy made between other religions and the religion of Old Testament Israel is a valid analogy.

184. Farquhar is more correctly understood as a missiologist than a theologian.

185 Cracknell, *Justice, Courtesy and Love*, 221.

Recent and Contemporary Use of the Israel Analogy and Fulfilment Theology

one of Christianity fulfilling these other religions. Kenneth Cracknell suggests the conference "was the moment of *apotheosis* of this idea."[186] The work of the Congregationalist missionary to India John Farquhar is emblematic of the fulfilment theology of this period. The most detailed account of his theology is given in his *Crown of Hinduism*,[187] which he wrote "to discover and state as clearly as possible what relation subsists between Hinduism and Christianity."[188] Farquhar maintains this relation is primarily one of fulfilment (of Hinduism by Christ).[189] According to Eric Sharpe, Farquhar understood fulfilment as comprising three distinct but related processes. First, fulfilment means replacement. In Farquhar's evolutionary scheme, a lower religious stage does not simply develop into a higher stage, but is replaced by this higher stage. Only then can its truths be realized and its quests reach fruition.[190] The second and third processes concern these "truths" and "quests." The truths in Hinduism are fulfilled by reappearing in a higher form in Christianity and Christ fulfils the quests of Hinduism, by providing an answer to its questions, a resolution of its problems, and a goal for its religions strivings: "In this third sense there need be no recourse to postulated 'truths', since a genuine quest can reach an illegitimate goal and an inadequate question receive a wholly wrong answer."[191] All three senses were used by Farquhar, sometimes together and sometimes separately.

Farquhar's approach is governed by two concerns: firstly, a recognition that every element of religion "springs from some genuine instinct, deep seated in the mystery of our common religious nature," and secondly, the conviction that Christianity represents the pinnacle of humanity's religious development—the "final religion."[192] It is with these two principles in mind that he proposes his fulfilment approach. Both principles he believed are held together in the New Testament theme of fulfilment (Matt 5:17). Farquhar acknowledges the primary

---

186. Ibid.

187. Farquhar, *Crown of Hinduism*.

188. Ibid., 3.

189. Sharpe, *Not to Destroy but to Fulfil*, 339. Sharpe notes that Farquhar stresses that it is *Christ* rather than *Christianity* that is the fulfilment of Hinduism.

190. Ibid., 336–37.

191. Ibid., 339.

192. Farquhar, "Christ and the Religions of the World," in *Student Movement* 12, 196, quoted in Satyavrata, "God Has Not Left Himself without Witness," 71.

application of this concept to the Judaeo-Christian tradition, but sees adequate grounds for including non-Christian religions within its scope also.[193] He writes "Christ's own attitude to Judaism ought to be our own attitude to other faiths, even if the gap be far greater and the historical connections absent."[194] Thus, his understanding of how Christ fulfils the Old Testament serves as a controlling model for the relationship of Christian faith to other religions. Indeed, Farquhar observes a greater correlation between some corresponding truths in Hinduism and Christianity than between some aspects of Judaism and Christianity.[195]

Farquhar's understanding of the relationship between other religions and Christianity is primarily one of continuity, but also incorporates elements of discontinuity. The basis for the continuity rests on three principles. Firstly, the universal Fatherhood of God.[196] This Fatherhood is a personal relation between the supreme Spirit and every human being: "God created man in His own image; so that the spirit of man is a finite copy of the infinite Spirit . . . God made man like Himself, so that he might be fit for the immediate, personal, spiritual intercourse of a son with his Heavenly Father . . . God loves every human being with the tender love of a father. Thus, God's relation to every individual human soul is truly that of Father."[197]

Secondly, Farquhar argues that there is an underlying unity in all religions: "The human heart and mind are the same everywhere. Hence there is something which links the lowest religion to the highest. There are gleams of light, suggestions of truth, in the most degraded faith."[198]

And thirdly, Farquhar maintains that Christ is the universal light, the light which lightens every human being.[199] However, he does

---

193. Ibid. Satyavrata does not state what these grounds are.

194. Farquhar, *Papers Submitted to Commission Four of the World Missionary Conference*, Edinburgh, 1910, # 153, 17, quoted in Hedges, *Preparation and Fulfilment*, 286 n. 347.

195. Satyavrata, "God Has Not Left Himself without Witness," 73. Satyavrata refers to Farquhar, "Christ and the Religions of the World," 197, as his source for this assertion.

196. Sharpe, *Not to Destroy*, 340. Sharpe argues that one of the keys to understanding Farquhar's theology is to be found in his use of the historical method, in which the influence of Harnack is to be seen.

197. Farquhar, *Crown of Hinduism*, 119–20.

198. Ibid., 26.

199. Ibid. (Farquhar cites John 1:9 here.)

acknowledge that various religions possess different degrees of light and truth. He also stops short from saying non-Christian religions *themselves* are true. In considering the issue of whether the religions are "true in part" or whether "each is wholly true" or whether "each is the very truth of God," he judges that "Clearly it can only be the former; for these great religions contradict each other very seriously on many points."[200]

According to Paul Hedges, Farquhar viewed non-Christian religions not as divinely inspired, but as of human origin.[201]

> But if all religions are human, and yet men can in the long run hold only Christianity, clearly it must be in some sense, the climax of the religious development of the world, the end and culmination of all religions. If all the great religious instincts, which have created the other faiths, find ultimate satisfaction in Christianity, then Christianity stands in a very definite relation to every religion.[202]

This assessment of non-Christian religions implies some discontinuity between these religions and Christianity. Hedges continues, suggesting: "While he [Farquhar] recognised the reality of the non-Christian's religious yearnings, there is still a Barthian-style radical distinction between true and false religion."[203]

At the heart of Farquhar's argument is his understanding of progressive revelation. "God's method of revelation is not the presentation, once for all, of a complete system of truth expressed in a book from all eternity, but a gradual and historical process."[204] Thus Jesus could affirm the faith of Israel and yet seek to transform it into a new religion. The religion given to Israel was given for the training of Israel, a preparation for the gospel.[205] In the construction of this argument he

---

200. Ibid., 29.

201. Hedges notes that this matter is passed over in Farquhar, *Crown of Hinduism* and most of Farquhar's other works (Hedges, *Preparation and Fulfilment*, 300).

202. Farquhar, *Papers Submitted to Commission Four of the World Missionary Conference*, # 154, 13–145 in Hedges, *Preparation and Fulfilment*, 300–301. Hedges makes the interesting observation that "Quite how, drawing this distinction and denying divine inspiration in the non-Christian religions, Farquhar can argue for the evolution of religions, is a matter unresolved in his thought" (301).

203. Ibid., 333.

204. Farquhar, *Crown of Hinduism*, 51.

205. Ibid.

cites Clement: "Philosophy tutored the Greeks for Christ as the Law did the Hebrews,"[206] and then extends this principle to the religion of India saying: "Thus it will be with India."[207] In this way, Farquhar applies this principle analogously to Hinduism, contending that just as Christ did not come to destroy the Old covenant, so he does not come to destroy anything of value in the Hindu religion.[208]

I noted above, that Farquhar does not give non-Christian religions "inspired" status. Nevertheless, he believed these religions and their scriptures had some revelatory value. However, he likens the light of revelation in these scriptures to the light of the "stars" as contrasted with the light of the "Sun" in Christ.[209] An important dimension of Farquhar's fulfilment approach is the provisional status he grants non-Christian religions. Once the non-Christian has truly encountered Christianity their former religion ceases to be of value for their relationship with God.[210]

I have noted above Farquhar's reliance on a progressive understanding of revelation. His understanding of progression, is in turn, partially based on an evolutionary understanding of reality. Humans need to "upgrade" from lower religions to higher religions.[211] The evolutionary dimension is evident in the definition of fulfilment theology offered by Hedges, who suggests that it represents the most developed and widespread form of fulfilment theology, in this period.[212]

---

206. Ibid., 53. quoting Clement, *Stromata*, 1.28.

207. Ibid.

208. Ibid., 54–55. "Christ provides the fulfilment of each of the highest aspirations and aims of Hinduism . . . Every line of light which is visible in the grossest parts of the religions reappears in Him set in healthy institutions and spiritual worship . . . In Him is focused every ray of light that shines in Hinduism. He is the crown of the faith of India" (457–58).

209. Farquhar writes: "Christ's authority will be maintained supreme in all things. Everything must pass the scrutiny of His Spirit . . . Thus the New Testament will remain the focus of all Revelation, the central sun in the light of which everything must be read and estimated. But the greater books of Hinduism will form a sort of second Old Testament, set like stars around the sun." Farquhar, "The Crown of Hinduism," in *The Contemporary Review* (1910) 98:535: 67–68, quoted in Satyavrata, "God Has Not Left Himself without Witness," 71.

210. Farquhar, *Crown of Hinduism*, 28.

211. Ibid., 27–28.

212. The period of Hedges study was 1840 to 1914, thus encompassing most of Farquhar's important writings. (*The Crown of Hinduism* was published in 1910.)

> Fulfilment theology involves the belief that man has certain innate religious yearnings which can only be satisfied by the full revelation of God; however, it was necessary that mankind was first prepared for this revelation, so a series of lesser religions were given to man. These religions were themselves at different levels, and were made known to man as he became ready to receive them, with "lower" religions being replaced by "higher" religions, until, at last, the 'highest' religion became known. Each of these religions answered man's religious needs, though to differing degrees, and in this way they may be seen as "evolutionary," in that there is a developing progression of religions from a lower to a higher form, each being more suited to man's needs. Further, each religion is held to be ordained by God for the purpose of leading mankind towards his final revelation.[213]

This form of fulfilment theology is less prominent now than in the nineteenth and early twentieth century, partially due to its reliance on an evolutionary interpretation of religion which is now largely discredited.[214]

Farquhar's approach bears some resemblance to both Daniélou's and Rahner's. With Daniélou, he views other religions as of human origin, but with Rahner he attributes to them some revelatory value. With Daniélou, he makes a clear distinction between natural and supernatural. With Rahner, he grants other religions, only provisional value—once the non-Christian has truly encountered Christianity their former religion ceases to be of salvific value. Farquhar incorporates elements of both continuity and discontinuity in his model, and it is difficult to determine which is dominant. In common with Daniélou, Rahner and Dupuis, Farquhar maintains a progressive understanding of salvation history. However, he incorporates an element here that is not evident in the former three, namely an evolutionary understanding of progress. For this reason it is not simple to locate Farquhar's fulfilment within the typology established above (F1–F3), as the evolutionary dimension is not apparent in any of the theologians studied so far.[215] With this quali-

---

213. Hedges, *Preparation and Fulfilment*, 40–41.

214. Race, *Christians and Religious Pluralism*, 57.

215. Indeed, according to Whaling's schema (see section 1.2.), the evolutionary model is a completely separate form of fulfilment to the "promise-fulfilment" or "preparation-fulfilment" model discussed so far. This highlights the difficulty in establishing a rigid typology.

fication in mind, I would propose Farquhar's approach as lying between F1 and F2, but with an evolutionary modification.

2.2.2. Carl Braaten (b. 1929)

As illustrative of more recent mainline Protestant use of the Israel analogy and fulfilment concept, I will outline the use made of these by the Lutheran theologian Carl Braaten. The starting point for Braaten's theology of religions is the reality of revelation in the religions. This reflects the Lutheran emphasis placed on the doctrine of creation. Lutheran theology affirms in the religious experience of humankind an original and continuing revelation that can be considered as a kind of natural theology. "Lutheran orthodoxy clearly taught a twofold revelation and knowledge of God: the general revelation of God through creation and law, and the special revelation of God through Christ and the gospel."[216]

The soteriological core of Lutheran theology consists of the necessity of Christ and the relationship between law and gospel. Because of the necessity of Christ, Lutherans see the gospel of Christ as the "final medium of revelation and therefore the critical norm in a theology of the history of religions."[217] Regarding the role of religion—both other religions and Christianity are relativized "in light of the absolute future of the kingdom that Christianity is to serve."[218]

Braaten states: "The basis and starting point of a Lutheran understanding of the world of religions other than Christianity is neither primarily nor exclusively the revelation of God in the history of Israel, Jesus and the Church."[219] Instead he affirms a general revelation of God apart from the Bible and the history of salvation culminating in Christ. There is in the religions "an echo of God's activity."[220] The religions owe their life to the ongoing activity of God.[221] The reality of God and his revelation "lie behind the religions of humanity as anonymous mystery and hidden power."[222] In the sacred writings of the various religions,

---

216. Braaten, *No Other Gospel!* 70. Cf. Martensen, "Lutheranism and Interfaith Dialogue," 176.

217. Braaten, *No Other Gospel!* 74.

218. Martensen, "Lutheranism and Interfaith Dialogue," 177.

219. Braaten, *No Other Gospel!* 67.

220. Ibid.

221. Ibid., 68.

222. Ibid.

voices pointing to the revelation of God's power and glory can be perceived.²²³ The subsequent quote highlights how Braaten's scheme employs a direct analogy between the Old covenant and other religions:

> In Romans 2 and 7 Paul speaks of the law written on the hearts of the Gentiles, which is nothing else than the law of God working universally through the conscience of people who know not Christ. *Although the understanding of this law may be dark and confusing apart from Christ, its fundamental content is the same as the law given to Israel, in relation to which Christ is announced as its end and fulfilment.* From this point, Lutherans have been able to spell out some analogies. Just as the church fathers could say that Greek philosophy was a preamble to the gospel analogous to the function of Jewish law, so also every religion may play a similar role in the history of humanity. Every religion has prophets who are similar to John the Baptist preparing the way for the coming of Christ. If this were not so, the gospel of Christ would drop like a stone from heaven and could not be translated into other religiocultural settings.²²⁴

Braaten sees the *Logos* (John 1) as "the source of light and life of all people."²²⁵ It is a "principle of universal enlightenment of all people in all times. Thus, wherever truth is found, it will function as a witness to the truth of God incarnate":²²⁶ "The God who comes in Christ has been hiddenly present to all epochs prior to Christ as the power of their end, both in the sense of judgement and of fulfilment. The eschatological light of God's coming kingdom, which shines in Christ, flashes back upon all the religions as the end to which God has been directing them unawares."²²⁷

Braaten's model sees Jesus Christ as the revelation of the eschatological fulfilment of the religions. The gospel does not destroy but fulfils the religions. There is a strong eschatological thrust in this fulfilment— "it is being worked out through the interaction of the religions and will be established for all eyes to see only at the end of history."²²⁸

---

223. Ibid., 69.
224. Ibid. (italics added).
225. Ibid.
226. Ibid., 69–70.
227. Ibid., 7.
228. Ibid., 80.

The material available on Braaten's theology of religions is less extensive than that available for the theologians already studied. Therefore, it is difficult to offer a precise assessment of his fulfilment model. However, based on the brief outline above, it is evident that Braaten's model includes a positive assessment of other religions—they owe their life to the ongoing activity of God, and there is here, an "echo of God's activity." For Braaten, the religions play a role in salvation history—the reality of God and his revelation "lie behind the religions of humanity as anonymous mystery and hidden power." Braaten emphasizes the need for preparation for the gospel in every religion. On the basis of these attributes, his model can be located on the fulfilment continuum between the discontinuity and continuity poles, probably in the proximity of "F2."

2.3. Evangelical Use of the Israel Analogy and Fulfilment Theology

2.3.1. Clark Pinnock (b. 1937)

Pinnock's theology of religions takes as axiomatic the two fundamental principles of a) the universal salvific will of God; b) made known in the particular work of Jesus Christ.[229] These two principles are of course also Rahner's starting point. Pinnock strives to defend an "optimism of salvation."[230] He believes this is possible because of the "faith principle" which is the basis of universal accessibility.[231] His defense of the faith principle is based on two categories of Old Testament believers: the people of Israel and "Holy Pagans."[232] The former are members of the covenant community, the latter, those individuals outside this community, who nevertheless are recorded in scripture as having saving faith.[233] He equates these temporally pre-messianic believers with

---

229 Pinnock, *Wideness in God's Mercy*. Pinnock devotes the first two chapters of this book to defending these axioms. For a significant analysis of Pinnock's inclusivism, see Strange, *Salvation among the Unevangelized*. I concur with Strange's treatment of this subject.

230 Pinnock, *Wideness in God's Mercy*, 17–19.

231. Ibid., 93, 157.

232. Ibid., 93.

233. Pinnock considers that Old Testament "Holy Pagans" include Abel, Enoch,

modern religious peoples who are informationally or epistemologically pre-messianic, for both categories know nothing of Christ: "A person who is informationally premessianic, whether living in ancient or modern times, is in exactly the same spiritual situation."[234] Indeed, Pinnock asks whether it would make any difference if Job had been born in AD 1900 in Outer Mongolia in terms of how God would deal with him.[235] He argues the analogy is valid because both categories of people fall under the universal covenant with Noah.[236] The cosmic covenant made with Noah is the basis for the universal accessibility of salvation.[237] People can relate to God through this cosmic covenant, the Old covenant established with Abraham, or the New covenant through Christ—the content of faith varying in these different epochs. "Before Jesus came, the nation of Israel had to 'make do' with an 'Old Testament'. Sometimes it seems like the nations also had to make do with one."[238] Pinnock asserts that Old Testament believers were saved without professing Christ, their theological knowledge was deficient measured by New Testament standards, and their understanding of God limited—nonetheless they were saved.[239] Here, Pinnock's three-stage salvation-history bears close resemblance to that of Daniélou.

With regard to the fulfilment paradigm there appears to be a development in Pinnock's views. In *A Wideness in God's Mercy* (1992), he dismisses the fulfilment paradigm: "There are so many evil sides to religion that a fulfilment paradigm (the idea that religions point people to Christ) is out of the question. Religions are not ordinarily stepping stones to Christ. More often they are paths to hell . . . Rahner's theory of lawful religion . . . is naïve speculation."[240]

However in *An Inclusivist View* (1995), he supports the fulfilment theory. In his defense of inclusivism (which is the approach Pinnock adopts), he writes:

Daniel, Noah, Job, Melchizedek, Abimelech, Jethro, and the Queen of Sheba. See ibid., 26–27.

234. Ibid., 161.
235. Ibid.
236. Ibid., 105.
237. Ibid., 21, 92.
238. Pinnock, "Religious Pluralism: A Turn to the Holy Spirit," 5–6.
239. Pinnock, *Wideness in God's Mercy*, 163.
240. Ibid., 91.

> The conviction of inclusivism is that the Christian message is the fulfilment, not only of Old Testament religion, but in some way of all religious aspiration and of the human quest itself. The aspirations of the ancient world, the messianic hope of Israel, the quest of the Greek people, and the longings of the Orient can find fulfilment in Jesus Christ. They are among the many and varied ways by which God has spoken to the nations . . . Positive values of non-Christian religions prepare for and are perfected by the light and power of God's revelation in Jesus Christ.[241]

And in *Flame of Love: A Theology of the Holy Spirit* (1996), Pinnock argues, "The history of Israel, for example, led to the coming of Jesus. Here God was at work apart from Jesus Christ but leading up to him. By analogy with Israel, we watch for anticipations in other faiths to be fulfilled in Christ."[242]

Pinnock argues rightly that inclusivism is not a "single, tightly defined position," but rather that there is a spectrum of opinions focusing on the activity of the Spirit in other religions and their precise salvific status.[243] At one end of the spectrum is a "cautious attitude" and at the other, a "less cautious attitude."[244] He calls the former "modal inclusivism." This approach "does not claim that God must or always *does* make positive use of religion in drawing people."[245] Pinnock's modal inclusivism is oriented to the Spirit as graciously present in the world among all peoples "preparing the way of the Lord."[246] The less cautious view does consider other religions to possess salvific status. Pinnock argues that the cautious view is exemplified by the Second Vatican Council, and by his own approach. Indeed, he acknowledges "an enormous debt of gratitude to the Council for its guidance on this topic."[247] He believes the Second Vatican Council "was wise not to declare religions to be ways of salvation."[248] Commending the "spirit and wisdom" of the Second Vatican Council, Pinnock writes: "The Council knows how to distinguish the ontological necessity of Christ's work of redemption from

---

241. Pinnock, "Inclusivist View," 115.
242. Pinnock, *Flame of Love*, 208.
243. Pinnock, "Inclusivist View," 98.
244. Ibid., 99.
245. Ibid., 100.
246. Ibid.
247. Ibid., 97 n. 94.
248. Pinnock, *Wideness in God's Mercy*, 107.

the epistemological situation of sinners. There is no salvation except through Christ, but it is not necessary to possess conscious knowledge of Christ in order to benefit from redemption through him."[249]

The less cautious view is exemplified by the theology of Karl Rahner.[250] Pinnock is critical of Rahner's "anonymous Christianity" as it tends to obscure the differences that Jesus makes when he is known through faith in the gospel: "The believing Jew of the Old Testament was not a Christian, and the believing pagan was not a Jew."[251] However, while he is critical of the term "anonymous Christian," he does affirm that salvation is available to adherents of other religions. He writes: "All inclusivists recognize that there are pagan saints in other religions, but not all would call them 'anonymous Christians' as Rahner does. I myself think it would be better and more biblical to speak of them as believers awaiting messianic salvation."[252]

There are close parallels between aspects of Pinnock's approach and the approaches of Daniélou and Rahner. The pertinent points have been highlighted above. On the fulfilment continuum, it is clear that Pinnock is closest to the position of Daniélou (F1). However, it is arguable that he adopts a more positive assessment of other religions than Daniélou. Nevertheless, he does not proceed as far as Rahner, who considers that the non-Christian religions mediate salvation.

2.3.2. TERRANCE TIESSEN (B. 1944)

Terrance Tiessen has developed the most comprehensive systematic treatment of the subject of Christianity's relationship to other religions from a Reformed perspective.[253] As noted above (section 1.1), he describes his overall position as "accessibilism," which he contrasts with "ecclesiocentrism" and "religious instrumentalism."[254] He is critical of

---

249. Ibid., 74–75.
250. Pinnock, "Inclusivist View," 99.
251. Pinnock, *Wideness in God's Mercy*, 91.
252. Pinnock, "Inclusivist View," 119.
253. Tiessen, *Who Can Be Saved?* This book has been commended as "One of the most satisfactory comprehensive treatments of salvation ever attempted by an evangelical in the Reformed tradition . . . This book will serve as the benchmark reference on the subject for evangelical teachers, pastors, missionaries and students for years to come" (Jonathan Bonk on back cover).
254. Ibid., 33–34. See my discussion of these terms in section 1.1.

religious instrumentalism because "it finds its rationale less in the explicit teaching of Scripture or tradition, than in a desire to view other religions in a more positive light than Christians have often done."[255] He distances himself from the view that "Non-Christian religions have a positive saving potential similar to Judaism in the Old Testament . . . They can be the means by which God's salvation reaches those who have not yet heard the gospel."[256] However, as this brief exposition will show, he does adopt a qualified and nuanced version of the Israel analogy and the fulfilment concept.

In his discussion of the vital issue of salvation and the basis on which individuals will be judged, Tiessen maintains that individuals are only held accountable for their response to the revelation they have received.[257] Of considerable import here is one's understanding of the New Testament concept of the "times of ignorance" (Acts 17:30). Tiessen asserts that this period did not end with the incarnation, but ends with the time of the *knowledge of the incarnation*, i.e., when the gospel is effectively proclaimed to an individual.[258] In this respect, his position is similar to that of Karl Rahner. Tiessen quotes the New Testament theologian I. Howard Marshall, with approval here: "Until the coming of the revelation of God's true nature in Christianity, men lived in ignorance of him. But now the proclamation of the Christian message brings this time to an end *so far as those who hear the gospel are concerned*; they no longer have an excuse for their ignorance. God was prepared to overlook their ignorance, but now he will do so no longer."[259]

With regard to the knowledge necessary for saving faith Tiessen asserts that knowledge of Jesus Christ is not necessary if one is ignorant of him through no fault of their own.[260] There are clear parallels here with the theologies of the Roman Catholic theologians already studied, and with the theology of Vatican II. Tiessen supports this position by referring to the work of Christ outside of the incarnation "the activity

---

255. Ibid., 43.

256. Shenk, *Who Do You Say That I Am?* 43; quoted in Tiessen, *Who Can Be Saved?* 43. Note that Shenk does not support this position either but is merely expressing a common notion among inclusivists.

257. Tiessen, *Who Can Be Saved?* 123–37.

258. Ibid., 132–37.

259. Ibid., 133, quoting Marshall, *Acts*, 289–90 (italics added).

260. Tiessen, *Who Can Be Saved?* 123–37.

of Christ, although crucially related to the events of his life, ministry and death in Palestine, is not confined to that short segment of history. Jesus is the incarnate embodiment of the cosmic Christ who is at work enlightening all people (Jn. 1:9)."[261]

Tiessen suggests it is in light of this reality that we can understand the faith of Abraham, who Paul identifies as the model of the justified believer—even though he had never heard the gospel about Jesus: "If one has to know about Jesus of Nazareth to be saved, then Abraham could not have been saved. Abraham did not have such knowledge, yet he was saved; hence it must be possible to be saved without knowing about Jesus."[262]

In arguing this, Tiessen is drawing an analogy between the Old covenant and the situation today for those who have not heard the gospel. At this point, he qualifies this analogy by acknowledging believers in the Old covenant were a special case: "The saving faith of people within the old covenant community was a response to very significant self-disclosures by God through his messengers. The situation of these old covenant believers is relevant to our situation today in a very limited way, namely, when we contemplate the situation of Jewish people to whom the Spirit has not made clear the identity of Jesus but who have the faith that Abraham had."[263]

With this qualification, the analogy being made is between Old covenant believers and *Jews* today who have not heard of Jesus—it is not extended to adherents of other religions. However, elsewhere in his work, Tiessen makes another analogy. This is an analogy between Old Testament believers who were *not* recipients of the revelation given in Scripture, and people today who are unaware of this revelation: "The people who lived between Adam and Moses—those who lived without the special forms of revelation experienced by the likes of Noah, Enoch and Abraham—then become a category of people whose counterpart may still exist in parts of the world. If we need not assume that those people before Moses were completely outside God's saving work, then we need not assume the same today of people in an analogous situation."[264]

---

261. Ibid., 168, quoting Abraham, *Logic of Evangelism*, 219.
262. Tiessen, *Who Can Be Saved?* 167, quoting Abraham, *Logic of Evangelism*, 220.
263. Tiessen, *Who Can Be Saved?* 168.
264. Ibid., 155.

Tiessen argues here that it is people *outside* the covenant with Abraham and his descendents, who had a saving relationship with God who are analogous to the unevangelized today. Here his position resembles Daniélou's theory of the "Holy Pagans." However, Tiessen seems to contradict this qualification elsewhere in his work. He states that the death of Christ is always the ground of salvation, but suggests some people who are ignorant of it still live under the revelational terms of the Old covenant—even though they are historically living in the New covenant.[265] He refers to the argument presented by a fellow evangelical, the late Norman Anderson:

> I believe that Anderson is right to draw an analogy between the situation of Old Testament believers and that of the unevangelized today. He posits that 'their repentance and faith (themselves the result of God's work in their hearts) opened the gate, as it were, to the grace, mercy and forgiveness which he always longed to extend to them, and which was to be made for ever available at the cross.' Anderson then asks, 'Might it not be true of the follower of some other religion that the God of all mercy had worked in his heart by his Spirit, bringing him in some measure to realise his sin and need for forgiveness, and enabling him, in the twilight as it were, to throw himself on the mercy of God?'[266]

It should be noted that Anderson is specifically referring here to *Jews in the Old covenant*.[267] This is an important distinction, and is one that Tiessen does not take into account at this point. It is apparent that although the precise nature of the analogy being drawn by Tiessen is unclear, he evidently does perceive there to be some kind of analogical application of the Old covenant to other religions today. In correspondence with the current writer he confirmed that the analogy should be made between *those outside the covenant with Israel and the*

---

265. Ibid., 198.

266. Ibid., quoting Anderson, *Christianity and World Religions*, 148–49.

267. Indeed Anderson refers here to the "multitudes of Jews who, in Old Testament times, turned to God in repentance. He also acknowledges, "It is true that they had a special divine revelation in which to put their trust" (148). Anderson does not suggest (as Tiessen does) that some people today live under the revelational terms of the Old covenant. While I disagree with the way Tiessen uses Anderson's argument, I see no reason to deny Anderson's proposal itself. However, the fact that Old Testament believers were saved should not be used as the basis for this proposal.

unevangelized today, but as I have shown, he also extends this using the Israel analogy.[268]

With this in mind, it is interesting to note that Tiessen is critical of fulfilment theology because he believes it undermines the unique role of Israel:[269] "It was Israel's unique role to be the people from whom the Messiah would come, the one through whom God's promise to Abraham of blessing for the whole world would be fulfilled. There is only one such Savior of the world and, therefore, no other people share an analogous position or have other prophets or scriptures that are preparatory to the Lord Christ."[270]

Tiessen maintains that objective special revelation, of the universally normative kind ceased with the apostles, because God's revelation in Christ was complete—he spoke his last word in Jesus (Heb 1:1–3).[271] Thus, the Scriptures of other religions are not parallel to the Old Testament as God's revelation for them, preparing them for Christ, nor are they additional revelation that supplements or even supplants the New Testament as religious authority.

> I am made decidedly uneasy, for instance, by the kind of proposal put forward by Steve Charleston when he suggests that "instead

---

268. Tiessen writes: "In my own understanding, God's saving work in the world after Christ's ascension is not best viewed by analogy with his work within Israel under the old covenant. Rather, we need to contemplate God's saving work outside of Israel in the old covenant. It is that work which I see as having continuity with God's saving work outside of the new covenant community. It is true that I think that the faith of Abraham can still save, in the case of Jews whom God has not illumined concerning the identity of Jesus, and who have, therefore, not rejected Christ. In this regard, I find contemplation of the experience of Jews during the time of Jesus on earth to be very instructive. As I have noted in my book, I do not think that the point of salvation in their lives is easy to discern. It is particularly not possible to demonstrate that no one of Jesus' contemporaries was saved until they reached a fully developed acknowledgment that he was their promised Messiah, and that (contrary to most prior expectations) the Messiah was himself God. So, the Jews are indeed a special case then and now. This in no way discourages evangelism among the Jews. But, I do not think that the Old Testament will support an 'Israelocentrism' in regard to salvation and it is in continuity with that reality that I do not find ecclesiocentrism in the New Testament" (e-mail from Tiessen, 9 September 2004).

269. Tiessen's understanding of the unique place of Israel is not entirely clear. He evidently recognizes some uniqueness, but as I have argued, he does not apply this sufficiently or consistently.

270. Tiessen, *Who Can Be Saved?* 378.

271. Ibid., 370.

of speaking about Native American spirituality," we should begin to speak of "an Old Testament of Native America."²⁷²

However, Tiessen does advocate a modified form of preparation and fulfilment, which he calls "providential preparation." This concept maintains that God is not intentionally developing other religions *themselves* in preparation for the gospel, but has placed "types" in them—in the sense of Old Testament types, pointing forward to Christ. These types may be stepping stones or preparations for the gospel. This is not to argue for direct continuity between other religions and Christianity, but allows that God may be preparing people from within their current religious context to receive Christ.²⁷³ His argument here draws on the work of Gerald McDermott who gives the example of the concept of grace. McDermott contends that "the idea that human beings are accepted by the divine on the basis of divine love rather than human effort" is taught by Mahayana Buddhists and Hindu *bhaktas*.²⁷⁴ However, McDermott observes: "the grace taught by these communities is not the same as the grace shown by the God of Jesus Christ. Humans are sometimes expected to do something to merit this grace, and the Hindu and Buddhist deities do not manifest the holiness of the God of Israel. Hence the grace is not as costly as for the Christian Trinity. Nevertheless, the basic idea of divine love overruling legal demands is present."²⁷⁵

These types are not the product of "general revelation," but they are also not "special revelation" of the "universally normative, covenantal type"²⁷⁶ for they do not reveal salvation through Jesus Christ.²⁷⁷

Tiessen proposes an approach to other religions which he calls the "point-of-contact" approach.²⁷⁸ In brief, this perspective grants that

---

272. Ibid. Tiessen is here referring to Charleston, "The Old Testament of Native America: Constructing Christian Theologies from the Underside," 72.

273. Tiessen, *Who Can Be Saved?* 380. Influential in Tiessen's proposal is the writing of the eighteenth-century Reformed theologian Jonathan Edwards. Edwards used the idea of *prisca theologia* (ancient theology) to argue that there were vestiges of true religion in non-Christian traditions. See Tiessen, *Who Can be Saved?* 60. For further discussion of *prisca theologia*, see section 9.3.2. of the current volume.

274. Ibid., quoting Dermott, *Can Evangelicals Learn Form World Religions?* 113.

275. Tiessen, *Who Can Be Saved?* 382, quoting Dermott, *Can Evangelicals Learn from World Religions?* 113 n. 138.

276. Tiessen, *Who Can Be Saved?* 381.

277. Ibid.

278. Ibid., 303.

there is no fundamental agreement or continuity between the religions, but there are common points from which dialogue and evangelism can take place. These common points can be expected because the grace of God is at work in the lives of many devout people in the other religions, even though that does not assure a saving response in all such cases.[279]

During my exposition of Tiessen's approach I have highlighted parallels with the approaches of Daniélou and Rahner. With Rahner, Tiessen does not consider "the times of ignorance" to have ended with the Advent, but rather with historical and existential encounter with the gospel. However, contrary to Rahner he does not attribute non-Christian religions with any salvific validity. In contrast to Daniélou, Tiessen does attribute non-Christian religions with some revelatory function. They contain elements that can be seen as "providential preparation," but the religions themselves have not been raised up intentionally by God. There is no direct continuity between the other religions and Christianity, and the relationship is primarily characterized by discontinuity. Nevertheless, this is not a complete discontinuity either, for there are "points of contact." With these characteristics Tiessen's model can be located on the fulfilment continuum closest to the F1 (Daniélou) position.

2.4. Summary

The purpose of this chapter has been to offer an exposition of how the Israel analogy and fulfilment theology are commonly employed in the theology of religions, particularly in inclusivist and other accessibilist theologies. I have surveyed seven theologians from across the confessional spectrum and have found that the way in which fulfilment theology is employed varies greatly. To illustrate this variety, I have developed a simple typology, a "fulfilment continuum" along which the various theologies can be located. The typology is not precise but provides a helpful framework for the ongoing discussion. Among the theologians here studied, the fulfilment approaches of Daniélou (F1) and Rahner (F2) are dominant. The approach taken by Dupuis (F3) was shown to be a more radical development, going beyond both Daniélou and Rahner. The development of a fulfilment typology has been a worthwhile exercise in order to distinguish the various types of fulfilment, which is

279. Ibid.

something the existing literature on fulfilment theology does not do. However, I will argue in later sections that all these forms of fulfilment are invalid, for all misapply the relationship between Old and New covenants to the relationship between other religions and Christianity. For this reason I will not distinguish between these fulfilment types in the subsequent discussion.

Among the various theologians here studied there is much variety, but it is important to note that all without exception employ, and arguably rely on, the Israel analogy. A further interesting observation concerns the way in which this analogy is used. A common feature is the acknowledgment of the unique relationship between Old and New covenants, but then the apparent downplaying of this unique relationship by the analogical extension of this relationship to other religions.[280] I will argue later that the use of the Israel analogy seriously undermines the *sui generis* relationship between Old and New covenants and so between Israel and the Church. I will go on to show that this in turn has important implications for understanding salvation history and consequently for the whole theology of religions. If, as I will argue, fulfilment theology and the Israel analogy are seriously flawed due to a range of biblical and theological considerations, there are important consequences for inclusivist and other accessibilist approaches to the theology of religions.

Before proceeding to examine these biblical and theological considerations, it is necessary to establish a correct understanding of the place of Israel in Christian theology.[281] This is the task to which we now turn.

---

280. Rahner, Dupuis, Farquhar, and Tiessen all explicitly make reference to the unique relationship between Old and New covenants but nevertheless believe the analogical extension of this relationship to other religions is valid. However, none specify in any detail why they believe this move to be valid.

281. Refer to the introduction for an explanation of how I am using the concept of "Israel."

Part II

Israel and the Church

INTRODUCTION

Chapters 1 and 2 of this book have outlined the way in which the relationship between the Old and New covenants is often analogically applied to the relationship between other religions and Christianity. As this work develops, I will argue that this analogical application is in fact a misuse of the relationship, and is only possible if the primary relationship between Israel[1] and the Church (or between Old and New covenants) is itself misunderstood. I will demonstrate that the affect of this misunderstanding is not only apparent in the use of the Israel analogy and fulfillment concept but has important implications for the entire theology of religions.

The primary objective of this part of the book (chapters 3–5) is to demonstrate that Israel is an essential topic for a Christian theology of religions. It has often been incorrectly handled, and there continues to be much debate about the role of Israel and its relationship to Christianity. It is essential to have a correct understanding of Israel itself before one can develop a correct understanding of its relationship with Christianity, and a failure to understand this prior relationship is an important contributory factor in the misunderstanding of the relationship between other religions and Christianity, which I suggest is evident in the use of the Israel analogy.

---

1. See the introduction to this volume for an explanation of how I am using the term "Israel."

3

WHY ISRAEL MATTERS FOR CHRISTIAN THEOLOGY

> We believe that Jesus Christ is the Saviour of all mankind. In Him there is neither Jew nor Greek, but we also believe that God elected Israel for the carrying out of His saving purpose. Jesus Christ as Man was a Jew. The Church of Jesus Christ is built upon the foundation of the Apostles and Prophets, all of whom were Jews, so that to be a member of the Christian Church is to be involved with the Jews in our one indivisible hope in Jesus Christ. Jesus, the Messiah of Israel, was accepted by Gentiles but rejected by His own people. Nevertheless God is so gracious and mighty that He even makes the crucifixion of His Son to be the salvation of the Gentiles (Rom 11:11). Whether we are scandalized or not, that means we are grafted into the old tree of Israel (Rom 11:24), so that the people of the New Covenant cannot be separated from the people of the Old Covenant.[1]

This statement, drafted by a group of delegates at the Second Assembly of the World Council of Churches (1954), helpfully summarizes some of the reasons why Israel "matters" for Christian theology.[2] Israel is not incidental to the task of Christian theology and cannot be understood merely as historical background to Christianity, or as another world religion sharing some common features with Christianity (most notably, the Scriptures known as the Hebrew Bible or the Old Testament, to

---

1. World Council of Churches, "The Second Assembly of the World Council of Churches," 10–11.

2. According to the accompanying notes, this statement was made by a number of delegates to the Second Assembly who were unhappy that the formal statement did not include a section on the hope of Israel in its statement on *Christ our Hope*. See World Council of Churches, *The Theology of the Churches and the Jewish People*, 10.

Jews and Christians respectively).[3] The question of Israel does not just have bearing on limited aspects of Christian theology such as eschatology and it needs treatment in its own right—not just as an adjunct to a theological position such as dispensationalism or covenant theology.[4] The way in which Israel is understood has profound implications for the whole range of Christian theology,[5] including the construction of a Christian theology of religions. Being a Christian implicitly demands one adopts a stance towards the Jewish People. This must be so, because Christianity concerns the God of the Hebrew Scriptures, Jesus was a Jew, Christianity began as a Jewish phenomenon, Jesus and the disciples preached first to Jews, and the first people to believe that Jesus was the Messiah were Jews. According to the understanding of these first Christians, the *place* of revelation was the land of the Jews, the *source*

---

3. Pontifical Biblical Commission, "The Jewish People and Their Sacred Scriptures in the Christian Bible" (hereafter JPSSCB). This document properly states that "Without the Old Testament, the New Testament would be an unintelligible book, a plant deprived of its roots and destined to dry up and wither" (par. 84).

4. Dispensationalism recognizes the continuing importance of Israel, and in contrast to historical (or covenantal) premillennialism, it maintains that the title Israel should not be applied to the church, because Jewish Israel is a distinct people of God separate from the church. A fuller definition is given below (chapter 4). Covenant theology is considered in chapter 8.

Diprose writes: "It seemed to me that the question of Israel had become some kind of theological football that two opposing teams of theologians kicked about in accordance with their particular agendas. For dispensationalists it was apparently important that ethnic Israel be given a high profile while for reformed theologians it was apparently important to show that, with the advent of the Church, ethnic Israel's significance had been irrevocably eclipsed. The result: to affirm that there are institutional distinctions between Israel and the Church was another way of declaring oneself to be a dispensationalist while denial of such distinctions was a sign of reformed orthodoxy" (Diprose, *Israel in the Development of Christian Thought*, xi). This thesis will argue such a polarization is unnecessary, and it is quite reasonable to affirm a continuing place for Israel in Christian theology without necessarily adopting a dispensational approach. The Reformed theologian Willem VanGemeren proposes that "The exegetical and theological issues surrounding the modern nation of Israel may lead the church to renewal as it faces the question of how best to respond to a living situation. While some communities may want to right every wrong of Israel, others avoid the issue altogether out of theological bias. The time for covenant, promise-fulfillment, and dispensational theologians is now! With the rise of interest in Messianic Judaism, Christians and Jews have a unique opportunity to build bridges, develop dialogue, and renew the discussions between church and synagogue that have been suspended since the second century A.D." (VanGemeren, *The Progress of Redemption*, 442).

5. Diprose, *Israel in the Development of Christian Thought*, xi. Diprose highlights the impact on ecclesiology, eschatology, soteriology, and missiology.

of revelation was the God of Israel, the first *recipients* of revelation were the Jews and the main *character* of revelation was the Jew—Jesus.[6] Furthermore, a central Christian conviction is that the Christian faith is for all—and hence this includes the Jews.[7] So, the issue has never been *whether* Christians should speak and act with reference to the Jewish people—the question is *how* they should.[8]

Bruce Marshall rightly maintains that the Church until the end of time remains linked to and dependent on Israel, in that a knowledge of Israel's narrated history from Abraham to Jesus is indispensable for Christians: "Without a grasp of Israel's history, and so without Jewish scripture, Christians cannot locate the Father of the Lord Jesus Christ, and so cannot know whom they are to worship."[9]

Jakob Jocz highlights the underlying reason why Israel is so important for the church, noting that the unique nature of the Jewish people is ultimately not due to *who they are*, but because of *who God is*: "The significance the Church attaches to the Jews over and above any other people is not occasioned by what the Jews are in themselves, but by what God is. The faithfulness of God, the Church does not call into question: God's gifts are without repentance (Rom 11:29). Blindness in part has fallen on Israel, but this is not God's final word. God's purposes are never defeated and his triumph is the last. It is because the Church clings to the God of Israel that she also clings to Israel."[10]

However, affirming the uniqueness of this people and this relationship, is but a start. Understanding the *nature* of the relationship, and its implications for Christian theology is a complex matter in which there are widely varying positions. At the heart of this complexity is the reality that the relationship is neither one of complete continuity nor one of complete discontinuity, but incorporates aspects of both.[11] This

---

6. Zaretsky, *Jewish Evangelism: A Call to the Church*, 11.

7. Soulen, *God of Israel*, 1.

8. "Ever since Christians first appeared on the scene, they have confessed that the God of the Hebrew Scriptures acted in Jesus of Nazareth for all the world. That is the center of Christian faith. All the rest turns on this" (ibid.).

9. Karl Barth has clearly affirmed the importance of the Israel-church relationship. He makes the striking statement that Christianity is nothing but a "balloon trip [if] separated from the history of Israel" (Barth, *Dogmatics in Outline*, 75). Cf. Marshall, "Christ and the Cultures: The Jewish People and Christian Theology," 84.

10. Jocz, *The Jewish People and Jesus Christ*, 314.

11. See the excellent compilation of essays from the perspectives of continuity

opens up an vast array of theological and exegetical considerations, as Carl Amerding points out, "When the question of a Christian view of Israel is introduced, the discussion is necessarily moved to the level of historic and contemporary exegetical and theological concerns that are unique to Christian consciousness as a community which has derived its major identity from its continuity or discontinuity with the Israelites of the old covenant."[12]

Similarly, David Holwerda rightly states that the varying viewpoints on the status and role of Israel in Christian theology "are not so much a matter of this or that isolated text as it is a matter of disagreement concerning foundational perspectives."[13] The issue of Israel goes right to the heart of Christian theology.

In the following discussion I shall argue that much Christian theology misrepresents or neglects Israel, and will assert that these errors are not a new development but have deep historic roots.[14] This has had a major affect on important aspects of systematic theology, and particularly on the Christian theology of religions. During the second half of the twentieth century there has been a monumental change in attitudes to Israel and the Jewish people among many churches and theologians of all denominations. The Holocaust, and the founding of the Jewish Nation in 1948 raised the profile of the Jewish People to a level unprecedented in modern history. Holwerda states that "the twentieth century . . . has become a watershed in Christian thinking about the relationship of Jesus to Jewish Israel. Never since the second century have Christian theologians devoted so much energy to rethinking this question as in the present century."[15]

Prior to this time, Israel was generally either almost ignored by Christian theology or received a very negative assessment, often characterized by a harsh and simplistic supersessionist paradigm, which has as its fundamental premise the assertion that the Gentile Church has

---

and discontinuity in Feinberg, *Continuity and Discontinuity: Perspectives on the Relationship between the Old and New Testaments*.

12. Amerding, "The Meaning of Israel in Evangelical Thought," 119.

13. Holwerda, *Jesus and Israel: One Covenant or Two?* x.

14. For some excellent historical accounts, see the relevant chapters in Holwerda, *Jesus and Israel: One Covenant or Two?*; Diprose, *Israel in the Development of Christian Thought*; and Soulen, *God of Israel*

15. Holwerda, *Jesus and Israel*, 1.

permanently replaced ethnic Israel in God's purposes for the world.[16] However, this supersessionist paradigm is being supplanted by a variety of other paradigms for the relationship between Israel and the church.[17] Before considering the dominant views on the nature of this relationship, I will first offer a brief overview of the neglect of Israel by Christian theology.

The systematic theologian Hendrikus Berkhof suggests the Church has seemed to forget Israel almost completely: "This is especially the case in creedal statements and systematic theology handbooks. An example is the structure of the Apostles Creed: the confession jumps directly from the Creator to Christ . . . In the study of faith . . . usually . . . one proceeds directly from the doctrine of sin to Christology. There is hardly any room and interest for God's history with Israel."[18]

Kendall Soulen's analysis of the prevalence of supersessionism in Christian theology argues that overcoming this legacy requires an evaluation of how Christians have understood the theological and narrative unity of the Bible as a whole. He contends that the standard "canonical narrative" is "structurally supersessionist."[19] He supports this assertion by explaining that the standard model turns on four key episodes: Creation; Fall; Incarnation and the inauguration of the church; and Final Consummation. Such an approach, he maintains, neglects the Hebrew Scriptures, with the exception of Genesis 1–3. The model "unifies the Christian canon in a manner that renders the Hebrew Scriptures largely indecisive for shaping conclusions about how God's purposes engage creation in universal and enduring ways."[20] I believe Soulen overstates his case, but the general thrust of his argument is valid.[21]

---

16. Supersessionism is addressed in chapter 4, where a full definition can be found.

17. See chapter 5 for a consideration of these developing paradigms.

18. Berkhof. *Christian Faith: An Introduction to the Study of the Faith*, rev. ed., 225, quoted in Fackre, *The Doctrine of Revelation*, 107. Cf. Diprose, *Israel in the Development of Christian Thought*, 2.

19. Soulen, *God of Israel*, 31. A "canonical narrative" is "an interpretive instrument that provides a framework for reading the Christian Bible as a theological and narrative unity" (12).

20. Ibid.

21. Soulen overstates his case because although Christian theology's meta-narrative may be presented as proceeding from creation and fall (Gen 1–3) to redemption, as Soulen suggests, Christian theology is reliant on much of the Old Testament for understanding salvation history, the nature of God, the reality of sin, the inability

According to some theologians, this ignoring of Israel can be traced back to the church's earliest days, when the opinion that the Jews had been disowned by God as a result of their rejection of Christ, was widely held.[22] According to Craig Blaising, supersessionism first arose after the suppression of the Bar Kochba revolt in AD 135. It was then expressed in the writings of second-century Christians such as Justin Martyr, Melito of Sardis, and in the *Letter of Barnabas*. This view quickly spread and became the prevailing viewpoint of the church.[23]

This general view dominated the patristic and medieval periods of Church history.[24] Diprose states: "The negative stance of Christians against Jews and Judaism consolidated into an *Adversus Judaeos* tradition which permeated much of the writings of the church fathers, favouring *replacement theology*."[25] Even the major renewal of interest in the Old Testament resulting from the Protestant Reformation did not significantly change the prevailing attitude. Indeed, Martin Luther's harsh polemic concerning the Jews, is well known.[26] Luther ranked the Jews with "Turks, fanatics, and papists" as agents of Satan in the final assault on the Church before Christ's return and he advocated the complete elimination of Jewish worship from Christian territories.[27] Calvin's attitude toward the Jewish people is more tolerant, but is, according to Holwerda, still largely negative.[28] Part of the reason for his more tolerant stance was his positive use of the Old Testament and law in his theology, but more because of his understanding of Romans 11:26–29,

---

of humankind to meet God's righteous demands, the need of a sacrificial substitute and representative who will take the place of sinners and satisfy God's justice, the nature of such substitute, and so on. I also disagree with the end result of Soulen's anti-supersessionist approach regarding the salvific status of the Jews, and about Christian mission to the Jews; for Soulen maintains that evangelistic mission is unnecessary. See ibid., 170–72.

22. Holwerda, *Jesus and Israel: One Covenant or Two?* 2.

23. Blaising, "The Future of Israel as a Theological Question," 435.

24. See Harrelson and Falk, *Jews and Christians: A Troubled Family*, 46–47. Cf. Holwerda, *Jesus and Israel*; Diprose, *Israel in the Development of Christian Thought*, 73–103.

25. Diprose, *Israel in the Development of Christian Thought*, 75 (emphasis original).

26. See for example, Luther, "On the Jews and Their Lies" (1543).

27. See Holwerda, *Jesus and Israel*, 2–3. Holwerda notes that many in the Reformation disagreed with Luther regarding the elimination of Jewish worship from Christian territories.

28. Ibid., 2–4.

which Calvin believed affirmed the continuing election of the Jewish people.[29] Based on Israel's election, Calvin maintained a future conversion of Jewish Israel. However, his belief in this future conversion never received much prominence in his theology or in that of his followers—instead the emphasis fell on the Church as the New Israel. Indeed, some developed a theology of election that no longer left room for any significant use of election with regard to Jewish Israel.[30] A study by the World Alliance of Reformed Churches (WARC) argues that Puritanism and its derivatives are the one stream of the Reformation that deal explicitly with the question of Israel.[31]

The concept of covenant is central for the Reformed tradition. It is also key in Jewish theology.[32] Reformed theology emphasizes similarity rather than difference, continuity rather than discontinuity between the Old and New covenants. The WARC study suggests that this allows for a positive evaluation of God's covenant with Old Testament Israel, for the old covenant, like the new, is founded on grace and love, and is eternal and inviolable. It concludes that this reality could have been a good basis for building a positive "Israel theology," especially when combined with the doctrine of election. However the study observes that covenant theology was worked out in a way that made the Jews "invisible."[33] "For the general conception of the reformers is that the covenant people of the Old Testament were Christians before Christ." Israel in its own identity disappeared.[34] The Westminster Confession (1647)[35] is silent on the future of the Jewish people and gives only gen-

---

29. See *Institutes*, IV.16.14. Calvin's view of the status of Israel and its relationship with the Church is variously interpreted. See section 4.1 n. 19, of the present volume.

30. Holwerda, *Jesus and Israel*, 4.

31. Leer, "Aspects of Historical Reformed Theology," 5. Sell does not specify how Puritan theology deals with the question of Israel. He refers to the following works: Iain Murray, *The Puritan Hope* (London, 1971) and Peter Toon, ed., *Puritans, the Millennium and the Future of Israel: Puritan Eschatology 1600 to 1660* (London, 1970).

32. Ibid., 6.

33. Ibid., 10. The study argues that election in the Reformed documents seems to be almost entirely individualistic—not corporate.

34. Ibid.

35. The Westminster Confession is the most influential Reformed confession in the English-speaking world. It has been adopted by Presbyterian churches as well as by many Congregational and Baptist churches. Frame, "Westminster Confession," 1168.

eral guidelines on the relationship between the covenants.[36] The Belgic Confession (1561) is likewise silent on the question of Israel.[37]

According to Carl Braaten and Robert Jenson, the founding theologians of modern Protestantism—Friedrich Schleiermacher, Georg W. F. Hegel, and Adolf von Harnack continued this supersessionist approach.[38] In *The Christian Faith,* Schleiermacher wrote: "Christianity does indeed stand in a special historical connection with Judaism, but so far as concerns its historical existence and its aim, its relations to Judaism and Heathenism are the same."[39] Harnack adopts a "neo-Marcionite" approach to the Old Testament, expressed in this oft-cited extract from his volume on Marcion: "To reject the Old Testament in the second century was a mistake which the Great Church rightly rejected; to keep it in the sixteenth century was a fate which the Reformation could not yet avoid; but to retain it after the nineteenth century as a canonical document in Protestantism results from paralysis of religion and the Church."[40]

Within Hegel's dialectical interpretation of history, Judaism represents a primitive stage in the history of religions, superseded by Christianity as the absolute religion.[41]

One notable exception to this general picture of the marginalizing of Israel is that of the minority view of premillennialism,[42] which has

---

36. VanGemeren, "Israel as the Hermeneutical Crux (1)," 132.

37. The Belgic Confession together with the Heidelberg Catechism and the Canons of Dort provided the confessional foundation of Dutch Reformed churches and remain the basis of the North American Christian Reformed Church. Engen, "Belgic Confession," 132. Only one article of this confession gives any guidance on the relationship between the Old and New covenants. Article 25 reads, "We believe that the ceremonies and figures of the law ceased at the coming of Christ, and that all the shadows are accomplished; so that the use of them must be abolished among Christians: yet the truth and substance of them remain with us in Jesus Christ, in whom they have their completion. In the meantime we still use the testimonies taken out of the law and the prophets, to confirm us in the doctrine of the gospel, and to regulate our life in all honesty to the glory of God, according to his will." quoted in VanGemeren, "Israel as the Hermeneutical Crux (1)," 132.

38. Braaten and Jenson, *Jews and Christians: People of God,* vii–viii.

39. Schleiermacher, *The Christian Faith,* 60 quoted in Braaten and Jenson, *Jews and Christians,* vii–viii.

40. Adolf von Harnack, *Marcion: Das Evangelium vom fremden Gott* (Leipzig, 1921), (page number not given) as cited in Baker, *Two Testaments, One Bible,* 49.

41. Braaten and Jenson, *Jews and Christians,* viii.

42. Historic/covenantal premillennialism is the view that the millennium will follow the return of Christ. Historic proponents include Irenaeus, Tertullian, and Justin.

persisted throughout the history of the church. This historic or covenantal premillennialism received fresh impetus in the nineteenth and twentieth centuries through the influence of dispensationalism (also known as dispensational premillennialism). Dispensationalism recognizes the continuing importance of Israel and in contrast to historical (or covenantal) premillennialism, it maintains that the title "Israel" should *not* be applied to the Church because Jewish Israel is a distinct people of God separate from the church. The approach distinguishes between God's eternal purposes for Israel and the Church in separate dispensations: Israel is seen as God's earthly people, and the Church is his heavenly people. When Israel did not accept Jesus as their Messiah, the fulfilment of Old Testament prophecy was interrupted. During this interruption the gospel goes out to the Gentiles and the Church is formed. However, dispensationalists maintain that this was not God's original purpose and that the Church does not fulfil the Old Testament promises for the Church is not Israel. Only after the Church is removed from history by the rapture, and Jesus returns to rule over a converted Jewish nation will the clock of prophecy begin again and move toward fulfilment. Since the promises were given to the literal descendents of Abraham, they must be fulfilled by them.[43] With the founding of the State of Israel in 1948, this view has become very popular among fundamentalists and some evangelicals.[44]

This brief historical survey serves to demonstrate the prevalence in Christian theology of a tendency to either ignore Israel or give it a very negative assessment. This has serious consequences for Christian theology: "For the church to attempt to dispense with Israel [is] perilously like playing Hamlet without the Prince of Denmark."[45] The next chapter provides an outline and critique of supersessionism, and in doing so begins to lay the foundations for the understanding of Israel adopted in this thesis. This will be an important component in the subsequent critique of the Israel analogy.

This view teaches that God's future purposes for a restored Israel depend on faith in Jesus Christ and involve a close relationship with the worldwide church, both enjoying God's blessings together during the millennium.

43. See Poythress, *Understanding Dispensationalists*; and Blaising and Bock, *Progressive Dispensationalism*.

44. Holwerda, *Jesus and Israel: One Covenant or Two?* 4–5.

45. Gerald Sloyan. "Who Are the People of God?" quoted in Goldingay, *Theological Diversity and the Authority of the Old Testament*, 82.

4

AN OUTLINE AND CRITIQUE OF SUPERSESSIONISM (REPLACEMENT THEOLOGY)

Supersessionism[1] has as its fundamental premise the assertion that the Gentile Church has permanently superseded or replaced ethnic Israel in God's purposes for the world. Israel does not have a future in the plan of God and the role of the Jewish people in the economy of salvation was purely preparatory. It is important to recognize that "replacement theology" and "supersessionism" are generally not theological systems consciously advocated by theologians, but are more often terms coined by opponents. However, the theology of replacement has been implicit in most traditional systematic theologies. The terms are also somewhat misleading because they do not reveal the range of positions that exist within this general approach. Instead, they suggest that replacement or supersessionism entails the permanent and total replacement of Israel by the Church. However, supersessionism exists in a number of forms—all maintain that the Church has replaced Israel, but there are wide variations on what this replacement entails.[2]

---

1. Also known as replacement theology. I will use these terms interchangeably.

2. Kendall Soulen develops a threefold typology. See Soulen, *God of Israel*, 30–31. "'Punitive supersessionism" maintains that "God abrogates his covenant with Israel . . . on account of Israel's rejection of Christ and the gospel . . . Because the Jews obstinately reject God's action in Christ, God in turn angrily rejects and punishes the Jews." "Economic supersessionism" maintains that Israel is not replaced because of its disobedience, but rather because its role in the history of redemption has finished with the advent of Christ. This approach "logically entails the ontological, historical, and moral obsolescence of Israel's existence after Christ" (30). The third supersessionist approach identified by Soulen is "structural supersessionism." This form exists at a

An Outline and Critique of Supersessionism (Replacement Theology)

In this chapter and in chapter 5, I will argue that according to the New Testament much of what was formerly true of Israel *is* now true of the Church. Israel enjoyed a special relationship with God based on election and so also does the Church. Just as Israel was called to be a light to the nations, so Christ entrusted a missionary mandate to the Church. According to Diprose, Jesus' choice of 12 disciples was a sign to the Jews that the continuation of salvation history was, from the time of Pentecost, to be linked primarily with the Church. "Thus no one can deny that the Church stands in continuity with Israel in the working out of God's plan. The question is whether this implies the *cessation* of Israel's special elective status and thus the eclipse of her significance in salvation history."[3]

Therefore, the position I adopt can be described as "modified replacement" because I do affirm a continuing role for the Jewish People in the plan of salvation. The approach I adopt is broadly in line with the positions of Herman Ridderbos and Steve Motyer. Motyer describes his approach as broadly "replacementist," but acknowledges the term covers a range of positions "in which either Jesus, or the church, or the new covenant are held to 'replace' Israel or the old covenant."[4] The term is not well chosen according to Motyer: "The problem with it is its overtone of 'terminate,' which gives the unfortunate impression that those who take this view perforce believe that God has 'finished' with Israel, and written off the old covenant. This is not true."[5]

Similarly, Ridderbos could be described as fitting this "modified replacement" model. He believes there is a "tension-filled unity" concerning Israel's rejection and its election.[6] The Church takes the place of Israel as the historical people of God,[7] and yet Israel has not been permanently replaced: "Thus on the one hand Paul is able to see the church of the Gentiles as endowed with all the privileges and blessings

---

deeper level than either punitive or economic supersessionism in Christian theology, because it "unifies the Christian canon in a manner that renders the Hebrew Scriptures largely indecisive for shaping conclusions about how Gods purposes engage creation in universal and enduring ways" (31). Cf. Fackre, "Perspectives on the Place of Israel in Christian Faith," 7–17; Fackre, *Revelation*, 108.

3. Diprose, *Israel in the Development of Christian Thought*, 32.
4. Motyer, "Israel in God's Plan," 1.
5. Ibid.
6. Ridderbos, *Paul: An Outline of His Theology*, 356.
7. Ibid., 333–34.

of Israel, and to see it occupy the place of unbelieving Israel, and yet on the other hand to uphold to the full the continuation of God's original redemptive intentions with Israel as the historical people of God."[8]

According to Michael Vlach other theologians who hold a "dualist" replacement view (i.e. a view that incorporates aspects of replacement *and* continuing election) are John Calvin, George Ladd, Millard Erickson and Wayne Grudem.[9] With these, I affirm that it is possible to adopt a position that incorporates aspects of replacement and continuing election, that is, aspects of discontinuity and continuity.

The *permanent* replacement of Israel by the Church is, as already noted, a fundamental premise of supersessionism. This view is often justified on the basis of some biblical texts that are interpreted in such a way to suggest that all that had formerly pertained to ethnic Israel now pertains to the Church.[10] However, Vlach argues careful exegesis of these texts shows that none of these passages necessarily support replacement theology. Rather, replacement theology arose out of historical circumstances that led the Church to believe it had replaced Israel. It did not arise out of a careful study of Scripture and it has led to a careless use (or non-use) of Israel in Christian theology. Theologically the case for replacement theology is very weak and does not hold up to exegetical scrutiny.[11] Similarly, Blaising argues that supersessionism lives today purely on the momentum of its own tradition, as developments in the twentieth century have undercut its supposed historical and biblical bases.[12] A full assessment of replacement theology and the

---

8. Ibid., 360–61.

9. Vlach, "Variations within Supersessionism."

10. Vlach, "Has the Church Replaced Israel in God's Plan?" 12, lists the following: verses that supposedly apply the terms *Israel* and *Jew* to the Church (Gal 6:16; Rom 2:28–29; 9:6), passages that apply the language used of Old Testament Israel to the Church (1 Pet 2:9; Phil 3:3), Verses that refer to members of the Church as "sons of Abraham" or "seeds of Abraham" (Gal 3:7, 28–29), a passage that shows equality between Jews and Gentiles (Eph 2:11–15, 19), a passage that applies the New covenant to the Church (Heb 8:8–13).

11. Ibid., 32.

12. Blaising, "Future of Israel," 436. Blaising does not specify what these developments are, but given the context of his argument, it is likely that he is referring to exegetical developments. Likewise, Diprose contends that although there are verses that are compatible with replacement theology (such as Gal 6:16 and 1 Pet 2:4–10.), these fall far short of requiring this position (Diprose, *Israel in the Development of Christian Thought*, 70).

An Outline and Critique of Supersessionism (Replacement Theology)

passages listed above is outside the scope of this thesis. However, I will now outline two key New Testament affirmations that are in conflict with the view that Israel has been permanently replaced by the Church. These two have been selected due to the importance they will play in my developing argument.

Chapters 9–11 of Paul's letter to the Romans are particularly important here, and I will base my critique on this passage (though not to the exclusion of other relevant texts).[13] As I have already stated, I do believe a modified replacement view *is* compatible with the biblical witness, and therefore modified replacement is not the subject of this critique.

4.1. The Jewish People Are Still in a Covenant Relationship with God

I consider the New Testament to clearly support a future for ethnic Israel, and it is therefore at variance with any kind of replacement theology that denies this. Without doubt, the most important passage of the New Testament to affirm this is Romans 9–11. As C. E. B. Cranfield declares:

> It is only where the Church persists in refusing to learn this message where it secretly—perhaps quite unconsciously!—believes that its own existence is based on human achievement, and so fails to understand God's mercy to itself, that it is unable to believe in God's mercy for still unbelieving Israel, and so entertains the ugly and unscriptural notion that God has cast off His people Israel and simply replaced it by the Christian Church. These three chapters [Romans 9–11] emphatically forbid us to speak of the Church as having once and for all taken the place of the Jewish people.[14]

It is clear from Paul's letter that God has not rejected Israel, as some Gentile Christians in Rome seem erroneously to have supposed. Paul teaches that Israel has not lost all distinctive significance in God's

---

13. E. P. Sanders states: "It is only in Romans, and explicitly in Romans 9–11, that Paul directly addresses the question of the status of the Jews [that is, their salvific status]" (Sanders, quoted in Johnson, "A New Testament Understanding of the Jewish Rejection of Jesus," 229).

14. Cranfield, *Romans*, 448.

plan.[15] He states that as far as the gospel is concerned, the Jewish people are "enemies of God for your [that is the Gentiles] sake," but as far as election is concerned, they are loved on account of the patriarchs, for God's gifts and his call are irrevocable (Rom 11:1–2, 28–29). Therefore, although it is tragic that many Jews do not enter into the blessings of the gospel, this does not mean God has abandoned his commitment to Israel.[16] Israel has stumbled (9:32b–33; 11:9–11), but, Paul says, it has not stumbled so far as to fall beyond recovery (11:11).[17] The fall is not total (for a remnant remain), and neither is it final, for there will be a recovery.[18] Calvin states, "Nor, however great the contumacy with which they persist in warring against the gospel, are we therefore to despise them. We must consider, that in respect of the promise, the blessing of God still resides among them; and, as the apostle testifies, will never entirely depart from them, seeing that 'the gifts and calling of God are without repentance' (Rom. xi. 29)."[19]

According to Karl Barth, the Jews were, are, and will remain the chosen people of God—nothing can alter this divinely ordained fact.[20] For Bruce Marshall, the main problem with supersessionism is that if it is true, then God cannot be trusted. For Christians believe God has, in Jesus Christ, promised salvation to all humanity, by grace through faith. This promise is permanent and irrevocable. God will never do anything to take it back or supersede it. However, the same God made a similar promise to Abraham prior to this. God promised Abraham that he and his descendents would be God's people forever (Gen 17:7). Both promises are permanent and irrevocable. To cast doubt on one

---

15. Motyer, *Israel in the Plan of God*, 164–67. Similarly, Walter Kaiser states, "The New Testament clearly teaches that God has not cast off disobedient Israel, for they are the natural branches into which the Church has been grafted" (Kaiser, "An Assessment of 'Replacement Theology,'" 10).

16. Motyer, *Israel in the Plan of God*, 40.

17. Moo, *The Epistle to the Romans*, 686–89.

18. Ibid.

19. *Institutes*, IV.16.14. However, Calvin's views on the nature of Israel and its relationship with the church are complex (and sometimes apparently contradictory). According to VanGemeren, "Some have seen utter rejection of Israel in Calvin's writing, whereas others have also viewed the hope for national Israel" (VanGemeren, "Israel as the Hermeneutical Crux (1)," 142).

20. Barth, *Dogmatics in Outline*, 75. Cf. Marshall, "Christ and the Cultures," 89. "The election of Israel . . . is as much in force after Christ as it was when Israel was poised to enter the promised land."

undermines both; "if God's pledge of salvation to the world in Jesus Christ is unsurpassable, then the election of Israel is unsurpassable. Christians cannot therefore be supersessionists about Israel unless they are willing to be supersessionists about Jesus—which is to say, unless they are willing to stop being Christians."[21]

Therefore, Paul's teaching in Romans 9–11 that Israel is an enemy of the gospel but still the elect of God is contrary to the suggestion that Jewish Israel has been completely rejected by God: "God's hardening of his disobedient people is not his negation of their election."[22] In Romans 11:1–6, Paul introduces the idea of a believing remnant of Israel as evidence that God has not rejected his people. However, Holwerda rightly points out that:

> We err if we assume that the significance of the remnant pertains only to elect individuals and no one else. If we assume that the people of God in 11:1 is now restricted to the elect remnant, we undercut the rest of Paul's argument. Nowhere in Romans 11 does the apostle withdraw from unbelieving Jewish Israel the reality of being the people of God or the fact of their election. Instead, Paul points to himself and other Jewish Christians as evidence that God has not withdrawn his grace from Jewish Israel. This remnant is a sign that God is still faithful to his election of Jewish Israel. The remnant signifies to the whole of Israel the essential nature of true Israel and what Israel is always called to be because the Jewish Christian remnant exists as the Israel of God, whose status is based not on works but on grace.[23]

To understand the argument Paul is developing here, it is important to recognize the connection that exists between chapters 9–11 and the preceding chapters (1–8). Chapter 8 functions as a climax to the proclamation contained in chapters 1–7. This proclamation concerns the Apostle's absolute confidence that nothing can separate the believer from the electing love of God. Then there is an abrupt change of tone

---

21. Marshall, "Christ and the Cultures," 88.

22. Holwerda, *Jesus and Israel*, 166.

23. Ibid. Holwerda notes Calvin's distinction between the election of a people as distinct and the election of individuals (*Institutes* III.21.7) and suggests that while this distinction has some validity, one must not make this distinction into a separation that denies the bonds of corporate solidarity—for the remnant represents and is significant for the rest of Israel. 164 n. 18. Cf. Diprose, *Israel in the Development of Christian Thought*, 16–17. For further elaboration of the differences between corporate and individual election see below, section 5.3.

in Romans 9; for given the reality of Jewish resistance to the gospel, the question of whether election is a reliable guarantee arises. If Israel can apparently fall away, then perhaps this casts doubt on the Christian's confidence in God's electing love in Jesus Christ. However, the apostle's confidence concerning the salvation of unbelieving Jewish Israel rests precisely on the *same* foundation as his certainty concerning the salvation of those who are in Christ, namely, that nothing can frustrate the purposes of God's electing love.[24] It should be noted that Paul's argument is not focused primarily on the destiny of *individual* unbelievers but rather on the *corporate* destiny of Jewish Israel and of the Gentile world in the history of redemption.[25] Paul is not accounting for the present status of unbelieving Israel by arguing that the true Israel was always less than the total number of Abraham's descendants (although this is true); instead he is primarily establishing the essence of what it means to *be Israel*. If Israel forgets its true nature and tries to establish another basis for its existence, then it lives outside the promise and gifts of God.[26]

The Gospels and Acts speak of judgment for all who reject the claims of Jesus. They reject any appeal to the patriarchs by those in Jewish Israel who refuse to acknowledge these claims (e.g., Matt 21:43, John 5:46; 8:34–59).[27] Because of this, many theologians wrongly conclude that there is no future for ethnic Israel. However, Holwerda rightly observes that "the Gospels and Acts never explicitly make a definitive judgment on the *future* for unbelieving Jewish Israel. Instead, they focus on the *present* manifestation of unbelief, the judgment that necessarily falls on such unbelief, and the consequent *present* loss of covenant blessings."[28]

Furthermore, Holwerda makes the important observation, that for God's chosen people to be subject to God's judgment for failing to believe is not a novel New Testament development. Judgment does not mean rejection or replacement and this same principle is evident in the witness of the Old Testament prophets. Paul's answer to the question about the status of unbelieving Israel is precisely the same as that given by the Old Testament prophets during other times of Israel's disobedience.

---

24. Moo, *Romans*, 547–51, 555–74.

25. The salvation-historical orientation of Paul's theology will be considered further in section 7.2.2 of this book.

26. Moo, *Romans*, 570–76. Cf. Holwerda, *Jesus and Israel*, 156.

27. Holwerda, *Jesus and Israel: One Covenant or Two?* 54–55, 148.

28. Ibid., 149.

From this, Holwerda concludes that "If their [the Gospels' and Acts'] language of judgment assumes Old Testament covenant perspectives, there is nothing in the Gospels or Acts that either biblically or logically entails an absolute or definitive rejection of Jewish Israel."[29] Moreover, these judgments are not detached from God's plan of salvation—but are intended to further his purposes. In this case it serves the salvation of the Gentiles: "all peoples will be blessed through you" (Gen 12:3, 26:4, 28:14). However, this is not the ultimate end. God's ultimate intention is to save Israel by making it jealous. The gathering of the Gentiles does not definitively displace Jewish Israel, rather, it serves God's purpose of achieving Israel's full inclusion.[30]

The assertion that the Church has replaced Israel is sometimes based on an incorrect understanding of fulfilment. A more complete analysis of the biblical concept of fulfilment will be considered in chapter 9 of this work, but it first requires brief comment here. At the heart of the relationship between Old and New covenants is the concept of fulfillment—in its true sense. The New Testament clearly portrays Christ as the fulfilment of the Old Testament. In Jesus, the law and prophets are fulfilled and "all the promises of God find their 'yes'" (2 Cor 1:20). However, the "new" should not be interpreted as a rejection of the "old," namely, God's covenant relationship with Israel.[31] Commenting on this error, Isaac Rottenberg argues, "When the church declared itself to be the 'New Israel,' it usually did so not in order to acknowledge in gratitude God's new initiatives in Jesus Christ, but rather to reinforce false notions about the church's calling. Ecclesiastical claims that run counter to the biblical witness (for example, Paul's affirmation in Romans 11:29 that the gifts and the call of God are irrevocable) became accepted as New Testament doctrine."[32]

Rottenberg argues that many incorrect representations of fulfilment "have found their basic source in a loss of eschatological perspective."[33] The fulfilment of the Old by the New is a full and complete fulfilment—but at present has been realized only in part—the full realization

29. Ibid., 150.

30. Moo, *Romans*, 710–12.

31. The New covenant fulfils the Abrahamic and Mosaic covenants in different ways. This important theme will be unpacked in chapter 8 of this book.

32. Rottenberg, "Fulfillment Theology and the Future of Christian-Jewish Relations," 67.

33. Ibid., 68

awaits the eschaton. The emphasis of the New Testament is on foretaste, not the full realization of divine redemption in present history.[34] Since the notion of the Church's replacing rejected Israel is incorrect, it follows that it is also inappropriate to refer to the Church as the "New Israel."[35] Colin Chapman points out that since Gentile believers are grafted into Israel, "The church should never be described as 'the new Israel.'"[36] According to Jocz, the idea of a "New" or "Spiritual" Israel has no New Testament basis: "There can be no plural to Israel. The idea of another Israel is utterly alien to the NT, as alien as the idea that beside the God of Israel there can be another God."[37]

Thus, I suggest that rather than "replacement" the present relationship of the Church to Israel represents an "expansion."[38]

4.2. God's Purposes for Israel Will Be Fulfilled. Israel Still Serves a Purpose

My second main argument refuting the traditional supersessionist view takes the point just established a step further. Not only does Scripture testify to the ongoing validity of the covenant relationship between God and the Jewish people, but it also affirms that they are still serving a purpose in God's plans for the world. Despite Israel's rejection of their Messiah, the Apostle Paul claims that God's Word concerning Israel will be fulfilled (Rom 9:6, 27–29; 11:1–5, 26–29). This fulfilment will be accomplished in a twofold manner. At the present time, God is fulfilling

---

34. Enzo Bianchi declares that "Israel is the church's eschatological goad and it is no accident that the church has lost the sense of eschatological tension; this happened as the church increasingly lost sight of the mystery and permanence of Israel." This statement was made in November 1987 by the Roman Catholic scholar Enzo Bianchi, at a seminar on the topic "Twenty years after *Nostra Aetate*"; cited in Diprose, *Israel in the Development of Christian Thought*, 141.

35. Although I believe the term "*r*enewed Israel" could be adopted without the unhelpful connotation of permanent replacement.

36. Chapman, "'Israel and Palestine: Where Is God in the Conflict?'" 11. Cf. Blaising, "Future of Israel," 446–47.

37. Jocz, *A Theology of Election*, 120.

38. Klett, "Not Replacement . . . Expansion!" Fred Klett explains: "God has not replaced the Jewish people with the church. Quite the contrary, God has grafted Gentile branches into the tree of believing Israel, a tree made up of all true believers, both Jewish and Gentile, a tree rooted in the faith of the patriarchs (Romans 11:17–24), God has expanded Israel, not replaced it."

the word that promised the salvation of a remnant according to God's gracious election which includes Israelites such as himself, as opposed to the whole of Israel. (Rom 11:1–2, 5).[39] On the most part, the hearts of the Jewish people have been hardened, but even this present hardening serves the broader purposes of God. This is the way God has chosen to extend the riches of salvation to the Gentiles (Rom 11:25).[40] This is a mystery in that whereas one might have expected Israel to be blessed in full prior to blessing being extended to Gentiles, in actual fact God will bring in the fullness of the Gentiles first while Israel is for the most part hardened. This astonishing reversal of expectations is the intention of Israel's God and, according to Bruce Marshall, it is a great mystery which the Gentiles must ponder in awe.[41]

The second aspect of the fulfilment of God's purposes for Israel is a future one, in which the fullness of Israel will be saved. Israel's rejection of God in the present time means the reconciliation of the Gentiles to God, however, their future acceptance will mean "life from the dead" (Rom 11:15), "All Israel will be saved" (Rom 11:26–27). There is considerable debate regarding the meaning of "all Israel," however, I believe the context indicates that the reference is to ethnic Israel as a corporate entity.[42] Such a view is supported by Murray who states that the references to "Israel" throughout Romans are to ethnic or national Israel and clearly so in verse 25, therefore the word could hardly take on a different meaning in the very next verse (26).[43] Moo concurs, stating that the reference is to ethnic Israel as it has been throughout the passage.[44]

---

39. Blaising, "Future of Israel," 437.

40. Moo, *Romans*, 713–19. Cf. Marshall, "Christ and the Cultures," 89; Holwerda, *Jesus and Israel: One Covenant or Two?* 157.

41. Marshall, "Christ and the Cultures," 89. Cf. The First Assembly of the World Council of Churches (1948), official report on "The Christian Approach to the Jews," reprinted in World Council of Churches, *The Theology of the Churches and the Jewish People*, 6: "For many the continued existence of a Jewish people which does not acknowledge Christ is a divine mystery which finds its only sufficient explanation in the purpose of God's unchanging faithfulness and mercy (Rom 11:25–29)."

42. Contra N. T. Wright, who considers "all Israel" to be a reference to the Church as a redefined Israel. See Wright, *Climax of the Covenant*, 246–51.

43. John Murray, states, "It is exegetically impossible to give to 'Israel' in this verse any other denotation that that which belongs to the term throughout this chapter" (Murray, *Epistle to the Romans*, 96). Cf. Das, *Paul and the Jews*, 109–13. Cf. Williamson, *Sealed with an Oath*, 189–91.

44. Moo, *Romans*, 710–37, esp. 722–23.

However, the meaning of this phrase needs to be related to the earlier reference to the "full inclusion" of Israel in Romans 11:12. Full inclusion does not necessarily imply the salvation of every individual who ever belonged to ethnic Israel, for full inclusion is being contrasted with the current remnant—it is not suggesting Jewish universalism.[45] This full inclusion will only transpire when the time of hardening has ended.[46] This event is eschatological, and will occur at the time of the second coming of Christ.[47] Thus, Scripture affirms a future of glorious blessing for ethnic Israel in the plan of God. The eschatological salvation of Israel as a whole will mean even greater riches for the world.[48] They will not form a separate program or separate entity next to the Church,[49] but their salvation will represent their "full inclusion" in the one community (Rom 1:12) of which they remain the elected root (Rom 11:16–24).[50]

Supersessionism requires a negative judgment of Israel's corporate election. A vital distinction that must be recognized here, is that between corporeal election and individual election. The entire Jewish people are elect in the former sense, and are in a covenant relationship with God. However, affirming this does not imply that all individual Jews are elect to salvation and are in right standing before God.[51] Paul is aware that "not all who are Israel are Israel" (Rom 9:6), but that does not mean that only part of Israel is the elect people of God.[52] Therefore, I believe any form of supersessionism that denies the elect status of Israel, and denies Israel has any future in the plan of God, is at variance with the teaching of Scripture. However, putting Israel back into the "theological equation" is not straightforward. The rejection of replacement theology has resulted in a number of other approaches to the place of Israel in Christian theology, which now need to be considered.

---

45. Ibid., 722–23.

46 Holwerda, *Jesus and Israel: One Covenant or Two*, 169.

47. Diprose, *Israel in the Development of Christian Thought*, 61.

48. Blaising, "Future of Israel," 438.

49. Woudstra, "Israel and the Church," 237.

50. Marshall, "Christ and the Cultures," 90.

51. I will cover this subject more fully in section 8.3.2, where I consider the different roles of the Abrahamic and Sinaitic covenants in salvation history.

52. Glaser, "Critique of the Two-Covenant Theory," 59.

5

OUTLINE AND CRITIQUE OF THE "NEW MAJORITY VIEWS"[1]

This chapter will consider some of the developing paradigms that are taking the place of replacement theology. These challenges have developed in the second half of the twentieth century primarily in the context of Jewish-Christian dialogue. The emerging new majority views are highlighted well by a statement made by a group of Jewish scholars in 2000. The Statement, *Dabru Emet* (Hebrew: "Speak the Truth"), declares that recent years have witnessed "a dramatic and unprecedented shift in Jewish and Christian relations."[2] This transformation is attributed, by this statement, to Christians who no longer characterize Judaism "as a failed religion, or, at best, a religion that prepared the way and is completed in Christianity."[3] Many denominations, and interdenominational bodies such as the World Council of Churches have during these past few decades, issued important declarations on the relationship between Christians and Jews.[4] Typically, these declarations express remorse for

1. I adopt the term "new majority views" from Ronald Diprose (see for example, Diprose, "Israel and Christian Theology"; *Israel in the Development of Christian Thought*; "Jewish-Christian Dialogue and Soteriology"). The term is used to describe the prevailing paradigms for the Israel-Church relationship that have developed in opposition to supersessionism.

2. Frymer-Kensky et al., "Dabru Emet."

3. Ibid.

4. See for example, World Council of Churches, *Theology of the Churches and the Jewish People* for a collection of statements from the WCC and its member Churches, including the Synod of the Evangelical Church in Germany (1950), the Netherlands Reformed Church (1951 and 1970), the General Conference of the United Methodist Church, USA (1972), the General Convention of the American Lutheran Church (1974), the Council of the Evangelical Church in Germany (1975), the Central Board

historic Church complicity in anti-Semitism, most notably the *Shoah*.[5] They emphasize the common roots of Judaism and Christianity, and affirm the continuing election of Israel. They also often encourage support for the state of Israel.

The Roman Catholic Church has arguably pioneered this new development. One particularly influential event in this process was the Second Vatican Council (1962–1965). Of all the declarations produced by this Council, the most significant for the Church's relationship with the Jewish People is *Nostra Aetate*. John Pawlikowski argues that this document, together with many parallel Protestant documents "fundamentally changed Christianity's theological posture relative to Jews and Judaism that had permeated its theology, art, and practice for nearly eighteen hundred years. Jews were now seen as integral to the ongoing divine covenant."[6] However, he also notes that the affect of *Nostra Aetate* and the parallel Protestant documents has yet to be fully realized.[7] Another commentator, Jaroslav Pelikan, judges that it was "The most forceful official Christian affirmation of the permanence of the covenant with Israel, at least since the ninth, tenth and eleventh chapters of the Epistle to the Romans."[8]

What have emerged as the "new majority views" have also been described as a theology of recognition,[9] or a theology of continuity.[10] All reject supersessionism and affirm the ongoing election of Israel but there is a great deal of diversity regarding the implications of affirming this ongoing election.[11] "Anti-supersessionism" has champions ranging from conservative evangelicals to radical pluralists.[12] Some theologians

---

of the Swiss Protestant Church Federation (1977), the Norwegian Bishops' Conference (1977), and the General Assembly of the Presbyterian Church, USA (1987).

5. *Shoah* is the Hebrew term for the Holocaust. It is translated "desolation."

6. Pawlikowski, "Reflections on Covenant and Mission," 3.

7. Ibid., 5.

8. Pelikan, *Christian Tradition* 5:334; quoted in Diprose, *Israel in the Development of Christian Thought*, 33.

9. Joann Spillman adopts this term, defining it as "a particular kind of Christian theology that recognizes the enduring role of Judaism in God's plan for revelation and salvation and thus sees Judaism as genuinely revelatory and salvific." Spillman, "The Image of Covenant in Christian Understandings of Judaism," 63–65

10. Ibid. Spillman suggests the term was introduced by Roy Eckardt.

11 Holwerda, *Jesus and Israel*, 5, 151.

12. Fackre, *Doctrine of Revelation*, 109–12

state that there is now no need for the Jewish people to accept Jesus Christ as their Messiah. Others reject supersessionism but retain the traditional christological claims.[13] Some contend that it is not possible to assert that there is an essential connection between Jesus and Israel, without straying into anti-Semitism and they argue that rejection of supersessionism is only possible with radical Christological revision.[14] However, according to Gabriel Fackre, all maintain the *noetic* as well as the *soteric* role of the Jewish people: there is a permanent place for Israel in the Christian faith.[15] This chapter will consider the two most prominent formulations of anti-supersessionism. These are the dual or two-covenant approach and the single-covenant approach.[16]

5.1a. The Dual- or Two-Covenant Paradigm

Dual- or two-covenant theology is a general label for a school of thought that now arguably represents the dominant position among the new majority views, particularly among those engaged in Jewish-Christian dialogue.[17] Proponents of this view include Franz Rosenzweig, James Parkes, John Pawlikowski, Peter von der Osten-Sacken, and Rosemary Radford Ruether.[18]

The paradigm is based on the premise that Jews and Christians are bound by two different but equal covenants. Jesus Christ is thus not the Messiah of the Jews, only of the Gentiles, and has saving relevance only

---

13. Marshall, "Christ and the Cultures," 81.

14. See, for example, Ruether, *Faith and Fratricide*, 64.

15. Fackre, *Doctrine of Revelation*, 109.

16. The term "single-covenant" can be rather misleading. As used here it applies to a particular understanding of the relationship between Judaism and Christianity. It should be noted that an entirely different understanding of "single-covenant" is found in Reformed or covenantal theology. There "single-covenant" maintains that the various biblical covenants are all part of an overall covenant of grace. (See chapter 8 of this book for an exposition of covenant theology.)

17. Blaising, "Future of Israel," 440. Cf. Glaser, "Critique of the Two-Covenant Theory," 56. Glaser argues that *Nostra Aetate* moved the Roman Catholic Church in the direction of the two-covenant theory.

18. Key works include Rosenzweig, *Star of Redemption*; Parkes, *Foundation of Judaism and Christianity*; Pawlikowski, *What Are They Saying about Jewish-Christian Relations?*; Von der Osten-Sacken, *Christian-Jewish Dialogue*; and Ruether, *Faith and Fratricide*.

for Gentiles.[19] The corporeal election of Israel is still in full force and the salvation of the Jewish People depends on their descent from Abraham,[20] while the salvation of Gentiles depends on how they respond to the gospel of Jesus Christ. There are in effect two parallel but not overlapping covenants which the God of Israel has made with humanity. The Jewish philosopher-theologian Franz Rosenzweig (1886–1929) has been credited as the originator of the two covenant theory.[21] He makes a sharp distinction between God's dealings with the *world* and his dealings with *Israel*: "We are wholly agreed as to what Christ and his church mean to the world: no one can reach the Father save through him . . . But the situation is quite different for one who does not have to reach the Father because he is already with him. And this is true of the people of Israel (although not of individual Jews)."[22]

Rosenzweig argues that while a mediator is essential in the Christian experience, the Jew stands in no need of mediation. This is so, because an individual is *born* a Jew, they do not need to *become* one in some decisive moment of their individual life.[23] A Jew is born into the faith community that was instituted between God and Israel on Sinai—it is a natural phenomenon: "The Christian is by nature or at least by birth—a pagan; the Jew, however, is a Jew."[24] However, despite this significant distinction between Israel and the Church, Rosenzweig is very positive about the Church's role in the world, and believes it is part of God's overall single plan: "Before God, then, the Jew and Christian both labor at the same task. He cannot dispense with either. He has set enmity between the two for all time, and withal has most intimately bound each to each. To us (Jews) he gave eternal life by kindling the fire of the Star of his truth in our hearts. Them (the Christians) he set on the

---

19. This is also true for the one-covenant view.

20. Mitch Glaser notes, however, that the two-covenant theory does not necessarily imply that every Jewish person will be saved—rather that they don't need to believe in Jesus to be saved (Glaser, "Critique of the Two-Covenant Theory," 44).

21. Wright, *New Testament and the People of God*, 437.

22. This is an extract from a letter from Rosenzweig to Rudolf Ehrenberg written after Rosenzweig had decided to remain a Jew. Cited in Glatzer, *Franz Rosenzweig*, 341.

23 Rozenweig, *Star of Redemption*, 396–97.

24. Ibid., 40

eternal way by causing them to pursue the rays of that Star of his truth for all time unto the eternal end."[25]

However, Rosenzweig maintains that Judaism is superior, and this attitude is highlighted by his assertion that Jews pursue the Star, whereas Christians pursue merely the rays of that Star.[26] Rosenzweig's crucial premise that God has ordained two separate covenants has become the starting point for much recent thinking on Jewish-Christian relations. According to Rabbi Jakob Petuchowski, "Rosenzweig conceded more than any Jew, while remaining a Jew, had conceded before him. He admitted the truth of John 14:6. This is immediately qualified though, by the assertion that 'the Jew does not have to come to the Father, He has been *with* the Father ever since Sinai.'"[27]

Of importance for the current study is the link between the dual covenant theory and the relationship between other religions and Christianity. Pawlikowski suggests the dual covenant approach will "profoundly alter Christianity's self-definition and make possible a more realistic relationship to Judaism and to all other non-Christian religions."[28] He suggests we "need to explore whether the realities expressed through the Sinai myth and the Christ myth may be present under different symbols in other world religions."[29] Pawlikowski calls for a Christology that does not claim to represent the totality of revelation, and therefore makes room for the ongoing validity of the Jewish covenant. He contends that "a similar approach needs to be developed with respect to the other world religions, especially Islam."[30] In doing

---

25. Ibid., 435–36.

26. Christians "are in any event already destined for all time to see what is illuminate, and not the light" (Ibid., 416).

27. Petuchowski, "The Christian-Jewish Dialog: A Jewish View," 383; quoted in Gudel, "To the Jew First," 4. Cf. Parkes, *Foundation of Judaism and Christianity*, 30, 326, 329–30; Pawlikowski, *What Are They Saying*, 43.

28. Pawlikowski, in Fleischner, *Auschwitz*, 168–69.

29. Pawlikowski, "Toward a Theology for Religious Diversity," 151.

30. Ibid., 149. See also Ruether, *Faith and Fratricide*, 251–57. Here Ruether calls for a "New Covenantal Theology" in which she likens Judaism and Christianity as to two brothers, and "two ways of carrying on the biblical inheritance" (254). They are different ways of "appropriating the biblical past and relating to its future hope" (255). Easter is a "reduplication" of the Exodus. The "story of Jesus parallels, it does not negate, the Exodus" (256). Furthermore what is said about Judaism and Christianity applies to all other religions as well. There are thus many covenants. Arguably, therefore, Ruether can also be considered as a proponent of the multi-covenant approach.

so, Pawlikowski is arguably moving from a dual-covenant position to a multi-covenant position.

The multi-covenant approach is in practice a development of the dual approach, and maintains that just as Jews and Christians are in different covenant relationships with God, so also are adherents of other faiths. There are in effect many covenants by which a divine-human relationship can be established. Paul van Buren is one theologian who adopts this stance. He rejects the traditional interpretations of central Christian claims such as the Trinity, and the divinity and humanity of Christ, and salvation by grace through faith in Christ because he believes these doctrines have supersessionist implications.[31]

5.1b. The Single-Covenant Paradigm

The single-covenant paradigm maintains that Christians (through the work of Christ) share in the *same* covenant as the Jews. In common with the dual-covenant approach, Jews and Christians are entrusted with different tasks and the latter do not replace the former. The single covenant approach begins at approximately the same starting point as the double covenant position: Jews and Christians continue to remain bonded despite their distinctive appropriation of the original covenantal tradition, but the main difference is the emphasis on the two separate communities and their distinctiveness in the dual approach and the emphasis on one people in the single covenant approach.[32] Proponents of this paradigm include Monika Hellwig, Clark Williamson, and Norbert Lohfink.[33]

The single-covenant model considers that the one ongoing covenant was in no way broken through the Christ-event. This event represents the moment when the Gentiles were able to enter fully into the relationship with God which was *already* enjoyed by the Jews—and is a relationship they continue to enjoy. Judaism and Christianity share a "simultaneous and complementary participation in the same covenant."[34] As the Sinai

---

31. Van Buren, "Covenantal Pluralism?," 21.

32. Pawlikowski, "Reflections on Covenant and Mission," 19.

33. Key works in include Hellwig, "Christian Theology and the Covenant of Israel"; Hellwig, "From the Jesus of Story to the Christ of Dogma"; Lohfink, *Covenant Never Revoked*; Williamson, *Guest in the House of Israel*.

34. Hellwig, "Christian Theology and the Covenant of Israel," 49.

Outline and Critique of the "New Majority Views"

covenant is still in force the Christ-event is not primarily the completion of Messianic prophecies but the possibility for all Gentiles to encounter the God of Abraham, Sarah and Isaac.[35] While the Christ-event enables non-Jews to enter the one ongoing covenant, some scholars argue that it does impact all people, including the Jews. However, it does not impact them in such a way that results in the breaking of already existing Jewish covenantal ties. Others would argue that the Christian appropriation and reinterpretation of the original covenantal tradition in and through Jesus applies primarily to non-Jews.[36]

Williamson suggests the Christ-event cannot be considered a "new" episode in salvation history, rather it was just a continuation of the salvific activity that began with the Jewish people and continues with them even today.[37] He rejects any idea of a "new," "better," or "improved" covenant made possible by Christ.[38] Similarly, Lohfink envisages a two-fold way of salvation within a single covenantal framework. Christians and Jews appropriate this single covenant in different ways. "There is a definite sense . . . in which the 'old covenant' of 2 Cor 3 is the 'new covenant' of the book of Jeremiah. We could say then that the contemporary Jewish people live in the 'old covenant' though it is at the same time now a 'new covenant.'"[39]

This brief account of dual-covenant and single-covenant theology reveals they have much in common, and indeed it has been argued that they are really nuances of the same position. Spillman writes: "the task [of assessing the two positions] is complicated by nuances introduced by proponents of the one-covenant and of the two-covenant models that effectively narrow the distance between the positions. Proponents of the one-covenant model include elements of duality in the singular covenant, while proponents of the two-covenant model tend to link the covenants very closely in a near unity. For example, advocates of one covenant write of two sides of the single covenant, two modes of participation in it; advocates of two covenants describe the two as closely related and complementary. Therefore, the difference between the

---

35. Hellwig, "From the Jesus of Story to the Christ of Dogma," 132. Cf. Pawlikowski, "Search for a New Paradigm for the Christian-Jewish Relationship," 29.

36. Pawlikowski, "Reflections on Covenant and Mission," 17.

37. Williamson, *Guest in the House of Israel*, 258.

38. Ibid., 250.

39. Lohfink, *Covenant Never Revoked*, 77.

one-covenant and two-covenant views is not a simple one, although it is, nonetheless, real."[40]

Pawlikowski does not think the single- or double-covenant approaches are entirely satisfactory, and he suggests that "a shift seems to be emerging at present within Christian theology towards a form of double covenant but with continued Jewish-Christian bonding."[41] He argues that the single covenant approach is problematic, because it is highly dependent on a linear understanding of the Jewish-Christian relationship. Pawlikowski suggests this can incorporate a form of theological fulfilment in Christianity that renders Judaism a second-class religion. He also asserts that the linear thrust is problematic in light of new scholarship which indicates the "co-emergence" of Judaism and Christianity from within a common religious revolution in Second Temple Judaism.[42]

This brief review of the double and single-covenant approaches is unable to reveal the complexity of these models, but has articulated

---

40. Spillman, "Image of Covenant in Christian Understandings of Judaism." Several considerations favor each model, according to Spillman. In favor of the one-covenant model are biblical and theological themes that speak of the unity of God's will and purpose, especially in his plan for salvation. The model also reflects the New Testament conviction that Jesus and the Church continue a history already begun in the great events of the Hebrew Scriptures. It also reflects the fact that Christianity arose within Judaism and that in its origins Christianity was intimately tied to Judaism. In contrast, the two-covenant model is supported by those biblical themes that emphasize the newness of the Christian message and the uniqueness of Christ. It is also supported by the fact that Judaism and Christianity are, in fact, markedly different traditions, despite the aspects they hold in common. Spillman continues, noting that "the considerations favoring the one-covenant model are not directly in conflict with those favoring the two-covenant model. One can simultaneously accept the validity of the considerations in favor of both models without contradiction. For example, one can acknowledge the biblical themes that speak of the unity of God's will and plan for salvation and still recognize the biblical themes that express the newness of the Christian message. One can recognize that Judaism and Christianity were intimately connected at the time of the origins of Christianity and still recognize the enormous differences between the two traditions that emerged as they developed. The difference between the considerations favoring the one-covenant and the two-covenant models is largely a matter of where one puts one's emphasis. This is one of the reasons why it is so difficult to decide between the two models. Support for one is not directly at odds with support for the other. The choice of models is not a matter of opposing evidence, and one cannot demonstrate that one model is closer to reality than the other" (Spillman, "Image of Covenant in Christian Understandings of Judaism," 73).

41. Pawlikowski, "Reflections on Covenant and Mission," 26.

42. Ibid., 18

Outline and Critique of the "New Majority Views"

their key themes. I will now critique these views. My critique of supersessionism relied heavily on Romans 9–11. The same passage also provides substantial material that is contrary to the new majority views, and it will be the focus of this critique. Many of the arguments presented in this chapter will be developed further in subsequent chapters.[43]

5.2 The Gospel Is for the Jews

The Church has traditionally proclaimed that the gospel is for all—including the Jewish People. Paul's argument in Romans turns on the assumption that the gospel which proclaims Jesus as Israel's Messiah is for Jews as well as Gentiles, indeed, it is for the Jews first (Rom 1:16).[44] The meaning of "first" (πρῶτος) is debated, there being two main opinions. Some theologians believe it refers to "first" in a merely chronological sense i.e. the gospel was preached to the Jews before it was preached to the Gentiles (e.g., Hodge).[45] Others, for instance Moo, understand "first" to refer not only to chronology, but also to a sense of priority: "Paul must intend more than a simple historical fact in light of the theological context here. If we ask what precedence Paul accords Israel elsewhere in Romans, we find that his emphasis is on the special applicability of the promise of God to that people whom he chose (3:2; 9–11). However much the church may seem to be dominated by Gentiles, Paul insists the promises of God realized in the gospel are 'first of all' for the Jew."[46]

---

43. See particularly section 8.3.2 ("The Abrahamic, Sinaitic, and New Covenants: Promise, Law, and Fulfilment"). There I emphasize the importance of a correct understanding of the place of the Abrahamic and Sinaitic covenants, and argue that the dual- and single-covenant theories have not properly understood the relationship between these covenants and the New covenant.

44. Marshall, "Christ and the Cultures," 90.

45. Charles Hodge "First, therefore, must refer to time: to the Jew in the first instance, and then to the Gentile." Hodge, *Romans*, 29. Moo suggests C. K. Barrett also fits this category (Moo, *Romans*, 69).

46. Moo, *Romans*, 69. Cf. Cranfield: "The word πρῶτον indicates that within the framework of this basic equality [i.e., the gospel is for both Jew and Gentile] there is a certain undeniable priority of the Jew. In view of chapters nine to eleven it is hardly admissible to explain this πρῶτον as referring merely to the historical fact that the gospel was preached to the Jews before it was preached to the Gentiles" (Cranfield, *Critical and Exegetical Commentary on the Epistle to the Romans*, 91.

However, the important point is that with either interpretation, πρῶτον is not understood in a *temporary* sense—thus the gospel is *still* for the Jews.[47] The following verses clearly suggest all people, Jews included, need the Christian gospel: John 3:36, 14:6, Acts 4:8–12, 1 Tim 2:5–6.[48] The missiologist David Bosch argues the early Church also believed the gospel was for the Jews: "Mass conversions of the Jews are again and again reported, particularly of Jews in Jerusalem . . . but also of those in the Diaspora. There is, moreover, a clear progression in these reports: in Acts 2:41, three thousand Jews are converted; in 4:4 there are five thousand; in 5:14 'multitudes both of men and women' are added; in 6:7 the number of disciples in Jerusalem has 'multiplied greatly'; in 21:20 Paul is informed about 'many thousands' . . . of believing Jews."[49]

The New Testament portrays Jesus Christ himself as giving priority to his Jewish ministry. He came to the Jew first (e.g., John 1:11; Matt 4:23–25; 9:35), and it was only in unusual circumstances that Jesus ministered to non-Jews (e.g., the Syrophoenician woman (Mark 7) and the Roman centurion's servant (Matthew 8). Furthermore, when the disciples were commissioned they were instructed: "Do not go among the Gentiles or enter any town of the Samaritans. Go rather to the lost sheep of Israel" (Matt 10:5–6). After the resurrection the disciples were instructed to start their ministry in Jerusalem (Acts 1:8).[50] Ironically, perhaps the supreme New Testament example of an apostle bringing the gospel of Jesus Christ to Jews is from the "apostle to the Gentiles," St Paul (Rom 11:13–14). It was the practice of Paul to take the gospel to Jews first. (e.g., Acts 9:20; 13:46).[51] It is not until Acts 10 that we find any attempt to begin taking the gospel to anyone other than the Jewish

---

47. Gudel, "To the Jew First: A Biblical Analysis of the Two-Covenant Theory of the Atonement," 10. He states that he does not know of any commentators who exegete "first "in a temporal sense.

48. Diprose, "The Jewish-Christian Dialogue and Soteriology," 31.

49. Bosch, *Transforming Mission*, 96.

50. Gudel, "To the Jew First," 11.

51. In Pisidian Antioch (Acts 13:13–52) the ministry of Paul and Barnabas is rejected by the Jews, prompting Paul and Barnabas to respond saying, "We had to speak the word of God to you first. Since you reject it and do not consider yourselves worthy of eternal life, we now turn to the Gentiles" (Acts 13:46). However, even after this incident it remained Paul's practice to go to the synagogue first when visiting a new town or region (e.g., Acts 14:1–3).

people.⁵² Paul repeatedly asks for prayers for the Jewish people that they may repent and be brought back into a relationship with God. The fact that they remain a covenant people is of no salvific help.⁵³ Paul states in Romans 9 that his concern is for his "brethren," his "kinsmen according to the flesh," (i.e., Israelites, Rom 9:3–5). He argues that Israel has failed to obtain the righteousness that is by faith (9:30–32; 10:2–21) and is consequently an enemy of the gospel (11:28). Paul nevertheless prays for them that they might be saved (10:1).⁵⁴ Motyer accurately conveys Paul's conviction that the Jews need the gospel: "Let us be clear from the outset: any Israel theology which does not start from a deep grief at the Jews' unbelief, and proceed to an intense longing that they should turn to their Messiah, cannot claim to be Pauline."⁵⁵ The New Testament clearly asserts that Jesus is the fulfilment of Old Testament expectations of a Messiah.⁵⁶ However, the "new majority views" effectively deny this. Diprose correctly states that whoever denies that Jesus is Israel's Messiah, is effectively denying the gospel which was announced in advance to Abraham (Gal 3:8–16; Rom 1:1–15, 16–17).⁵⁷

Bruce Marshall rejects the two-covenant paradigm by arguing that according to the New Testament, in the death and resurrection of the Jew Jesus, the God of Israel has acted definitively and unsurpassably on behalf of all humanity, Jews and Gentiles.⁵⁸ Thus, "It seems

---

52. Gudel, "To the Jew First," 11.

53. Ibid., 15. Strictly speaking, the Old covenant itself was never the source of salvation, even throughout the period of its duration. Its salvific efficacy was dependent solely on its relationship with the New covenant. See section 5.3 n. 75, for further elaboration.

54. Blaising, "Future of Israel," 437.

55. Motyer, *Israel in the Plan of God*, 33.

56. See section 9.1.1 for elaboration of this point.

57. Diprose, "Israel and Christian Theology," 66.

58. Marshall, "Christ and the Cultures," 90. However, Marshall adds the qualification that "the ways in which Jews and Gentiles are each related to what happens on the cross and the Emmaus road may differ quite significantly, but the New Testament seems deeply committed to saying that what happens here is decisive for the destiny of both" (90). I disagree with the conclusion that Marshall draws from affirming the permanent election of Israel. He argues that rejecting supersessionism allows for the reality of the certainty of salvation for the Jews—it's "in the bag" (89). "In Jesus Christ eschatological salvation comes to light as the ultimate blessing which God promised to Abraham's children, and through them to the nations; if God's gifts are irrevocable then this supreme blessing will not be withheld from those to whom it was first promised. This suggests that Christians may engage in a non-proselytising conversation

implausible to take Paul's insistence on the permanence of Israel's election as a repudiation of this conviction that salvation comes through Jesus Christ alone, or as a suggestion that the salvation of the Jewish people will come about, in the end, without their own recognition of Jesus as Israel's promised Messiah."[59] The New Testament is clear that Christ has universal significance. However, it is not only the vision of the New Testament that is universal. Blaising points out that both Israel in the Tannach and the Church in the New Testament see themselves as related to God through the covenant with Abraham. Thus, they both see their covenant relationship with God as in some way entailing all peoples, because the covenant with Abraham had universal import. The Tannach's eschatological vision is universal. Similarly, the Church in the New Testament sees itself as proclaiming New covenant blessings that flow from the covenant with Abraham. Both Jew and Gentile are in Christ united in this New covenant blessing (Gal 2:6–9).[60]

> The point is this: neither the vision in the Tannach of Israel's covenant relationship to God and God's plan to bless Gentiles, nor the NT view of Jews and Gentiles in the Church presents a view of dual, unrelated covenants, one for Jews as Jews and the other for Gentiles as Gentiles. What is more, both require evangelistic proclamation of covenant blessing to all peoples. Consequently, dual covenant theology is fundamentally incompatible with the Biblical foundations of Israel's and the Church's identities and missions . . . Dual covenant theology proposes that Christianity and Judaism see each other as legitimately distinct religions and this creates further incoherence at the Biblical level. Why? Because both Israel in the Tannach and the Church of the NT were profoundly exclusive—not of other peoples, but of other religions. There are no other religions sanctioned by God. To suggest that Christianity and Judaism see each other as validly separate religions insults both Christianity and Judaism at their fundamental, that is Biblical, levels . . . But the biggest problem

---

with Jews; since we do not have to assume that we are talking to the damned, we do not have to fell responsible for converting and thus saving them . . . Whether Paul or the New Testament as a whole permits, or even requires, the church to drop the idea of a mission to the Jews in view of their promised salvation remains in dispute, though even the most profoundly christocentric theologians have entertained doubts on this score" (89).

59. Ibid.

60. Blaising, "Future of Israel," 441.

Outline and Critique of the "New Majority Views"

with two-covenant theology is its claim that Israel is related to God by covenant apart from Jesus Christ.[61]

5.3. There Is No Special Way of Salvation for Israel

I have stated above (in 4.1 and 4.2) that Israel remains in a covenant relationship with God and that Israel still has a part to play in salvation history, and indeed that ultimately, "all Israel" will be saved. All who adopt the new majority views would agree with these assertions. However, they would deny that the gospel of Jesus Christ is for Jews, and would argue instead that there is a special way or "*Sonderweg*" of salvation for Israel.[62]

On the basis of Romans 9–11, it is very difficult to maintain that there is a special way of salvation apart from Christ for Israel. According to E. P. Sanders, "Paul in fact explicitly denies that the Jewish Covenant can be effective for salvation."[63] Moo likewise states the flawed exegetical base for a *Sonderweg* approach:

> The most extreme form of this [the Sonderweg] view finds in Rom. 11 the exegetical basis for a 'bi-covenantal' theology . . . But Paul knows nothing of it. He teaches that salvation can be found in one place only: within the one community made up of those who believe in Jesus Christ. There is only one tree, and one becomes attached to this tree by faith: Jews can be grafted back if they do not persist in unbelief (v. 23). Nor can the absence of the name of Christ in Rom. 11 justify the conclusion that this faith need not be faith in Christ. Paul has defined the faith he is taking about here quite adequately in the first ten chapters of the letter: it is faith in Jesus Christ (see esp. 3:22, 26; 10:4–13).[64]

---

61. Ibid.

62. See, for example, Stendahl, *Paul among Jews and Gentiles*.

63. Sanders, *Paul and Palestinian Judaism*, 551. Cf. N. T. Wright, *Climax of the Covenant*, 173. I have already noted (n. 53) that the Jewish covenant itself has never been "effective for salvation," and that its efficacy in this regard is dependent on its relationship with the New covenant, and the mediator of the covenant, Jesus Christ. This point is elaborated further in section 5.3 n. 75.

64. Moo, *Romans*, 725–26. For a full critique of the *Sonderweg* and dual covenant views see Vanlaningham, *Christ, the Savior of Israel*.

Terence Donaldson's critique of the *Sonderweg* reading of Paul highlights the difficulty such an approach raises for Jewish Christianity. If the *Sonderweg* approach is right, Donaldson observes, "then Jewish Christianity represents an anomaly. How are we going to locate a group that by virtue of its Jewish identity should be following the *Sonderweg* —or better, the *Toraweg*—but that by virtue of its religious allegiance has set itself on the *Christusweg*? Our investigation of how such a question, in its various dimensions, is addressed by proponents of a two-covenant reading of Paul has led to the conclusion that such a reading cannot be maintained."[65]

It is of interest that Ruether, who is a proponent of the two-covenant position, recognizes that Romans 9–11 cannot be used to support this position. She states that contemporary ecumenists speak "out of good intention, but inaccurate exegesis," when they use Romans 11 to defend the doctrine of two covenants.[66] Paul's grief in Romans 9:2–4 would make little sense if Paul considered belief in Jesus as unnecessary for Jewish people. John Johnson states that there is "almost unanimous consent" among scholars that Paul did not think salvation was guaranteed for the Jews on the basis of birth.[67] According to Johnson, Paul makes this clear in Romans 9:6–9, where his argument stands in oppo-

---

65. Donaldson, "Jewish Christianity, Israel's Stumbling," 52. Donaldson continues: "At the same time, however, I have attempted to argue that, while Paul does not hold out a special way to salvation for Israel, he nevertheless sees Israel as occupying a special place. It was to Israel, in the person of its progenitor Abraham, that the promise of universal blessing was given. It was within Israel, through the giving of the law, that the nature of the human plight was clarified. It was within Israel, in the person of Israel's Messiah, that sin and death were defeated and the eschatological age of the Spirit was inaugurated. It was to the remnant of Israel that the messianic blessings most properly belonged. It was by the agency of Israel's apostle to the Gentiles, himself a member of the remnant, that Israel's blessings were shared with the nations. And it was in the existence of the remnant that God's promise to save all Israel was most clearly demonstrated. While Paul does not envisage a *Sonderweg* for Israel, he nevertheless assigns his own people *a Sonderplatz* within God's single program of salvation" (52).

66. Ruether, *Faith and Fratricide*, 106. Cf. Gregory Baum, "Introduction," in Ruether, *Faith and Fratricide*, 6. Gregory Baum describes it as "wishful thinking" when Christian theologians attempt to base a two-covenant approach on Romans 9–11. However, both Ruether and Baum continue to support a two-covenant approach.

67. Johnson, "New Testament Understanding of the Jewish Rejection of Jesus," 243. Cf. Hvalvik, "A 'Separate Way' for Israel?" 12–29. According to Hvalvik, exegesis of the text suggests only the time of the salvation, not the means of the salvation, is different.

sition to the traditional Jewish understanding of his day, which maintained that all Jews were destined for salvation on the basis of birth.[68]

Holwerda also makes the important point that it is wrong to isolate the Jewish people as Israel from essential confessional beliefs. For both the Old Testament teaching on the relationship of covenant and people and the comparable New Testament understanding of what it means to be Israel imply that neither race nor physical descent provides a sufficient basis for understanding the identity of Israel."[69] With regard to the identity of Israel throughout history, he writes:

> Whenever those who claimed to be Israel assumed that Israel was a fixed and static entity, a people self-evident to all, the prophets issued strong warnings. The promises given to Israel were not like automatic guarantees to be received apart from faith and obedience. Consequently, because of Israel's historical disobedience, the prophets announced that in the end it will be the remnant who is saved (Isaiah 10:20–23; Amos 9; Micah 7:18). Therefore 'not all Israelites truly belong to Israel' (Romans 9:6) is not only a Pauline teaching but a summary of the prophetic warning of the entire Old Testament. Claiming Abraham as father was never a sufficient basis for claiming the covenant promises.[70]

The important distinction between corporate election and individual election is crucial here, as Jacob Jocz explains: Israel as a collective entity is the chosen race of God, a people elected to do his will. However, Jocz is insistent that this must be reconciled with the importance of an individual's response to Christ. The key here is a proper understanding of election. Paul uses election in a twofold manner—sometimes he speaks of election in personal terms and sometimes in collective terms. Israel's election is in respect of revelation; individual election is in respect of salvation.[71] His belief in the two types of election enables him to fully affirm a passage like Romans 9:4 which calls the Jews the recipients of the covenants, the law, and the promises of God, but also to take seriously Paul's emphasis on salvation through Christ alone. Regarding the way of salvation, there is "no difference between

---

68. Johnson, "New Testament Understanding of the Jewish Rejection of Jesus," 243. Johnson refers to Charles Talbert, "Paul on the Covenant," *Review and Expositor* (1987) 304.

69. Holwerda, *Jesus and Israel*, 25.

70. Ibid., 27.

71. Jocz, *Theology of Election*, 70. See also section 5.3 n. 75.

Jew and Gentile" (Rom 10:12).[72] So, in Romans Paul attempts to balance two different, yet related concepts: his belief in Israel's corporate election as the chosen people of God, and his belief that each person, Jew or Gentile, is elect only if they come to have personal faith in Christ.[73]

An important principle is established here, and is one that has significant bearing on the broader topic of this thesis.[74] Descent from Abraham alone does not guarantee truly belonging to "Israel" i.e., being a recipient of salvation.[75] This is not a New Testament development for

---

72. Johnson, "The Jewish Rejection of Jesus," 244.

73. Jocz, *A Theology of Election*, 138.

74. This subject will be given more extensive treatment in chapter 8 of this volume.

75. The failure to distinguish between corporate election and individual election results in a radically skewed theology of Israel, and soteriology. This error is evident in much Jewish-Christian dialogue. For example, John McDade, SJ, argues "If . . . Paul's axiom is right that 'the gifts and calling of God are irrevocable' (Rom 11.29), then the salvific gifts Paul lists earlier in the letter, 'the adoption, the glory, the covenants, the giving of the Torah, the worship and the promises' (9:4), are still in place and it is therefore impossible for *post Christum* Judaism to be deleted from the script of divine history . . . It follows that if salvation is still on offer to Israel, then we cannot think that 'old' Israel and been replaced by a 'new' Israel from which Jews are excluded . . . We might think that there is simply one *Israel of God* . . . composed of Jews faithful to God in the form of their covenantal charter at Sinai and Jews and Gentiles united through faith in Christ" (McDade, "Catholic Christianity and Judaism since Vatican II," 369). Here McDade has conflated corporate and individual election. Likewise, the new perspective on Paul also confuses corporate election with individual election. Peter O'Brian notes the important difference in the definition of Israel in the "traditional" view on Paul and in the new perspective, as represented by E. P Sanders: "For Paul 'not all who descended from Israel are Israel' (Rom. 9:6). Salvation was not promised to every individual Israelite in the Old Testament. The intended recipients of the divine promises were the remnant of Israel, a remnant preserved throughout history by God's electing grace . . . The notion that the majority of Israel was hardened in their sin . . . and excluded from God's righteousness (Rom 11:7–10), is integral to Paul's teaching on election, but does not sit well with Sanders's paradigm. The latter thinks that every individual [ethnic Jew], except those who commit apostasy, will attain salvation. '[T]he universal view [in Palestinian Judaism is] that *every individual Israelite* who indicates his intention to remain in the covenant by repenting, observing the Day of Atonement and the like, will be forgiven for *all* his transgressions.' With this election all were members of the people of God'" (O'Brien, "Was Paul a Covenantal Nomist?" 260, quoting Sanders, *Paul and Palestinian Judaism*, 182 (italics are Sanders's). On this subject, Mark Seifrid has shown that in the Old Testament the concepts of "righteousness" and "covenant" are only rarely associated, thus indicating that membership of the covenant community (i.e., being an ethnic Jew), should not be interpreted as necessarily implying one is considered righteous, i.e., "saved" (Seifrid, "Righteousness Language in the Hebrew Scriptures and Early Judaism," 415–42).

righteousness has always been received by faith (Rom 4:13ff.; 10:6ff.). The way of salvation for Jew and Gentile is the same—both must call on the name of the Lord to be saved (Rom 10:9–13). Nowhere in Scripture is it suggested that Israel's advantageous position guaranteed salvation to all members of the nation.[76] Romans 9:3–4 and 10:1 clearly indicate that Paul did not consider his Jewish "brothers" to be saved. They were zealous, but their zeal was misplaced—it was not according to knowledge. They sought to know God on their own terms.[77] Therefore, to maintain that God's covenant with Israel is still valid, and yet also maintain that this does not imply that Jewish people can be saved without personally accepting Christ, is not incongruous. The Jewish people were chosen to be servants of God—that was their divine vocation. Personal salvation was a matter between each individual Jew and God. The covenant ensured nationhood, but faith alone was still the only possible route to forgiveness.[78] According to Jocz this is one of Paul's central points in Romans. To claim that an individual is assured salvation as a matter of birthright would "make nonsense of faith" in the Pauline understanding of salvation.[79] Jocz makes this explicit: "The Jewish or the Christian attitude can neither be the result of history or of race, but entirely depends upon the personal response to Jesus Christ. Christian theology is the result of faith in Jesus of Nazareth, the Son of God. Jewish theology is the negation of that faith. The dividing line is not between Jews and Gentiles in the racial sense, but between men who accept and men who reject the Christian claim."[80]

Jocz refutes the idea that Jews will somehow "magically" be saved at the eschaton, simply by virtue of their Jewish heritage—they will need to exercise faith, for only individuals experience salvation, not

---

76. Diprose, *Israel in the Development of Christian Thought*, 18.

77. Cranfield, "Light from St. Paul on Christian-Jewish Relations," 24.

78. Glaser, "Critique of the Two-Covenant Theory," 59. Cf. World Evangelical Fellowship (WEF), "Willowbank Declaration on the Christian Gospel and the Jewish People": "We affirm that the biblical hope for Jewish people centers on their being restored through faith in Christ to their proper place as branches of God's olive tree from which they are at present broken off. We deny that the historical status of the Jews as God's people brings salvation to any Jew who does not accept the claims of Jesus Christ" (article 3.15).

79. Jocz, *Theology of Election*, 139.

80. Jocz, *Jewish People and Jesus Christ* (page number not given); quoted in Macleod, "Witness of the Church to the Jewish People," 79.

racial groups. Thus mission is essential. "Israel as a people cannot hear the word of the Cross; it can be heard only personally by the individual Jew."[81] This is the position adopted by the World Evangelical Alliance in their "Willowbank Declaration on the Christian Gospel and the Jewish people" which states: "We affirm that Jewish people have an ongoing part on God's plan . . . We deny that covenantal privilege alone can ever bring salvation to impenitent unbelievers." [82]

So, rather than suggesting separate arrangements or covenants for Jews and Gentiles, Romans 9–11 affirms that there is only one such arrangement—which depends as a whole on Jesus' death and resurrection (Gal 3:13–14).[83] This one way is now open to all who receive the gospel of Christ (Rom 1:17; 11:23).[84] Likewise, Stott states that the salvation that the Jews will experience is through faith in Christ. It is not a national salvation—nothing is said about a political entity or return to the land, "Nor is there any hint of a special way of salvation for the Jews which dispenses with faith in Christ."[85]

The new majority positions are at odds with this clear teaching on the vital nature of messianic faith and consequently they view mission (that is evangelistic mission rather than dialogue or social justice initiatives) to the Jews as unnecessary or even inappropriate and offensive. Paul van Buren, for example, has stated that the Church's duty is to witness the God of Israel to pagans only—not to Jews.[86] He claims that the only Jews who could ever be converted to Christianity are those who have already forgone allegiance to the Jewish People. However, Goldberg disagrees, and cites the existence of Messianic Jewish congregations as evidence that van Buren is wrong.[87] Van Buren and other proponents of the new majority views seem to discount the fact that there have always been Jews who have believed in Jesus as the Messiah—and, argues

---

81. Jocz, *Theology of Election*, 191.
82. World Evangelical Fellowship, "Willowbank Declaration," articles 3.12, 3.13.
83. Marshall, "Christ and the Cultures," 90.
84. Ibid.
85. Stott, *Message of Romans*, 304.
86. Van Buren, "Discerning the Way to the Incarnation," 298–99; cited in Goldberg, "Are There Two Ways of Atonement?" 21.
87. Goldberg, "Are There Two Ways of Atonement?," 22. Cf. Baumann, "Two Ways/Two Covenants Theory," 39.

Arnulf Baumann, in significant numbers.[88] N. T. Wright correctly observes: "The irony of this, is that the late twentieth century, in order to avoid anti-Semitism, has advocated a position (the non-evangelization of the Jews) *which Paul regards precisely as anti-Semitic.*"[89]

5.4. The Israel-Church Relationship and the Implications for a Christian Theology of Religions

I have stated above (sections 4.1 and 4.2) that theologians such as Ruether consider supersessionism to be rooted in New Testament Christology.[90] For such theologians rejecting supersessionism requires major Christological reformulation. Pawlikowski notes that after the Second Vatican Council, early attempts to eliminate a Christology rooted in supersessionism continued to insist on a central role for Christ in all human salvation, and on a fulfilment dimension in Jesus' incarnation and resurrection. More recent approaches recognize the difficulty of maintaining this tension, and recognize the unavoidable implications for Christological and soteriological reformulation. For example, The ecumenical statement *A Sacred Obligation* states that

> Affirming God's Enduring Covenant with the Jewish People has consequences for Christian understandings of salvation. Christians meet God's saving power in the person of Jesus Christ and believe that this power is available to all people in him. Christians have therefore taught for centuries that salvation is available only through Jesus Christ. With their recent realization that God's covenant with the Jewish people is eternal, Christians can now recognize in the Jewish tradition the redemptive power of God at work. If Jews, who do not share our faith in Christ, are in a saving covenant with God, then Christians need new ways of understanding the universal significance of Christ.[91]

---

88. Baumann, "Two Ways of Covenant Theory," 39.

89. Wright, *Climax of the Covenant*, 253 (emphasis original). Cf. Zaretsky, *Jewish Evangelism*: "God's continued covenant with the Jewish people does not annul their need of Jesus for salvation. Neither does the covenant imply that they are saved in a manner that differs from non-Jews. Faith comes through the proclamation of the gospel and therefore the gospel needs to be proclaimed to the Jewish people" (18).

90. See chapter 5 n. 14

91. Christian Scholars Group on Christian-Jewish Relations, "Sacred Obligation," article 9.

Another important document which seeks to understand the meaning of the Christ-event in the context of anti-supersessionism, is the Pontifical Biblical Commission's *The Jewish People and their Scriptures in the Christian Bible* (2001).[92] According to Pawlikowski, this document aims to express the universal significance of the Christ-event while leaving theological space for Judaism.[93] Pawlikowski considers the document to make an "important contribution to the development of a new constructive Christological understanding in the context of Jewish covenantal inclusion . . . Here we have the seeds of what appears to be a recognition of a distinct salvific path for the Jewish People as a theological principle."[94]

Pawlikowski recognizes that because Christology "stands at the very nerve centre of Christian faith, re-evaluation of Christological affirmations cannot be undertaken superficially."[95] He notes that among Christians "who are most open to general inter-religious understanding," the Christ-event is seen as "only one of several authentic revelations with no particular universal aspect."[96] Pawlikowski rejects such an approach and rightly asserts that "we must maintain from the Christian side some understanding that the Christ Event carries universal significance."[97] Pawlikowski believes the two documents considered above "provide space for exploring whether the Church can speak about the universal significance of the Christ Event in a way that allows for its articulation through religious symbols not directly connected with Christology, such as Jewish religious symbols. This might in fact prove the most fruitful way of developing a Christology that remains open to covenantal pluralism, particularly with respect to the Jews who are acknowledged to have authentic revelation from the Christian theological perspective."[98]

This brief discussion of some of the recent attempts to produce a Christian theology of Israel that is anti-supersessionist, and yet seeks to

---

92. Pontifical Biblical Commission, JPSSCB.

93. Pawlikowski, "Reflections on Covenant and Mission," 23.

94. Ibid.

95. Ibid., 22.

96. Ibid.

97. Ibid. However, I would argue that it is far from clear whether Pawlikowski achieves this.

98. Ibid., 24

retain traditional Christological affirmations, highlights the magnitude of the issues involved. I have included this material here to illustrate the reality that the Church cannot embrace the notion of a separate way for Israel without major implications, not only for its understanding of Israel, but also for its self-understanding and its theology of religions.

I have suggested above that misunderstanding the Israel-Church relationship is an important factor contributing to the Israel analogy and fulfilment model. I suggest all the theologians outlined in chapter 2 misunderstand the nature of Israel itself and its relationship with Christianity, to some extent at least, for their theology undermines the *sui generis* nature of the Israel-Church relationship. Later sections of the thesis will highlight various aspects of their theology that contribute to this error, but before proceeding further I will briefly highlight two examples from the theologians considered in chapter 2 which reveal the link between their (mis)understanding of Israel and their theology of religions. This link will developed further in subsequent chapters (especially chapter 8).

For Rahner, the Old covenant facilitated salvation and the same principle may apply to other religions, which remain lawful until the gospel is promulgated. In his four-stage thesis in which Rahner outlines his theology of religions there is a clear indication that he sees Judaism as salvifically efficacious (at least until the gospel is received). He writes: "Normally [in Catholic theology] the beginning of the objective obligation of the Christian message for all men—in other words, the abolition of the validity of the Mosaic religion *and* of all other religions—is thought to occur in the apostolic age. Normally, therefore, one regards the time between this beginning and the actual acceptance or the personally guilty refusal of Christianity in a non-Jewish world and history as the span between the already given promulgation of the law and the moment when the one to whom the law refers takes cognizance of it."[99] "Until the moment when the gospel really enters into the historical situation of an individual, a non-Christian religion (even outside the Mosaic religion) does not merely contain elements of a natural knowledge of God . . . It contains also supernatural elements arising out of the grace which is given to men as a gratuitous gift

---

99. Rahner, "Christianity and the Non-Christian Religions," 119. Rahner used the term 'law' here to refer to Christianity (from 1st thesis).

on account of Christ. For this reason a non-Christian religion can be recognized as a *lawful* religion."[100]

Similarly, Dupuis speaks in terms of "one covenant and two interrelated ways within one organic plan of salvation."[101] He does not consider the New covenant as being entirely new,[102] therefore, "The [Old] covenant remains even today a way of salvation, but not independently from the Christ-event."[103] As God has made a covenant with the Jews so also with human beings in many times and places. The covenant with the Jews is not abrogated in the New covenant made in Christ, so also the other covenants are not provisional or abolished by the Christ-event: "The apparent suppression of the 'first' covenant by the 'second' (in the Letter to the Hebrews) can 'hyperbolically' be understood likewise. The new covenant is no other than the first; it unveils the first by spreading abroad the splendour of the Lord which the first contained without revealing it fully."[104]

The close link between how the Jewish–Christian relationship is understood, and how the relationship between other religions and Christianity is understood, is also manifest in the "new majority views" outlined above. I have referred briefly to the multi-covenant approach of Paul van Buren (above, see 5.1a), who rightly contends that Jews and Christians believe God is the creator of the whole world and believe that he cares deeply about all his creatures, therefore once we begin to rethink the church's understanding of Israel, "we are already on a course that leads to rethinking how we see and relate to the rest of the world."[105] This leads van Buren to develop a model of "covenantal pluralism", in which the Old covenant (Sinai) and the faithfulness of Jesus can be seen as "evidence of the plurality of ways in which God relates to the plurality of different peoples and cultures."[106] Ronald Diprose,

---

100. Ibid., 121 (from 2nd thesis).
101. Dupuis, *Toward a Christian Theology of Religious Pluralism*, 232.
102. Ibid., 231.
103. Ibid., 233.
104. Ibid., 231.
105. Van Buren, "Covenantal Pluralism?" 21.
106. Ibid. Cf. ibid., 25: "This growing ability to say that the God who has bound God's self to the Jewish people has also shown his love to the Jewish community in the face of Jesus Christ, invites us to entertain the possibility that God could also have laid claim upon an Arab prophet and called the nation of Islam to obedience, and even that he might be found as emptiness by yet another people."

commenting on this development suggests: "Christianity's unqualified acceptance of Jewish monotheistic faith has become a strong factor in fostering religious pluralism. The general opinion that Israel's own covenant with God exempts her from needing to believe in Jesus in order to be saved implies that any number of peoples may have their own special relationship with God and hence be exempted from recognising in Jesus the only means of reconciliation."[107]

5.5. Summary

The preceding chapters have demonstrated that Israel is not incidental to the task of Christian theology. However, Israel has generally been neglected or mistreated by Christian theology. I have suggested that this is due in large part to the traditionally prevailing replacement paradigm which views the Jewish people as being rejected by God and permanently replaced by the Church. I have argued that such a view is contrary to the teaching of the New Testament, which clearly portrays the Jewish people as remaining in covenant relationship with God and still serving a purpose in salvation history.

The replacement paradigm is now being replaced by emerging "new majority views" (double-, single- and multi-covenant paradigms) which reject the supersessionist premises and affirm the ongoing covenant relationship. However, this is interpreted in such way that maintains the Jewish people have no need of the Christian gospel. The gospel is therefore for Gentiles only. I have argued that these new majority views are contrary to the biblical witness, which does not suggest that

107. Diprose, "Jewish-Christian Dialogue and Soteriology," 38. Likewise, N. T. Wright points out the close connection between the two-covenant approach and affording other religions salvific value. He judges that the two- covenant approach is a "half-way house" to a "fully-blown" relativism (Wright, *Climax of the Covenant*, 254 n. 52). "What is at stake in this debate is not the privileged position of this or that race or religion. It is the nature of monotheism itself. The two-covenant model claims the high ground of monotheism: all roads lead to the one god. But this is not the God of the Old Testament, who (in order to rescue his world) made an exclusive, binding and highly paradoxical covenant with Israel, nor the God of the new, who revealed himself fully and finally in the sending, 'giving up' and raising of Jesus Christ and in the sending of the Spirit." Wright, *Climax of the Covenant*, 254–55. While I agree with Wright on these points, I do not support his supersessionist approach. For a critique of Wright's supersessionism see Harink, *Paul among the Postliberals*, 152–54.

the validity of the covenant relationship in any way diminishes the need for Jewish people to respond to the gospel. With Diprose, I believe the new majority views require a selective use of Scripture; for example, Romans 9–11 are often used selectively, omitting the missiological challenge contained in chapter 10.[108] He rightly states that what is needed is not an emotional reaction to the effects of the *old majority view*, but rather a return to all that Scripture has to say about the place of Israel in redemption history. Blaising is more forthright in his criticism, stating that "dual-covenant theology takes its primary orientation not from the Bible but from modern pluralism . . . To claim that Israel can be related to God by covenant apart from Jesus Christ is nothing less than a repudiation of NT Christianity."[109]

The position I adopt has been termed "modified supersessionism." This position maintains the Old covenant has been fulfilled in Christ but does not maintain that the Church is the "new Israel" and does not consider God to have rejected the Jewish people. It insists the Jews are still in covenant relationship with God, and have a continuing and future place in God's plans for the world. However, this does not in any way remove the need for Jewish people to accept Christ as their Messiah for their salvation. A separate way of salvation for Jewish people does not exist. I have demonstrated that adopting a single or dual-covenant approach does not merely affect one's view of the Jewish-Christian relationship. The implications of such approaches extend to central Christian doctrines such as soteriology and Christology and to a Christian theology of religions. The importance of this issue is realized correctly by Spillman (himself an advocate of the dual-covenant model), who writes: "Theology of recognition calls for significant revisions in important Christian doctrines."[110] Similarly, Soulen claims that the rejection of supersessionism is "fraught with profound implications for the whole range of Christian theological reflection, and the full extent of these implications is still far from fully clear."[111]

---

108. Diprose, "Israel and Christian Theology," 66.

109. Blaising, "Future of Israel," 441–42.

110. Spillman, "Image of Covenant in Christian Understandings of Judaism," 72. I have noted above that "theology of recognition" is term sometimes used for the anti-supersessionist paradigms.

111. Soulen, *God of Israel*, x.

Outline and Critique of the "New Majority Views"

    In this part of the thesis I have laid the foundation for my understanding of the place of Israel in Christian theology. My understanding of the relationship between Old and New covenants will be developed in subsequent chapters (particularly chapter 8). This will then allow an assessment of the analogical application of this relationship to the relationship of other religions to Christianity.

Part III

Critique of the Israel Analogy and Fulfilment Model

INTRODUCTION

In part I of this work I have outlined the use of the Israel analogy and fulfilment model in the theology of religions. In part II I have demonstrated the importance of a correct understanding of Israel and the Israel–Church relationship for a Christian theology of religions. In part III I will develop some of the themes introduced in part II and will subject the Israel analogy and fulfilment model to sustained critique on further biblical and theological grounds. The first chapter of this critique (chapter 6) will establish the framework for much of the subsequent discussion, and successive chapters will assess key biblical and theological themes that are contrary to the Israel analogy and fulfilment model.

6

SALVATION HISTORY 1

Continuity and Unity

6.1. An Introduction to Salvation History

Salvation history can be defined as "the personal redemptive activity of God within human history to effect his eternal saving intentions. This activity finds fulfillment in the ministry of Jesus foreshadowed in various Old Testament writings and institutions and culminating in the New Testament message of his death, resurrection, and eventual return."[1]

The concept of salvation history will play a crucial role in the critique of the Israel analogy and fulfilment model. Reformed theology maintains the Bible is the record of salvation-history.[2] However, how the various parts of this history relate is complex, particularly the question of the relationship between Old and New Testaments. One of the most fundamental questions facing theology and the Church in every age is, does Christianity need an Old Testament? Bernhard Anderson suggests, "It is no exaggeration to say that on this question hangs the

---

1. Yarbrough, "Paul and Salvation History," 297.

2. "The Bible, as the record of salvation, is one complete whole, an organism throbbing with life, and a system of prophecy wrought out in history according to plan. It is a marvellous structure, of which the ground was prepared in advance, a harmonious graduated whole, with perfect proportion and accord in all its parts, and having Christ as its goal. And the theme of the kingdom of God, with the rhythm of its progressively developing epochs and periods, is the leading basic melody of this whole majestic divine symphony" (Sauer, *Dawn of World Redemption*, 12).

meaning of the Christian faith."[3] Similarly, Rodney Petersen states that "The first question in the interpretation of Scripture for the Christian after acknowledging the Lordship of Jesus Christ is how to relate the Hebrew Scriptures to the New Testament."[4] In evangelical theology the issue of the relationship between the Old and New Testaments is variously understood. Reformed theology[5] maintains that the relationship is marked by a prevailing continuity, and Dispensationalist theology emphasizes the elements of discontinuity.[6] In this chapter I shall argue that a fundamental problem with the Israel analogy and fulfilment model is their failure to appreciate the true nature of redemptive history, and as a result they have an erroneous "theological vision" of the present, particularly the place of other religions in the divine economy.

Willem VanGemeren rightly states that Reformed theology has always been interested in continuity, and that this continuity must reflect the results of exegesis.[7] The "Scripture principle" (*sola Scriptura* and *tota Scriptura*) is a defining characteristic of Reformed theology, and "therefore Reformed theologians ought to integrate the whole of Scripture into a coherent system of doctrine that does justice to the harmony of Scripture, the unity of the history of redemption, and the historical progress of revelation."[8] The concept of Salvation History[9] (*Heilsgeschichte*) is accepted in Reformed theology as an important framework for un-

3. Anderson, "Old Testament as a Christian Problem," 1.

4. Petersen, "Continuity and Discontinuity," 17. Cf. Feinberg, "Systems of Discontinuity," 63.

5. Reformed theology is sometimes also referred to as covenant theology, due to the major role the doctrine of the covenant plays in this theological system. See chapter 8 for a discussion of covenant theology.

6. For a comprehensive survey of these issues, see Feinberg, *Continuity and Discontinuity*. I concur with Richard Lints, who suggests that "unity in diversity" should be the governing paradigm for this relationship: "Some overstress the continuity between the epochs (à la theonomy); others overstress the discontinuity of the epochs (à la dispensationalism)" (Lints, *Fabric of Theology*, 278).

7. VanGemeren, "Systems of Continuity," 52. Cf. Lints, *Fabric of Theology*, 142. Lints argues that the Reformed wing of the Church (along with the Lutheran) has valued serious theological reflection more dearly than other branches of Protestantism: "This branch of the church has been self-conscious in its concern for matters of method, of the framework in which one moves from the biblical text to doctrine."

8. Klooster, "The Uniqueness of Reformed Theology," 50; quoted in VanGemeren, "Systems of Continuity," 52.

9. This is also described as "redemption history" or "redemptive history," and I shall be using these terms interchangeably.

derstanding the continuity of Old and New Testaments, and the progressive nature of revelation.[10] According to John Goldingay, the recent history of the concept is traced to J. C. K. von Hofmann (1810–77) of the so-called "Salvation history school" of Erlangen.[11] Scholars of this school regarded the Bible primarily as the witness to what God had done in saving history rather than as a repository of doctrine.[12] Von Hofmann's work has influenced much subsequent theology based on this concept.[13] However, while he may have been instrumental in its modern renaissance, the origins of the concept are far more ancient. Aspects of the salvation-history approach can, in embryonic form, be traced to some of the Church Fathers. Their contribution was in defending the inclusion of the Hebrew Scriptures in the Christian canon. This defense was directed primarily against Marcionites and Gnostics, who argued that the Hebrew Scriptures were not valid as divine revelation for the Christian.[14] In their defense of the inclusion of the Hebrew Scriptures the Fathers emphasized the unity of the revelation found in both Old and New Testaments.[15]

---

10. G. E. Ladd writes, "There is a widespread recognition that revelation has occurred in redemptive history, and that *Heilsgeschichte* is the best key to understanding the unity of the Bible" (Ladd, *Theology of the New Testament*, 4). It is also important to note that the motif of salvation history should not be used in a way that overshadows other important biblical themes. On this, see Goldingay, *Approaches to Old Testament Interpretation*, 200–202. John Frame issues a similar caution: "Theology . . . must *take account* of redemptive history but not of redemptive history only. It must also be concerned to do justice to Scripture as law, poetry, wisdom, gospel . . . Theology is not, therefore, to be controlled exclusively by redemptive history, in opposition to other aspects or perspectives" (Frame, *Doctrine of the Knowledge of God*, 210). Oscar Cullmann notes that the term *salvation history* is not found in the Bible, but the concept is (Cullmann, *Salvation in History*, 75).

11. Goldingay, *Approaches to Old Testament Interpretation*, 66.

12. Ladd, *Theology of the New Testament*, 4. Cf. Petersen, "Continuity and Discontinuity," 30.

13 Baker, *Two Testaments, One Bible*, 42.

14. Brown, *Heresies: Heresy and Orthodoxy in the History of the Church*, 62.

15. Petersen argues that it was with Irenaeus that deeper reflection on the relationship between Old and New Testaments began (Petersen, "Continuity and Discontinuity," 19). Irenaeus considered Christ to be the primary link between the testaments. While the Old Testament is, for Irenaeus, subordinate in the scheme of progressive revelation, it is nevertheless of real value for understanding God's activity in history. According to Emil Brunner, Irenaeus and Tertullian contended that rejection of the Old Testament sprang from a faith "wholly irreconcilable with Christianity" (Brunner, "The Significance of the Old Testament for Our Faith," 243). Similarly Justin

The salvation-history approach is characterized by its emphasis on the historical and theological continuity of the Testaments.[16] Such continuity and unity does not preclude elements of discontinuity and diversity, but the diversity that exists is complementary to that unity.[17] VanGemeren suggests, "The stress on the unity of Scriptures has given Reformed Theology its distinctive stamp."[18] Salvation history emphasizes clear progress from creation to new creation in the unfolding plan of redemption, each period of which has "redemptive-historical significance" for all the other stages.[19] Each epoch is distinct, but relates organically to preceding and succeeding epochs. Each reveals elements of

---

Martyr argued for the unity of God's revelation, with the Old Testament itself looking forward to the Messiah and the New covenant (Baker, *Two Testaments, One Bible*, 35). Oscar Cullmann writes: "It is no accident that among the theologians of the second century none fought Gnosticism with such acuteness as did Irenaeus, who with unyielding consistency carried through the time line of redemptive history from the Creation to the eschatological new creation. Down to the theologians of the 'redemptive history' school in the nineteenth century . . . there has scarcely been another theologian who has recognised so clearly as did Irenaeus that the Christian proclamation stands or falls with the redemptive history, that the historical work of Jesus Christ as Redeemer forms the mid-point of a line which leads from the Old Testament to the return of Christ" (Cullmann, *Christ and Time*, 56–57).

16 Baker, *Two Testaments, One Bible*, 241: "There is no one concept that can sum up the meaning of the whole Old Testament nor its relationship to the New Testament. Nevertheless 'salvation history' has the merit of effectively grasping and organizing the material of the Old Testament in such as way as to stress the centrality of elements which are undoubtedly central and the secondary nature of others which are not. Even Barr, while emphasizing that there are other important axes through the biblical material, admits that: 'there really is a *Heilsgeschichte* . . . we have been generally right in saying that this can be taken as the central theme of the Bible, that it forms the main link between Old and New Testaments, and that its presence and importance clearly marks biblical faith off from other religions" (Ibid., 159; Baker quotes from James Barr "Revelation through History in the Old Testament and in Modern Theology," *Interpretation* 17 [1963] 201). Baker's comment beginning with, "even Barr" reflects Barr's objections to some aspects of salvation history and the biblical theology Movement of his time.

17. Ibid., 243.

18. VanGemeren, "Systems of Continuity," 55. It should be noted though that among Reformed theologians there is some divergence regarding the degree to which this unity and continuity should be emphasized. This matter has been highlighted recently in the debate between the Reformed theologians Paul Blackham and Graeme Goldsworthy. See Blackham, "Faith in Christ in the Old Testament"; Goldsworthy, "A Response to Paul Blackham"; Blackham and Goldsworthy, "Blackham-Goldsworthy Debate: Question Time,"

19. VanGemeren, *Progress of Redemption*, 15.

continuity and discontinuity, and contributes to a greater appreciation of the overall plan of God.[20] Therefore, salvation history can be seen as "the major link between the two testaments: they relate the beginning and the conclusion of one story, Act I and Act II of the same drama. The Christ-event completes a story that would otherwise be truncated; the OT gives the pre-history of an event which would otherwise lack the context which makes it intelligible."[21]

The approach is biblical rather than systematic in orientation because it organizes its material historically rather than logically.[22] It shows an appreciation of God's Word as it has come to us in space and time.[23] Geerhardus Vos (1862–1949) has been described as the "father of a Reformed biblical theology."[24] His theological approach is instrumental in the approach I adopt, and I will therefore briefly outline its key elements. Vos states, "Biblical Theology deals with the material from the historical standpoint, seeking to exhibit the organic growth or development of the truths of Special Revelation from the primitive pre-redemptive Special Revelation given in Eden to the close of the New Testament canon."[25]

Willem VanGemeren has summarized Vos's approach as follows:

---

20. Ibid. VanGemeren identifies twelve such periods, although he notes that the number itself is not as important as the principle.

21. Goldingay, *Approaches to Old Testament Interpretation*, 67–68.

22. It should also be noted that the division between biblical theology and systematic theology should not be seen as absolute, and the two should not be portrayed as competing disciplines. I concur with John Frame, who describes these different disciplines as "related perspectivally—each embracing the whole of theology and therefore embracing the others . . . They differ from one another in focus and emphasis and in the way they organise their material, but each is permitted (and obligated) to use the methods characteristic of the others" (Frame, *Doctrine of the Knowledge of God*, 206(.

23 VanGemeren, *Progress of Redemption*, 17.

24 Gaffin, *Shorter Writings of Geerhardus Vos*, xiv. Lints states that Vos is the first evangelical proponent of what has come to be called biblical theology. Although Vos preferred to use the term "history of special revelation," he accepted the more manageable term, *biblical theology* (Lints, *Fabric of Theology*, 182 n. 89). Lints also notes that "Vos has begun to receive attention through the writings of several representatives of the evangelical movement, including Herman Ridderbos, Meredith Kline and George Eldon Ladd. Also of interest is some recent work by David F. Wells, Henri Blocher, E. P. Clowney, Richard, B. Gaffin, Vern Poythress and others who write on theological topics with a decidedly Vosian methodology" (n. 90). Lints also notes that "Unfortunately, he has received virtually no attention among nonevangelicals" (n. 90).

25. Vos, *Biblical Theology*, v.

1. the object of theology is the knowledge of God through his revelation;
2. the revelation of God is historical and therefore requires attention to the historical continuity. He acknowledges the individuality of the biblical authors and books, as the analysis gives fresh insights;
3. the revelation of God in historical continuity discloses progression with elements of continuity and discontinuity;
4. the revelation of God is multiform and varied; as the legal, historical, prophetic, poetic, gospel, and epistolary forms contribute to that multiformity. The multiformity enhances rather than deprecates "what Paul calls the much-variegated, the manifold wisdom of God";
5. the motifs and themes of biblical theology are also variegated as they all contribute to the progressive unfolding of the revelation of God in Christ;
6. the "structure" of biblical theology (redemptive revelation) is centered in Christ and resembles that of "an organically unfolding process of a maturing organism";
7. the goal of redemptive history is eschatological. The unity of perspective between the biblical author, the people of God, and the modern interpreter lies in the relation to the "redemptive-historical context" on the one hand and the eschatological perspective on the other.[26]

For Vos, "Biblical Theology deals with revelation as a divine activity, not as the finished product of that activity."[27] Therefore, the nature and method of biblical theology must keep in touch with, and so far as possible reproduce, the features of the divine work itself.[28] Vos outlines these as:

1. *The historic progressiveness of the revelation-process.* Revelation[29] has not completed itself in one exhaustive act, but in a series of successive acts. This is so because revelation does not stand alone but is

---

26. VanGemeren, "Systems of Continuity," 48. The internal quotations are from Vos, "Idea of Biblical Theology as a Science and as a Theological Discipline"; and Gaffin, "Introduction" in Vos, *Redemptive History*, xviii, xix.

27. Vos, *Biblical Theology*, 5.

28. Ibid.

29. Throughout Vos's explanation of the revelation process, he uses the term *revelation* to refer to special revelation.

(at least in the case of Special Revelation), inseparably attached to another divine act—redemption. And the act of redemption could not be otherwise than historically successive because it addresses itself to successive generations in time and space.[30] "Revelation is the interpretation of redemption, it must, therefore, unfold itself in instalments as redemption does."[31] However, the two processes are not entirely co-extensive, because revelation comes to a close[32] at a point where redemption still continues. Here, Vos distinguishes between the objective and subjective aspects of redemption. The former take place outside, but on behalf of the individual and are unrepeatable—these are the incarnation, atonement, and resurrection of Christ. The latter are repeated to each individual separately and involve the acts of regeneration, justification, conversion, sanctification, and glorification.[33] Revelation accompanies the process of objective redemption only, and there remains only one epoch of such objective redemptive activity, namely the eschatological event of the second coming of Christ.[34]

2. *The actual embodiment of revelation in history.* "The process of revelation is not only concomitant with history, but it becomes

---

30. Vos, *Biblical Theology*, 6.

31. Ibid.

32. Vos does not specify when precisely (special) revelation comes to a close, but Reformed theology maintains it ends with the writing of the New Testament Scriptures. See Reymond, *New Systematic Theology of the Christian Faith*, 11–12, 56–59, 407–9. Reymond comments: "Vos's insistence that special revelation has come to a close should disturb no one, especially when it is recalled that even the revelatory process that produced our Bible did not flow uninterruptedly. Between Genesis 49:1–27 and Exodus 3:4 there was a 'blackout' of divine communication for over four hundred years. Then with the passing of Malachi, another four-hundred year 'blackout' ensued before the angel Gabriel appeared to Zechariah the priest. These prior revelational 'blackouts' show the naturalness of the 'revelational blackout' that has been in place since the close of the New Testament canon" (408–9).

33. Vos, *Biblical Theology*, 6.

34. Ibid. A more recent advocate of this approach to the relationship between revelation and redemption is Richard Gaffin, who writes: "Revelation never stands by itself, but is always concerned either explicitly or implicitly with redemptive accomplishment. God's speech is invariably related to his actions. It is not going too far to say that redemption is the *raison d'être* of revelation. An unbiblical, quasi-Gnostic notion of revelation invariably results when it is considered by itself or as providing self-evident general truths. Consequently, revelation is either authentication or interpretation of God's redemptive action" (*Resurrection and Redemption*, 22).

incarnate in history."[35] It becomes incarnate in the acts and words of God. In the outstanding acts of redemption (i.e. the life, death and resurrection of Christ), revelation and redemption coincide. Vos describes these redemptive acts as "two-sided."[36] They did not take place primarily for the purpose of revelation—their revelatory character is secondary. Their prime purpose transcends revelation, having a God-ward reference in their effect.[37] Only secondarily do they posses a "man-ward reference for instruction" i.e. revelation. These "act-revelations are never entirely left to speak for themselves; they are preceded and followed by word-revelation."[38] Thus: "The Old Testament brings the predictive preparatory word, the Gospels record the redemptive-revelatory fact, the Epistles supply the subsequent, final interpretation."[39]

3. *The organic nature of the historic process observable in revelation.* Of Importance here is the emphasis not only on the historic nature of revelation, but the *organic* character of this historical progress. Because of this, revelation is perfect in each of its stages.[40] Vos likens this progress as to that from a seed to a tree. The seed is not qualitatively less perfect than the tree, and neither are the earlier epochs of revelation, less perfect than latter epochs.[41] This explains

---

35. Vos, *Biblical Theology*, 6.

36. Ibid., 7.

37. Vos does not specify the nature of this God-ward effect, but Reformed theology considers this God-ward reference to be that of the propitiation of God; that is, the satisfaction of the "demands of the glory of God's offended holiness and justice" (Reymond, *New Systematic Theology*, 640). Cf. Ibid., 639–43, 656–57.

38. Vos, *Biblical Theology*, 7.

39. Ibid.

40. Here Vos does not specify what demarcates these "stages," but given his later comments to the epochal nature of revelation and redemption, and given the covenantal framework for his exposition of biblical theology, he is almost certainly referring to the various biblical covenants.

41. Vos, *Biblical Theology*, 7. According to David Baker, Aquinas also likened the relationship of New and Old Testament as to that of a Seed and a Tree (Baker, *Two Testaments, One Bible, Two Testaments*, 36 [Baker does not cite his source.]). Gaffin writes that the biblical "process is not heterogeneous, involving ongoing self-correction. Nor does it have anything to do with a evolutionary movement from what is erroneous and defective to what is relatively more true and perfect . . . The movement of the revelation process is from what is germinal and provisional to what is complete and final" (Gaffin, "Systematic Theology and Biblical Theology," 289).

"how the soteric sufficiency of the truth could belong to it in its first stage of emergence: in the seed-form the minimum of indispensable knowledge was already present."[42] Also important here is the close connection between revelation and redemption. Because redemption is organically progressive, so also is revelation—they partake of the same nature. Redemption does not proceed in a uniform motion but is "epochal" in its onward movement. In the great epoch-making redemptive acts, revelation is accelerated and its "volume increased." Where redemption "takes slow steps, or becomes quiescent, revelation proceeds accordingly."[43]

Richard Lints highlights the importance of these principles for Vos's theological method: "The impact of these principles on Vos's actual practice of exegesis is enormous. Texts do not stand in isolation, only later to find their correlation and concatenation in the theological vision of the church. Rather, the texts stand in a teleological relation to one another because they have one divine author who has brought the facts of history into teleological relation to one another."[44]

Lints rightly argues that the principles of redemptive history are not just exegetical aids for the interpretation of past revelation as recorded in Scripture, but are key in developing a "theological vision" of the present: "A theological vision must be shaped by a careful and purposeful reading of the revelation of God's redemptive activity. We will understand ourselves only if we first understand Scripture. Once we understand the framework of Scripture, we may then interpret our own place in the historical unfolding of the redemptive activity of God. The Scriptures ought to interpret the modern era rather than vice versa."[45]

A fundamental problem with the Israel analogy and fulfilment model is their failure to appreciate the true nature of redemptive history, and as a result they have an erroneous "theological vision" of the present, particularly the place of other religions in the divine economy. As I proceed I will highlight some particularly pertinent aspects of salvation history that have bearing on this issue. These will be further developed in later chapters.

---

42. Vos, *Biblical Theology*, 7.
43. Ibid.
44 Lints, *Fabric of Theology*, 188.
45. Ibid., 189–90.

6.2. Two Testaments—One Salvation History

The salvation-historical approach highlights the importance of both testaments for the Christian faith. The believers of the early Church understood their identity and their mission in the world as rooted in a purposeful reading of the Hebrew Scriptures, in which God is seen pre-eminently as the Lord of history—the God of Abraham, Isaac and Jacob. He is the God who was constantly reminding Israel that just as he had acted in the past so he would do so in the future.[46] This, states Lints, was the defining principle for the Christian challenge to the pagan world in the first century. God's redemptive history had begun in the Old Testament and reached a climax in the mission of Jesus Christ, and it was this consistent thread of God's redemptive activity in history, both in the past and the present that provided the early Church with the resources for an effective response to the pagan communities surrounding it.[47] G.E. Ladd argues that an appreciation of redemptive history is important in Paul's understanding of the Old Testament. Paul frequently appeals to the Old Testament to support his teaching, quoting from it 93 times. However,

> His primary concern in using the Old Testament is not to gain biblical authority for specific doctrines so much as to show that redemption in Christ stands in direct continuity with the revelation in the Old Testament and is in fact the fulfillment of that revelation. It is significant that twenty-six of his quotations occur in Romans 9–11, where he is dealing specifically with the question of the *history* of salvation, showing that the church is directly continuous with Israel, and that the 'word of God' (Rom. 9:6) given to Israel is not frustrated by Israel's unbelief but is fulfilled in the church . . . Paul's use of the Old Testament is not so much to seek one-to-one equating of prophecy and fulfillment as to place the new redemptive events squarely in the stream of Old Testament redemptive history.[48]

Oscar Cullmann rightly asserts that acceptance of the Old Testament by the New is exceedingly important, because the Christian Faith is a faith in a "divine salvation happening" consisting in a sequence

---

46. Ibid., 263.

47. Ibid., 266–67.

48. Ladd, *Theology of the New Testament*, 433 (italics original). The salvation-historical orientation of Paul's theology will be discussed further in section 7.2.

of events especially chosen by God, taking place within an historical framework. The New Testament books clearly connect their message with the Old Testament.[49] Cullmann emphasizes the significance of this fact: "What does the acceptance of the Old Testament by the New Testament witnesses mean? First of all, that early Christianity does not see, as Marcion does, revelation and salvation in a *punctiliar* event, but in a *coherent* salvation happening. For Marcion the gospel is a punctiliar unbound event, vertical and not horizontal. It comes unprepared; it is the gospel of the 'strange God.'"

"This indicates that Christian faith, like Jewish faith, was distinguished from all other religions of the time by this salvation-historical direction. We must therefore ask whether the surrender of this specific aspect of Christian faith either by its complete exclusion or by demythologization, whether in favour of mythological reinterpretation in antiquity or an existential one in our time does not amount to the loss of what distinguishes Christian and Jewish faith from all other religions.[50]

Similarly, David Baker suggests it is significant that Jesus, Peter and Paul presupposed the *Old Testament* as the basis of their faith, and their challenge was to relate the *new events* in which they were involved (i.e. the events that would later be documented in the New Testament) to earlier events (i.e. those recorded in the Hebrew Scriptures/Old Testament). It was only with the post-New Testament Church that this challenge was reversed (that is, the challenge then became understanding how the Old Testament related to the New).[51]

I consider the Israel analogy and fulfilment model to have incorrectly understood this challenge, and this is evident in how the Old Testament is employed by these concepts. Understanding the relationship between the Old and New covenants as an analogical basis for the relationship of other religions to Christianity results in undermining the *sui generis* nature of the relationship between these covenants. However, the redemptive-historical approach to understanding the relationship between the Old and New covenants ensures both are afforded their full place and significance in the canon and in Christian theology, and

---

49. Cullmann, *Salvation in History*, 85.

50. Ibid., 24–25 (italics original). The context of Cullmann's writing here is his opposition to Bultmann and other existential theologians, but his argument can also be validly applied to the current issue.

51. Baker, *Two Testaments, One Bible*, 34.

the uniqueness of their relationship is affirmed. I fully concur with the results of Samuel Amsler's study of the New Testament's use of the Old Testament which showed that:

a) The significance of the gospel is seen clearly only in light of the Old Testament.
b) The New Testament authors recognize in the Old Testament a witness which corroborates their own.
c) The New Testament authors claim the Old Testament to be an advance witness, a promise which shows the theological significance of events within the history of salvation prior to their occurrence.
d) The New Testament authors interpret the Old Testament as a witness to God's revelation and salvation in history.[52]

Amsler points out that the Old Testament was *the Bible* of the early Church. The early Christians used the Old Testament not simply because in a Jewish context it was convenient to do so, but because they were convinced that the advent, life, death and resurrection of Jesus Christ were the fulfilment of the Old covenant and therefore inextricably related to it.[53] According to Cullmann, "The concept of fulfilment, so important for salvation-history, indicates that the new covenant does not bring an end to a chaotic situation of the past, but that the past remains very real in the present and determines the Church's 'self-understanding.'"[54]

However, I consider the fulfilment model for understanding the relationship between other religions and Christianity to imply that the use of the Old Testament (Hebrew Scriptures) by the early Church was really just a matter of historical and cultural convenience. For, in other contexts, other scriptures and other faiths are viewed as being similarly fulfilled in Christ. I have already made extensive references (see chapter 2) to a number of theologians who make this assertion, and will not repeat these here, but refer the reader back to this material for their consideration.[55]

---

52. Ibid., 28–29. This account is based on Baker's summary of Amsler's work. I have been unable to source the latter.

53. Ibid., 164.

54. Cullmann, *Salvation in History*, 87. The quotation finishes with, "so that it views itself as 'the new Israel.'" I have shown in part 2 that titling the Church "the New Israel" is problematic because of the implications of total replacement or termination of the Old covenant. But Cullmann's point is valid nonetheless.

55. A separate chapter will examine the evidence used by proponents of the fulfil-

6.3. The Structure of Salvation History

A guiding principle of the salvation history approach to the unfolding biblical revelation is that no part of this story can be understood without reference to preceding and following parts of the story. Interpretation of the Bible embraces the *total* context of the Bible, as Lints explains: "The essence of theology is the interpretation of the history of redemption. Correspondingly, our theological framework must see the totality of the movement of scriptural revelation as progressing toward a goal. No point in the history of redemption can be understood aright until its relationship to the origin and the consummation of this movement has been understood."[56]

The origin and consummation of this movement are the creation and the new creation at the eschaton, respectively. A correct understanding of the theological relationship of redemption and creation is important here, and it is essential that redemption is not treated in isolation from creation.[57] As Erich Sauer states, it was God's intention to redeem the world right from the start for the plan of salvation even pre-dates the creation of the world.[58] Seen this way, creation is the preamble to redemption, and VanGemeren argues that "The integration of creation and redemption opens up more fully the one purpose of God, because reflection on the many mighty acts of God in creation, redemption, and judgment bears witness to the unified purpose of God in Christ."[59] The unifying factor throughout the entire process is the Son of God, who is the mediator of world-creation, world-preservation, world-redemption and world-judgment.[60] Thus, "Scripture is united by one primary pervading purpose: the tracing of God's unfolding plan of redemption. It everywhere assumes that *this God acts coherently and purposefully in history.*"[61] This pervading theme is emphasized in the

---

ment model to support this understanding of the relationship of other religions to Christianity. This will be compared and contrasted with the biblical understanding of fulfilment. See chapter 9.

56. Lints, *Fabric of Theology*, 268.

57. I appreciate that there is considerable scholarly debate regarding the relationship of creation and redemption. This matter will be discussed further in chapter 7.

58. Sauer, *Dawn of World Redemption*, 20–25.

59. VanGemeren, "Systems of Continuity," 52.

60. Sauer, *Dawn of World Redemption*, 21.

61. Köstenberger and O'Brien, *Salvation to the Ends of the Earth*, 20 (italics original).

work of the Puritans who held that God's redemption of his people is the fundamental thread tying all of history together.[62] Jonathan Edwards argued that if creation is a stage, the purpose of which is to permit the drama of redemption to be played out, the outcome of the drama (and thus the reason for creation) is God's self-glorification.[63] According to Edwards, redemption is structured around three main periods: a) the period from the fall to the incarnation; b) the period from Christ's incarnation to his resurrection; and c) the period from the resurrection to the second coming. These phases represent periods of "preparation," "imputation," and "application" respectively.[64]

> The Work of Redemption with respect to the grand design . . . is carried on from the fall [of man to the end of the world] in a different manner, not merely by the repeating and renewing the same effect on the different subjects of it, but by many successive works and dispensations of God, all tending to the one great end and effect, all united as the several parts of a scheme, and together making up one great work. Like an house or temple that is building, first the workmen are sent forth, then the materials are gathered, then the ground fitted, then the foundation is laid, then the superstructure erected one part after another, till at length the topstone is laid. And all is finished.[65]

This emphasis on a clear structure to redemption history highlights the need to respect both the *content and structure* of the Scriptures in their interpretation. The structure of theology must be linked to the structure of Scripture otherwise the normative role of Scripture is undermined, as Lints explains:

> [T]he theological framework ought to be linked to the actual *structure* of the biblical text itself and not merely to the *content* of the Bible. The questions that the biblical text asks ought to be the primary questions of the theological framework . . . The

---

62. Lints rightly notes the similarities between the work of Vos and Edwards: "Although the historical record gives no indication that he [Vos] was familiar with Edwards's work, there are some remarkable similarities between the two on this point of emphasizing the centrality of redemption" (Lints, *Fabric of Theology*, 185 n. 97).

63. Wilson, "Introduction," in Edwards, *History of the Work of Redemption*, 31–32.

64. Ibid., 117. For an exposition of Edwards's three-stage salvation history, see Bombaro, "Dispositional Peculiarity, History, and Edwards's Evangelistic Appeal to Self-Love," 140–47.

65. Edwards, *History of the Work of Redemption*, 121.

sense of movement so critical to the biblical text ought to be part and parcel of the theological framework. The organic relations between the different episodes (or epochs) of the Scriptures ought to be developed in such a manner as to envelop the modern epoch and thereby bring the entirety of history under the interpretive umbrella of the Scriptures.[66]

I shall demonstrate in subsequent chapters that the Israel analogy and fulfilment model exhibit a deficient understanding of this structure. VanGemeren suggests there are three main facets to the structure: literary form; canonical place; and redemptive-historical significance. The first of these trifocal elements considers the "grammatical-historical" significance of the text. The second considers the function of the particular text or book within the context of its respective place in the canon, recognizing the progress of revelation. The third aspect provides a "framework for connecting the parts of Scripture into a coherent whole."[67] It pays "careful attention to the text, to the particular redemptive-historical period, and to the relationship of that period to the coming of Jesus as the Savior and Restorer of heaven and earth."[68] In this way each part of the Bible is related to the one history of redemption. It is this third aspect that is of particular importance for the current study, and it will be referred to frequently in subsequent chapters.

Redemption history emphasizes the progressive and organic nature of revelation. This progression is, as has already been noted, characterized by increasing clarity, and this is an important principle for understanding the Scriptures. Augustine recognized this principle, as evidenced by his oft-cited statement: "In the Old Testament the New is concealed, in the New the Old is revealed."[69] He perceived in Scripture a progressive line of divine history culminating in Jesus Christ.[70] A similar emphasis on the increasing clarity of revelation is found in the work of John Calvin.[71] Calvin traces the progress of redemptive history from

---

66   Lints, *Fabric of Theology*, 271

67.   VanGemeren, *Progress of Redemption*, 32.

68.   Ibid. Cf. Lints, *Fabric of Theology*, 293, describes these as the "textual horizon," "epochal horizon," and "canonical horizon."

69.   Cited in Petersen, "Continuity and Discontinuity," 23. Petersen does not cite his source. Cf. Edwards, *History of the Work of Redemption*, 290.

70.   See particularly Augustine, *City of God*, books 15–22, in Schaff, *St. Aurelius Augustin's "City of God" and "Christian Doctrine"*

71.   John Murray writes, "In John Calvin there is a distinct emphasis upon the

creation to new creation.[72] The Old Testament contains the promises of salvation and anticipates the revelation of God in Jesus Christ. The New Testament contains a better and fuller revelation of God. However, this does not mean the Old Testament can be set aside as containing a mere "shadow" of the substance of the hope. The Old covenant anticipates the fullness of the revelation in the New covenant, and is not complete by itself. Nevertheless, Calvin appreciates the beauty of the salvation experience of the Old Testament saints.[73] Their salvation was salvation by grace, just as it is for the New-Testament believer:

> The covenant made with all the fathers in [*sic*—read "is"] so far from differing from ours in reality and substance, that it is altogether one and the same: still the administration differs . . . *First*, That temporal opulence and felicity was not the goal to which the Jews were invited to aspire, but that they were admitted to the hope of immortality . . . *Secondly*, That the covenant by which they were reconciled to the Lord was founded on no merits of their own, but solely on the mercy of God, who called them. . . . *Thirdly*, That they both had and knew Christ the Mediator, by whom they were united to God, and made capable of receiving his promises.[74]

This stress on the similarity of the faith of Old- and New-covenant believers stands in contrast to the understanding of Old covenant faith suggested by the Israel analogy and fulfilment model. The faith of Old covenant believers is considered by these models to be of a very different type to New covenant faith, and can be considered in similar terms to the faith of adherents of other religions today.[75]

Calvin's emphasis on the unity of the Scriptures also acknowledges the differences that exist. He stated: "I readily admit the differences

---

historic progressiveness and continuity of redemptive revelation" (Murray, *Covenant of Grace*, 195; quoted in VanGemeren, 'Systems of Continuity', 53).

72. VanGemeren, "Systems of Continuity," 53

73. VanGemeren, "Israel as the Hermeneutical Crux in the Interpretation of Prophecy (1)," 137.

74. Calvin, *Institutes*, II.x.2. I elaborate further on the gracious nature of Old Testament salvation in section 8.3.2.

75. While soteriology is not the focus of this study, I will argue in chapter 8 that there is substantial continuity between saving faith in the Old and New Testaments. For a detailed defense of the confession of Christ by Old Testament believers see Strange, *Salvation among the Unevangelized*, esp. chapter 6, "The Covenant, Christ, and Confession of Christ."

Salvation History 1

which are pointed out in Scripture, but still hold that they derogate in no respect from the established unity . . . I hold . . . that they all belong to the mode of administration rather than to the substance."[76] Calvin viewed the two Testaments as two forms of one divine administration of grace, both being based on the one foundation of Christ, the mediator of the covenants. In this way, he holds in tension the unchangeable nature of God and the newness of the various redemptive stages.[77] These various redemptive stages are demarcated largely by God's acts and redemptive covenants.[78] Each covenant builds on those that precede it and God is consistent in intent between the various covenants. The different covenants are organically related to each other, and are interdependent. In fact, I suggest the various covenants are better thought of as one covenant with several administrations.[79] The various administrations are expressions of one covenant between the Father and the elect, whose mediator is Jesus Christ.[80] Throughout the Scriptures, "covenant" is the theological basis for the relationship between God and his people, making possible what Eichrodt calls "sacral communion."[81] Vos correctly states that these covenants should be "carefully heeded."[82]

However, I do not consider that the Israel analogy regards the nature of the various covenants and their interdependence correctly. I have outlined in Part 1 how theologians that use the Israel analogy consider a saving relationship with God to be possible in various ways depending on which covenant one lives under. The Noahic covenant, Abrahamic covenant and New covenant are portrayed as separate arrangements rather than part of the same unfolding plan. The unity of the one covenant of redemption is also at variance with the approaches to the Jewish-Christian relationship outlined in Part 2. Clearly, an understanding of the covenants and covenantal relationship is of key

---

76. Calvin, *Institutes*, II.xi.1.

77. VanGemeren, *Progress of Redemption*, 23. According to VanGemeren, his scheme is characterized by the tension between law and gospel, promise and fulfilment, and token and reality (24–25).

78. Lints, *Fabric of Theology*, 262–65.

79. I will consider the covenants and their relationship in chapter 8.

80. VanGemeren, "Israel as the Hermeneutical Crux in the Interpretation of Prophecy (2)," 289.

81. Eichrodt, *Theology of the Old Testament*, 1: 43.

82. Vos, *Biblical Theology*, 16.

significance to the current topic, and this will be the subject of a subsequent chapter (chapter 8).

6.4. The Christological and Eschatological Orientation of Salvation History

Both Testaments share a common Christological focus. Calvin recognized this, viewing the two testaments as witnesses to the one God in Jesus Christ as "the *scopus* of Scripture, the 'goal' to which it all points."[83] Christ is the mid-point of salvation history. His incarnation is described by G. E. Wright as "a historical event which was the climax of God's working since the creation. All former history had its goal in him because God has so directed it."[84] This Christological focus is particularly emphasized in the work of Oscar Cullmann, "According to the New Testament view, all the epochs which make up salvation-history are oriented towards the happening of the decisive period, the cross and resurrection of Jesus Christ. The *whole* salvation-history present in God's plan is latently contained in this one event. All the preceding history of salvation tends towards the occurrence of this period."[85]

"*The mutual connection of all the epochs* continually operates within the whole saving process. Because these epochs are all held together by the event of the decisive period, which provides an orientation, they are co-ordinated one with another. Although they are all placed in a continual forward movement toward a temporal end, and although one presupposes the other in a temporal sequence, there is nevertheless at the same time an influence of future events still to come upon preceding events, in the opposite direction. This is because of the co-ordination of the vertical and the horizontal."[86]

Here, Cullmann emphasizes the interdependence of what he calls the "vertical" and "horizontal" orientation of redemptive history. The Christ-event has required horizontal (i.e. historical) preparation, it has not appeared merely in a vertical fashion: "The whole struggle of the ancient Church, particularly of Irenaeus, against Marcion was meant to

---

83. VanGemeren, "Systems of Continuity," 56. VanGemeren does not cite his source.
84. Wright, *God Who Acts*, 13; quoted in Baker, *Two Testaments, One Bible*, 163.
85. Cullmann, *Salvation in History*, 166.
86. Ibid., 167 (Italics original).

defend the New Testament link of the Christ-event with the history of salvation against the Marcionite doctrine of the unknown God. In other words, the struggle was over the horizontal foundation of verticality."[87]

The interdependence of the vertical and horizontal orientation of salvation history is particularly important with regard to the topic of this thesis, because I suggest the Israel analogy and fulfilment model do not fully succeed in holding these two axes together. For, in treating other religions or other religious Scriptures as alternatives to the Old Testament, they reject the necessity of the particular "horizontal" (i.e. historical) preparation for the Christ-event (i.e. the "vertical" dimension of salvation history).

Not only do the two testaments have a common Christological orientation, they also share an eschatological orientation. Calvin's hermeneutical framework has been described as "triadic" by VanGemeren. The triad comprises Old Testament–New Testament–Completion; Shadow–Reality–Full reality.[88] According to VanGemeren, Calvin maintained that to appreciate the nature of OT salvation "one needs a proper view of promise. In the Old Testament the promise was concealed. In the NT it is revealed. But in each case it remains promise and it will continue to be promise until the final consummation."[89] This Christological and eschatological orientation to redemptive-history is recognized by VanGemeren:

> The progression of redemption did not culminate in Jesus' first coming but anticipates the coming of Christ in glory, when he will inaugurate the era of consummation, the new heavens and the new earth. Interpretation therefore, is both christological and eschatological. If it limits the fulfillment to Jesus' first coming, it tends to contrast the Old Testament with the New. If, however, it focuses on the restoration of all things as the goal of the history of redemption, then the Old Testament and the New Testament are brought more closely together as witnesses to the hope that this Jesus has been appointed to make everything subject to the Father (Acts 2:34–36; 1 Cor. 15:25; Heb. 1:13; 2:8; 10:13; Rev. 2:27; 12:5; 19:15).[90]

---

87. Ibid., 170.

88. VanGemeren, "Israel as the Hermeneutical Crux in the Interpretation of Prophecy (1)," 138.

89. Ibid., 137.

90. VanGemeren, *Progress of Redemption*, 32.

Therefore the OT is not completely fulfilled in the NT because the Scriptures have an eschatological focus, as Old and New together point forward to the era of consummation, when all things will be made new.[91] Torrance states this succinctly: "the *Heilsgeschichte* has been completed and only awaits its ultimate *epiphany* or *apocalypse* in the consummation of the Second Advent, but the Church has its life and mission between the penultimate event of the *Heilsgeschichte* at Pentecost, and the ultimate event at the *Parousia*."[92]

The Christological and eschatological orientation common to Old and New Testaments emphasizes the continuity of redemption history, as progressively revealed in the Christian Scriptures. This stands in contrast to how the Scriptures are understood by advocates of the Israel analogy and fulfilment model.

6.5. Summary

The salvation history approach highlights the organic, progressive nature of revelation and redemption, the historical and theological continuity of the Old and New Testaments and the clear progress of the drama of redemption from creation to new creation. Each period or epoch of this unfolding drama has "redemptive-historical significance" for all the other stages. I have emphasized the actual embodiment of revelation and redemption in history. This history is portrayed in both the Old and New Testaments, which together constitute one salvation-history, and therefore neither Testament can be set aside or replaced. I have stated that the fundamental problem with the Israel analogy and fulfilment model is their erroneous construal of salvation history which does not adequately recognize the importance of the historical and organic nature of revelation and redemption as portrayed in the Old and New Testaments. In short, they do not appreciate the "redemptive-historical significance" of each of the progressive stages of salvation history.

According to Cullmann, the salvation-history approach guards against syncretism.[93] He argues that the only thing that kept primitive

---

91. Ibid., 38.
92. Torrance, *School of Faith*, lviii.
93. Cullmann, *Salvation in History*, 25–26.

Christianity from ruin was the concept of salvation-history.[94] I consider the Israel analogy and fulfilment model also as challenges to the uniqueness of the Christian faith as historically revealed in Old and New Testaments. Cullmann's emphasis on the interdependence of the "horizontal" and "vertical" aspects of revelation and redemption is of key significance for the current issue, and as Cullmann states, the normative significance of the Christ-event (the vertical dimension) is rendered meaningless if severed from the horizontal dimension:

> Just as the whole plan of salvation encompassing every period of time is present *in God himself*, so this plan appears, in its entire fullness, as it were, compressed in that one event [the incarnation], only now in such as way that neither the past history, which is fulfilled in this event, nor the future, in which it unfolds, becomes superfluous ... *The event in the Word-made-flesh contains within itself the entire salvation history that comes before and that comes afterwards; but it also aligns itself with this history.* It is no good giving up the horizontal while appealing to the normative significance of the Christ-event, as happens today.[95]

This introduction to salvation history will provide the framework for the ongoing critique. Subsequent chapters will in turn develop important aspects of this salvation-historical approach and will apply these developments to the Israel analogy and fulfilment model. In the next chapter I will explicate the importance of a correct understanding of the universal decisiveness of the Christ-event in the unfolding of salvation history, and will consider the implications for a theology of religions.

---

94. Ibid., 27.

95. Ibid., 100 (italics original). While I fully agree with Cullmann's argument here, I do not fully concur with his eschatology. According to Cornelius Van Til, Cullmann "does not want this mid-point [the Christ-event] to be the invasion of the eternal into the temporal, but wants to render all of revelation a matter of history. The death and resurrection of Christ, for Cullmann, serves as a beacon to illuminate all of history, rather than being an eschatological invasion from another realm. So anxious is Cullmann to reverse the dialectical flight from history" (Van Til, *Great Debate Today*; quoted in Horton, *Covenant Eschatology*, 229). I would prefer to understand the Christ-event as both a historical and an eschatological event.

7

SALVATION HISTORY 2

Chronology and Crisis[1]

7.1. Christ the Midpoint of Salvation History[2]

As has been previously stated, the analogy made between other religions and Old Testament Israel relies on a correspondence between the chronologically pre-messianic (Israel) and the epistemologically pre-messianic (other religions). The seven theologians studied in Part 1 all make an analogy between Old covenant believers and the unevangelised today, and in so doing consider the "BC condition" as continuing today (at least for certain groups of people). I suggest that the Israel analogy undermines the significance of the Christ-event[3] in the unfolding plan of redemption by failing to appreciate the decisive effect of the Christ-event on history and the nature of existence. In a similar way, the fulfilment model views fulfilment as an ongoing process continuing

---

1. I use the term "crisis" in the sense of "a crucial stage or turning point in the course of something, esp. in a sequence of events" (*Collins English Dictionary*) Online: http://www.collinslanguage.com/results.aspx/.

2. I adopt the term "midpoint" from Cullmann. It should be noted that the term does not imply an equal period of time both before and after this point. Cf. Conzelman, *Theology of Saint Luke*. Throughout this work, Conzelman sees Jesus' ministry as the "centre of time." R. T. France describes Jesus as "the turning point of time" (France, *Matthew*, 197).

3. I use the term "Christ-event" to refer to the entire work of Christ in his incarnation, life, death, resurrection and exaltation. According to Herman Ridderbos, the resurrection is the "centre" of redemptive history (Ridderbos, *Paul*, 55).

after the Christ-event. It considers the historical and teleological relationship between the Old and New Testaments to be less than fully decisive in how fulfilment can be interpreted. It does not require there to be a historical or chronological relationship between that which is fulfilled (the contemporary religion) and the fulfiller (Christ) and therefore undermines the radical transition from BC to AD. In chapter 6 I outlined how the history of redemption is characterized by continuity and unity. I also emphasized the Christological and eschatological focus of revelation and redemption. In the current chapter I will develop this argument, showing that the Christ-event is the midpoint of the unfolding redemptive history and is of universal significance for all space and time and for all people. Therefore, the concept of a continuing "pre-Messianic" condition or state is seriously flawed, and should not be employed in developing an understanding of the relationship of other religions to Christianity.

7.1.1. An Eternal Purpose and a Mystery Revealed in the Fullness of Time

The times and ages of redemptive history have been ordained by God from eternity, in his divine decree.[4] This decree establishes God's ultimate intention for the world and his means of accomplishing this, thus giving a fundamental unity to the plan of redemption, for the whole created order ultimately serves this purpose.[5] Ephesians 3:11 refers to this "eternal purpose" (πρόθεσιν των αἰώνων) in the adjective-genitive tense indicating that there was never a time when God's plan with all of its parts was not fully determined.[6] The same verse states that this eternal purpose is realized in Jesus Christ (cf. Eph 1:9). "Here we learn that God's eternal plan, which governs *all* his ways and works in heaven and on earth, he *purposed* to fulfil in Christ. Christ, as God's Alpha and Omega, is at the beginning, the center and the end of his eternal

---

4. For a helpful introduction to the topic of the divine decree, see Feinberg, *No One Like Him*, 501–36. Cf. Helm, "Of God's Eternal Decree," 143–47.

5. Reymond, *New Systematic Theology*, 343. Cf. Westminster Confession of Faith 3.1. "GOD from all eternity did, by the most wise and holy counsel of his own will, freely and unchangeably ordain whatsoever comes to pass: (1) yet so, as thereby neither is God the author of sin, (2) nor is violence offered to the will of the creatures, nor is the liberty or contingency of second causes taken away, but rather established.(3)"

6. Reymond, *New Systematic Theology*, 463.

purpose."⁷ The outworking of God's eternal purpose is governed by his providential superintending activity over the created order and history, bringing creation to its divinely determined goal. All God's providential work is mediated through Christ (Col 1:16-17; Heb 1:3).⁸ From the very beginning God has ordered events toward Christ and his redemptive work.⁹ Indeed, the covenant of redemption precedes even the fall.¹⁰

Christ is the midpoint of the history of redemption. His death and resurrection are the unsurpassable and unrepeatable point of crisis, the "omega-point."¹¹ This historical reality has enormous theological import, for all history is to be understood and judged in light of this crisis. The centre of redemption in the period before the Christ-event is the future hope (of the promised Messiah), the centre of redemption after Christ's death and resurrection is the past event. Therefore, the Christ-event is of constitutive significance for all history and time. What was achieved by Christ through his life, death and resurrection cannot be divorced from what came before or after it. In any theological scheme therefore, the historical unfolding of events must be respected for these events follow a course decreed by God from eternity, and each is but a part of the one overarching purpose.¹²

---

7. Ibid.

8. While a distinction between ordinary (common or general) providence and special providence (or special grace) exists, care needs to be taken not to interpret these two kinds of providence to mean that God is conducting two works alongside each other with no relationship between them. Ordinary providence serves special (Ibid., 399–400).

9. See section 6.3, "The Structure of Salvation History."

10. Feinberg, *No One Like Him*, 531–36. Cf. Reymond, *Systematic Theology*, 379, 401. Within Reformed theology, a debate exists between those who support *supralapsarianism* and those who support *infralapsarianism*. "The difference concerns what happened in God's mind before the foundation of the world. It does not concern something that happened in time, but rather the *logical* order of God's thoughts. The question is whether, in logical order, (a) God decided first that he would *save some people* and second that he would *allow sin* into the world so that he could save them from it (the supralapsarian position), or whether it was the other way around, so that (b) God first decided that he would *allow sin* into the world and second decided that he would *save some people* from it (the infralapsarian position)" (Grudem, *Systematic Theology*, 679, footnote 12). However, both positions maintain that the covenant of redemption precedes the fall chronologically.

11. The "omega-point" is a term Richard Gaffin uses to describe the death and resurrection of Christ (Gaffin, *By Faith, Not By Sight*, 6).

12. Torrance, *Divine and Contingent Order*, 1. As Torrance argues, in every aspect of a theological account of God's interaction with us in the world, time and space

Salvation History 2

The death and resurrection of Christ is the center of redemptive history inaugurating a period of radical newness which cannot be overstated, for the Christ-event is the ultimate eschatological event.[13] Jesus is the mediator of a divine act of redemption, the Centre and End of all history, because in him the eternal God has entered time, and in so doing has revealed the "mystery" of the ages (Rom 16:25–26; 1 Cor 2:7; Eph 1:9–10, 3:4–5; Col 1:26, 2:2–3; 2 Tim 1:9–10; Titus 1:2–3). This "mystery" (μυστήριον) should not be understood as a secret revealed to a few intimates, but rather "in connection with the hidden counsel of God in relation to his redemptive work in history."[14] David Wells explains: "In the New Testament, 'mystery' is typically associated with what is revealed and proclaimed (1 Tim 3:9), never with what is obscure and unknown. The chief mystery is Christ (1 Cor 2:2), promised long ago (1 Cor 1:19), by whom the Gentiles now gain access to the Father (Eph 3:14–15), and to whom Paul was bound in service (1 Cor 9:16). To associate this mystery with the unknown rather than the known would be . . . to render God unthinkable."[15]

Thus, in addition to the noetic aspect, there is a historical connotation to the mystery revealed, it is that which for a time had not yet appeared, but is then made known.[16] The dawning of the messianic

---

constitute the orderly medium for divine revelation to man and human knowledge of God. Cf. Rust, *Salvation History*, 127. Here Rust highlights the meta-historical plan of redemption: "On the Biblical view, the time process must be measured in terms of the mighty acts of God and not of the evolutionary development of man . . . The phrase *preparatio evangelica* has come of recent years to be coloured with an evolutionary significance, imposing on the situation the false category of progress rather than the Biblical conception of crisis . . . The Biblical faith is based on the conviction that God is the Lord of history, able to control its events and movements in the interest of His purpose."

13. While the term "eschatology" is commonly employed to refer to the "last things," this excludes much that falls within the scope of the term. I use the term "eschatological" here and throughout this chapter in its broad sense, as defined by F. F. Bruce: Eschatology "may denote the consummation of God's purpose whether it coincides with the end of the world (or of history) or not, whether the consummation is totally final or marks a stage in the unfolding pattern of his purpose" (Bruce, "Eschatology," 362).

14. Ridderbos, *Paul*. Cf. Carson, "Mystery and Fulfillment"; see esp. 413–25.

15. Wells, *God in the Wasteland*, 132 n. 122.

16. Herman Ridderbos emphasizes this historical revelation: "The revelation of the mystery is nothing other than that which the fullness of the time brings to view; it is the fulfillment of the eschatological promise of redemption in the times appointed

age in the "fullness of time" (πλήρωμα τοῦ χρόνου, Gal 4:4; cf. Eph 1:10) also testifies to the important historical transformation that occurred with the Christ-event. The fullness of time centers on Christ as Messiah—when the fullness of time had come, God sent his Son. At the appropriate moment the Old age ended and the new age was ushered in. The age of the Law had run its course to be superseded by the age of the Spirit, inaugurated by the accomplishment of Christ's redemptive work.[17] The term "fullness" suggests, states A. A Hoekema, the thought of fulfilment, of bringing to completion, "from the Old Testament perspective, the New Testament era is the time of fulfillment."[18] This fulfilment is not only historical but profoundly teleological. As Ridderbos asserts, it is "not only the maturation of a specific matter in the great framework of redemptive history, but the fulfillment of the time in an absolute sense."[19] The new age actually arrives in Christ as the first fruits of a full cosmic salvation.[20]

Similarly, Vos observes that the fullness of time means more than the time was ripe for the introduction of Christ into the world: "the fullness of the time means the end of that aeon and the commencement of another world-period."[21] This new "world-period" is unfolding in two stages, the present age, starting with the resurrection, and the age to come, consummated by Christ's return. However, the two stages should not be seen as separate, for the New Testament's outlook is that the Messiah's coming is one (eschatological) coming which unfolds in two episodes, one already having happened, and one still to come. However, the Age-to-Come had already dawned.[22] "The Messianic Age is divided

---

for it, its 'own times,' that is denoted in this fashion" (Ridderbos, *Paul*, 47). Ridderbos (ibid., 48) points out that Paul is echoing what Jesus proclaims as the "fulfillment of time (Mark 1:15)."

17. Bruce, "Salvation History in the New Testament," 82.

18. Hoekema, *Bible and the Future*, 17. Hoekema supports this assertion with reference to 1 Cor 10:11; Heb 9:26 and 1 John 2:18.

19. Ridderbos, *Paul*, 44.

20. "This is the new, overpowering certainty, that in the crucified and risen Savior the great turning-point has come. This is the main theme of Paul's ministry and epistles. 'Old things are passed away; behold they are become new' (2 Cor. 5:17) . . . And of the 'fullness of the times' (Gal. 4:4), of this now now the day of salvation (2 Cor. 6:2), Paul is the herald (Eph. 3:2ff.)" (Ridderbos, *When the Time Had Fully Come*, 48).

21. Vos, "Eschatological Aspect of the Pauline Conception of the Spirit," 93.

22. Rust, *Salvation History*, 158. Cf. Hoekema, *Bible and the Future*, 18–20.

into two parts—the first supervening upon and overlapping the historical process, and ushered in by the life, death and resurrection of Jesus Christ; the second, the eternal and otherworldly consummation of what has already been begun, ushered in by the second advent of the exalted Messiah who had been appointed by God to judge the quick and the dead."[23]

The eschatological in-breaking has commenced, and with it there is not only a horizontal/chronological transformation, but also one that Horton describes as vertical/cataclysmic.[24] The resurrection is the crucial sign that the "last days" are here.[25]

According to Gaffin, "The clearest, most explicit biblical warrant for this fundamental redemptive-historical, history-of-revelation construct is the overarching assertion with which Hebrews begins (1:1–2a). . . . 'Long ago, at many times and in many ways, God spoke to our fathers by the prophets, but in these last days he has spoken to us by his Son.'"[26]

Therefore, the manifestation of Jesus Christ, is not in the first place made known as a "noetic piece of information, but has happened as an historical event."[27] For that reason, it should not be construed primarily as an existential matter but an historical/eschatological event with cosmic significance.[28] This fact will be seen to be of decisive significance for this chapter as it proceeds.

---

23. Rust, *Salvation History*, 138

24. Horton, *Covenant and Eschatology*, 40. See section 6.4 for more on this theme.

25. Frame, "Doctrine of the Christian Life," 262. Cf. Gaffin, *Resurrection and Redemption*, 91–92, 116. Gaffin states that the resurrection and ascension are separate occurrences, but the resurrection is integral to Christ's subsequent mode of existence. What Christ is and continues to be, he became at the resurrection and at no other point. His resurrection marks the completion of the once for all accomplishment of redemption.

26. Gaffin, *By Faith, Not By Sight*, 6–7. Here Gaffin notes how this declaration, which embraces the entire message of Hebrews, captures three interrelated factors concerning God's "speech": "(1) Revelation is expressly in view as a historical process. (2) The diversity involved in this process is accented, particularly for old covenant revelation . . . by the two adverbs, translated 'at many times and in various ways,' at the beginning of the construction in the Greek original. . . . (3) Christ is the 'last days' endpoint of this history, the nothing-less-than eschatological goal of the entire redemptive-revelatory process."

27. Ridderbos, *When the Time Had Fully Come*, 50.

28. Ridderbos writes, "When the approach is made from man, then it is no more the analysis of the history of redemption in Jesus Christ which reveals the real

7.1.2. Cosmic Atonement

The works of God-in-Christ in the creation and in the new creation are necessarily cosmic in extent. So too, I suggest, is Christ's atonement—his incarnation, death and resurrection. Herman Bavinck rightly argues that if Christ is the incarnate Word, then the incarnation is the central fact of the entire history of the world, and it must have been prepared from eternity and have its effects throughout eternity.[29] Similarly, Ridderbos contends that in Paul's theology resurrection is nothing less that the counterpart of creation: "The resurrection of Christ is the beginning of the new and final world-order, an order described as spiritual and heavenly. It is the dawn of the new creation, the start of the eschatological age. In terms of the conceptual framework with which Paul views the whole of history, it is the commencement of the 'age-to-come.'"[30]

Within Christian theology there is much debate concerning the extent and nature of the atonement. Briefly put, the question concerns whether Christ died to save all (unlimited or universal atonement), or just to save the elect (limited/particular atonement).[31] Within Reformed theology the emphasis is on limited atonement.[32] It must be acknowl-

---

existence of man, but it is the analysis of man in his actual situation that serves as the criterion for what is acceptable in the history of salvation" (Ibid., 59).

29. Bavinck, *Reformed Dogmatics* 3:274.

30. Ridderbos, *Paul*, 90.

31. For some recent accounts of the debate between unlimited and limited atonement positions, see Letham, *Work of Christ*, 246, 225–48; Blocher, "Scope of Redemption and Modern Theology," 80–103; Bavinck, *Reformed Dogmatics* 3:460–61; Blacketer, "Definite Atonement in Historical Perspective," 304–23; Bloesch, *Jesus Christ: Saviour & Lord*, 167–68.

32. Although there are exceptions such as Benjamin B. Warfield. In his exposition of 1 John 2:2, he writes, "It is the great conception which John is reflecting in the phrase, 'he is the propitiation for our sins, and not for ours only but for the whole world.' This must not be diluted into the notion that he came to offer salvation to the world, or to do his part toward the salvation of the world, or to lay such a basis for salvation that it is the world's fault if it is not saved. John's thinking does not run on such lines; and what he actually says is something very different, namely that Jesus Christ is a propitiation for the whole world, that he has expiated the whole world's sins. He came into the world because of love of the world, in order that he might save the world, and he actually saves the world. Where the expositors have gone astray is in not perceiving that this salvation of the world was not conceived by John—any more than the salvation of the individual—as accomplishing itself all at once. Jesus came to save the world, and the world will through him be saved; at the end of the day he will have a saved world to present to his father. John's mind is running forward to the completion of his saving work; and he is speaking of his Lord from the point of view of this

Salvation History 2

edged that one's position on this issue will have significant bearing on one's development of a Christian theology of religions. One example must suffice to illustrate this point. Those who argue for unlimited atonement need to develop a theory of how the redemption accomplished through the atonement can be mediated to the unevangelized, that is, how it can be applied. For this reason they may be inclined towards inclusivism. Todd Magnum recognizes the clear link between soteriology and atonement theology. He explains that one's view of the state of the unevangelized is influenced considerably by whether one is a Calvinist or Arminian. "Simply put, the more classically Reformed (particular redemptionist) is one's Soteriology, the more exclusivist is one likely to be regarding the destiny of the unevangelized."[33] However, what is important for the current topic is a recognition that the atonement has a cosmic and eternal effect. Nothing is the same after the cross. Barth appreciated this: "The human speaking and acting and suffering and triumphing of this one man directly concerns us all, and his history is our history of salvation which changes the whole human situation, just because God himself is its human subject in His Son."[34]

A distinction between creation and redemption must be preserved, but because God's purpose from before the foundation of the world is one and the same purpose, it is important not to completely dissociate redemption from creation.[35] Bavinck rightly maintains that the incarnation, aside from its rootedness in the Trinity, also has its pre-

---

completed work. From that point of view he is the Savior of the world . . . He proclaims Jesus the Savior of the world and declares him a propitiation for the whole world. He is a universalist; he teaches the salvation of the whole world. But he is not an 'each and every' universalist: he is an 'eschatological' universalist" (Warfield, *Selected Shorter Writings of Benjamin B. Warfield*, 176–77). Cf. Shedd, *Dogmatic Theology*, 739–40. More recently the Calvinist Neal Punt has defended unlimited atonement. See his, *What's Good about the Good News?* Cf. Crisp, "Augustinian Universalism." Here Crisp outlines a version of universalism and shows "that it is both coherent and plausible to claim that someone could be both a traditional Augustinian and a universalist" (127).

33. Magnum, "Is There a Reformed Way of Getting the Benefits of the Atonement to Those Who Have Never Heard?" 121.

34. Barth, *Church Dogmatics*, IV/2, 51; quoted in *Christology in Conflict*, 162. Cf. O'Donovan, *Resurrection and Moral Order*, 15.

35. Daniel Strange argues that overstressing continuity undermines the need for incarnation and atonement: "If the cross is not the source of God's saving grace, then why is it needed? Does it effect salvation or does it merely reveal (albeit normatively) something already presupposed? Is it representative or constitutive" (Strange, *Salvation among the Unevangelized*, 207)?

supposition and preparation in the creation.[36] O'Donovan, highlights the cosmic reach of redemption, seeing it as the recovery of something given and lost: "At the same time, however, we must go beyond thinking of redemption as a *mere* restoration, the return of a *status quo ante*. The redemption of the world, and of mankind, does not serve only to put us back in the Garden of Eden where we began. It leads us on to that further destiny to which, even in the Garden of Eden, we were already directed. For the creation was given to us with its own goal and purpose, so that the outcome of the world's story cannot be a cyclical return to the beginnings, but must fulfil that purpose in the freeing of creation from its 'futility' (Rom 8:20)."[37]

This eschatological transformation "is neither the mere repetition of the created world nor its negation. It is its fulfilment, its *telos*, or end."[38] Therefore, while a fundamental connection between creation and redemption is recognized, aspects of continuity and discontinuity must both be acknowledged. They are inseparable, for Christ is agent of creation and new creation (Eph 1:10; Col 1:15–20). Creation itself has a Christological focus, and it anticipates a *telos*.[39] The plan of God the Father involves Jesus the Son as the cosmic redeemer. The Garden of Eden is a prototype of the world planned by God and the new creation will be superior to the original creation. Christ is the very purpose of God's creation and the incarnation was in view when God created the world. Creation is therefore the beginning or the preamble of the history of redemption. As O. Palmer Robertson explains: "The very words that pronounce the curse of the covenant of creation also inaugurate the covenant of redemption. From the very outset God intends by the covenant of redemption to realize for man those blessings originally defaulted under the covenant of creation."[40]

The impact of the incarnation and resurrection is not limited to a small section of time and space but is of universal significance. As Thomas Torrance states: "Through Jesus Christ there takes place a restoration of man's proper interaction both with the Creator and the creation, for in

---

36. Bavinck, *Reformed Dogmatics*, 3:277.

37. O'Donovan, *Resurrection and Moral Order*, 55. Italics original.

38. Ibid.

39 VanGemeren, *Progress of Redemption*, 62.

40. Robertson, *Christ of the Covenants*, 91. Covenant theology is the subject of chapter 8 of this volume.

Christ a creative centre of healing and integration has been set up within the structure and destiny of human contingent being, which cannot but affect the whole created order with which man has to do."[41]

Indeed, such is the significance of the incarnation and resurrection, that they can be equated to the act of creation itself. In the incarnation, God the creator, the transcendent one, has himself become a creature within time and space.[42] Jonathan Edwards describes the incarnation in these terms: "Christ's incarnation was a greater and more wonderful thing than ever had yet come to pass. The creation of the world was a very great thing, but not so great as the incarnation of Christ. It was a great thing for God to make the creature, but not so great as for the Creator himself to become a creature."[43]

In a similar way, the resurrection signifies an event which even surpasses God's original creative activity. The resurrection is also the work of the creator, now himself incarnate and at work in fallen creation. It takes place in space and time, in physical and historical existence. However, the New Testament indicates, states Torrance, that it is

> not merely a great event upon the plane of history, but an act that breaks into history with the powers of another world. It is akin to the creation in the beginning; and the Gospel is the good news that God is creating a new world . . . Such a resurrection of the incarnate Word of God within the creation of time and space which came into being through him is inevitably an event of cosmic and unbelievable magnitude. So far as the temporal dimension of creation is concerned, it means that the transformation of all things at the end of time is already impinging upon history, and indeed that the consummation of history has already been inaugurated. And so far as the spatial dimension of creation is concerned, it means that the new creation has already set in, so that all things visible and invisible are even now in the grip of the final recreation of the universe. The resurrection of Jesus heralds an entirely new age in which a universal resurrection or transformation of heaven and earth will take place, or rather has already begun to take place, for with the resurrection of Jesus that new world has already broken into the midst of the old.[44]

41. Torrance, *Divine and Contingent Order*, 136. Cf. Rust, *Salvation History*, 148–49.
42. Torrance, *Space, Time and Resurrection*, 21.
43. Edwards, *The Works of Jonathan Edwards*, 1:573.
44. Torrance, *Space, Time and Resurrection*. Torrance is quoting A. M. Ramsey, *The Resurrection of Christ*. (1945), 31. Cf. Torrance, *Space, Time and Resurrection*, 32–35.

Thus, the renovation of the entire universe is grounded in the death and resurrection of Christ. In this once-for-all triumph of the cross a new situation has been created objectively in history, independent of the circumstances of individuals.[45] The decisive battle has been fought and the ultimate outcome is sure.[46] The resurrection is a deed "so decisively new" that the whole of creation existing both before and after the cross is affected.[47] It has a "creative and constitutive character, and as such cannot but transform our understanding of the whole relation of God to the universe of things visible and invisible, present and future."[48]

7.1.3. Historical Atonement

To present the Christ-event as an event of cosmic and eternal significance should not be interpreted as portraying the historical dimension as less important. There is a profound paradox at the heart of this matter. The eternal, transcendent God enters time and space at a particular place

---

45. However, I accept that it is not entirely clear how exactly this new universal situation actually changes the circumstances of individuals who are unaware of Christ.

46. Rust, *Salvation History*, 214.

47. The effect of the atonement is of such proportions that all benefit from it. John Murray, a prominent defender of limited atonement, also argues that "The unbelieving and reprobate in this world enjoy numerous benefits that flow from the fact that Christ died and rose again. The mediatorial dominion of Christ is universal. Christ is head over all things and is given all authority in heaven and in earth." Murray, *Redemption Accomplished and Applied*, 61. Cf. Demerest, *Cross and Salvation*, 183; Blocher, "Scope of Redemption," 101. Here Blocher says, "Calvinists who hold to a particular atonement can add that Christ died, in some respects, 'for all human beings', even for the reprobates: he did not settle their juridical debt, but he secured for them the benefits of this earthly life (the reprieve which God grants to the 'old' sinful world logically depends on redemption), and his sacrifice validly grounds an offer of salvation which they could receive—if only they wanted to." Cf. Bavinck, *Reformed Dogmatics* 3:470–75: "The Universal Significance of Particular Atonement."

48. Torrance, *Space, Time and Resurrection*, 36.Cf., 58. Here Torrance declares Jesus Christ was "none other than the Creator Word of God come as a creature within the world he had made. In the resurrection of Jesus we see that the saving act of God in the expiation of sin and guilt, in the vanquishing of death and all that destroys the creation, is joined to God's act of creation. Redemption and creation come together at the resurrection . . . The vast significance of the crucifixion and resurrection emerges only as we see that here *redemption and creation come completely together*, in such a way that they gather up all the past and proleptically include the consummation of all things at the end" (italics original). Cf. Torrance, "Atonement, the Singularity of Christ, and the Finality of the Cross: The Atonement and the Moral Order," 234.

and time, but in such a way that affects all time and space.[49] Reformed theology recognizes both the eternal and historical dimensions of the atonement. The drama of redemption began in eternity, before history (2 Cor 8:9; Gal 4:4; Phil 2:5–8; Heb 2:17; 5:5-6),[50] and Christ was our mediator even before his condescension in human form—but his saving work was not accomplished until the cross. It is his death that is atoning.[51] John Murray declares the incarnation and the redemption wrought are both historical events. The atonement is historically objective in character, it is not "supra-historical nor is it contemporary."[52] However, Murray rightly recognizes that Jesus Christ is above history "as regards his deity and eternal Sonship."[53] He is eternal and transcends all conditions and circumstances of time. But the atonement was made in human nature and at a "particular time in the past and finished calendar of events . . ."[54]

"History with its fixed appointments and well-defined periods has significance in the drama of divine accomplishment. The historical conditioning and locating of events in time cannot be erased nor their significance under-estimated."[55]

The cross is the intersection of the divine and the human, the eternal and the temporal. Although it was a once-and-for-all particular event in the space-time continuum, it was also a once-and-for-all event in an absolutely decisive sense. The cross derives from and is grounded in the eternal love of God. God was in Christ reconciling the world to himself.[56]

Therefore, the effect of the atonement cannot be limited to one strand of subsequent history, namely that which is coextensive with the

49. Marshall, *Christology in Conflict*, vii.

50. Bloesch, *Jesus Christ*, 161.

51. Ibid. Bloesch notes that the suffering of Christ during his life was also atoning but only in an anticipatory sense (Heb 5:8–9).

52. Murray, *Redemption*, 52.

53. Ibid.

54. Ibid., 52–53.

55. Ibid., 53.

56. Torrance, " Atonement," 234–35. "It is the oneness of the sacrifice of God the Father with the sacrifice of his incarnate Son that stamps the cross with its decisive and ultimate finality. It was at once eternal and historical in its once-for-all character—that is why the New Testament can speak of the Lamb of God who bore our sins on the cross as slain before the foundation of the world."

Church or knowledge of the gospel. Redemption has been accomplished concretely through the objective act of Christ crucified and raised. It is a historical reality, and not one that occurs contemporaneously through an existential encounter with the gospel.[57] The ontological basis for all salvation is the grace "given us in Christ Jesus before the beginning of time" but revealed historically in his incarnation (2 Tim 1:9–10; Titus 1:2). The work of Christ has a "timeless efficacy that renders its benefits potentially and retroactively operative for all people of true faith, whatever their time or place."[58]

Torrance helpfully elucidates the relationship of the eternal and the historical, the divine and the human, atonement and incarnation:

> [W]e must think of the incarnation as the eternal Word and the eternal Act of God become human word and human act without ceasing to be divine, moving and operating creatively and redemptively within the space and time of our world in the acutely personalised form of the Lord Jesus Christ. It is surely in this way that we are to understand the teaching of the New Testament that the Lord Jesus Christ *is himself* our *justification, redemption, mediation and propitiation; he is himself the resurrection and the life*—he who is, who was and who is to come, the incarnate *I am* of the ever-living God. His incarnate life as the one Lord and Saviour of the world and his atoning work on the cross and in the resurrection cannot be separated from one another. Incarnation and atonement intrinsically locked into one another constitute the one continuous movement of God's saving love for the world. Therein lies the absolute singularity of Christ, but therein also lies the absolute finality of the Cross.[59]

Therefore, the Christ-event is of constitutive significance for the atonement. It is not merely a demonstration of God's redemptive will, but the means of redemption. As Calvin put it, the love of the Father is the "efficient cause," the obedience of the Son, the "material cause," and the illumination of the Spirit, (that is, in faith) the "instrumental cause."[60]

---

57. However, redemption is *applied* contemporaneously (see below).

58. Clendenin, *Many Gods, Many Lords: Christianity Encounters World Religions*, 125. The Westminster Confession of Faith (8.6) succinctly articulates this great truth:
"Although the work of redemption was not actually wrought by Christ till after his incarnation, yet the virtue, efficacy, and benefits thereof were communicated unto the elect, in all ages successively from the beginning of the world."

59. Torrance, "Atonement," 233 (italics original).

60. Calvin, *Institutes*, III.XIV.21.

Salvation History 2

Because the incarnation is of constitutive significance for the atonement, it follows that Christ's redemptive work is finished (τετέλεσται, John 19:30). All that was necessary to reconcile humankind to God has been accomplished. Reconciliation is already achieved and enjoyed.[61] In Romans 5:10–11 reconciliation is spoken of as a work achieved decisively by the one act of Christ's death.[62] Alan Stibbs notes that in contrast to this position on the finished work of Christ, some maintain that Christ's incarnate work "was but an expression in time or history of something which happens only fully in eternity; and that the eternal Son of God is, therefore, to be thought of as continually offering Himself to God in order to secure our acceptance in God's presence."[63]

However, Stibbs responds to such views by contending that Christ's atoning work has to deal with the effects of sin, which are exposure to divine wrath and exclusion from the divine presence, and "Such consequences demand for their remedy a single decisive action rather than a continuous and eternal one."[64]

---

61. Forsyth, *Work of Christ*, 86. P. T. Forsyth writes: "Reconciliation was finished in Christ's death. Paul did not preach a gradual reconciliation. He preached what the old divines used to call the finished work . . . He preached something done once for all—a reconciliation which is the base of every soul's reconcilement . . . What the Church has to do is to appropriate the thing that has been finally and universally done." Cf. Edwards, *History of the Work of Redemption*, 333: "Christ finished the purchase of redemption while in his state of humiliation here on earth."

62. Stibbs, *Finished Work of Christ*, 38–40.

63. Ibid., 5.

64. Ibid., 9. Cf. Murray, *Redemption*, 11–13. Murray considers why the atonement was necessary, and suggests there are two main answers to this question. The first he calls "hypothetical necessity"—God could forgive sin and save the elect without atonement or satisfaction—but he chose to do it through the vicarious sacrifice of his Son because this is the way in which "the greatest number of advantages occur and the way in which grace us more marvellously exhibited" (11). The second is termed "consequent absolute necessity"—consequent because God's choice to save some was his free choice and was not of absolute necessity. However, it is absolute in that having elected some to salvation, there was the necessity to accomplish this purpose through the sacrifice of his Son—a necessity arising from the perfections of his own nature. "[W]hile it was not inherently necessary for God to save, yet, since salvation had been purposed, it was necessary to secure this salvation through a satisfaction that could be rendered only through substitutionary sacrifice and blood-brought redemption" (12). Cf. Stibbs, *Finished Work of Christ*, 9. Stibbs draws on the work of Oscar Cullmann's *Christ and Time* here. "'Here,' he says, 'in the final analysis lies the "offense" of the primitive Christian view of time and history, not only for the historian, but for all "modern" thinking, including theological thinking: the offense is that God reveals Himself in a special way, and effects "salvation" in a final way, within a narrowly lim-

In contrast to this Reformed view of salvation history, Leonardo De Chirico argues that Roman Catholic theology blurs time distinctions with respect to the incarnation. This blurring of time distinctions is particularly apparent in the theology of Daniélou, Rahner and Dupuis. De Chirico suggests the significance of the difference between *hapax* (once and for all) and *mallon* (for evermore) is not sufficiently appreciated in Roman Catholic theology, and in contrast he argues for an approach that recognizes "the work of God, both *hapax* and *mallon*, has significant temporal meaning in the history of salvation. Both of these elements can be seen in the divine plan, and as long as their boundaries are maintained, any unjustifiable blurring is avoided... The incarnation of Christ is a *hapax* in the work of God which is so uniquely related to the person and mission of the Son that it does not require any supplement or continuation, integration or representation."[65]

This is of significance for the issues addressed in this chapter because it helps to substantiate the central assertion that atonement occurred in space and time, as a single historical event forming the midpoint of salvation history, and having an impact on all time and space.

---

ited but continuing process.' [23] Also: '... all points of this redemptive line are related to the one historical fact at the midpoint, a fact which precisely in its unrepeatable character, which marks all historical events, is decisive for salvation. This fact is the death and resurrection of Jesus Christ.' (32–33) Again, this idea of a 'kairos', or definite point of time especially favourable for an undertaking, and central in the divine plan of salvation, is found connected with the work which the incarnate Christ performed not only in the subsequent faith of the Church. 'Rather,' says Cullmann, 'Jesus Himself, according to the Synoptic witness, characterizes His passion as His "kairos."' [30–41]. Similarly, 'in the numerous Johannine passages in which Jesus speaks of His "hour" ... in every case the hour of His death is meant.' [43–44] So Oscar Cullmann would have us realize on the one hand, that Jesus really 'regarded His own death as the decisive point in the divine plan of salvation,' [148–49] and, on the other hand, that what he calls the one great Christological heresy both of ancient and modern times is that wider Docetism, which has at its root 'the failure to respect the historically unique character of the redemptive deed of Christ.' [127]" (Stibbs, *Finished Work of Christ*, 9–11, quoting Cullmann, *Christ and Time*; Cullmann page numbers in brackets).

65. De Chirico, "Blurring of Time Distinctions in Roman Catholicism," 40. De Chirico notes that Roman Catholic theology views the Church as an extension of the incarnation. It is the permanent incarnation of the Son of God (41). The ascension is not the end of the incarnation but a change from physical presence to mystical presence. Time is re-presented in the Eucharist (42). "Since the church is involved in the time of the incarnation of the Son, she is also active in his redemption which is accomplished on the cross. Both the incarnation and redemption are seen in light of *mallon*, instead of *hapax*" (43).

The preceding discussion has highlighted the historical and objective nature of the atonement. However, there is also a subjective dimension to atonement.[66] Christ's work of redemption is accomplished already, but it is only in the subjective experience of faith in Christ that the atonement is appropriated by the individual: "The saving effect of Christ's redemptive work only becomes effective in the life of a person, however, when it is appropriated by faith. The faith that unites people to Christ is itself a fruit of Christ's saving work, distributed to the elect by the Spirit of God."[67]

The seventeenth-century Protestant expression "Dempta applicatione, redemption non est redemption [sic]"[68] (without application redemption is not redemption), succinctly expresses this.

7.2. The Impossibility of Being Pre-Messianic in Post-Messianic Times

The preceding discussion has asserted the decisive cosmic impact of the Christ-event. The implications of this assertion on the Israel analogy and fulfilment model will now be considered. I will argue here that the concept of "pre-messianic" is invalid this side of the cross, and therefore the Israel analogy and fulfilment model are rendered implausible. I will focus my initial analysis on two texts (Acts 14:16–17 and Acts 17:30–31), for these are widely cited by those who consider the pre-messianic condition to be an ongoing condition.[69] Two issues need examining: First, what is *the nature* of the times of ignorance, and second, what is *the duration and extent* of these times—do they continue today, and if so for whom?

7.2.1. The Nature of the Times of Ignorance

The reference in Acts 14:16, "In past generations he [God] allowed the nations to walk in their own ways," parallels the statement in 17:30, "The times of ignorance God overlooked." With regard to the nature of these

---

66. See, for example, Bloesch, *Jesus Christ*, 162.

67. Tiessen, *Who Can Be Saved?* 257.

68. Cited by Gaffin, *By Faith, Not by Sight*, 20. (Note: Here, "redemption" should be "*redemptio*.")

69. See the references in the following discussion, particularly those in section 7.2.2.

times, it is commonly argued, for example by Pinnock, that God did not consider culpable, those who failed to trust him and come to terms with him out of ignorance.[70] However, I dispute this interpretation, and maintain that the Scriptures suggest all people everywhere (including the "ignorant") are considered culpable.[71] As McGiffert explains: "The 'overlooking' of ignorance which is here referred to does not imply that in pre-Christian days God regarded the idolatry of the heathen with indifference or saved them from the consequences of their sins, denounced so vigorously in Rom. i., but simply that the time for the final judgement had not come until now, and that they were, therefore, summoned now to prepare for it as they had not before."[72]

Rather than indicating non-culpability these two addresses suggest that even in these former times, God held accountable all who rejected him, for he did not leave himself without witness (14:17). This witness is evident in the works of creation and providence which testify to the existence and nature of the true God.[73] Therefore, any ignorance that did exist should not have been as great as it was.

What Paul is arguing in these passages is that until the full revelation of God came to the Gentiles, God "overlooked" the errors that arose through ignorance of his will. However, this overlooking "betokened not indifference but patience."[74] Therefore, although God did allow the nations to "go their own way," this should *not* be taken as an indication that he condoned their guilt, but rather an acknowledgement that his redemptive plan was targeted in the former times, at Israel.[75] During

---

70. Pinnock, *Wideness in God's Mercy*, 101. Many Acts commentators also suggest this. For example, I.H. Marshall suggests: "In time past he had let the Gentiles live in their own ways, the implication being that he did not regard their ignorance of himself as culpable." Marshall, *Acts*, 239. Cf. Williams, *Acts*, 250: "The implication seems to be that their ignorance of God in the past was not culpable . . . though this would no longer be so now that the Good News had been announced."

71. For example, all are subject to the wrath of God (John 3:19; Eph 2:3), and are already under condemnation (Rom 3:19).

72. A. C. McGiffert. *History of Christianity in the Apostolic Age*, 260, quoted in Little, *The Revelation of God among the Unevangelized*, 27.

73. Bruce, *Book of the Acts*, 277. Cf. Johnson, *Message of Acts in the History of Redemption*, 193, 198.

74. Bruce, *Book of the Acts*, 277.

75. Reymond writes "In Old Testament times God had "let the nations go their own way" (Acts 14:16) as he prepared Israel to be the repository of special revelation and the racial originator of the Messiah, and he had "overlooked the nations' ignorance"

Salvation History 2

these former times, there is a strong distinction between Israel as the covenant people of God and Gentiles outside God's covenant.[76] C. K. Barrett explains that God was unknown to the Gentiles because with the exception of his own people, Israel, he had withdrawn from human affairs to the extent of leaving the Gentiles to manage their own, and *to this extent* they may be excused.[77] God did not fully reveal himself to the Gentiles, but neither did he completely annihilate them, as their sins deserved.[78]

This interpretation is confirmed by the first three chapters of Romans, which make it clear that even before Christ all were subject to God's wrath.[79] In Rom 1:19–20, Paul explains that if humankind had paid heed to the works of God in creation, they might have found indications of his existence and nature. Therefore, no one has ever been absolutely ignorant. God has made himself known through general revelation, providing sufficient evidence of himself to hold accountable all who reject that revelation.[80] Knowledge of God's eternal power and

---

(Acts 17:23) in the sense that he had taken no direct steps to reach them savingly. But now that Christ has come God commands all people everywhere to repent (Acts 17:30) and to put their faith in Christ." Reymond, *New Systematic Theology*, 1091, footnote 40. Cf. Witherington, *Acts of the Apostles*, 427.

76. This former division between Jew and Gentile and the overcoming of it in the events described in Acts is a fundamental theme in redemptive history, and has great significance for how these passages should be understood. It should be noted that although Gentiles were not formerly the target of God's redemptive program and were generally ignorant of God's purposes—they were not excluded from redemption. Examples recorded in the Old Testament such as Ruth make it clear that through faith Gentiles could also become part of the covenant community.

77 Barrett, *Acts*, 1: 681. Cf. Lewis and Demerest, *Integrative Theology*, 1:306.

78. Little, *Revelation of God among the Unevangelized*, 22. Cf. Henry, *Matthew Henry's Commentary*, 489; Harrison, *Acts*, 223.

79. See particularly Romans 1:18 ("the wrath of God is revealed from heaven against all ungodliness and wickedness of men") and Romans 2:12 ("those who have sinned without the law will also perish without the law"). Douglas Moo writes "Rom. 1:18-2:20 has sketched the spiritual state of those who belong to the old era: justly condemned, helpless in the power of sin, powerless to escape God's wrath" (Moo, *Romans*, 221).

80 Mounce, *Romans*, 77. Cf. Edwards, *Romans*, 50–53. "Verses 19–21 . . . assert that the problem of human guilt is not God's hiddenness and therefore humanity's ignorance, but rather God's self-disclosure and humanity's rejection of it" (Edwards, *Romans*, 50). Cf. Cranfield, *Romans: A Shorter Commentary*, 32–33. Cranfield writes: "The result of God's self-manifestation in His creation is not a natural knowledge of God on men's part independent of God's self-revelation in His Word, a valid though

divine nature is manifest, but is suppressed and the truth is exchanged for a lie (Rom 1:21-26).[81] With regard to Acts 17, Barrett writes: "From nature the Greeks have evolved not natural theology but natural idolatry. That this should have been permitted was a mark of God's forbearance (cf. 14.16; also and especially Rom 3:26). God did not will or approve this ignorant idolatrous worship, but he did not suppress it; he overlooked it."[82]

Therefore, the guilt of humanity is not due to absence of the truth—but to its suppression. "If guilt were due to ignorance it would be an intellectual problem, but in reality it is a problem of the will which is sin."[83] Although all are culpable, God's judgment is impartial and proportionate. Romans teaches that those with the Mosaic law (the Jews) and those without (Gentiles) will both be judged impartially (Rom 2:12-16). "The Mosaic legislation will play no part in the judgement of those who have not heard."[84] However, those without the Mosaic law, still have "law"—in the sense of a moral conscience—written on their hearts (2:14–15), and they will be judged according to this. Neither the Jews nor the Gentiles keep their respective laws and therefore this universal sinfulness demands judgment (1:18—3:20).[85] Tiessen rightly argues that judgment is in accordance to the revelation an individual receives. With regard to Acts 14:16-17,

Tiessen explains: "It is highly implausible that Paul is suggesting that God accepted all the various forms of worship and conduct that the nations chose in their ignorance of God through lack of revelation. His point is twofold: First, God had given them some revelation in the form of his providential care for them. As indicated in Romans 1:21, this left

---

limited knowledge, but simply the rendering excuseless of their ignorance" (32). Cf. Osborne, *Romans*, 46–47.

81. See, for example. Bahnsen, "Encounter of Jerusalem with Athens," 11. Paul identifies the "basic schizophrenia in unbelieving thought when he described in the Athenians *both* an awareness of God (v.22) and ignorance of God (v.23) . . . Knowing God, the unregenerate nevertheless suppresses the truth and follows a lie instead."

82. Barrett, *Acts*, 2:851.

83. Edwards, *Romans*, 51. Cf. Rom 1:18–23, which indicates that the natural human relation to God is more that a simple straightforward *agnoia*. Cf. Watson, *Text and Truth*, 248; Bahnsen, "Encounter of Jerusalem with Athens," 13. The unbeliever is "responsible because he possesses the truth, but he is guilty for what he does with the truth" (Bahnsen, "Encounter of Jerusalem with Athens," 13).

84. Mounce, *Romans*, 93.

85. Edwards, *Romans*, 70.

Salvation History 2

them culpable if they did not respond by honouring God as God and giving him thanks. And second, in Paul's generation, they were receiving a clearer revelation of God's truth and of his will, so their obligation was increasing accordingly."[86]

Pinnock adopts a different position on this, suggesting Paul was positive about the religious practices of the Lystrans and Athenians, and by extension is similarly positive about the potential of contemporary non-Christian religious practices. He suggests Paul's Lystran sermon "represents a gracious and understanding appreciation of their past and their culture. In a later vignette, Paul is described in Athens as acknowledging the good intentions of the Greeks in worshipping the unknown God . . . Evidently Paul thought of these people as believers in a certain sense, in a way that could be and should be fulfilled in Jesus Christ." [87]

In the same way, Rahner also suggests Paul's speech shows he held a positive view of pagan religion.[88] Similarly, Dupuis interprets this passage as evidence that "Paul praises the religious spirit of the Greeks and announces to them the 'unknown God' whom they worship without knowing . . . the message surely seems to be that the religions of the nations are not bereft of value but find in Jesus Christ the fulfillment of their aspirations."[89]

However, I believe Pinnock, Rahner and Dupuis are mistaken here. Paul argues that God was worshipped in ignorance precisely because he was *unknown*—not that God was known but was somehow worshipped in ignorance. There are clear indications in the text that this is what Paul meant. William Larkin asserts that the use of neuter instead of masculine pronouns here shows that Paul is not simply going to proclaim to them the identity of the one whom they worship ignorantly. "Here is no basis for contending that non-Christian religionists, who are seeking him but don't know his name, are in a saving relation with God."[90] Similarly, Simon Kistemaker maintains

> They worship without knowledge, which in Athens, the bastion of learning, was a contradiction in terms. They concede that this

---

86. Tiessen, *Who Can Be Saved?* 128–29. Tiessen is referring to general revelation in his use of the expression "some revelation."

87 Pinnock, *Wideness in God's Mercy,* 32.

88. Rahner, "Christianity and the Non-Christian Religions," 122, 125.

89 Dupuis, *Toward a Christian Theology of Religious Pluralism*, 49.

90. Larkin, "Contribution of the Gospels and Acts to a Biblical Theology of Religions," 82–84. Cf. Caragounis, "Divine Revelation," 229–30.

unknown god exists, but they have no knowledge of him. And they must acknowledge that their approach to proper worship is deficient because of their ignorance. Paul, however, does not equate the unknown god of the Athenians with the true God. Notice that he says 'what you worship' not 'whom you worship.' Paul calls attention only to their lack of knowledge and thus takes the opportunity to introduce God as Creator and Judge of the universe. Paul intimates that the Athenians' ignorance of God is blameworthy and this ignorance demands swift emendation.[91]

This interpretation is supported by the word "ignorance" (ἀγνοίας) which occurs here in the present participle active form thus suggesting the Athenians were continually worshipping without knowledge, that is, in ignorance. Bultmann explains that the verb is "used with all the nuances of knowledge [and] denote[s] 'being mistaken' or 'in error' as the character of action (cf. 1 Tim 1:13). Ignorance of self is meant in Heb 5:2. 'Not recognizing' in 1 Cor 14:38 means rejection ('not being recognized' by God). Not knowing God is meant in Rom 10:3, and Christ in 1 Tim 1:13. This ignorance entails disobedience (Rom 10:3); hence it is not just pardonable lack of information but a failure to understand that needs forgiveness."[92]

The statement "if perhaps they might grope for Him and find Him" (17:27 NIV) should not be understood as suggesting individuals are able to reach a true knowledge of God unaided by special revelation, for the words "grope" and "find" are in the optative mood, that is the mood of strong contingency or possibility.[93] "It contains no definite anticipation of realization, but merely presents the action as conceivable. Hence it is one step further removed from reality than the subjunctive."[94] So this statement does not suggest a divine pattern for

---

91. Kistemaker, *Exposition of the Acts of the Apostles*, 632. Cf. Ladd, *The Wycliffe Bible Commentary*, 1157. Cf. Witherington, *Acts*, 524.

92. Bultmann, "Ignorance," 18. Cf. John Calvin "God cannot be worshipped rightly unless he be first known." *Commentary on the Acts of the Apostles*. (Edinburgh: Edinburgh Printing Company, n.d.), vol. 2, 157; quoted in Little, *The Revelation of God among the Unevangelized*, 26 Cf. Bock, "Athenians Who Have Never Heard," 124. Bock writes: "Ignorance and "God-fearing devotion" in themselves provide no hope that one can enter God's presence outside of Jesus, as the New Testament shows. Devotion to God must be according to knowledge."

93. The Greek reads: εἰ ἄρα γε ψηλαφήσειαν αὐτὸν καὶ εὕροιεν.

94. H. E. Dana and Julius Mantey, *Manual Grammar of the Greek New Testament*, 172; quoted in Little, *Revelation of God among the Unevangelized*, 26–27. Cf. Bahnsen, "Encounter of Jerusalem with Athens," 13. Cf. Marshall, *Acts*, 288.

successfully finding God and salvation apart from special revelation. Rather, it points to the effect of sin causing all to become as those who are blind in their search for God.[95]

According to Paul, non-Christian religious worship is rebellious, it is evidence of each culture going its own way, autonomously developing its religion without reference to the one true God. [96] If this were not so, the times of ignorance would not have to be overlooked and Paul's message would not have climaxed in a call to repentance.[97] Further confirmation of Paul's negative assessment of non-Christian religious practices is seen in the description that "his spirit was provoked within him" (17:16) which "at the least . . . means that Paul was very irritated by what he saw."[98]

In conclusion, the texts examined here indicate that the "times of ignorance" are not to be interpreted as a period during which sin was not punished, or as a period when non-biblical religions functioned as instruments of salvation. Rather, all people at all times are culpable for their sin, and worshippers of non-biblical religions are worshipping in ignorance and rebellion.

7.2.2. Duration of the Times of Ignorance

Having established the *nature* of the times of ignorance, the next matter for consideration is the *duration* of these times, namely, have they ended with the objective act of the Christ-event, or is their end associated with an individual's existential encounter with the gospel? Proponents of the Israel analogy and fulfilment model believe the latter to be the case. For example, Rahner writes: non-Christian religions are "overtaken and rendered obsolete by the coming of Christ and by his

---

95. Larkin suggests the fact that God is "not very far away" (v. 27) shows that the human lack of success is not a function of how God has set up the search but of an intervening factor—sin. Larkin, "The Contribution of the Gospels and Acts," 82. Cf. Caragounis, "Divine Revelation," 227–30; Bahnsen, "Encounter of Jerusalem with Athens," 13. Bahnsen argues that this groping is not an innocent matter—but is unrepentant ignorance.

96. Larkin, "The Contribution of the Gospels and Acts," 83. Paul's negative attitude toward pagan worship is also shown by the meaning of the word "provoke" in v. 16. Little asserts it meaning is to rouse to wrath. Little, *The Revelation of God among the Unevangelized*, .25.

97. Larkin, "Contribution of the Gospels and Acts," 83.

98. Witherington, *Acts*, 512. Cf. Bahnsen, "Encounter of Jerusalem with Athens," 6.

death and resurrection." However this moment in time "is arrived at the point at which Christianity in its explicit and ecclesiastical form" becomes "an effective reality, making its impact and asserting its claims in history in the relevant cultural sphere to which the non-Christian religions concerned belonged."[99]

"Normally [in Catholic theology] the beginning of the objective obligation of the Christian message for all men—in other words, the abolition of the validity of the Mosaic religion *and* of all other religions—is thought to occur in the apostolic age. Normally, therefore, one regards the time between this beginning and the actual acceptance or the personally guilty refusal of Christianity in a non-Jewish world and history as the span between the already given promulgation of the law and the moment when the one to whom the law refers takes cognizance of it."[100]

Rahner wants to "leave it . . . an open question (at least in principle) at what exact point in time the absolute obligation of the Christian religion has in fact come into effect for every man and culture."[101] I shall argue in this section that the times of ignorance have ended objectively, coinciding with the Christ-event.

The place of the events of Acts in the unfolding history of redemption provides the necessary framework for a proper understanding of these times.[102] Luke, in his second volume, recounts the historical origins of the Christian movement, the founding of the Church, and the spread of the gospel. He addresses the universal claims of the gospel and the nature of the Church—a Church for both Jew and Gentile. He writes concerning the climax of God's redemptive acts in history[103] and has

---

99. Rahner, "Church, Churches and Religions," 47.

100. Rahner, "Christianity and the Non-Christian Religions," 119. Rahner uses the expression 'law' here to refer to Christianity.

101. Ibid., 120.

102. See in this volume section 6.3 for an outline of redemptive-historical hermeneutics. Cf. Gaffin, *Resurrection and Redemption*, 13. Gaffin rightly states that dealing with the biblical writers in terms of their respective places in redemptive history is necessary.

103. See, for example, Johnson, *Message of Acts*: "Luke invites us again and again to walk back and forth across the bridge linking old covenant promise with New Covenant fulfilment in Christ—to see, compare and discover afresh the manifold wisdom of God in his plan of redemption, glimpsed in many parts and ways in the words of the prophets, but now blazing from the glorious face of the Son" (122).

been described as *par excellence* the "theologian of redemptive history."[104] Redemptive history is fundamental in Paul too. While Reformed Pauline studies have rightly placed much emphasis on the doctrine of justification by faith, this emphasis has at times overshadowed the centrality of redemptive-history in Paul. Ridderbos maintains a redemptive-historical or eschatological orientation governs Paul's theology.[105]

"It is this great redemptive-historical framework within which the whole of Paul's preaching must be understood and all of its subordinate parts receive their place and organically cohere . . . It is from this principal point of view and under this denominator that all the separate themes of Paul's preaching can be understood and penetrated in their unity and relation to each other."[106]

Whatever treatment Paul gives to the application of salvation to the individual (the *ordo salutis*) is controlled by his redemptive-historical outlook, that is, how salvation was accomplished (the *historia salutis*).[107]

"The center of Paul's teaching is not found in the doctrine of justification by faith or any other aspect of the *ordo salutis*. Rather, his primary interest is seen to be in the *historia salutis* as that history has reached its eschatological realization in the death and especially the resurrection of Christ."[108]

---

104. Bruce, "Salvation History in the New Testament," 78. Bruce is quoting Lohse, "Lucas als Theologe der Heilsgeschichte," *Evangelische Theologie* 14 (1954–55) 254. Cf. Flender, *St. Luke: Theologian of Redemptive History*.

105. Ridderbos uses the designations redemptive-historical and eschatological interchangeably. Ridderbos states "the central motive of justification by faith can be understood in its real pregnant significance only from this redemptive-historical viewpoint." Ridderbos, *When the Time Had Fully Come*, 50 Cf. Ridderbos, *Paul and Jesus*, 64–5 'Before everything else, he [Paul] was the proclaimer of a new time, the great turning point in the history of redemption' Cf. Yarbrough, "Paul and Salvation History," 297–342.

106. Ridderbos, *Paul.*, 39 Cf. 44, 49, 65, 162, 208, 429–30, 516.

107. Gaffin notes that this distinction (*historia salutis*—*ordo salutis*) appears to originate with Herman Ridderbos, being found first in *Time Fully Come* (1957), 48–49. Gaffin, *By Faith, Not by Sight*, 8 n. 2.

108. Gaffin, *Resurrection and Redemption,* 13. Gaffin notes the term "*ordo salutis* can have two distinct senses, one more general, the other more elaborated. The latter sense, more detailed and technical, is its usual, more common usage. It has in view the logical and/or causal, or even chronological 'order' or sequence of various discrete saving acts and benefits, as these are unfolded in the life of the individual sinner. However, the expression *ordo salutis* may also be used . . . more generally, to the ongoing application of salvation, in distinction from its once-for-all accomplishment." It is this

Michael Horton cautions that separating the *ordo salutis* from the *historia salutis* results in a "failure to recognize the revolutionary logic of biblical (especially Pauline) eschatology, in which the future is semirealized in the present and the individual is included in a wider eschatological activity."[109] However, when the *ordo salutis* is seen in relationship to the *historia salutis*, then "that which God is doing in the experience of believers will be treated as derivative of that which God is doing in the world, in history."[110] Paul's redemptive-historical outlook is clear in the Paul of Acts,[111] and is more fully expounded in his Epistle to the Romans.[112] There are clear parallels between Paul's speeches in Acts 14 and 17, and Rom 3:21–26 and these three texts will be considered in unison in the following discussion.[113]

Paul's speeches in Acts 14 and 17 embrace the ideas of the creation (the past), of God's dominion over the world (the present) and of the judgment (the future).[114] Paul presents the Christ-event, as an event of acute temporal decisiveness. Referring to Acts 17, F. F. Bruce rightly observes: "The claim that the fact of Jesus marks the end of the time of ignorance and the irrevocable declaration of God's will, with the accompanying summons to repentance, is underlined by the framework of universal history in which it is set."[115] Paul's reference to the "times of ignorance" was, as Francis Watson states, motivated by the need to

---

latter sense that is being used here. Cf. Gaffin, *By Faith, Not By Sight*, 18. Cf. Horton, *Covenant and Eschatology*, 6. Horton rightly observes that often (even in Reformed theology) the various loci of the *ordo salutis* (calling, regeneration, repentance and faith, justification, sanctification and glorification) have been separated from the *historia salutis*.

109. Horton, *Covenant and Eschatology*, 6–7.

110. Ibid., 7.

111. Bruce, "Salvation History in the New Testament," 81. Bruce suggests this is true for his speeches at Pisidian Antioch and Athens.

112. Ibid., 84.

113. My use of Rom 3:21–26 is given further weight by the importance it plays in Romans. Luther notes in his Bible margin that it was "the chief point, and the very central place of the Epistle, and of the whole Bible." quoted in Moo, *Romans*, 218. Cf. Cranfield, *Critical and Exegetical Commentary on the Epistle to the Romans*, 199. Cranfield notes it is "the centre and heart of the whole of Romans."

114. Conzelman, *Theology of Saint Luke*, 168. Cf. Bahnsen, " Encounter of Jerusalem with Athens," 17.

115. Bruce, "Salvation History in the New Testament," 81.

Salvation History 2

assert the radical newness of the present moment.[116] The former times correspond to the ages in which the mystery of Christ has been kept secret, the period before the fullness of time was revealed.[117] But now, the Lordship of Christ is a present reality, extending over the whole world, as Oscar Cullmann explains: "The result of Christ's death and resurrection is that the Lordship over all things is committed to him. The entire creation is affected by this redemptive event. Ever since the ascension Christ sits at the right hand of God, and everything is put under his feet. With this is connected the fact that since reaching this mid-point the world process is drawn into the redemptive history in a decisive manner."[118]

In the cross an eschatological process is taking place. The Kingdom of God becomes manifest in Christ's resurrection which marks the boundary where the two aeons collide. The Eschaton has come and the world has been opened up for the Kingdom of God.[119]

There is therefore a dichotomy of "before" and "after" the Christ-event, and a radical newness to the present age.[120] The "but now" (τὰ νῦν) of Acts 17:30b balances "the times" (τοὺς χρόνους) in the first part of the sentence. It is the "now" that is the subject of the last part of the sentence. All has changed *now* that Christ has come with the full knowledge of God. Through Christ, God has dealt definitively with the problem of sin, but for that very reason, he has laid humanity under a new accountability. The day of the gospel begins with the resurrection, and the Old Testament aeon ends here. Now that Christ has come, God calls the unbelieving world into judgment through the One whom he raised from the dead.[121] God "overlooked" sin during the former times,

---

116. Watson, *Text and Truth*, 248.

117. See section 7.1.1.

118. Cullmann, *Christ and Time*, 185. Cf. Cullmann, *Salvation in History*, 163.

119. Ridderbos, *When the Time Had Fully Come*, 17. Cf. Ridderbos, *Coming of the Kingdom*, xxviii: "The coming of the kingdom of God is most certainly to be looked upon as the realization of the great drama of the history of salvation. . . . This realization is not merely a matter of the future, however, it has started. The great change of the aeons has taken place. The center of history is in Christ's coming, in his victory over the demons, in his death and resurrection." Ridderbos states that the cosmic and historical meaning of the Kingdom of heaven must be fully acknowledged (xxiv). The idea of the Kingdom of Heaven implies the participation of all created life in the coming of the kingdom. The proportions of the Kingdom are universal (46).

120. Poythress, *Understanding Dispensationalists*, 43.

121. Lewis and Demerest, *Integrative Theology*, 2:87.

but this overlooking was possible only because these times were for a period only, a period allocated by God from eternity, to be followed by a course of action which would deal with sin finally and fully through the cross.[122] As Bruce argues, "God's overlooking people's earlier ignorance of himself is seen to have had in view the full revelation now given in the advent and work of Christ. 'But now' in the present context is parallel to 'but now' in Rom. 3:21. If ignorance of the divine nature was culpable before, it is inexcusable now." [123]

Romans 3:21–26 also testifies to the radical newness of the current age, an age inaugurated when "this righteousness from God" was made known in Christ. The "but now" of v.21 indicates a change of tone from the preceding section (1:18—3:20).[124] This change is both logical and temporal, marking a decisive shift, not just in Paul's argument, but in God's economy. It is logical because of its place in the strategy of Paul's argument—concluding the teaching of the previous section. It is temporal—shifting the emphasis from the old situation of Jews and Gentiles under sin to the new age of salvation inaugurated by Christ. Grant Osborne considers the temporal sense to be most important: "Paul tells us here that as a result of Christ's sacrificial act a new era, one of salvation, has dawned. As Schreiner says, this indicates 'a salvation-historical shift between the old covenant and the new.' God's 'saving righteousness' has been 'actualized in history.'"[125]

The temporal sense is reinforced by the expression "has been made known" (πεφανέρωται).[126] The perfect tense used here specifies

---

122. Cranfield, *Romans: A Shorter Commentary,* 74. John Calvin points out that Paul gives no explanation for why God allowed the times of ignorance to last so long, but that even during this time ignorance cannot be excused because of the reality of general revelation (Calvin, *The Acts of the Apostles*, 12, 124).

123. Bruce, *Book of the Acts*, 340. Cf. Witherington, *Acts,* 535: "Both the Paul of his letters . . . and the Paul of this speech (17:31) see the resurrection as a decisive divine demonstration or proof of God's intentions in regard to humankind, and the decisive shift in the ages which turns times of ignorance or sin into the age of accountability."

124. Osborne, *Romans,* 92.

125. Ibid., 92. The reference is to Schreiner, *Romans,* 180. Cf. Mounce, *Romans,* 114, footnote 2. Mounce notes that "Most contemporary writers take Νυνι δὲ as temporal rather than logical and emphasize that it marks the transition to a new stage in salvation history." Cf. Moo, *Romans,* 221: "This contrast between two eras in salvation history is one of Paul's most basic conceptions, providing the framework form many of his key ideas." Cf. Carson, "Atonement in Romans 3:21–26," 121 Carson states the "but now" is "salvation-historical."

126. Edwards, *Romans,* 98.

something which began in the past but which is still valid now—that which was made manifest in Christ's redemptive work has ever since remained manifest, and is the means of salvation for all people henceforth.[127] At a given point in history, God intervened to consummate the plan of redemption.[128] The decisive once-for-all redemptive act of God, the revelation both of righteousness and wrath, has taken place. Thus, verse 21 "points to the decisiveness for faith of the gospel events in their objectiveness as events which took place at a particular time in the past and are quite distinct from and independent of the response of men to them."[129]

This does not mean that God failed to punish sins committed before the Christ-event, or that God was unable to fully forgive sins committed by Old Covenant believers. According to Moo, "Paul's meaning is rather that God 'postponed' the full penalty due sins in the Old Covenant, allowing sinners to stand before him without their having provided an adequate 'satisfaction' of the demands of his holy justice (cf. Heb 10:4)."[130]

The reference to passing over former sins (3:25), refers to sins committed before the Christ-event—not sins committed before a person's individual justification.[131] This is clear from the context, which Paul presents as the *historia salutis* rather than the *ordo salutis*. This is indicated by the reference to the revelation of the *righteousness of God* that is now revealed (v.26), rather than the righteousness that is given to those who believe. This latter sense cannot be what Paul intends as in the next chapter (chapter 4) he demonstrates that Abraham and all true believers whether Jew or Gentile are reckoned righteous by faith. "If in 3:21 Paul is talking about individual soteriology, there would be no 'but now' about it. Justification has always and ever been by faith."[132] Rather,

---

127. Cranfield, *Romans: A Shorter Commentary*, 70. Cf. Edwards, *Romans*, 98.

128. Edwards, *Romans*, 98.

129. Cranfield, *Romans: A Shorter Commentary*, 69.

130. Moo, *Romans*, 240.

131. A different interpretation is offered by Davies, *Faith and Obedience in Romans*, 110. Davies suggests it was the sins of the righteous that God formerly passed over, thus enabling the Old Testament saints to enjoy the experience of forgiveness. However, this is a minority view among the commentators, and seems unlikely given the historical-redemptive framework of Paul's argument here.

132. Leithart, "Paul on God's Righteousness."

what is new, what is "now" is that God has revealed his righteousness through Christ.[133]

The temporal decisiveness of the Christ-event is given further weight by Paul's assertion that the divine act of righteousness has now been made known "apart from the law" (v. 21a). In one sense this refers to the fact that righteousness cannot come by keeping the law (3:20 cf. 2:1—3:8), but the primary meaning here is given by the salvation-historical orientation of Paul's argument. That is, it refers to the new era inaugurated by Christ. "Paul's purpose is to announce the way in which God's righteousness has been manifest rather than to contrast two kinds of righteousness."[134] This is clear from the developing argument - Paul has already established that the law is powerless to save (Rom 2:12—3:20), and as I have already mentioned, chapter 4 makes clear that justification has always been by faith, apart from the law. For the argument to make sense the reference has to be to the manner in which God's righteousness is manifested, not the manner in which it is received.[135]

This then indicates that the "law" (νόμου) (v. 21a) is not primarily a set of rules required by God for humans to keep—but the law as a system, that is, as a stage in God's unfolding plan. If this is so, then it refers to the Mosaic covenant, a temporary administration established by God for the period leading to its fulfilment in Christ.[136] There is therefore a discontinuity between the former times and the present times.[137] However, as Paul proceeds, the emphasis changes from discontinuity to continuity. For while this righteousness comes apart from the law, the "Law and Prophets bear witness to it" (v. 21b). The Old Testament as a

---

133. See section 8.3.2 for a fuller exposition of the continuity of justification by faith in Old and New Testaments.

134. Moo, *Romans*, 222. Moo notes here (footnote 16) that this is how most English translations interpret this verse. Cf. Osborne, *Romans*, 93. "[A]part from the law modifies made known more than it does a righteousness from God and so refers to the process by which it is revealed rather than the way it is received by us."

135. Moo, *Romans*, 222–23. Cf. Carson, "Atonement in Romans 3:21–26," 123. Carson states the reference "focuses attention not on the *reception* of righteousness . . . but on the disclosure of this righteousness."

136. Moo, *Romans*, 223. Cf. Carson, "Atonement in Romans 3:21–26," 121, 123. I elaborate further on the temporary nature of the Mosaic covenant in sections 8.3.2 and 9.1.4.

137. Carson, "Atonement in Romans 3:21-26," 123 "There is a dramatic shift in salvation-history."

whole is understood by Paul, as anticipating and preparing for this new age of justification and fulfilment.[138]

On the basis of the discussion outlined above, it is clear that the "times of ignorance" are a period in the *historia salutis* and therefore have ended with the objective, historical and decisive Christ-event. These times should not therefore be understood in reference to a person's existential encounter with the gospel or to any other time after the Christ-event. If one does not accept the definite turning point of the Christ-event, it leads to speculative and rather arbitrary predictions of when the "times of ignorance" might have ended. The focus of many commentators on when these times might have ended is due in part, I suggest, to a misunderstanding of the nature of the times of ignorance and the nature of saving faith. Many consider saving faith to have changed between the Old Testament and New Testament eras, and this leads them to speculate how this change affects the existential circumstances of individuals. I maintain that the nature of saving faith has always and everywhere been essentially constant, that is, trust in the covenant-making God, made possible by his special revelation. This revelation is Christocentric, and consequently saving faith has always been Christ focused, and has not changed at any point in terms of its object and essential characteristics.[139]

Scripture gives no grounds for suggesting saving faith has changed or for suggesting that a believer who lived during the "times of ignorance" will no longer be saved after the Christ-event, for failing to respond to the "new content" of saving faith. But this is exactly what is discussed by some theologians.[140] For Pinnock, the times of ignorance end only when an individual receives the gospel.[141] Similarly, Tiessen argues Acts 17:30–31 indicates there is an ignorance that is not culpable, but when the gospel is preached and the Spirit illumines the hearers, the ignorance is dispelled and God's overlooking is therefore no longer appropriate.[142] Tiessen concurs with Marshall who considers that "until the coming of the revelation of God's true nature in Christianity, men lived in igno-

---

138. Moo, *Romans*, 223. Moo comments (footnote 21) that the "law and prophets" denotes the entire Old Testament. Osborne, *Romans*, 93

139. That is not to say that all believers at all times have known and understood the same details.

140. See below.

141. Pinnock, *Wideness in God's Mercy*, 101.

142. Tiessen, *Who Can Be Saved?* 129. Cf. 178–79.

rance of him. But now the proclamation of the Christian message brings this time to an end *so far as those who hear the gospel are concerned;* they no longer have an excuse for their ignorance. God was prepared to overlook their ignorance, but now he will do so no longer.'"[143]

For Tiessen, the "critical question" is, "when (if ever) does salvation cease to be possible for Jews with an Old Testament faith and for God-fearing Gentiles who do not know of Jesus? Ronald Nash suggests 'that whole first century community of Believers in Yahweh was a kind of transition generation.' But why must the transition be limited to one generation? Why may it not extend throughout this age to all who remain ignorant of Jesus and of his identity and work? Why might people today who have the faith of an old covenant believer or of a Gentile god-fearer be saved today, just as they were then?"[144]

"Ecclesiocentrists face a particularly sticky problem in regard to Jews at the time of Jesus who had the faith of Abraham or in regard to Gentile God-fearers who did not know about Jesus. Did such people *lose* their salvation? And, if so, at what point—at the moment of Christ's resurrection, at the ascension or at Pentecost? . . . Some theologians might cover such people under a 'grandfather clause,' but this is problematic within the principles of Ecclesiocentrism."[145]

Likewise, Sanders claims:

> A major problem for this understanding of faith [that knowledge of Jesus Christ is necessary] is the salvation of those who lived before and just after Jesus. Those who take a restrictive approach generally allow for the salvation of those who lived before Jesus but claim that since the time of Jesus one has to know about him in order to be saved. God-fearing Jews and Gentiles who died ten minutes after Jesus died but who had no knowledge of that fact or no understanding of its atoning value are thus left in a most pitiful position—damned to hell for not living long enough for Christian theology to be developed! But if we concede that such people are exceptions, then why aren't the rest of the unevangelized exceptions as well?[146]

---

143. Ibid., 133, quoting Marshall, *Acts*, 289–90 (italics Tiessen's).

144. Tiessen, *Who Can Be Saved?* 178. The reference is to Nash, "Restrictivism," 22.

145. Tiessen, *Who Can Be Saved?* 199. (See section 1.1 of this volume for a definition of "ecclesiocentrism.")

146 Sanders, *What about Those Who Have Never Heard?* 37 n. 18. Sanders highlights here the particular problems that the dispensational system presents for the situation of those living at a time of transition between different dispensations. "When

Salvation History 2

These accounts demonstrate the problem that results, if it is argued that saving faith is substantially different before and after Christ. In chapter 2, I showed that Tiessen draws an analogy between Old covenant believers and Jews today who do not know Jesus is their Messiah—these he proposes are "in the same position as were their forebears who lived prior to Messiah's coming."[147] Tiessen makes this proposal to support his thesis that knowledge of Christ is unnecessary for salvation. However, on the contrary, I suggest his proposal is broadly right, but should be understood as supporting my position that saving faith has not changed. A believing Jew living at the time of Christ would have faith in the Messiah (anticipated). If such a Jew died before hearing of the advent of the Messiah, then there is no reason to suggest they would be denied saving faith now that greater information (which they have not received) about the Messiah is available. In theory then, it is possible to be saved "by Old covenant anticipation" after the Christ-event, if that anticipation is according to special covenantal revelation. With regard to the Gentile "God-fearers" that Tiessen and Sanders refer

---

do the new requirements of the "specific content of salvation" take effect? For instance when did the requirement for belief in Jesus become obligatory? At the resurrection? At the ascension? . . . If a 'grace period' is granted to people who are a dispensation behind (in terms of hearing), then why not a grace period for those unevangelized, who may be five or six dispensations behind." Sanders is right to identify this as a problem. Pinnock writes favorably regarding dispensationalism, with its emphasis on the difference between the nature of saving faith in the different dispensations. He writes, "Charles Ryrie spoke of a dispensation where God accepted pagans like Job on the basis of faith but without knowledge of either Moses or Christ. I felt this was biblical and found it appealing. I remember thinking how helpful it would be if this arrangement were still true for today for people in the same situation. I keep hoping dispensational theology will progress in this direction too and that a dispensational inclusivist will come forward to help people burdened by restrictivism" (Pinnock, "Inclusivist View," 108). However, he continues, "It hasn't happened yet, and I'm not holding my breath" (Ibid.). The dispensational theologian Ramesh Richard has provided a useful critique of inclusivism, showing that even *if* the nature of saving faith in Old Testament and New Testament times differed, (with Old Testament believers not confessing Christ), this no longer holds true now that Christ has come. See Richard, *Population of Heaven*. Dispensational inclusivists attempt to resolve the problem by proposing "transdispensationalizing"—treating people in a particular dispensation as though they live in another dispensation, in terms of the requirement of salvation. Tony Evans uses the concept of "transdispensationalizing" in his book *Totally Saved*. This problem is overcome for covenantal theologians for saving faith has been constant in its essential nature at all times.

147. Tiessen, *Who Can Be Saved?* 168.

to, I maintain that these too, were only ever saved by contact with and response to special covenantal revelation.[148]

Don Carson responds to the suggestion that the times of ignorance end only when an individual hears the gospel by declaring, "This is an astonishing inference. It would mean that the Athenians were better off before they heard Paul's preaching about Jesus: they were nicely spared any blame because they were ignorant, but now, poor chaps, for the first time they are held accountable."[149]

While Carson is right to highlight the error of the individual/existential interpretation of the ending of the times of ignorance, his response is itself rather misleading.[150] He presents a hypothetical scenario (that people would be better off not hearing the gospel), which given his wider Reformed theological convictions he does not consider valid, for he maintains that all people everywhere are culpable, and he accepts therefore that no-one will be saved through their ignorance. Therefore, although the "times of ignorance" should not be confused with an individual's personal knowledge or ignorance, Scripture does seem to suggest that judgment is according to the revelation one receives (see section 7.2.1). Indeed, Jesus speaks of greater judgment on those to whom more has been revealed (Matt 11:20–24; John 9:39–41; 15:22). John Frame contends that "there is some indication in Scripture that greater knowledge can be an aggravating circumstance (Luke 12:47–48). From whom much is given, much is required."[151] This indicates, suggests Frame, that it would better not to hear of Christ than to hear of him and reject him. Matthew 26:24 and 2 Peter 2:21 say this in specific contexts.[152]

---

148. See Strange, *Salvation among the Unevangelized*, 163–88 for an insightful critique of the concept of "pagan saints."

149. Carson, *Gagging of God*, 310. Likewise, Darrell Bock suggests that if the times of ignorance end with the hearing of the gospel then "at Mars' Hill Paul puts nonhearers at risk. In their ignorance they had a chance, but now that he has told them about Jesus they must respond or be destroyed. We are driven to the absurd conclusion that Paul should never have mentioned Jesus, because as "nonhearers" they had a chance!" (Bock, "Athenians Who Have Never Heard," 122).

150. Carson and Bock possibly intend their statements to be understood rhetorically. Nevertheless, my assertion that they are misleading is warranted.

151. E-mail from John Frame, "Does the BC Condition still exist today?" 22 August 2006.

152. Ibid.

Salvation History 2

Piper defends the assertion that the times of ignorance have ended with the Christ-event by stating,

> But 'now'—a key word in the turning of God's historic work of redemption—something new has happened. The Son of God has appeared. He has revealed the Father. He has atoned for sin. He has risen from the dead. His authority as universal Judge is vindicated. And the message of His saving work is to be spread to all peoples. This turn in redemptive history is for the glory of Jesus Christ. Its aim is to put Him at the center of all God's saving work. And therefore it accords with this purpose that henceforth Christ be the sole and necessary focus of saving faith.[153]

Larkin makes a similar statement: "Formerly humankind lived in a sinful ignorance that God in his mercy passed over. Now, after sin has been judged in Jesus' death and resurrection, comes the 'day of salvation' in a gospel proclaimed in his name, calling for repentance and promising forgiveness. Today there is no room in God's economy, as Paul preaches it, for so-called B. C. Christians—persons saved without knowledge of Christ and his saving work."[154]

While I concur with both Piper and Larkin, that the times of ignorance have ended with the Christ-event, these quotes give the unhelpful impression that saving faith has changed. On the contrary I maintain that Christ has always been the "sole and necessary focus of saving faith"[155] and there has never "been room in God's economy for so-called B.C. Christians." The intervention of God to inaugurate a new era, means that all who respond in faith—not only after the cross, but as Romans 4 shows, before it also—will be transferred into the new era from the old era.[156]

---

153. Piper, *Let the Nations Be Glad!* 134–35. While I agree with the general thrust of Piper's statement, it must be noted that it does unhelpfully infer that salvation was different before Christ. However, Piper makes it clear elsewhere that this is not what he means to suggest. He notes that there is continuity between God's path to salvation in the Old Testament and New Testament, and that before Christ people were not saved apart from special revelation. General revelation was not effective in producing faith before Christ but ineffective after Christ (Piper, *Let the Nations Be Glad!* 164 footnote 23).

154. Larkin, *Acts*, 259–60.

155. I do accept, however, that New Testament believers have greater knowledge of Christ than Old Testament believers.

156. Moo, *Romans*, 221.

7.3. Summary

Christ is the midpoint of salvation-history. The Christ-event constitutes the centre of salvation-history and is of universal and decisive significance. It marks a radical turn in salvation-history, a crisis point, rendering the BC period complete and fulfilled. It ushers in the new eschatological age, and forms a dividing line between "BC" and "AD." A new situation has been created objectively in history independent of the circumstances of individuals. The effect of the atonement cannot be limited to one strand of subsequent history, namely, that which is coextensive with the Church or knowledge of the gospel. Therefore it is impossible to exist in a "BC condition" this side of the cross.

The "times of ignorance" are a period in salvation-history and not a period before an individual's existential encounter with the gospel. They are a category in the *historia salutis*—not the *ordo salutis*. The "times of ignorance" must not be confused with an individual's personal knowledge (or lack of it). To do so conflates ontology and epistemology. Maintaining the existence of a pre-messianic condition fails to recognize the epochal nature of the unfolding redemptive history and represents a form of under-realized eschatology. The first coming of Christ is an eschatological event around which the culmination of history centers. It is a breaking in of the future events of the day of the Lord which has yet to come. It has now been revealed that God's final wrath against sin, which is to come at the end of history, has been poured out upon Christ in the middle of history. It is therefore an event that allows no practical reality of any pre-cross paradigm continuing, or of an alternative track being presently employed. The question of when the times of ignorance end is the question of whether the history of salvation or individual application of salvation is the ultimate governor. *Historia salutis* always underlies *ordo salutis,* and never the reverse. The final and once for all saving act of Christ is more ultimate with its attendant historical transition than an individual's personal experience and appropriation of the benefits of this.

The Israel analogy relies on a correspondence between the chronologically pre-messianic and the epistemologically pre-messianic, and in so doing requires the "BC condition" to continue today. I have shown that there is no sense in which the "BC condition" can exist after the cross, and therefore, the Israel analogy and fulfilment model, with their reliance on a present continuation of a pre-messianic paradigm is substantially weakened.

8

COVENANT CONFUSION

8.1 Introduction

So far my critique has focused largely on the nature of salvation history. The major structural divisions of this history are governed by the biblical covenants. In this chapter I shall argue that the Israel analogy and fulfilment model rely in large part on a misunderstanding of these biblical covenants. In particular, the nature of the Old covenant and its relationship with the New covenant is misconceived. Furthermore, the nature and relationships of the various biblical covenants that constitute the Old covenant are also erroneously conceived. I will argue that covenant theology correctly understood invalidates the Israel analogy and fulfilment model and will demonstrate that the Israel analogy does not sufficiently recognize the elements of continuity and discontinuity between the various biblical covenants, and that the analogy made between the "Old covenant" and other religions is problematic in that it fails to appreciate the different types of Old Testament covenant and how these are variously fulfilled by the New covenant. The first part of the chapter will introduce covenant theology and outline the aspects of this theology most pertinent to salvation history. The second part will assess the implications of this covenant theology for the Israel analogy and fulfilment model.

8.2. An Introduction to Covenant Theology

This thesis critiques the Israel analogy and fulfilment model from a Reformed theological perspective. Reformed theology is synonymous with covenant theology[1]; however, covenant theology should not be seen as an innovation of the Reformation, rather as a renovation of a far more ancient tradition in Christian theology. Indeed, the canonical nomenclature for the Old and New *Testaments* bears witness to an early concept of covenant.[2] A helpful definition for Covenant theology is offered by Jürgen Moltmann, and is adopted in this study: "One defines covenant theology as a theological method which utilizes the biblical theme of the covenant as the key idea for a) the designation of the relationships of God and man, and b) the presentation of the continuity and discontinuity of redemptive history in the Old and New Testaments."[3]

The doctrine achieved early dogmatic significance because the Christian church had to understand its relation to and distinction from Judaism. Over against Gnosticism and Marcionism, the church had to maintain the *unity of* the Old and New covenants, and over against Judaism, the *distinction between* the Old and New covenants.[4] Thus, covenant theology can be traced to the early Fathers where the doctrine was "present but undeveloped."[5] It is also clearly present in the writings of Augustine (354–430)[6] and Calvin (1509–1564).[7]

---

1. The doctrine of the covenant has been referred to by one of its leading proponents as a "peculiarly Reformed doctrine" (Vos, "Doctrine of the Covenant in Reformed Theology," 234).

2. Horton, *God of Promise*, 11. Cf. Kline, *Structure of Biblical Authority*, 45–48; Williamson, *Sealed*, 19. It should be noted however that Covenant and Testament should not be treated as synonymous. I will address the differences below; see this chapter, n. 114.

3. Moltmann, "Foderaltheologie," in *Lexicon fur Theologie und Kirche*. (1960), 190; quoted in Lillback, *Binding of God*, 27 (Lillback's translation). See ibid., 26–39 for other definitions for *covenant theology*.

4 Bavinck, *Reformed Dogmatics* 3:207. See, for example, Irenaeus, *Against Heresies* IV; Tertullian, *Against Marcion*, V, 11.

5. Clark, "Brief History of Covenant Theology." Cf. Golding, *Covenant Theology*, 13–47, for a historical survey of the origins of covenant theology.

6. See e.g., *City of God*, 16:27. Here, according to Clark, Augustine "clearly taught the outlines of what would become central elements in classic Reformed theology, the covenant of works and the covenant of grace" (Clark, "Brief History of Covenant Theology."

7. See particularly Calvin, *Institutes*, II.ix–xi. Calvin does not use the covenant concept as the architectonic principle for his *Institutes*, as this work is organized in a Trinitarian fashion; however, all the elements of covenant theology are present. Peter Lillback states "While the covenant does not provide the organizational structure for the *Institutes*, it clearly is an integral feature of Calvin's theology" (Lillback, *Binding of God*, 137). Lillback explains that for Calvin the essence of covenant is the mutual

Covenant Confusion

Within covenant theology there is much debate concerning the definition of "covenant" (*berît*).[8] Possibly more helpful than attempting a precise definition is to identify the key features of the biblical covenants. These are threefold: An oath or promise including stipulations, a curse for violation, and a cultic ceremony that represents the curse symbolically.[9] Meredith Kline argues that "covenant" is the most basic aspect of Scriptural revelation.[10] However, as Horton rightly cautions, this does not mean everything in Scripture should be reduced to the covenant motif. Rather, treating the covenant concept as of "architectural significance" recognizes the "rich covenantal soil in which every biblical teaching takes root."[11] While covenant theology is central to reformed theology, there is in this tradition some diversity regarding the nature and number of the covenants. The approach adopted here draws on a wide cross-section of Reformed theologians, and although a consensus cannot be reached on all points, the application of this covenant theology to the critique of the Israel analogy and fulfilment model could *mutatis mutandis* be supported by all Reformed theologians. I will not describe in detail each of the biblical covenants or offer an exegesis of the passages where these are presented. Rather, the focus

---

binding of God and people. With respect to God, the covenant is unconditional; with respect to people, it is conditional upon obedience (Lillback, *Binding of God*, 137–39). Cf. Helm, "Calvin and the Covenant." According to Robert Reymond, Johann Heinrich Bullinger's (1504–1575) *Of the One and Eternal Testament or Covenant of God* is the first full treatise on covenant. Here Bullinger argues that the "entirety of Scripture must be viewed in the light of the Abrahamic covenant in which God graciously offers to give himself to men and in turn requires that men "walk before him and be perfect" (Reymond, *New Systematic Theology*, 504, summarizing Bullinger).

8. Baker, "Covenant: An Old Testament Study," 22. *Berît* is used 290 times in the Old Testament. Some recent covenant theologians offer the following definitions: Paul Williamson has defined covenant as "a solemn commitment, guaranteeing promises or obligations undertaken by one or more parties, sealed with an oath" (Williamson, *Sealed with an Oath*, 43); John Murray defined covenant as "a sovereign administration of grace and promise" (Murray, *The Covenant of Grace*, 29); O. Palmer Robertson prefers the definition, a "bond in blood sovereignly administered" (Robertson, *Christ of the Covenants*, 15). Michael Horton prefers "a relationship of 'oaths and bonds' and [that] involves mutual, though not necessarily equal, commitments" (Horton, *God of Promise*, 10). I do not consider any of these definitions to be entirely satisfactory, as they are either too vague (e.g., Murray) or too narrow (e.g., Robertson—his definition would exclude the covenants with Adam as they did not involve blood).

9. Bavinck, *Reformed Dogmatics*, 3:203.

10. Kline, *Structure of Biblical Authority*, 25.

11. Horton, *God of Promise*, 23.

will be on the part each of the covenants plays in salvation history and on their inter-relationships.

Covenant theology teaches that God has structured his relationship with humanity according to covenants (*contra* Dispensationalism), and these covenants function as the major stages in redemptive history. Prior to the historical covenants there existed an eternal "covenant of redemption," sometimes referred to as the *pactum salutis* ("counsel of peace"). This eternal intratrinitarian pact takes the fall of the human race into account prior to its occurrence, and provides the basis for all the historical covenants. Each person of the Trinity cooperates in this pact with each performing a particular task.[12] Some Reformed theologians prefer not to refer to any pre-temporal intratrinitarian arrangement as a covenant, as they suggest such a covenant cannot be defended on the basis of exegesis.[13] However, while not explicit, proponents argue convincingly that such a covenant is implied in Scripture.[14]

8.2.1. The Covenants with Adam: A Covenant of Works and a Covenant of Grace

The first historical covenant is that made with Adam before the fall. This "covenant of works" is also referred to as the "covenant of nature, the covenant of life, [or] the Edenic covenant."[15] More recently, the epithet

---

12. "The Father promises to redeem an elect people. In turn, the Son volunteers to earn the salvation of his people by becoming incarnate (the Spirit having prepared a body for him), by acting as the surety of the covenant of grace. . . . for and as mediator of the covenant of grace to the elect. In his active and passive obedience, Christ fulfills the conditions of the *pactum salutis* and fulfills his guarantee . . . , ratifying the Father's promise, because of which the Father rewards the Son's obedience with the salvation of the elect. And because of this, the Holy Spirit applies the Son's work to his people through the means of grace" (Van Drunen and Clark, "Covenant before the Covenants," 168).

13. E.g., Williamson, *Sealed with an Oath*, 28–31. For a survey of Reformed theologians who oppose the designation "covenant of redemption," see Van Drunen and Clark, "Covenant before the Covenants," 177–80.

14. For a biblical and theological defense of the covenant of redemption, see Horton, *God of Promise*, 79–81. Horton notes that some who reject the "covenant of redemption" do so because they are operating with a definition of covenant that is too restrictive (Horton, *God of Promise*, 82). For a survey of the historical development and scriptural support for this covenant see Bavinck, *Reformed Dogmatics*, 3:212–15. Cf. Baugh, "Galatians 3:20 and the Covenant of Redemption."

15. Berkhof, *Systematic Theology*, 211.

"Adamic Administration" has been proposed.[16] Within this covenant, humanity is considered to have been on trial before the fall "neither sinful nor confirmed in righteousness."[17] The Westminster Confession of Faith states "life was promised to Adam; and in him to his posterity, upon condition of perfect and personal obedience."[18] If Adam had perfectly obeyed God during this "probationary period" he would have become incapable of transgression and would have gained eternal right standing with God. However, Adam failed to meet the requirements of this covenant, thereby subjecting himself and all his descendents to condemnation. With the fall humanity became "incapable of life."[19]

Among Reformed theologians some are reluctant to refer to any arrangement with Adam before the fall as a covenant, as it is not expressly stated in Scripture as being a covenant, the first such reference being in Genesis 6:18, in relation to the Noahic covenant.[20] However, I concur with Reymond, who offers a convincing defense of the covenant of works based on four scriptural observations: First, the word *berît* does not have to be used at the time a covenant is made in order for a covenant to be present. For example, in 2 Samuel 7, *berît* is not used, but we are clearly to understand this passage in covenantal terms because Psalm 89:19-37 portrays God as having covenantally promised David that his dynastic house would rule over Israel.[21] Second, the necessary covenant elements are present: parties, stipulation, promise and threat. Third, Hosea 6:7 refers to the fall of Adam as being a transgression of the covenant. Fourth, the New-Testament parallels between Adam and Christ (Rom 5:12-19; 1 Cor 15:22, 45-49) imply that Adam and Christ are federal heads—Adam being head of the covenant of works and Christ head of the covenant of grace (Luke 22:20; Heb 9:15).[22]

---

16. Murray, "Adamic Administration." A recent proponent of Murray's terminology is McGowan, "In Defence of 'Headship Theology,'" 189.

17. Horton, *God of Promise*, .83

18. Westminster Confession of Faith VII.ii The Westminster Confession of Faith is perhaps the confessional epitome of covenant theology. See Williamson, *Westminster Confession of Faith: For Study Classes*, 83.

19. Ibid., VII.iii. See Williamson, *Westminster Confession of Faith: For Study Classes*, 83.

20. For a survey of detractors of the covenant of works, see Estelle, "The Covenant of Works in Moses and Paul," 92 n. 7.

21. See especially vv. 28 and 34, where the term "covenant" is used.

22. Reymond, *New Systematic Theology*, 430-32. Federal headship involves the imputation of sin or righteousness, and the Reformed tradition rightly recognizes

With the fall, the first covenant was broken and the covenant of grace commences.[23] In the words of the Westminster Confession of Faith "the Lord was pleased to make a second [covenant], commonly called the covenant of grace; wherein he freely offereth unto sinners life and salvation in Jesus Christ; requiring of them faith in Him that they may be saved."[24] The requirement of perfect obedience has not been withdrawn in the covenant of grace—but is now fulfilled on behalf of his own by the second Adam—Jesus Christ. The covenant of grace is "made with Christ as the second Adam, and in him with all the elect as his seed."[25] Indeed, the covenant of works and the covenant of grace primarily differ in that Adam is "exchanged for and replaced by Christ."[26] This bifurcation of covenantal terminology has been termed "federal theology" (from *foedus*, Latin for "covenant").[27]

The covenant of grace thus fulfils the covenant of works and is the outworking of the pre-temporal, intratrinitarian covenant of redemption. The covenant of grace executed and revealed in the various historical covenants rests on this eternal unchanging foundation as Bavinck explains:

> This pact of salvation, however, further forms the link between the eternal work of God toward salvation and what he does to that end in time. The covenant of grace revealed in time does not

---

the parallel between Adam and Christ here. Schreiner argues that to deny that Adam would have gained eternal life through his obedience is to question how Christ could function as a substitute because of his obedience (Schreiner, *Law and Its Fulfillment*, 250–51). Vos defends the ancient pedigree of the covenant of works (at least in seminal form) in Vos, "Doctrine of the Covenant," 234–67. Cf. Bavinck, *Reformed Dogmatics* 3:201–3, 209–11.

23. Bavinck, *Reformed Dogmatics* 3:197: "God's first encounter with fallen humanity is both proof of his wrath and a revelation of his grace," because the punishment threatened in Gen 2:17 is not fully implemented, for Adam and Eve did not die on that day.

24. Westminster Confession of Faith, VII.ii. See Williamson, *Westminster Confession of Faith: For Study Classes*, 83.

25. Westminster Larger Catechism Q/A.31.

26. Bavinck, *Reformed Dogmatics*, 3:226.

27. This federal schema is not an innovation of the Reformation, for it can be traced to the early Fathers. For example, Horton maintains Irenaeus distinguished between a covenant of law and a covenant of promise. The former he identifies with the first arrangement with Adam (works) and with the Sinai covenant. The latter is identified with the *Protoevangelium*, Abraham, and the New covenant (*Against Heresies* 4.25; 5.16.3; 4.13.1; 4.15.1; 4.16.3; Horton, "Which Covenant Theology?" 208).

hang in the air but rests on an eternal, unchanging foundation ... It is a false perception that God first made his covenant with Adam and Noah, with Abraham and Israel, and only finally with Christ; the covenant of grace was ready-made from all eternity in the pact of salvation of the three persons and was realized by Christ from the moment the fall occurred.[28]

This covenant is a unilateral promise made to Adam (Gen 3:15),[29] and is not based on human performance, rather, it is an unconditional divine promise to send a Messiah who will crush the serpent and overturn the curse of the first covenant.[30] This covenant with Adam contains the first reference to two lines of development in humanity—the seed of Satan and seed of the Woman.[31] Genesis 4–11 sketches the development of these two lines. This bifurcation of humanity is an important element in the development of salvation history and covenant theology as will be seen below.

All the historical post-fall covenants are different administrations of this single overarching covenant of grace, which, therefore, provides a crucial unifying factor between Old and New covenants.[32] This single covenant of grace implies an essential unity in God's dealings with humanity after the fall that should guard against a reading of salvation

---

28. Bavinck, *Reformed Dogmatics*, 3:215 Cf. ibid., 194, 212–14.

29. I concur with Bavinck, who acknowledges that Genesis 3 does not use the term "covenant" but considers the concept to be implicit (ibid., 193).

30. Horton *God of Promise*, 116. A number of Reformed theologians reject the covenant-of-works/covenant-of-grace distinction. For example, O. Palmer Robertson writes, "To speak of a covenant of 'works' in contrast with a covenant of 'grace' appears to suggest that grace was not operative in the covenant of works. As a matter of fact, the totality of God's relationship with man is a matter of grace. Although 'grace' may not have been operative in the sense of a merciful relationship despite sin, the creational bond between God and man indeed was gracious" (Robertson, *Christ of the Covenants*, 56). However, Horton responds to such charges by persuasively arguing it is anachronistic to require grace or mercy as the foundation of creation and covenant in the beginning (Horton, *God of Promise*, 84).

31. Describing Cain's line as the seed of the serpent/Satan does not indicate that "Cain's line has been physically sired by Satan; rather, the Bible commonly describes people figuratively as children of those whose characteristics they emulate" (Hamilton, "Skull Crushing Seed of the Woman," 33).

32. For a substantial defense of the unity of the covenant of grace, see Reymond, *New Systematic Theology*, 512–16. Cf. Robertson, *Christ of the Covenants*, 27–29. Robertson describes the Abrahamic, Mosaic, Davidic, and New covenants as the main, "epoch making" (27) covenants of redemptive history, and he argues that there is structural and thematic unity between these covenants (28–29).

history that overemphasizes the distinction between God's work of redemption in Old and New Testaments. The Old is characterized by promise, shadow, and prophecy, the New by fulfilment, reality, and realization.[33] The covenantal framework of Scripture unifies what is often divided or confused.[34] Covenant theology therefore begins with continuity rather than discontinuity because "Scripture itself moves from promise to fulfillment, not from one distinct program to another and then back again."[35] The covenants should not be seen in a purely chronological relationship, for as Vos explains the link is transcendental as well as linear, and this provides a unifying factor to the covenants and to the nature of salvation in all periods of redemptive history: "the bond that links the Old and New Covenant together is not a purely evolutionary one, inasmuch as the one has grown out of the other; it is, if we may so call it, a transcendental bond: the New Covenant in its pre-existent, heavenly state reaches back and stretches its eternal wings over the Old, and the Old Testament people of God were one with us in religious dignity and privilege; they were, to speak in a Pauline figure, sons of the Jerusalem above, which is the mother of all."[36]

Furthermore, Christ's mediatorial role in all covenant administrations unites these various administrations of the covenant of grace: "In the covenant with Adam, Noah, Abraham, David, and others, he is the mediator, the guarantor who takes responsibility for the implementation of the covenant, realizes it in the hearts of humans by his Spirit, administers it to sinners, bestows its benefits, and incorporates his own in the covenant. From start to finish, the whole covenant is entrusted to him."[37]

However, covenant theology is equally able to affirm the aspects of discontinuity that exist because of the different types of covenant that exist. Some covenants are unconditional (unilateral), some conditional (bilateral), some are temporary and others permanent.[38] The implica-

---

33. Robertson, *Christ of the Covenants*, 57

34. Reymond, *New Systematic Theology*, 506. The Westminster Confession of Faith clearly affirms the unity of the covenant of grace and the oneness of the people of God in both Old and New Testaments (Westminster Confession of Faith VII. v, vi). See Williamson, *Westminster Confession of Faith: For Study Classes*, 81ff.

35. Horton, *God of Promise*, 20.

36. Vos, "Hebrews, the Epistle of the Diathēkē," 199.

37. Bavinck, *Reformed Dogmatics*, 3:228.

38. Farris, *Mighty to Save*, 64.

tions of the different types of covenant for our understanding of salvation history will be addressed below (section 8.3).

8.2.2. The Noahic Covenant: The Covenant of Preservation[39]

The first biblical use of the term "covenant" (*berît*) is in relation to the Noahic covenant in Genesis 6:17–22, which is the first of four passages that narrate the covenant with Noah.[40] The revelation of God's promises to Noah commences *before* the flood (Gen 6:17–22), however it should be noted that the pre- and post-diluvian commitments of God to Noah do not constitute two different covenants: "Preliminary dealings precede formal inauguration procedures. God's commitment to 'preserve' Noah and his family prior to the flood relates integrally to the 'preservation' principle, which forms the heart of God's covenantal commitment after the flood."[41]

This covenant must be understood in the context of the fall and the subsequent corruption of humanity resulting in the flood judgment.[42] In the development of salvation history, Noah and his family are by this stage the sole representatives of the "seed of the woman." The rest of humanity can be considered as the "seed of Satan."[43] Genesis 4–11 sketches the development of these two lines, and the covenant with Noah manifests God's attitude to both lines—destruction for one and gracious deliverance for the other. The judgment of the flood is not only a punishment for the sin of Noah's generation, but can be seen as a virtual reversal of creation.[44] However, the narrative does not stop there,

---

39. I borrow the nomenclature of the Noahic, Abrahamic, Sinaitic, Davidic, and New covenants from Robertson, *Christ of the Covenants*.

40. The three other passages are Gen 8:20–22; 9:1–7; 9:8–17.

41. Robertson, *Christ of the Covenants*, 110 n. 2. Cf. Williamson, *Sealed with an Oath*, 59. Here Williamson states that the suggestion that there are two covenants (Gen 6:18 and Gen 9) is wrong because the mention of covenant at 6:18 is proleptic. It "simply anticipates the covenant ratified in Genesis 9 and discloses God's purpose in the divine selection and preservation of Noah and his family."

42. Vos, *Biblical Theology*, 45–51.

43. Strange, *Salvation among the Unevangelized*, 174–76.

44. "Whereas Genesis 1 depicts creation in terms of separation and distinction, in Genesis 6–7 such distinctions are eradicated. In Genesis 1:6–8 God establishes a firmament to keep the heavenly waters at bay, but the opening of the 'windows of heaven' in Genesis 7:11 (ESV) tears this protective canopy apart. Likewise, the distinction

for its climax can be understood in terms of a recreation, a restoration of divine order—although in its postdiluvian state it is now marred by human sinfulness: "Thus understood, this post-diluvian covenant (Gen 8:20—9:17) reaffirms God's original creational intent that the flood had placed in abeyance and that humanity's inherent sinfulness would otherwise continue to place in jeopardy."[45] Humanity's creational mandate is here renewed (Gen 9:8–17), with Noah being the founder of this new humanity.[46] The post-diluvian revelation to Noah is presented in three stages: The first recites the purposes of God, expressed in a monologue instituting a new order of affairs (Gen 8:20-22). The second describes the measures taken that give content and security to this order (9:1–7) and the third relates how the new order was confirmed in the form of a covenant (9:8–17).[47]

Two major principles can be derived from the narrative outlining the Noahic covenant. These principles are important for the subsequent progress of salvation history and covenant development. First, there is a close relationship between God's creative and redemptive purposes. God's covenant with Noah entails a renewal of the provisions of creation. The language used is similar and there is a repetition of the cultural mandate that expands the vistas of redemption's horizons.[48] As Robertson points out, "God does not relate to his creation through Noah apart from his on-going program of redemption."[49] The covenant with Noah binds together God's purposes in creation with his purposes in redemption. Noah, his seed, and all creation benefit from this gracious relationship. Therefore, although the covenant with Noah ratified after the flood does not relate directly to the prosecution of redemption, there is an indirect bearing on redemption here, for "If appropriate relief from sin's corruption is to appear, the earth must be preserved free

---

between subterranean waters and the earth established in Genesis 1:9 is obliterated by the 'fountains of the deep' bursting out in Genesis 7:11. In the flood, the creative process (bringing order out of watery chaos) is thus reversed. Therefore, as Clines (1997:81) aptly concludes, 'The flood is only the final stage in a process of cosmic disintegration that began in Eden'" (Williamson, *Sealed with an Oath*, 60; the internal reference is to Clines, *Theme of the Pentateuch*, 2nd ed., 81).

45. Ibid., 61. Cf. Fackre, *Doctrine of Revelation*, 62.
46. Bavinck, *Reformed Dogmatics*, 3:218.
47. Vos, *Biblical Theology*, 51–53.
48. Robertson, *Christ of the Covenants*, 110.
49. Ibid., 111.

Covenant Confusion

of devastating judgments such as the flood for a time."[50] After the fall God might legitimately have disowned his creation—but for the eternal and unconditional agreement of the Trinity for the redemption of a people. However, to redeem this people, he has chosen to care for the rest of hostile humanity through his unconditional pledge of common grace. This covenant is unilateral, although it does incorporate bilateral obligations.[51] While not a universal covenant of redemption, the Noahic covenant does have a universalistic dimension. This covenant provides the assurance that God will sustain the creation order. Every living creature lives under the sign of the rainbow, and ultimately the entire universe will be delivered from the curse (Rom 8:22–23). This covenant "provides the biblical-theological framework within which all subsequent divine-human covenants operate"[52] and thus "its universal scope is undoubtedly significant."[53]

This covenant has not always been given sufficient attention in considerations of salvation history due to the primary focus being God's dealings with Israel. However, it provides the "biblical-theological framework within which all subsequent divine-human covenants operate."[54] However, although the covenant with Noah must not be divorced from God's redemptive purposes the provision of the covenant itself was limited to a guarantee that there would never again be a flood to destroy the earth (Gen 9:11).

"We will not find here . . . a promise to redeem sinners or to reconcile them to him [God] through the gift of the Messiah. This is a unilateral oath that does not depend on what humans do, but it is not redemptive. It is a promise to uphold creation in its natural order, not to release it from sin and death."[55]

---

50. Ibid., 114.

51. Williamson, *Sealed with an Oath*, 63. These are the basic principles that make life together possible. In the second century, Gamaliel identified these as the "Noachian precepts."

52. Ibid., 68.

53. Ibid.

54. Ibid. Cf. Robertson, *Christ of the Covenants*, 122: "This universal character of the covenant with Noah provides the foundation for the worldwide proclamation of the gospel in the present age. God's commitment to maintain faithfully the orderings of creation displays his long-suffering toward the whole of humanity."

55. Horton, *God of Promise*, 114.

As Strange comments, "This is the explicit covenantal basis of a universal but non-salvific 'common grace' that benefits believers and non-believers alike."[56] However, common grace is not special grace.[57] Therefore, the significance of the revelation of the Noahide period is not primarily in the sphere of redemption—but in the natural development and preservation of the race (although it ultimately has an important bearing on the subsequent progress of redemption).[58] God's common grace means he has not left himself without witness; however, "Of an essentially different character was the preparation of salvation in Israel."[59]

Secondly, the Noahic covenant reveals the particularity of God's redemptive grace. "Nothing indicates that Noah's favoured position arose from anything other than the grace of the Lord himself."[60] Thus, the calling of Noah is particularistic in character—just as the revelation to Noah's forebears was particularistic, occurring in the line of Seth. The principle of particularity in God's choice of Noah represents an "early manifestation of a theme which continues throughout the covenant of redemption."[61] When understood in the context of the two seeds introduced above, the continuity of the particularity theme is evident. Therefore, those who seek to use the Noahic covenant as a basis for universal salvation history disregard the context of this covenant—it takes place *after* God's wrath is universally demonstrated. Only Noah and his family are saved, and in this is demonstrated the exclusivity of salvation-history, for even those who did not have opportunity to heed the warning were judged. As Ramesh Richard points out "Jesus uses

---

56. Strange, *Salvation among the Unevangelized*, 175–76.
57. Horton, *God of Promise*, 118.
58. Vos, *Biblical Theology*, 45.
59. Bavinck, *Reformed Dogmatics*, 3:218–19.
60. Robertson, *Christ of the Covenants*, 111–13. Robertson points out that "Although Gen. 6:9 affirms that Noah was 'a righteous man,' structural considerations characteristic of the book of Genesis forbid the conclusion that Noah received 'grace' because of a previously existing righteousness. The phrases 'these are the generations of . . .' which begins Genesis 6:9 occurs 10 times in Genesis. Each time the phrase indicates the beginning of another major section of the book. This phrase decisively separates the statement that 'Noah found grace' (Gen. 6:8) from the affirmation that Noah was a 'righteous man' (Gen. 6:9). God's grace to Noah did not appear because of this man's righteousness, but because of the particularity of God's program of redemption" (112–13).
61. Ibid., 113.

[the term] 'Noah's day' to speak of judgement and not salvation (Matt. 24:36-41; cf. Luke 17:37)."[62]

8.2.3. The Abrahamic Covenant: The Covenant of Promise

After the Noahic covenant, the Abrahamic covenant is the next biblical covenant. It does not abrogate the former covenant, but develops it. Like the Noahic covenant, this covenant is made in the context of universal human sinfulness. Abraham, being a descendent of Shem stands in the lineage in which the knowledge and worship of God had been preserved most purely and for the greatest duration.[63] Although made with the one man Abraham, its ultimate scope is universal, it is the basis of God's redemptive work within human history, the start of a recurring pattern of promise-fulfilment, fresh promise-fresh fulfilment that repeats and amplifies through Old Testament history.[64] The Abrahamic covenant is an everlasting covenant (Gen 17:7, 13; 19:1; Chron 16:15–17), it continues even though Israel would transgress its stipulations many times. It is a unilateral covenant of promise and in the covenant ceremony it is significant that Abraham does not pass through the symbolic divided flesh—only the Lord does, indicating that God takes full responsibility for seeing that every promise of the covenant shall be realized.[65] The establishment of this covenant is presented in Scripture as lying in Yahweh's choosing and promising, and the sole foundation of the covenant is his promise and faithfulness to it.[66]

The covenant of grace is, as I noted above, inaugurated in Gen 3:15, but the period until Abraham "saw only a minimal demonstration of restraining and saving grace."[67] This delay in implementing the plan of redemption is explained by Vos in this way:

> Had God permitted grace freely to flow out into the world and to gather great strength within a short time period, then the true nature and consequences of sin would have been very

---

62. Richard, *Population of Heaven*, 33.
63. Bavinck, *Reformed Dogmatics*, 3:220.
64. Wright, *Knowing Jesus through the Old Testament*, 72.
65. Robertson, *Christ of the Covenants*, 145. Cf. Horton, *God of Promise*, 42. The command to circumcise is not a condition of inheriting the Abrahamic promise. Rather it is a sign and seal of the inheritance for the heir, who is already entitled to it.
66. Hart, "Christ the Mediator," 73.
67. Reymond, *New Systematic Theology*, 512.

imperfectly disclosed. Man would have ascribed to his own relative goodness what was in reality a product of the grace of God. Hence, before the work of redemption is further carried out, the downward tendency of sin is clearly illustrated [by the flood] in order that subsequently in the light of this downgrade movement the true divine cause of the upward course of redemption might be appreciated.[68]

However, with the call of Abraham, "the covenant of grace underwent a remarkable advance, definitive for all time to come . . . So significant are the promises of grace in the Abrahamic covenant found in Genesis 12:1–3; 13:14–16; 15:18–21; 17:1–16; 22:16–18, that it is not an overstatement to declare these verses, from the covenantal perspective, as the most important verses in the Bible."[69]

The entire redemptive work of God since this time has been to fulfil his covenant to Abraham (and thereby his eternal covenant of redemption).[70] It is primarily this covenant that becomes the basis of the prophecies of a New covenant in the future (Jer 31:31–34, etc.).[71] This covenant is "the foundation and core . . . of the Sinaitic covenant,"[72] and it continues in the epoch of the Sinaitic covenant, although it takes on a different form during that period.[73] Indeed, Vos rightly considers that this promissory Abrahamic covenant is presented by the writer to the Hebrews as underlying "the whole subsequent development; it is the broad basis on which the two successive [Sinaitic and New] covenants rest; the New Testament believers have an equal interest in it with the saints of the old dispensation, and in this way the uninterrupted continuity of grace is recognised (6:13–18)."[74] Such is the significance of the Abrahamic promise that the New covenant itself is "simply the admin-

---

68. Vos, *Biblical Theology*, 56; quoted in Fuller, *Unity of the Bible*, 253–54. Fuller is citing the 1961 edition of Vos.

69. Reymond, *New Systematic Theology*, 513.

70. Ibid.

71. Baker, "Covenant: An Old Testament Study," 25.

72. Bavinck, *Reformed Dogmatics*, 3:220.

73. By describing the Abrahamic covenant as "foundational," I do not intend to undermine the significance of the other covenants. Indeed, I would argue that all the covenants play a vital role in salvation history. However, the Abrahamic covenant does perform a particularly crucial role in this history.

74. Vos, "Hebrews, the Epistle of the Diathēkē," 226. Similarly, Reymond states that throughout the Bible after Genesis 12, the Abrahamic covenant is repeatedly cited as the basis of other redemptive activity (Reymond, *New Systematic Theology*, 514–18).

istrative 'extension and unfolding of the Abrahamic covenant.' Thus the temporal and spiritual reach of the Abrahamic covenant establishes and secures the organic unity and continuity of the one church of God composed of the people of God living both before and after the cross."[75]

8.2.4. THE SINAITIC COVENANT: THE COVENANT OF LAW[76]

The former covenant with Abraham and the subsequent deliverance of the people of Israel from Egypt is the hermeneutical key for understanding this Sinaitic/Mosaic covenant. Exodus begins (Exod 1:1–7) by setting out how the promise to Abraham has been initially fulfilled, and Exodus 2:24 establishes this connection explicitly.[77] Torah is inseparably bound to the Abrahamic covenant and the Mosaic administration rests on a covenantal rather than legal relationship for covenant commitment precedes the giving of the law.[78] Indeed, through the requirements of the law, Israel was constantly reminded of her inclusion in the covenant.[79] The Mosaic covenant does not supersede the Abrahamic promise, for the covenant with the ancestors continues even when at Sinai it takes a different form.[80] At Mount Sinai the promise heads for its next stage of fulfillment—the gift of the land.[81] This covenant is national in scope,

---

75. Reymond, *New Systematic Theology*, 518. The internal reference is to Murray. *Christian Baptism*, 46. Cf. Gal 3:15–16. Here Paul argues that the "promises to Abraham were originally given with an orientation to their fulfillment in Christ, who came in fulfillment of the Abraham covenant (Luke 1:72–73) . . . Paul says as much when he points out in Gal 3:8 that the promise was originally announced to Abraham as a 'pre-preaching of the gospel' (προευηγγελίσατο) with a future orientation to the 'fullness of times' when God would send his own Son . . . This orientation to future fulfillment in the original revelation to Abraham undergirds Paul's interpretation of the 'seed' promises as having their center in the Messianic Seed" (Baugh, "Galatians 3:20 and the Covenant of Redemption," 58).

76. This variously referred to as the Mosaic covenant and the Sinaitic covenant, and I shall use the terms interchangeably.

77. Murray, *Covenant of Grace*, 20, comments: "The only interpretation of this [Exod 2:24] is that the deliverance of Israel from Egypt and the bringing of them into the land of promise is in fulfillment of the covenant of promise respecting the possession of the land of Canaan (Exod 3:16, 17; 6:4-8; Ps 105:8–12. 42–45; 106:45)."

78. Robertson, *Christ of the Covenants*, 170–71. "Whatever concept of law may be advanced, it must remain at all times subservient to the broader concept of covenant" (171).

79. Scott, *Jewish Backgrounds of the New Testament*, 273.

80. Bavinck, *Reformed Dogmatics* 3:220.

81. Wright, *Jesus through the Old Testament*, 73. Initially, there is failure at Kadesh

but not in an exclusive sense, for it is established to take forward the ultimate goal of the Abraham covenant—blessing to all nations.

I have highlighted above the unity of redemption history, and even at this stage this unity can be perceived. The Exodus exhibited the same salvific principles which governed Christ's work of atonement "thereby teaching the elect in Israel about salvation by grace through faith in the atoning work of Messiah's mediation."[82] The biblical text portrays the exodus as a redemptive event. In the Exodus God revealed salvific principles that regulate all true salvation, taught Israel about faith in Christ, and bind the soteriologies of Old and New Testaments indissolubly together into one "great salvation."[83] Reymond identifies four such principles: First, the exodus in both purpose and execution originated in the sovereign, loving, electing grace of God (Deut 7:6-8); Second, it was accomplished by God's almighty power and not by the strength of man (Exod 3:19-20). Third, it actually delivered only those who availed themselves of the expiation of sin afforded by the efficacious covering of the blood of the paschal lamb (Exod 12:12-13, 21-23, 24-27); and fourth, it resulted in the formation of a new community liberated from slavery in order to serve its redeemer and lord.[84]

At the heart of the Old Testament Israelite faith is the conviction that Israel is the people of God by election. This was expressed through the Abrahamic covenant and reaffirmed through Moses at the time of the Exodus and then echoed throughout the Old Testament. God chose the people of Israel and redeemed them from Egypt not because of their own righteousness, but because of his mercy (Deuteronomy 6-8). Their being saved from Egyptian captivity and brought into the Promised Land is a matter of grace (Gen 26:5). So also is the status of every Israelite as a justified person in God's sight: "all by grace alone, through faith alone, in Christ alone, *according to the Abrahamic covenant.*"[85] However, once in the land, it is up to Israel *as a nation* to determine whether it will remain in God's land or be evicted from it. The unilateral and utterly prom-

---

Barnea; then under Joshua the next generation realize the promise, *but* not fully because they did not have "rest" in the land (Heb 4:8)—i.e., they were *in* the land but not fully in control and possession of it.

82. Reymond, *New Systematic Theology*, 518.

83. Ibid., 519.

84. Ibid., 519-25.

85. Horton, *God of Promise*, 50 (italics added).

issory character of the Abrahamic covenant yields to the conditional arrangement at Sinai even while the former is never (and can never be) revoked by the oath-taking God.[86] With the Abrahamic covenant Yahweh is depicted as swearing an oath to Abraham. However, with the Sinaitic covenant the roles of the partners are markedly different, with Israel committing to keep the terms of the covenant.[87] Thus, unlike the Noahic and Abrahamic covenants, this covenant is bilateral in nature; it is conditional, detailing the type of nation Israel were to be if it were to remain in the land. It is gracious in respect to justification, but it also possesses a "works element" regarding Israel's residence in the promised land; for it is a temporary, legal, superimposition upon the covenant of grace.[88] Thus, the Sinai covenant, as with all post-fall covenants was founded on a historical prologue that was gracious in character and aspects of grace are evident in its sacrificial provision for appeasing God's wrath. However, what happens at Sinai itself is not wholly gracious and ultimately Israel's tenure is lost by disobedience.[89] The pact between God and the Israelites establishes personal obedience to every commandment as the basis for life in the land and the land promises are temporary and conditional—just as Adam's probation was.[90]

The nature of the relationship between law (exemplified by the Mosaic covenant) and promise (exemplified by the Abrahamic covenant) is the subject of much debate.[91] Some reformed theologians, such as Murray emphasize continuity,[92] others such as Kline, discontinuity.[93] However, as VanGemeren states the debate shows the necessity of maintaining the tension between law and grace.[94] Thus, the law should not be seen as wholly negative. Indeed, in creation and in the institution

---

86. Ibid., 50.

87. Ibid., 42.

88. Clark, "Brief History of Covenant Theology."

89. Bavinck, *Reformed Dogmatics* 3:55. Some Reformed theologians dispute this distinction, suggesting the covenant of Sinai remains a covenant of grace (e.g., Bavinck, *Reformed Dogmatics* 3:220–22).

90. Horton, *God of Promise*, 54.

91. Robertson, *Christ of the Covenants*, 167: "The precise relationship of the Mosaic covenant to the promises that preceded it and to the fulfillment that followed has been proven to be one of the most persistent problems of biblical interpretation."

92. Murray, *Covenant of Grace*, 31.

93. Kine, *By Oath Consigned*, 36.

94. VanGemeren, "Law Is the Perfection of Righteousness," 49.

of the theocracy at Sinai, law as the basis for the divine-human relationship is wholly positive.[95] Baker rightly does not completely distinguish the Abrahamic and Mosaic covenants—preferring to see the latter as a "confirmation and elaboration of that made with Abraham, not something new or different."[96] The two are part of the same covenant that God initiates with Abraham and then confirms and elaborates.[97] Israel does not become the people of God at Sinai for their election is established already in the early chapters of Exodus (e.g., 3:7–10; 4:22; 5:1, etc.). Thus "the covenant at Sinai is a specific covenant within the context of the Abrahamic covenant" made with an already existing covenant community.[98] While standing in basic unity with the prior covenants, the Mosaic covenant does have some distinctive features, most notably its nature "as an externalized summation of the will of God."[99] The emphasis in the Pentateuch on the Decalogue and the explicit identification of these laws with the covenant indicate the distinctiveness of this covenant.[100] This covenant's nature as a "covenant of law" has led some reformed theologians to see it as a "republication" of the pre-fall covenant of works,[101] but this assessment is much contested.[102] However, for the

---

95. Horton, *God of Promise*, 88.

96. Baker, "Covenant: An Old Testament Study," 25

97. Ibid., 26

98. Ibid.

99. Robertson, *Christ of the Covenants*, 172

100. Ibid.

101. See, for example, Kline, *By Oath Consigned*, 22–24 and Clark, "Brief History of Covenant Theology."

102. See, for example, Murray, "Adamic Administration," 50: "The first or old covenant is the Sinaitic. And not only must this confusion in denotation be avoided, but also any attempt to interpret the Mosaic covenant in terms of the Adamic institution. The latter could apply only to the state of innocence, and to Adam alone as representative head. The view that in the Mosaic covenant there was a repetition of the so-called covenant of works, current among covenant theologians, is a grave misconception and involves an erroneous construction of the Mosaic covenant, as well as fails to assess the uniqueness of the Adamic administration" Cf. Robertson, *Christ of the Covenants*, 173–74. Here Robertson contends the Mosaic is not a republication of the covenant of works, for the covenant of works refers to the situation at creation in which man in his innocence was required to obey God perfectly in order to enter the state of eternal blessedness. But the Mosaic covenant is addressed to humanity in sin. It "never intended to suggest that man by perfect moral obedience could enter into a state of guaranteed covenantal blessedness. The integral role of a substitutionary sacrificial system within the legal provisions of the Mosaic covenant clearly indicates a sober awareness of the distinction between God's dealings with man in his innocence and man in sin."

purposes of the issues addressed in this thesis the matter is largely irrelevant, for my covenantal critique of the Israel analogy and fulfilment model is not altered by the question of whether the Mosaic covenant is a republication of the covenant of works.

The Sinaitic covenant is the most prominent covenant in the Old Testament in terms of the proportion of these Scriptures devoted to it, and the large number of echoes and renewals of this covenant throughout the Old Testament. As a result, the Old covenant is often treated as synonymous with the Mosaic covenant. For example, McKenzie suggests "This [i.e. the Mosaic] is the one considered *the* Old Testament covenant."[103] While this is partially true such an association is insufficiently conditioned and distorts salvation-history. Indeed, in some ways the Abrahamic covenant is *the* Old covenant.[104] This lack of clarity concerning the nature of the Old covenant will be shown to contribute significantly to the errors of the Israel analogy and fulfilment model.

8.2.5. THE DAVIDIC COVENANT: THE COVENANT OF THE KINGDOM

It is under David that the Abrahamic promise receives its next stage of fulfilment. At last, after two centuries of tribal infighting a unified Israel emerges in possession of the whole land, as promised to Abraham. And now the promise receives fresh impetus with the pledge of an heir for David (echoing the promise to Isaac), and the promise that his descendents would reign over Israel for ever.[105] The Davidic covenant is unconditional in that God promises "not to remove from him my steadfast love or be false to my faithfulness. I will not violate my covenant or alter the word that went forth from my lips" (Ps 89:33–34). However, Psalm 89 also indicates that the unfaithfulness of the covenant people would invite the judgment of God (vv. 30–32).

The context of the Davidic covenant (2 Samuel 7)[106] echoes aspects of the Abrahamic and Sinaitic covenants.[107] Continuity with the Abrahamic covenant is evident in the summaries of the Abrahamic and Davidic covenants. Graeme Goldsworthy highlights the relationship:

---

103. S. L. McKenzie, *Covenant*, 4; quoted in Williamson, *Sealed with an Oath*, 94.
104. See section 8.2.3 for elaboration of this point. See especially footnotes 72–75.
105. Wright, *Jesus through the Old Testament*, 73.
106. Cf. 2 Samuel 23:1–7; Psalms 89, 132.
107. Wright, *Jesus through the Old Testament*, 89–91. Cf. Williamson, *Sealed with an Oath*, 144–45.

"I will be their God, they will be my people' sums up God's purpose in the covenant with Abraham and after him, with Israel (Gen 17:7–8; 26:12; Jer 7:23; 11:4; 30:22). Now the promise concerning David's son, the one who will represent the many, is given as 'I will be his father, and he shall be my son' (2 Sam 7:14). Thus, David's son is also the son of God, and his house, throne and kingdom are established forever (2 Sam 7:16)."[108]

Indeed, the lack of covenant ceremony associated with the Davidic covenant may be explained on the basis that this covenant functions primarily as an extension of the Abrahamic covenant.[109] Continuity with the Sinaitic covenant is apparent from the context of the Davidic covenant. The chapter preceding the account of the Davidic covenant (2 Sam. 6) records how David brought the ark of the covenant into Jerusalem. The ark represented all that the Sinai covenant meant to Israel. David hereby demonstrates his allegiance to Israel's historic faith.[110] The promises made to Abraham become more focused in the Davidic covenant for this covenant identifies the royal dynasty from which the promised seed would come.[111] In this covenant God's plan to redeem a people reaches its climactic stage of realization so far as the Old Testament is concerned.

8.2.6. THE NEW COVENANT: THE COVENANT OF CONSUMMATION

The promise to David of his line ruling over Israel forever, at one level appeared to be terminated by the defeat by the Babylonian forces and the subsequent exile of 587 B.C. However, by that stage the Davidic covenant "had been given fresh impetus which survived and transcended that catastrophe, by the prophetic vision of a future true son of David who would reign over his people in an age of justice and peace. And additionally, out of the wreckage of the exile arose the promise of future redemption, but still fuelled by the original ingredients of the promise—a new *exodus*, a new *covenant*, a fresh appropriation of the *land* under the blessing and presence of God himself."[112]

---

108 Goldsworthy, *According to Plan*, 167.
109. Williamson, *Sealed with an Oath*, 122.
110. Wright, *Jesus through the Old Testament*, 89–90.
111. Williamson, *Sealed with an Oath*, 144–45.
112. Wright, *Jesus through the Old Testament*, 73 (italics original).

Covenant Confusion

God's intention to redeem a people for himself will not be thwarted. A New and better covenant is promised. Jeremiah prophesies that under the New covenant, the divine-human relationship will be very different to the Old—that is the national one that was formally ratified at Sinai.[113]

The relationship between Old and New covenants is complex and includes aspects of continuity and discontinuity. The complexity is due in large part to the fact that the Old covenant itself is not to be conceived simply as a single uniform administration, but includes various covenantal arrangements. Thus the New covenant variously fulfils, replaces, completes, and continues the Old covenant, and this demands some clarity when using the designation "Old covenant." I will later show that within the Israel analogy and fulfilment model this clarity is lacking.[114]

In the Old Testament, the term "New covenant" itself occurs only in Jeremiah 31. However, the complex of ideas depicting the future

---

113. Williamson writes "It is clear from Jer 31:32 that the superseded covenant is the national covenant, not the Abrahamic-Mosaic covenant" (Williamson, *Sealed with an Oath*, 152). Here Williamson rightly disputes Robertson's suggestion (Robinson, *Christ of the Covenants*, 272) that the New covenant supersedes all God's previous covenantal administrations.

114. A simplistic equating of the Old covenant with the Old Testament is also problematic, for it masks the complexity and multiplicity of the Old Testament covenants and does not sufficiently recognize the organic connection between Old and New covenants. The Old covenant is not to be conceived as simply that which precedes and prepares for the New covenant. This complexity is contributed to by the fact that the terms "covenant" and "testament" are often used synonymously. However, "testament" and "covenant" are *not* interchangeable. *Berît* is generally translated by *diathēkē* ("testament") in the Septuagint and New Testament. However, *diathēkē* is *not* strictly speaking a translation of *berît*; rather, *synthēkē* is; for *diathēkē* refers to a last will or testament whereas *berît* refers to a formal agreement or treaty, and therefore *synthēkē* would be a more accurate translation (Horton, *God of Promise*, 62–64). Vos judges that the conception of *berît* as testament (*diathēkē* "is utterly foreign to the intent of the Hebrew Scriptures." Vos, "Hebrews, the Epistle of the Diathēkē," 166. However, the unilateral divine origin and character attributed to the covenant in the Hebrew is the reason why the LXX prefers *diathēkē* ("testament") to *synthēkē* ("covenant") (Bavinck, *Reformed Dogmatics*, 3:205–6). Cf. Williamson, *Sealed with an Oath*, 37–39. Last, the Old Testament and Old covenant are not chronologically identical, for they do not cover exactly the same periods of salvation history. The Old Testament includes the entire period from creation to approximately 400–450 BC. However, the Old covenant, strictly speaking, denotes the period initiated with the covenant with Abraham and then formalized in the covenant with Moses to the death of Christ. The New covenant starts with death of Christ as may be inferred from Luke 22:20 and 1 Corinthians 11:25 (Wyngaarden, "Testament," 1079).

expectation of God's people has a very broad base.[115] The future age is characterized by the prophets as having a covenantal structure, corresponding to the whole of the Lord's past dealings with his people.[116] The New covenant is "arguably the climactic covenant that all other divine-human covenants anticipate and foreshadow."[117] The comprehensive nature of fulfilment wrought in the New covenant is indicated in the Old Testament prophecies of this New covenant. Jeremiah combines a reference to the New covenant with an allusion to the Abrahamic covenant (Jer 32:39–41) and by so doing indicates that these two covenants unite to form a single expectation for God's people.[118] Other prophecies addressing the New covenant contain allusions to other Old Testament covenants. For example, Ezekiel's prophecy of a new covenant combines allusions to the Abrahamic, Mosaic and Davidic covenants:

> He anticipates by divine inspiration the day in which 'my servant David will be king over them, and they will have one shepherd [an allusion to the Davidic covenant], and they will walk in my ordinances, and keep my statutes, and observe them [an allusion to the Mosaic covenant]. And they shall live on the land that I gave to Jacob My servant, in which your fathers lived [an allusion to the Abrahamic covenant] . . . and I will make a covenant of peace with them; it will be an everlasting covenant with them [an allusion to the New covenant] (Ezek. 37:24–26).[119]

Here, the major Old Testament covenants combine with the New covenant into a single divine ordering, "The New covenant does not appear in the promises of the Old Testament as some novelty previously unknown to God's people. Instead, the New covenant represents the collation of all the Old covenant promises in terms of a future expectation."[120] There is a "clear pattern of promise-fulfilment-fresh

---

115. Other key passages include Ezekiel 34–37 and Isaiah 40–55. For a substantial overview of other Old Testament allusions to a New covenant, see Williamson, *Sealed with an Oath*, 158–62.

116. Robertson, *Christ of the Covenants*, 278.

117. Williamson, *Sealed with an Oath*, 146. Cf. Robertson, *Christ of the Covenants*, 41.

118. Robertson, *Christ of the Covenants*, 41.

119. Ibid., 42. On this see also Wright, *Jesus through the Old Testament*, 94–98, who elaborates the allusions to the four preceding historical covenants in the New covenant as depicted in Isaiah, Jeremiah, and Ezekiel.

120. Robertson, *Christ of the Covenants*, 42.

promise in the Old Testament, built into the ongoing historical relationship between God and Israel over the centuries. This means that when the New Testament talks about Jesus fulfilling the Old Testament promise it is not doing something new or unprecedented. Rather it sees Jesus as the final destination of an already well recognized pattern or promise-fulfilment."[121]

Furthermore, not only do the Old-Testament covenants *look forward* to the New covenant, but the New covenant *looks back* to the former covenants. In particular, the New Testament identifies the New covenant with the promissory oaths made to Noah, Abraham and David.[122]

In Jeremiah's prophecy of a New covenant, discontinuity with the Old is indicated by the expression "New" and by the contrastitive clauses (v. 34). Covenant renewal ceremonies are found throughout the history of Israel in the Old Testament,[123] however something more radical was needed than a renewal, and therefore the New covenant should not be conceived as simply a renewal of the Sinaitic covenant as suggested by some. For example, Holmgren states, "The 'new covenant' is not completely new or different; it is the Sinai covenant presented ironically under another designation. Jeremiah 31:31–34 was directed to Israel, and the plain meaning of the text found fulfilment in that community . . . Nowhere in 31:21–24 or in its broader context is there any indication that this announcement of a new covenant is to have its fulfilment hundreds of years later."[124]

However, I suggest a more accurate understanding of Jeremiah's prophecy is to see the fulfilment on two levels. The post-exilic restoration of Israel partially fulfils it, but it has an eschatological fulfilment in Jesus Christ.[125] Jeremiah 31 promises a New covenant in which the

121. Wright, *Jesus through the Old Testament*, 74.

122. Horton, *God of Promise*, 68.

123. Wright, *Jesus through the Old Testament*, 93. Wright lists the following: the first was less than two months after the Sinai covenant, while still at Sinai. (Exod 34), then by Moses on plains of Moab (Deut.), by Joshua after the conquest (Josh 23–24), by Samuel at the institution of the monarchy (1 Sam 12), by Hezekiah (2 Chr 29–31), and by Josiah (2 Kgs 22–23).

124. F. C. Holmgren, *Old Testament and the Significance of Jesus*, 75; quoted in Williamson, *Sealed with an Oath*, 148.

125. Ibid., 149, 208–10. James Dunn takes a similar view to Holmgren. See Dunn, "Judaism and Christianity: One Covenant or Two?" 41–43. However, this leads him ultimately to the related conclusion that "the relation of Christianity to Judaism has more the character of an *ecumenical* than an *interfaith* issue." Mark Bonnington judges

blessings of the Abrahamic covenant will finally be realized. It is not a *renewal* of the Old covenant made at Sinai—but an entirely different covenant with a different basis.[126] To describe the "New covenant" of Jeremiah 31 as a "renewal" of the covenant would, as Mark Bonnington points out, "be a substantial diminution of the depth and radicality of the disjunction that Jeremiah envisions. If we ask, 'Does Jeremiah intend two covenants or one?' the answer is, emphatically, 'Two.' Anything less would be to condemn God's people to the endless spiral of failure endemic in the history of God's people in the post-Sinai period."[127]

Among some[128] proponents of the Israel analogy, the New covenant is treated as a renewal of the Old. For example, Dupuis considers the Old covenant not to be abolished by the New covenant—but "unveiled" by it. He writes: "The apparent suppression of the 'first' covenant by the 'second' (in the Letter to the Hebrews) can 'hyperbolically' be understood likewise. The new covenant is no other than the first; it unveils the first by spreading abroad the splendour of the Lord which the first contained without revealing it fully."[129]

For this reason, Dupuis prefers to refer to the Old and New Testaments as the "First" and "Second" Testaments and suggests, "Paul himself bears witness that the Mosaic covenant has not been abolished by that which God established in Jesus Christ . . . Paul expresses his firm conviction with regard to the permanent nature of God's election of the Israelites . . . Accordingly, several recent documents of the magisterium

---

that Dunn's claim that for Paul the New covenant is the making effective of the Old covenant is not adequate, for Paul is clear that in the New covenant law keeping is not necessary for members of the New-covenant community (Bonnington, "Is the Old Covenant Renewed in the New?" 62–65).

126. Horton, *God of Promise*, 53. A different position is taken by the Reformed theologian Willem VanGemeren, who states "The Hebraic use of the word 'new' signifies confirmation or restoration rather than replacement." Thus, there is an organic connection between Old and New. The Old was not a failure. (VanGemeren, "Law Is the Perfection of Righteousness," 377–78). However, VanGemeren fails here to recognize that although the Old covenant *itself* was not a failure, people were unable to keep it, and therefore a New covenant was needed.

127. Bonnington, "Is the Old Covenant Renewed in the New?" 60. Cf. Rad, *Old Testament Theology*, 2:212.

128. It may be the case that *all* proponents of the Israel analogy consider the New covenant to be a renewal of the Old covenant rather than being completely new. However, I have been unable to ascertain if this is the case.

129. Dupuis, *Toward a Christian Theology of Religious Pluralism*, 231.

state with a certain insistence that the Mosaic covenant remains valid and efficacious, even though God has established a 'new covenant' in Jesus Christ, and in a parallel fashion the 'First' Testament maintains its validity in relation to the New Testament."[130]

It is apparent from these remarks that Dupuis has misunderstood the basis of the election of the Jews—which is the permanent Abrahamic covenant rather than the temporary Mosaic covenant.[131] This failure to distinguish adequately between the functions of the Abrahamic and Mosaic covenants is a significant contributing factor to the error of the Israel analogy, as I will elaborate further below (section 8.3.2).

While there is therefore an aspect of discontinuity between the Old and the New, continuity is also evident in that the New covenant encompasses the same people (Israel and Judah), involves the same obligation (Yahweh's law) and has the same objective (a divine-human relationship).[132] However, God will facilitate the obedience required by the New covenant, the obligations will now be internalized making the permanent divine-human relationship attainable.[133] Now everyone in the New-covenant community would be affected, now everyone would know God—without the need for a human priestly mediator. The biggest difference between the covenants is the way in which the sin problem is finally dealt with—without the need for repeated sacrifices. Thus, there is no possibility of breaking the New covenant.[134] Jeremiah's prophecy indicates the superiority of the New covenant over "the covenant which I made with their fathers in the day I took them by the hand to bring them out of the land of Egypt" (31:32), that is the Sinaitic covenant.[135] However, this superiority does not necessarily relate to the content of the covenants. As Robertson contends, "the newness of the new covenant must not stand in absolute contradiction

---

130. Ibid., 331. Cf. Watson's assessment of the terms "Old" and "New" and "First" and "Second" to denote the Testaments. See this volume, section 9.3.1 n. 172, for details.

131. See this chapter (section 8.3.2) for elaboration.

132. Williamson, *Sealed with an Oath*, notes that Jeremiah (like Ezekiel—see 37:15–23) is emphasizing the comprehensive scope of the restoration in view here because the reference to "Israel and Judah" extends the hope beyond the circle of God's people then extant. (153).

133. Ibid., 154.

134. Ibid., 157.

135. Wilson, "Luke and the New Covenant: Zechariah's Prophecy as a Test Case," 161.

to the previous covenants. A factor of continuity must be recognised."[136] However, the New is not a renewal of the Old; *new* implies a break with the past.[137] This New covenant is different to the Old (Mosaic) because it is a unilateral promise. However, although it is unilateral it does not mean New-covenant people have no obligations, as Dumbrell rightly observes, "The tendency to see the covenant of Jeremiah as a New covenant because it replaces obligation by promise drives a wedge between promise and law."[138]

In 2 Corinthians 3 Paul draws a contrast between the Old and New, and in so doing echoes the themes of Jeremiah 31:31–34. The "old" here is clearly the Sinaitic covenant—as indicated by the association with "tablets of stone" (v. 3), "engraved in letters of stone," "Moses" (v. 7), etc.[139] Here, the Old is shown to be inferior to the splendor of the New, although it is not inherently bad.[140] Indeed, the Mosaic code is described as glorious (2 Cor 3:7, 10). However, it did not provide power for obedience, for the giving of the law was not coterminous with the giving of the Holy Spirit.[141] Thus, although law itself does not need to be changed, it needs to be written on the heart so that it can be obeyed.[142] The ultimate problem says Paul is not with the law itself but with human inability.[143] Here the New covenant is presented as replacing the Old, i.e. the Sinaitic, which is temporary (2 Cor 3:7–11).[144]

The most developed New-covenant theology in the New Testament is in the book of Hebrews.[145] In Hebrews 8–10 the superiority of the New over the Old serves as the writers framework. The two covenants

---

136. Robertson, *The Christ of the Covenants*, 281.

137. Ibid., 280.

138. Dumbrell, *Covenant and Creation*, 178.

139. Schreiner, *The Law and Its Fulfillment: A Pauline Theology of Law*, 129

140. Williamson, *Sealed*, 193. Cf. Schreiner, *Law and Fulfillment*, 81–82.

141. Schreiner, *Law and Fulfillment*, 250.

142. Ibid., 81–82

143. Ibid., 85.

144. Ibid., 132. The reference in Rom 10:4 ("Christ is the end of the law ") supports this interpretation. Schreiner notes the debate concerning the interpretation of *telos* as "end" or "goal," but considers "end" to be more likely for in the New Testament *telos* often contains temporal meaning but only once (1 Tim 1:5) does it indisputably mean goal. 134. I concur with this judgment. Cf. Thielman, *Paul and the Law*, 113.

145. See especially Heb 7:22; 8:6—10:31; 12:18–24; 13:20. See Vos "Hebrews, the Epistle of the *Diathēkē*." Cf. Williamson, *Sealed with an Oath*, 201–4.

being contrasted are the Mosaic and the new. In saying that the New covenant makes the first one obsolete (Heb 8:13), the writer is suggesting replacement rather than covenant renewal.[146] The contrast here (as in 2 Corinthians 3) is not between something bad and something—but between something good and something better.[147] The New is not like the Old in that it coalesces around a son rather than a servant in God's house, it is a better covenant, one enacted on better promises: "In speaking of a new covenant, he makes the first one obsolete" (Heb 8:13a). In Hebrews 10:28–29 the writer explains that the blessings of being in Christ (i.e. the New covenant) are greater than under the Old covenant—but so too are the curses for those who still place their faith in the shadows of the law rather than the promises of the gospel.

8.3. Covenant Confusion: A Reformed Covenantal Critique of the Israel Analogy and Fulfilment Model

From a Reformed perspective, Horton points out that failure to understand the nature of the Old-Testament covenants results in the errors of dispensationalism and of covenantal nomism.[148] I concur with Horton and consider this failure to be a major factor contributing to the single- dual- and multi-covenant theories prevalent in Jewish-Christian dialogue,[149] and in the erroneous analogical application of the relation-

---

146. Williamson, ibid., 201–2.

147. Ibid., 207.

148 Horton, *God of Promise*, 101. Here Horton is referring firstly to *older* dispensationalism, which considered Old Testament believers basis of justification to be different to that of New Testament believers. He then refers to covenantal nomism, a major element of the so-called new perspective on Paul, which "regards the conditions for preservation in the earthly land as conditions for enjoyment of everlasting life, either for the Israelites or for new covenant believers." The term "covenantal nomism" was first proposed by E. P. Sanders in 1977. See Sanders, *Paul and Palestinian Judaism*, 16 and passim. Sanders describes the "pattern" or "structure" of covenantal nomism as follows: "(1) God has chosen Israel and (2) given the law. The law implies both (3) God's promise to maintain the election and (4) the requirement to obey. (5) God rewards obedience and punishes transgression. (6) The law provides for means of atonement and atonement results in (7) maintenance or re-establishment of the covenant relationship. (8) All those who are maintained in the covenant by obedience, atonement and God's mercy belong to the group which will be saved" (Sanders, *Paul and Palestinian Judaism*, 16).

149. See this volume, sections 5.1a and 5.1b. Note especially the priority that the dual- and single-covenant theories give the Mosaic covenant over the Abrahamic

ship between Old and New covenants to the relationship between other religions and Christianity.

To misunderstand the scope, intention, duration, or nature of fulfilment of the various Old Testament covenants results in a fundamental misunderstanding of the nature of the Old Testament faith and its relationship with Christianity.[150] In this critique I will demonstrate that it is problematic to consider *the* Old covenant as a single entity (often identified most closely with the Mosaic covenant, or simplistically as the period before Christ) with no internal variation. A failure to understand the diverse ways in which "covenant" is used in the Scriptures results in serious error.[151] I will also show that the covenants should not be understood as separate means of establishing a divine-human relationship.

8.3.1. Noah and Salvation History

Salvation history is structured covenantally. Therefore, misunderstanding the covenants distorts salvation history. I contend that the Israel analogy and fulfilment model misconstrue the Noahic covenant. I have

---

covenant. See section 8.3.2 for further discussion of the relationship of the Abrahamic and Mosaic covenants.

150. In considering the nature of Old Testament faith, it is vital to distinguish between the covenantal religion of Old Testament believers and later Judaism which formed the context for the New Testament Church. Failure to recognize this distinction results in a projection of the faith of first century Palestinian Judaism onto the Old Testament Israelite religion, which then results in a distorted understanding of the nature of saving faith. I discuss the discontinuity between Old Testament Judaism and later Judaism/s in the introduction to this volume. Richard Gaffin rightly acknowledges the importance of this distinction in considering the theology of Paul, and he highlights the failure of the new perspective on Paul to sufficiently recognize this: "One overall effect of the 'new perspective' tendency to reduce or moderate the distance between Paul and the Judaism of his day is that it appears to assume a basic continuity between the OT and the various mainstreams within Judaism. For both Dunn and Wright the OT roots of Paul's theology and its roots in Second Temple Judaism seem to be more or less interchangeable or at least continuous . . . There is little recognition or even appreciation that OT revelation and Jewish religion and theology are not the same thing and [are] often in conflict, even in OT times and especially in Paul's day" (Gaffin, "Review Essay: Paul the Theologian," 133–34).

151. Dennis J. McCarthy criticizes Walter Eichrodt (who was recognized for his emphasis on the covenantal architecture of Scripture) for this error: "The historical relationships, and ideological differences, of the Abrahamic, Mosaic and Davidic covenants are glossed over [in the work of Eichrodt] in the necessity to subordinate the entire Old Testament to the one covenant of Mount Sinai." McCarthy, *Old Testament Covenant: A Survey of Current Opinions*, 5.

argued above (section 8.2.2) that the Noahic covenant is a covenant of preservation rather then redemption. However, proponents of the Israel analogy present this covenant as a cosmic covenant of redemption which provides the basis for a "universal-" or "general salvation history."[152] Such a view rests on the assertion that salvation history does not begin with the Mosaic or Abrahamic covenants but with the Noahic covenant, and that particularism is a late development, associated with the Abrahamic, and particularly the Mosaic covenants prior to which the cosmic covenant of redemption operated. For example, Rahner maintains the Noahic covenant is a covenant of redemption: "the scriptures tell [the Christian] expressly that God wants everyone to be saved (1 Tm 2:4); the covenant of peace which God made with Noah after the flood has never been abrogated: on the contrary, the Son of God himself has sealed it with the incontestable authority of his self-sacrificing love embracing all men."[153]

Similarly, Pinnock states: "by this pledge [the Noahic covenant] we understand that God is concerned not with a single strand of history, but with the entire historical tapestry, including all the earth's people."[154] While this basic statement is true, Pinnock goes on to argue that with this covenant "God announces . . . his saving purposes are going to be working, not just among a single chosen nation but among all peoples sharing a common ancestry with Noah. [i.e. all people]"[155] For Pinnock, there is no disjunction between salvation-history and world history, rather, they are coextensive, and universality is the tenor of the Old Testament revelation.[156] He maintains it is unfortunate that the Noahic covenant is commonly interpreted "in a minimalist way" as a covenant of physical preservation and not of redemption.[157] Pinnock

---

152. See, for example, Rahner, "History of the Word and Salvation-History," 107–8. and passim. Here Rahner distinguishes between special and general salvation history.

153. Rahner, "Anonymous Christians," 391.

154 Pinnock, *Wideness in God's Mercy*, 21. Cf. D'Costa, *Meeting of the Religions*, 154: "The Christian (and Jewish) tradition has always recognized the beginnings of the covenant as a covenant of cosmic dimensions, made with all humanity represented by Noah (Gen 9:8–16). This means that all creation is in covenant with God, without negating the specific and particular covenants made later with Abraham, Moses and eventually Jesus."

155. Pinnock, *Wideness in God's Mercy*, 21.

156. Ibid., 20-28.

157. Ibid., 21.

views Gentiles outside the covenant with Abraham such as Melchizedek to have a relationship with God based on this cosmic covenant.[158] However, as Strange persuasively argues, such figures were recipients of special revelation, and Pinnock's proposal for the Noahic covenant is erroneous when seen in its proper place in the "redemptive-historical index."[159] The Noahic covenant is not a redemptive covenant but provides the framework for the work of redemption. It has "important dissimilarities with the *protoevangelium* before it and the Abrahamic administration after it."[160]

Dupuis also presents salvation history as universalistic, and as not starting with the Abrahamic covenant.[161] In a sense, Dupuis is correct to state salvation history did not start with Abraham, for as I have already outlined it has its origins in the eternal covenant of redemption, and was first announced to Adam in the *protoevangelium* of Genesis 3:15. However, in terms of the work of God in calling a people for himself through whom he would work to bring about his plan of redemption, it is with Abraham that he starts. For Dupuis, salvation history has tended to be too restrictive and should allow for a more positive assessment of other religions than has been the case:[162] "Against all reduction of the history of salvation-revelation to the Hebrew-Christian tradition it must be affirmed that salvation history coincides and is coextensive with the history of the world. It consists of human and world history itself, seen with the eyes of faith as a 'dialogue of salvation' freely initiated by God with humankind from creation itself and pursued through the centuries until the fulfillment of God's Reign in the eschaton."[163]

---

158. Ibid., 24.

159. Strange, *Salvation among the Unevangelized*, 173–76.

160. Ibid., 175. Here Strange quotes Grudem, who highlights the differences: "the covenant with Noah, although it certainly does depend on God's grace or unmerited favour, appears to be quite different in the parties involved (God and all mankind, not just the redeemed), the condition name (no faith or obedience is required of human beings), and the blessing that is promised (that all the earth will not be destroyed again by flood, certainly a different promise from that of eternal life)" (Grudem, *Systematic Theology*, 520).

161 Dupuis, *Toward a Christian Theology of Religious Pluralism*, 216. Rahner too presents salvation history as universalistic. See for example, Rahner, *Foundations of the Christian Faith*,145.

162 Dupuis, *Toward a Christian Theology of Religious Pluralism*, 211.

163. Ibid., 217.

Dupuis considers the religious traditions of humanity as testimony to this universal covenant.[164] The Noahic covenant and the extra-biblical religions "cannot but bear an imprint of the economic Trinity."[165] He suggests "pagan saints" (whether before Israel or outside Israel) are evidence of this universal salvific covenant,[166] and lists Abel as an example.[167] However, this is a flawed proposal, not least because Abel precedes Noah.[168]

Rahner correctly affirms that the "tremendous distance in time between 'Adam' and the Mosaic revelation . . . cannot simply be conceived of as empty of divine revelation."[169] However, Rahner is mistaken in his interpretation of the significance of this affirmation, for he perceives the reality of revelation in this period as providing warrant for other religions. He continues "And this [the reality of revelation in the Adam-Moses period] cannot simply be cut off *per se* from the whole history of specific religions."[170] In the same way, Ishanand Vempeny considers the

---

164. Ibid., 33. Cf. 226. Here Dupuis quotes B. Stoeckle, "Die ausserbiblische Menschheit und die Weltreligionen." in *Mysterium Salutis*, ed. J. Fiener and M. Löhrer, 2:1053–54: "The covenant with Noah constitutes the lasting foundation for the salvation of every human person . . . The particular characteristics recorded in the Scripture concerning the Noah covenant make it clear that there is no question here of a true event of salvation, marked by grace . . . Israel and the nations have thus a common base: they are in a state of covenantship with the true God and under the same salvific will of that God" (226).

165. Ibid., 227. Cf. Bühlmann, *Chosen Peoples*, 20. Here Bühlmann argues that as Noah was not an Israelite, the covenant made with him can be seen as "a legitimation of all non-Israelite religion that goes back to God himself. For the author of this account, both the people of the covenant with Noah—the "pagans"—and the people of the covenant with Abraham—Israel—come within the scope of God's salvific will, albeit in different fashions."

166. Dupuis, *Toward*, 34–37.

167. Ibid., 35.

168. Hywel Jones rightly states that it is not possible that ante-diluvian believers were saved by the Noahic covenant—because this covenant had not yet been established (Jones, *Only One Way*, 68).

169. Rahner, "Jesus Christ in the Non-Christian Religions," 42.

170. Ibid., 42. Similarly, Mariasusai Dhavamony argues that in the Judaeo-Christian tradition there has always existed a more inclusive view of the extent of God's grace and redemption, besides the exclusive covenant with Israel, there is in the Old Testament the covenant with Noah which embraces all, and this "certainly rules out all exclusive claims in the Church today" (Dhavamony *Christian Theology of Religions*, 82–83). For Dhavamony, "Religion as a universal datum can be presented as a first revelation, as cosmic revelation to which the covenant with Noah in the Old Testament bears witness and to which St Paul makes reference (Acts 14:15–16)" (ibid., 88).

history of salvation in universalistic terms: "In fact, Israel as a nation was born not with Abraham but with Moses, though the promise was made to the former . . . in that promise the nations too were included. Hence, it seems legitimate to conclude, according to the salvific truths expressed in the Bible, that every religion in the world is heir to God's covenant with Adam, Noah and Abraham and so every religion partially shares in these interventions of God in history, and so in public historical revelation."[171]

For Vempeny non-Christian religions are direct heirs of the covenants with Adam, Noah, and Abraham, and indirect heirs of the covenant with Israel. God's universal salvific love is equally and effectively manifested in all the nations.[172]

On the contrary, I contend that there is no biblical basis for such a proposal, and I consider Bavinck's assessment of non-Christian religions to be closer to the biblical witness. Bavinck judges that all "pagan religions are self-willed and legalistic. They are the after effects and adulterations of the covenant of works."[173] That is, they are heirs not of the covenant with Noah, but with the covenant made with Adam before the fall. Therefore, the Noahic covenant should be seen as a covenant of preservation rather than redemption, and is the basis for God's continued providential care of the created order. This distinction is vital in understanding salvation history as Horton cautions, "Just as the failure to distinguish between law covenant from promise covenant leads to manifold confusions in our understanding of salvation, tremendous problems arise when we fail to distinguish adequately between God's general care for the secular order and his special concern for the redemption of his people."[174]

---

171. Vempeny, "Approach to the Problem of Inspiration in the Non-Biblical Scriptures," 138.

172. Ibid., 144.

173 Bavinck, *Reformed Dogmatics*, 3:220.

174 Horton, *God of Promise*, 116. Cf. Fackre, *Doctrine of Revelation*, 116. "Yes, the covenant with Noah promises common grace. No, this chapter does not close the Tale. The depth of the fall and the lengths to which God must go to overcome its noetic (and soteric) effects is not understood by those who settle for a foreshortened journey." Cf. Shenk, *Who Do You Say That I Am?* 76–77. Cf. Goldingay and Wright, " 'Yahweh Our God Yahweh One,'" 46. "[H]uman beings in the covenant relationship initiated with Noah are still prohibited from entering fullness of life in the presence of God and tend to resist the fulfillment of their human destiny."

Rahner maintains that the Old Testament gives witness to the universal salvific will of God outside the history of the Old covenant, and the Old Testament is aware of a "real covenant" between God and the whole human race. However, "The Old Testament covenant is only a special instance of the former [cosmic covenant] which has reached a special level in the historical consciousness of Israel."[175] Similarly, Vempeny concedes that there is an element of particularity in the salvation history that prepared for the coming of Christ, but he fails to comprehend the full significance of the relationship between Israel and Christ. He writes, "as a concrete step towards the fulfilment of His one and only plan of salvation and in order to prepare a definite people at a particular period of history for the sending of His Son, God's dealings with Israel were not identical because of Israel's geographical and historical immediacy to the Christ."[176]

What Rahner and Vempeny do in effect is reduce the uniqueness of Israel to a historical and geographical detail. This is deeply unsatisfactory, for it is not primarily the geographical and historical immediacy that give cause to the *sui generis* relationship between Israel and the church, but far more importantly it is the theological continuity and unity of redemptive history.[177] Similarly, Dupuis contends that whatever lies outside and before the sacred history of Israel belongs to general salvation history "while the immediate and express historical preparation for the Christ-event in Israel inaugurates special salvation history."[178] However, I suggest that Scripture presents no duality in salvation history. There is only one history of salvation.

The proposal for a general and a special salvation history is due in part to a misreading of the book of Genesis. The commonplace division of Genesis into chapters 1–11 and 12–50 has contributed to an unhelpful bifurcation of the Old Testament in which the story of Israel (along with the associated particularity theme) is seen as starting in Genesis 12. However, the events that occur in the primeval history are central to the story that follows. These events are more than simply a prologue to the story of Israel. Indeed, they are in many ways paradigmatic, for they

---

175. Rahner, *Foundations of the Christian Faith*, 148.

176. Vempeny, "Approach to the Problem of Inspiration in the Non-Biblical Scriptures," 144.

177. I refer the reader to chapter 6, above, for further elaboration of this point.

178. Dupuis, *Toward a Christian Theology of Religious Pluralism*, 219.

reflect the progress from sin to exile to restoration, as so often appears in the remainder of the Old Testament.[179] The unity and particularity of God's plan of redemption both in the period before Israel is constituted, and then in and through Israel is not sufficiently recognized by proponents of the Israel analogy.

Dupuis argues that Israel's monotheism was a gradual development,[180] and maintains that the term "particularism" is totally inadequate to account for the thought of the Old Testament for God does not limit his action to the one people of Israel—he is the Lord of universal history. The Old Testament manifests a universalism where everything is placed under God's providence and Israel's election had a universal intent.[181] Dupuis is certainly correct to assert Israel's election had a universal intent, but he fails to recognize the relationship between a universal goal and the particular means.

This error is made also by the Anglican Board of Mission and Unity Report *Towards a Theology for Interfaith Dialogue,* which asserts that the Sinaitic covenant between God and Israel, which is particularistic, must be understood in the context of the Adamic, Noahic and Abrahamic covenants which it considers to be universalistic: "To understand the covenants with Adam, Noah and Abraham as primary rather than the Mosaic covenant, leads to a dramatically different reading of the Old Testament and points the direction of salvation history in a different way. It leads to the recognition that all humanity is the people of God and that the God of the Jewish and Christian revelation is the God of all peoples."[182]

It is correct to assert that the Mosaic must be understood in the context of the others, and is right to state God is concerned with the whole world; however, the report is wrong to claim that by treating the covenants with Adam, Noah and Abraham as primary rather than the Mosaic covenant, one avoids being exclusivistic in the theology of religions. As Chris Wright points out in his critique of the report: "instead of preserving the biblical balance by seeing the Mosaic covenant and God's special relationship with Israel as the means of realizing this

---

179. Pate et al., *The Story of Israel,* 29.

180. Dupuis, *Toward a Christian Theology of Religious Pluralism,* 38–40.

181. Ibid., 40.

182. General Synod Board for Mission and Unity, *Towards a Theology for Inter-Faith Dialogue,* para.33.

universal goal—i.e., holding together both the ultimate, inclusive, missiological, 'all nations' intention, and the interim exclusive relationship, 'through Israel' as the means—the report effectively substitutes one for the other and relegates what it calls 'the more exclusive view of things' to the position of a post-exilic degeneration."[183]

This error results in a "dramatic obliteration of a primary Old Testament concept, namely the distinction between the people of God and other peoples within history, and the uniqueness of the covenant relationship."[184] Wright continues: "That 'all humanity is the people of God'—if by that is meant, as it seems to be, 'people of God as Israel were'—is no recognition, but a distortion, in the present context. If it were true, there would have been no need of 'salvation history' in any 'direction.'"[185] The report's authors have failed to understand the relationship between the *universal goal* and the *particular means* elected for that goal. God's promise to Abraham that "all peoples shall be blessed" entailed that this would happen through Abraham's seed, namely Israel. God's promise that "they shall be my people and I shall be their God" is an expression common to *both* the Abrahamic and Mosaic covenants. "The tension of this paradox and polarity runs right through the Old Testament from Abraham onwards, and it is wrong therefore to regard the 'exclusive view of things' as merely a post-exilic development. The tension between history and eschatology in Scripture cannot so easily be disposed of."[186]

8.3.2. The Abrahamic, Sinaitic and New Covenants: Promise, Law and Fulfilment

Two very different covenant types together constitute the Old covenant, and these are exemplified by the Abrahamic and Mosaic covenants representing the unconditional and conditional, the permanent and temporary covenant forms, respectively. I submit that in order to understand how the Old and New covenants relate it is vital for there to be a robust understanding of how the Abrahamic and Sinaitic covenants relate to

---

183. Wright, "Inter Faith Dialogue," 239.
184. Ibid., 239.
185. Ibid., 239–40.
186. Ibid., 241.

one another and to the New covenant.[187] I shall here argue that the Israel analogy does not recognize the very different roles that the Abrahamic and Sinaitic covenants play in salvation history.

In his letter to the Galatians, Paul emphasizes the differences between these two covenant traditions and Paul's contribution here will be the focus of the following analysis. Paul insists that his opponents, the "Judaizers" (who believe that salvation not only comes from the Jews, but only comes to those who themselves become Jews), have failed to recognize in the Hebrew Scriptures this contrast between the covenants of Abraham and Moses. Paul believed confusion of the two covenants lay at the heart of the Galatian heresy—a charge repeated by the Protestant reformers against the Roman Catholic Church.[188] I believe it is a major flaw of the Israel analogy too. Paul elaborates two formulae of equivalences spanning the history of redemption, and explains that two antithetical alternatives for realizing acceptance by God face the Galatians (Gal 4:21–26). The first traces its lineage back to Abraham's slave-son Ishmael, who was born out of the patriarch's efforts to assure the fulfilment of God's promises on the basis of his own resources. This alternative for justification manifests itself again in the law-covenant of Sinai which corresponds to the "present Jerusalem" (v. 25). The second formula of equivalences runs from Sarah through the covenant of promise to the "Jerusalem above" (v. 26).[189]

Paul's reference to Sinai here must be understood in the context of the equivalences which he develops. The covenant of "law" corresponds to the "present Jerusalem" i.e. the Jerusalem of the Judaizers. It is the legalistic misapprehension of the Sinai law-covenant, and slavery inevitably results from resorting to natural human resources as a means of gaining right standing before God. Ishmael, the current Judaizers and unbelieving Israel together find themselves to be slaves. Thus, the understanding of Mosaic law with which Paul is dealing cannot be viewed

---

187. I have already briefly introduced this matter in section 8.2.6 but will develop it at much greater length here.

188. Horton, *God of Promise*, 35. Cf. Horton, *Covenant and Eschatology*, 175–76. The Reformers believed the Roman Catholic Church confused the Mosaic and Abrahamic covenants (law and gospel), and my limited study of the Roman Catholic sources confirms this observation.

189. Robertson, *The Christ of the Covenants*, 181. Cf. Williamson, *Sealed with an Oath*, 199–200.

Covenant Confusion

as the divinely intended purpose of the giving of the law at Sinai. Vos explains the difference between these two systems:

"Paul speaks of two contrasting διαθηκαι, i.e., two great religious systems operating by diverse methods and with opposite results, the one a Hagar-diatheke geographically associated with Mount Sinai, the other a Sarah-diatheke having its local center in the heavenly Jerusalem. There is a difference between this and II Corinthians 3 insofar as there the Old and the New were contrasted in their original God-willed and God-given character, whilst here in Galatians the Sinaitic-Hagar-diatheke is the old system as perverted by Judaism."[190]

It is evident from Gal 3:24 that Paul's negative remarks about the law do not relate to the original intention of law giving. Here Paul explains that the law was given to lead to Christ and the fundamental issue Paul is grappling with here is that the misapprehension of the law has led the Judaizers *away* from Christ. In considering the relationship of other religions to Christianity therefore, it must not be assumed that these religions lead to Christ, for even the Jewish tradition (misappropriated) can lead away from Christ.

Paul contrasts the legalism of the Judaizers with the graciousness of the New covenant (Gal 2:14–16; 3:1; 4:31—5:2). In order to heighten this distinction Paul sets up two secondary contrasts which must be understood as they relate to his primary purpose. The first contrast is of the period before Christ from the age of the New covenant (Gal 3:23, 25). The Judaizers' error here is that they have not taken into account adequately the radical difference Christ's coming has made. However, Paul modifies this contrast by stressing that the way of salvation is the same in both periods. Indeed, the same gospel was preached beforehand to Abraham (Gal 3:8).[191] The second contrast is that made between the Abrahamic and Mosaic covenants (Gal 3:15-19). The inheritance of God's blessing is based on promise not law. Law was never intended to function apart from promise, and separated from this promise dimension which reached its fulfilment in Jesus Christ, law never could justify. Promise as under Abraham was the only effective way by which sinners could be justified through the Old covenant.[192] Paul modifies this

---

190. Vos, "Hebrews, the Epistle of the *Diathēkē*," 163. The original and transliterated Greek appear in Vos.

191. Robertson, *Christ of the Covenants*, 58–59.

192. Ridderbos, *Paul*, 149.

contrast however, by establishing a basic unity between the Abrahamic and Mosaic covenants in contrast to the legalistic proposals of the Judaizers. Thus, the ultimate contrast here is not between the Abrahamic and Mosaic covenants but between the way of justification advocated by the Judaizers and the way of justification provided by Christ. The antithesis between law covenant and promise covenant (which give rise to antithetical forms of religion) must not detract from the unity of God's dealings under the covenant of grace.[193] Paul's main argument here can therefore be summarized as follows: "Old and new covenants merge into a basic harmony. Abrahamic and Mosaic covenants unite in the purposes of God's grace. But no unifying factor whatsoever arises to harmonize the message of the Judaizers with the message of Christ. The antithesis is absolute."[194]

For the covenant of law to function as a way of salvation, the covenant of promise would first have to be suspended, but this is not the case for the Mosaic covenant is clearly established in the context of the Abrahamic.[195] The covenant of law neither annulled the covenant of promise, nor offered a temporary alternative to the covenant of promise.[196] The covenant with Abraham has been in effect since its inauguration until the present time. The principle of "justification by faith" (Gen 15:6) has not been interrupted. Throughout the Mosaic period, as in all periods of salvation history God considered righteous anyone who believed in the promise of redemption.[197] In Romans 3, Abraham is presented as the paradigm case of justification through faith alone apart from the law (Rom 3:28). Abraham received forgiveness because he believed the Lord, and this was credited to him as righteousness (Gen 15:6; cf. Rom 4:3, 23; Gal 3:6; Jas 2:23).[198] As Walter Kaiser correctly asserts,

---

193. Robertson, *Christ of the Covenants*, 60. I concur with Robertson who here counters Kline's assertion that inheritance under the Mosaic covenant was based on works.

194. Ibid., 61.

195. See section 8.2.4 above.

196. Baugh, "Galatians 3:20 and the Covenant of Redemption," 65–68.

197. Robertson, *Christ of the Covenants*, 174.

198. Fuller, *Unity of the Bible*, 254. Cf. ibid., 251–57. According to Peter O'Brien, the Judaizers with whom Paul is disputing in Galatians, claimed Abraham was justified by works. However, O'Brien rightly concludes that Paul's interpretation of Genesis 15:6 in Romans 4 makes it clear that he opposes the Jewish understanding of Genesis 15:6, i.e., that Abraham was forgiven as a wage that God the employer paid to Abraham

keeping the law never led to justification, and Paul excluded even the hypothetical possibility of keeping the law, on the basis of Gal 3:21.[199]

The contrast between the righteousness that is by the law and the righteousness that is by faith is also prominent in Paul's letter to the Romans (e.g., Rom 10:5-8; 9:30-32).[200] Some theologians such as Wayne Strickland maintain Paul is not so much arguing that the law *never* saved, but is contending that the Jews had not understood the salvation-historical change that had occurred with the Christ-event, which now meant law was not a means of salvation.[201] However, Moo rightly responds:

"Failure to understand the shift in salvation history is certainly part of the problem ([Rom] 10:4). But this cannot be the entire problem, since, as Strickland himself insists, righteousness had always been by faith. This was not something new with the coming of Christ, as Abraham and David attest (Rom 4:1-8). Criticism of the Jews for misusing the law as a means of righteousness cannot therefore be removed from Paul's discussion of 'law righteousness.'"[202]

There is therefore a fundamental continuity in the nature of saving faith at all times.[203] The church of Jesus Christ is the present-day

---

the worker, in compensation for service rendered. This view is found in various non-canonical Jewish writings (O'Brien, "Was Paul Converted?" 376-79). Cf. Fuller, *Unity of the Bible*, 256-57.

199. Kaiser, "Law as God's Gracious Guidance for the Promotion of Holiness," 74, 190. On the contrary, Moo argues that texts such as Matt 19:17; Rom 2:13b; and 7:10 imply that perfect obedience of the law would hypothetically procure one's salvation. However, the law was not given to bring Israel or individuals to salvation (Moo, "Law of Christ as the Fulfillment of the Law of Moses," 311, 324-26). Cf. Schreiner, *Law and Fulfillment*, 44. Schreiner correctly asserts that no one can be justified by the law firstly because no one can keep it perfectly; and second, because of the salvation-historical shift. "Old Testament sacrifices no longer atone since Jesus has provided definitive atonement on the cross. In fact, his atoning work casts light back on the Old Testament sacrifices showing that they were defective because they could not provide effective and final forgiveness."

200. Moo, "Law of Christ as the Fulfillment of the Law of Moses," 312. Paul is here demonstrating that Jews have falsely pursued a relationship with God based on works (9:32) and the law (9:31).

201. See Strickland, "Inauguration of the Law Of Christ with the Gospel of Christ," 229-319.

202. Moo, "Law of Christ as the Fulfillment of the Law of Moses," 313.

203. See O'Brien, "Was Paul Converted?" 387-90 for an account of the similarity of Abraham's faith and Christian faith. I acknowledge the debate concerning the exact nature of Old Testament faith, and in particular the question of whether Old

expression of the one people of God whose roots go back to Abraham.²⁰⁴ The requisite condition for salvation is identical in both the Old and New Testament: the elect were saved, are saved and will be saved only by grace through faith in the work of the Messiah (anticipated or accomplished).²⁰⁵ Jonathan Edwards considered that the condition of salvation remained the same in both Old and New covenants, being faith in the Son of God as mediator, and that all parts of the Old Testament point to the future coming of Christ. In sum, the religion of Israel "was essentially the same religion with that of the Christian Church."²⁰⁶

It is evident from the preceding discussion that the Abrahamic covenant is foundational for salvation history in a way that the Sinaitic is not.²⁰⁷ It is the fundamental covenant of the entire history of salvation. As Bullinger states this covenant is "the chief point of religion."²⁰⁸ Lillback shows that for Bullinger all of Scripture is to be referred to Genesis 17.²⁰⁹ For Calvin, the Abrahamic covenant is operative today,²¹⁰ and it distinguishes believers from unbelievers.²¹¹ Jesus Christ is its

---

Testament believers were indwelt by the Holy Spirit. For a comprehensive survey of views on this issue see Hamilton, *God's Indwelling Presence: The Holy Spirit in the Old and New Testaments*. Hamilton concludes that Old Testament believers were regenerate but not indwelt.

204. Reymond, *New Systematic Theology*, 525.

205. Ibid., 528–30. Cf. Kaiser, "Law as God's Gracious Guidance," 182–83.

206. Edwards, *History of the Work of Redemption*, 443: "The church of God from the beginning has been one society; the Christian church that has been since Christ's ascension is manifestly the same society continued with the church that was before Christ came. The Christian church is grafted on to their root; they are built on the same foundation." Cf. Yarbrough, "Paul and Salvation History," 313–14. Here Yarbrough cites Hofmann, who argues that justification through faith is "a primeval realization" present at the earliest levels of Genesis (10), and describes Israel as "the people of salvation-historical calling" (11). Hofmann references are from J. C. K. von Hofmann, *Biblische Theologie des neuen Testaments* (Nördlingen: C. H. Bexk, 1886).

207. Ridderbos, *Paul*, 149. See the current chapter, n. 73, for clarification on how I am using the term "foundational."

208. Heinrich Bullinger, *De Testamento Seu Foedere Dei Unico et Aeterno* (1534), quoted in Lillback *Binding of God*, 110 (full reference not given.)

209. See ibid., 115–17.

210. See, for example, Calvin, *Institutes*, IV.xvi.6: "For it is most evident that the covenant, which the Lord once made with Abraham, is not less applicable to Christians now that it was anciently to the Jewish people, and therefore that word has no less reference to Christians that to Jews."

211. See, for example, ibid., I.vi.1, "Let the reader then remember, that I am not now treating of the covenant by which God adopted the children of Abraham, or of

seed,[212] and justification and sanctification are its two major redemptive benefits."[213]

Its promissory character is underscored three times in Gal 3:16–20.[214] Paul explains that the Judaizers, through their exaltation of the law effectively (but unintentionally) gave priority to the Mosaic rather than the Abrahamic covenant. In their scheme the Mosaic law covenant cancels out the promissory character of the Abrahamic covenant, and if the Mosaic is primary then inheritance is to be gained through obeying the law rather than through God's gracious promise. However, Paul's response is to stress that the Mosaic covenant does *not* teach a different way of salvation to the Abrahamic promise.[215]

Paul emphasizes that salvation is always based on promise and not law. "For if the inheritance comes by the law, it no longer comes by promise; but God gave it to Abraham by a promise" (Gal 3:18). All "who believe" (Gal 3:7) are therefore Abraham's genuine heirs for they like him were justified by faith rather than the law (Gal 3:6,11). The Mosaic covenant could *never* make anyone righteous because it merely indicated the righteousness required by God—not the means of achieving such righteousness (Gal 2:15–18), it thereby underlines the necessity of becoming righteous by faith.[216] Thus, the law covenant is inferior to the Abrahamic promise, and this inferiority is underscored by its temporary nature (Gal 3:19).[217] The covenant of law pertains to the nation's remaining in the earthly land; the covenant of promise pertains

---

that branch of the doctrine by which, as founded in Christ, believers have, properly speaking, been in all ages separated from the profane heathen."

212. See for example, ibid., II.vi.2, "For although God embraced the whole posterity of Abraham in his covenant, yet Paul properly argues (Gal. iii. 16), that Christ was truly the seed in which all the nations of the earth were to be blessed, since we know that all who were born of Abraham, according to the flesh, were not accounted the seed."

213. See for example, ibid., IV.xiv.5, "the circumcision of Abraham was not for justification, but was an attestation to the covenant, by the faith of which he had been previously justified." and IV.XVI.3, "The Lord . . . covenants with Abraham, that he is to walk before him in sincerity and innocence of heart: this applies to mortification or regeneration."

214. Schreiner, *Law and Fulfillment*, 124.

215. Ibid., 126.

216. Alexander, "Abraham Reassessed Theologically." Cf. Schreiner, *Law and Fulfillment*, 127.

217. Carson, "Mystery and Fulfillment," 411–12. Cf. Longenecker, "Pedagogical Nature of the Law in Galatians," 57.

to the eternal inheritance in Jesus Christ, Abraham's seed. No Israelite was ever justified by works, but the nation had to keep the conditions of the law in order to remain in possession of the earthly type of the heavenly rest.[218] Old Testament saints were justified by faith *according to the Abrahamic promise*, but the theocracy itself was to be maintained and vindicated by adherence to the Torah.[219]

It is vital to distinguish between the typological and conditional aspects of the Old covenant (based on the law) and the reality to which they point (based on promise). Therefore, the Sinai covenant should not be understood as involving timeless principles of blessing and cursing—for this would confuse this covenant concerning a national geopolitical entity—Israel, with the eternal plan of redemption carried forward in the unconditional divine promise made to Abraham and fulfilled in Jesus Christ.[220]

All who seek to be justified by the law no longer seek salvation as Abraham's heirs. Ironically, the very people who "seek the closest affinity to Moses and Sinai end up missing the fulfillment of the *prior* covenant of promise in the seed who is received through faith alone."[221]

> Israelites under the old covenant and believers under the new are justified by grace alone through faith alone because of Christ alone. The difference is the theocratic parenthesis of redemptive history in which the typological kingdom is front and center. But this tutelage gives way to adulthood when the reality appears in Christ, who not only fulfills the law in our place but pours out his Spirit on the true children of Abraham, Jew and Gentile. Thus, they are correct who insist upon the continuity of God's covenant of grace from Adam to Noah to Abraham to Moses to David to Christ as to the terms of eternal blessedness in God's covenant.[222]

The temporary Sinaitic covenant was a *paidagogos* leading to Christ by types and shadows and by revealing human inability to meet God's

---

218. Horton, *God of Promise*, 131.

219. Ibid., 74–75.

220. Ibid., 20. Cf. ibid., 38: "As Paul's critics had confused the principles of law and promise, they had also confused the *relative* fidelity required in the *national* covenant and thus they *remain in the typological land* with the *absolute* faithfulness required of *every person* in order to fulfill all righteousness and thus appear safely in God's *heavenly* presence."

221. Ibid., 39.

222. Ibid., 101–2.

righteous standards.[223] Humankind needed preparation in order to recognize and appreciate the benefits of Christ.[224] The law covenant was added 430 years after the promise to Abraham was limited in duration, it is now obsolete, having been fulfilled in the New covenant.[225] The Hebrew Scriptures themselves qualify the Sinaitic covenant in strictly conditional terms: "This is the witness of the Law and the Prophets as well as Jesus and Paul, not to mention the radical Jewish communities of Second Temple Judaism . . . Furthermore, the New Testament treats the old covenant (largely identified with the Sinaitic pact) as obsolete, having fulfilled its temporary function of providing the scaffolding for the building of the true and everlasting temple."[226]

The Mosaic covenant was made specifically with the Jews, and contained laws that separated Jews from Gentiles, it was therefore abolished when the New covenant was realized, as this New covenant constituted the fulfilment of God's covenant with Abraham which was established to bless *all nations*.[227] Once the Messiah appears the Sinai covenant is no longer necessary—the reality displaces the types and shadows.[228] As Mendenhall explains:

"The harmonization of the two covenant traditions [Abrahamic and Mosaic] meant that great emphasis had to be placed upon the divine forgiveness, and this becomes the foundation of the New Covenant predicted by Jeremiah. . . . The New Covenant of Christianity obviously continued the tradition of the Abrahamic-Davidic covenant with its emphasis upon the Messiah, Son of David. Paul uses the covenant of Abraham to show the temporary validity of the Mosaic covenant."[229]

---

223. For further discussion on the role of the Mosaic covenant as a *paidagogos* see section 9.1.4 of this volume.

224 Bavinck, *Reformed Dogmatics* 3:222: "The necessity of this upbringing and preparation does not arise, objectively, in God as though he were variable; nor in Christ as though he were not the same yesterday and today and forever; nor in the spiritual benefits as though they did not exist and could not be communicated by God. But it arises, subjectively, in the state of the human race, which, precisely as a race, had to be saved and hence had to be gradually prepared and educated for salvation in Christ."

225. Schreiner, *Law and Fulfillment*, 79.

226. Horton, *God of Promise*, 47.

227. Schreiner, *Law and Fulfillment*, 142.

228. Ibid., 123.

229. G. E. Mendenhall, *Law and Covenant in Israel and the Ancient Near East* (Pittsburgh: The Biblical Colloquium, 1995), 49, quoted in Horton, *God of Promise*, 48.

Thus in Galatians Paul counters the notion that the Mosaic covenant represented the apex of God's revelation to his people; instead it is an interim covenant before the promise is fulfilled. The Galatian believers have experienced the fulfilment of God's promises to Abraham, and to turn back to the law regresses to an era in which the law functioned apart from the Spirit.[230]

Paul highlights the continuity and discontinuity between these two covenant types and the New covenant. There is fundamental continuity between the covenant promise to Abraham and its fulfilment in Christ. But this continuity highlights the discontinuity between the Mosaic-law covenant and the New covenant.[231] While the Old law covenant has passed away the Abrahamic promise has not.[232] This distinction is of crucial significance to my critique of the Israel analogy.[233]

This rather prolonged elaboration of the Abrahamic and Sinaitic covenants and their relationship with the New covenant has been necessary to highlight the different nature, purpose and duration of these covenants, and therefore to reveal the flaw in simplistic analogies between other religions and *the* Old covenant, for such analogies do not recognize the aspects of continuity and discontinuity that characterize the relationship between Old and New covenants, and between Israel and the church, or the *sui generis* relationship of these covenants.

Proponents of the Israel analogy commonly present the various biblical covenants as separate or alternative arrangements under which a divine-human relationship can be established. For example, although Dupuis rightly states that the various biblical covenants need to be viewed as distinct but also as interrelated and inseparable,[234] he evidently mishandles their interrelationships for he asks the question "Is God's grace-filled relation today with persons belonging to the Jewish people to be assigned to an enduring efficacy of the Mosaic covenant or to be assigned to the New covenant established in Jesus Christ?"[235] and he

---

230. Schreiner, *Law and Fulfillment*, 124.

231. Bonnington, "Is the Old Covenant Renewed in the New?" 64.

232 Horton, *God of Promise*, 60. Cf. Schreiner, *Law and Fulfillment*, 142, 145–47, 160–63.

233. As I have already noted, it also highlights a major flaw in the dual- and single-covenant theories popular in Jewish-Christian dialogue.

234. Dupuis, *Toward a Christian Theology of Religious Pluralism*, 212.

235. Ibid., 229.

offers a positive answer to the "vexing question of the abiding efficacy of "pre-Christian" covenants."[236] Dupuis argues that just as the Mosaic covenant has not been suppressed by coming to fullness in Christ, neither has the cosmic covenant with the nations been obliterated by reaching in the Christ-event the goal for which it was ordained.[237] However, to equate the two covenants in this way shows he does not understand the differences between the Noahic and Mosaic, and the nature of their fulfilment in Christ. Furthermore, it is the Abrahamic covenant that is the basis of God's "grace-filled relationship with the Jewish people," not the Mosaic covenant. Those who use the Israel Analogy have not recognized this, for in seeing the Old covenant as analogous to other religions today they indicate they have not understood the temporary nature of the Old i.e. the Mosaic covenant. It has served its purpose and is now superseded.

A similar error is made by Pinnock, who states: "According to the Bible, persons can relate to God in three ways and covenants: through the cosmic covenant established with Noah, through the Old covenant made with Abraham, and through the New covenant ratified by Jesus."[238] However, this claim reveals a fundamental flaw in the way the covenants are perceived by Pinnock. While Pinnock rightly identifies these as separate covenants, they should not be seen as isolated arrangements for the divine-human relationship, or as having any intrinsic salvific efficacy. There is an essential organic unity to the covenants and the divine-human relationship at all times has been on the basis of the work of Christ. Only Christ, as federal head of the covenant of grace saves, and Christ unites the various administrations of the covenant of grace.

8.4. Summary

I have introduced covenant theology and outlined the salvation-historical significance of the biblical covenants. I have considered the relationships of the Old Testament covenants and the nature of their fulfilment in the New covenant and have then applied these principles in my critique of the Israel analogy and fulfilment model. I have demonstrated that the various biblical covenants are not separate arrangements

---

236. Ibid., 212.
237. Ibid., 233.
238. Pinnock, *Wideness in God's Mercy*, 105.

under which a divine-human relationship may be established. They are all part of the one covenant of grace of which Christ is the federal head. The covenants do not operate independently, and with the exception of the replacement of the Sinaitic covenant by the New covenant, the successive covenants do not replace preceding covenants, rather there is an organic unity and continuity, and this unity is ultimately based on the eternal covenant of redemption. The covenants should not be seen in a purely chronological relationship, for the link is transcendental as well as linear, and this provides a unifying factor to the covenants and to the nature of salvation in all periods of redemptive history. Furthermore, Christ's mediatorial role in all covenant administrations unites these various administrations of the covenant of grace.

I have asserted that the covenant with Noah is a covenant of preservation rather than redemption, and should not be interpreted as the basis for a universal, general, or cosmic salvation history. I have maintained that salvation history is characterized by particularity. However, the Israel analogy fails to maintain the tension between the particular means (as outworked in history) and the universal goal of this salvation history (as realized at the Eschaton). I have highlighted the problem caused by failing to distinguish adequately between the various Old Testament covenants and the nature of their fulfilment in the New covenant, and have highlighted the foundational and enduring role of the Abrahamic covenant but the provisional and temporary role of the Sinaitic covenant.

My critique of the Israel analogy and fulfilment model has revealed that proponents of these models have incorrectly understood the scope, nature and duration of the various Biblical covenants and their function in salvation history. Therefore, these paradigms are fundamentally flawed for they have not sufficiently comprehended the relationship between Old and New covenants, and this has facilitated the erroneous analogical application of this relationship to the relationship between other religions and Christianity.

9

A BIBLICAL, HISTORICAL, AND THEOLOGICAL CRITIQUE OF THE FULFILMENT MODEL

In chapter 1 I introduced the fulfilment model and noted how many proponents of this model claim strong support from a number of key biblical texts. They also claim some of the early Church Fathers shared a similar approach. In this chapter I will consider these claims and will contend that although fulfilment is indeed a key biblical concept, the biblical understanding of fulfilment is very different from that employed by the fulfilment model. The biblical concept of fulfilment is an exclusive one—fulfilment of the Old Testament by the New Testament, and this is a *sui generis* relationship. I will also argue that contrary to much contemporary thought, the Church Fathers did not endorse fulfilment theology as understood today. They were not proto-inclusivists. They did not consider the relationship between Old and New covenants as an analogical basis for the relationship of other religions to Christianity.[1] In the course of examining the biblical and patristic material, a number of key theological themes emerge, which will be developed in the final part of this chapter. While the focus of this chapter is on the fulfilment model, many of the conclusions apply more widely to the Israel analogy too.

---

1. I acknowledge that my treatment of the biblical and patristic material does not constitute original research. However, the inclusion of this material is warranted due to its value in countering the Israel analogy and fulfillment model.

9.1. Biblical Arguments Outlined and Assessed

Proponents of the fulfilment model suggest the approach is endorsed by the New Testament. A small number of biblical texts are relied on for support. Paul Hedges suggests the most commonly cited by fulfilment theologians are Matthew 5:17; Galatians 3:24; Acts 10, 14, and 17; and John 1—and the literature reviewed for the current study confirms this.[2] While a full exegesis of these passages is beyond the scope of this chapter, the following section will assess whether these texts are employed correctly in the fulfilment model.

9.1.1. Fulfilment in Matthew 5:17–20

Jesus' statement in Matthew 5:17: "Do not think that I have come to abolish the Law or the Prophets; I have not come to abolish them but to fulfil them,"[3] is the verse from which fulfilment theology derives its title.[4] Despite the text explicitly referring to fulfilment of "the law and the prophets," fulfilment theologians interpret this verse in a "broad" sense—extending it to suggest Christ is the fulfilment of other religions also.[5] This, I suggest, is an invalid extension of the fulfilment here presented. "The law" (τόν νόμον) in verse 17 is a reference to the Pentateuch. When used in conjunction with "the prophets" (τοὺς προφήτας), the entire Hebrew Scriptures are the referent.[6] The exegetical evidence and context indicate the passage should be understood in a specific or "narrow" sense—that is, limited to fulfilment of the Old Testament Israelite

---

2. Hedges, *Preparation and Fulfilment*, 17–21. Farquhar, appeals to John 1:9; Acts 10:34, 35; 14:17; and Romans 2:15; 10:12 for support (Farquhar, *Crown of Hinduism*, 27).

3. The passage continues, (v.18): "For truly, I say to you, until heaven and earth pass away, not an iota, not a dot, will pass from the Law until all is accomplished."

4. Indeed *Not to Destroy But to Fulfil* is the title of a major study on the fulfilment theologian John Farquhar by Eric Sharpe (Uppsala: Gleerup, 1965).

5. See for example, Farquhar, *Crown of Hinduism*, 27

6. Morris, *Gospel according to Matthew*, 107. In the following verse (18), "law" (νόμου) refers to the Old Testament Scriptures as a whole. Thus, Jesus is not referring to commandments alone; he is referring also to the covenant to which the commands belong, and to the patterns of God's dealings with Israel presented in the historical narratives of Old Testament Scripture. This adds further weight to my assertion that the biblical understanding of fulfilment emphasizes the unique place of the Old Testament in the Christian faith.

A Biblical, Historical, and Theological Critique of the Fulfilment Model

tradition. The preceding chapters (1–4) have already established Jesus Christ as fulfiller.[7]

> Matthew 1–4 shows a host of parallels with the events of the Exodus and Israel's experiences in the wilderness and sums up the significance of these parallels in the announcement of the coming kingdom. Matthew 1–4 thereby shows that Jesus fulfills the purposes and meanings contained in the earlier history of Israel. Since it is a narrative, Matthew 1–4 concentrates on the narrative portions of the five books of Moses. Matthew 5–7, by contrast, contain a large amount of teaching of Jesus. It thereby shows most specifically Jesus' fulfillment of the didactic portions of the books of Moses.[8]

Matthew's narrative clearly indicates that Jesus' *life* was to be understood as a fulfilment of scriptural expectations, and the instances of Jesus' *teaching* which follow in 5:21–48 will show this is a fulfilment of Old Testament demands and expectations also.[9] Robert Banks highlights this fulfilment expressed in the life and teachings of Christ: "The prophetic teachings point forward (principally) to the actions of Christ and have been realized in them in an incomparably greater way. The Mosaic laws point forward principally to the teachings of Christ and have also been realized in them in a more profound manner."[10]

Matthew, along with the other Gospel writers, presents Jesus as the Messiah who fulfils the Old Testament. Matthew wants his readers to see that Jesus was not only the completion of the Old Testament story at a historical level, as his genealogy portrays, but also that he was in a much deeper sense its fulfilment.[11] The genealogy does not merely provide historical background, but as Chris Wright states has a profound theological function: "The very form of the genealogy shows the direct continuity between the Old Testament and Jesus himself . . . This continuity is based on the action of God. The God who is manifestly

---

7. All four Gospels show that Jesus fulfils the Old Testament promises regarding the coming of the Messiah. Matthew does so in particular detail because of his Jewish audience.

8. Poythress, *Shadow of Christ in the Law of Moses.*, 255.

9. Davies, *Matthew*, 51.

10. Robert Banks, *Journal of Biblical Literature* 93 (1974) 231; quoted in Morris, *Matthew*, 108 (full reference not given).

11. C. J. H. Wright, *Knowing Jesus through the Old Testament*, 55–58; cf. France, *Matthew*, 168.

involved in the events described in the second half of Matthew 1 was also active in the events implied in the first half. In Jesus he brought to completion what he himself had prepared for. This means that it is Jesus who gives meaning and validity to the events of Israel's Old Testament history. So the person who accepts therefore, the claims of this chapter about *Jesus* (that he is indeed the promised Messiah . . . etc.), also accepts its implied claim about the *history* which leads up to him."[12]

Therefore, the fulfilment here considered is fulfilment of God's special revelatory and redemptive activity in the Old Testament, it is not fulfilment of unspecified truths or general revelation that exist outside the Old Testament. Christ's fulfilment is not only the completion and transcending of a large number of specific prophecies, but at a deeper level is also the fulfilment of the entire revelatory work of God leading up to this time. R. T. France emphasizes this:

> The essential key to all Matthew's theology is that in Jesus all God's purposes have come to fulfilment. This is, of course, true of all New Testament theology, but it is emphasized in a remarkable way in Matthew. Everything is related to Jesus. The Old Testament points forward to him; its law is 'fulfilled' in his teaching; he is the true Israel through whom God's plans for his people now go forward; the future no less than the present is to be understood as the working out of the ministry of Jesus. History revolves around him, in that his coming is the turning-point at which the age of preparation gives way to the age of fulfilment. Matthew leaves no room for any idea of the fulfilment of God's purposes, whether for Israel or in any other respect, which is not focussed in this theme of *fulfilment in Jesus*. In his coming a new age has dawned; nothing will ever be quite the same again.[13]

France highlights the main options for the meaning of the term "fulfil" ($\pi\lambda\eta\rho\acute{o}\omega$) as a) to accomplish or obey; b) to bring out the full meaning; c) to complete / to bring to its destined end, by giving the final revelation of God's will to which the Old Testament pointed forward, and

---

12. C. J. H. Wright, *Knowing Jesus through the Old Testament*, 27. Cf. Herter, *Abrahamic Covenant in the Gospels*, 24–26.

13. France, *Matthew*, 38.

A Biblical, Historical, and Theological Critique of the Fulfilment Model

which now transcends it.[14] He observes that no single translation can do justice to it but that the third option "points in the right direction."[15]

I concur with France who maintains that the usage of the term in the introductory formulae of the formula-equations (and in Matt 26:54, 56), is determinative for its use here.[16] Ten times in Matthew's gospel the formula-quotations are used. These follow the standard format: "This was to fulfil (or "then was fulfilled") what was spoken by the prophet, saying . . . ," followed by a quotation from an Old Testament prophet (or in one case the Psalmist). The study of the textual peculiarities indicates, asserts France, that behind these texts

> lies some quite original and sophisticated study of the Old Testament in order to discover points of correspondence much more subtle than the direct fulfilment of clear prophetic predictions. Sometimes the subtlety results in an application of the Old Testament text which is "to our critical eyes, manifestly forced and artificial and unconvincing"; but C. F. D. Moule, goes on to argue that this "vehicular" use of Scripture "is a symptom of the discovery that, in a deeply organic way, Jesus was indeed the fulfiller of something which is basic in the whole of Scripture."[17]

Therefore, what Matthew emphasizes is that Christ is the fulfiller not only of specific predictions but also the broader pattern of God's Old Testament revelation.[18] Similarly, Grant Osborne argues "fulfil" here means that "the meaning of the Old Testament is completed by being fulfilled in Jesus; in both his deeds and his teaching he lifted the Old Testament to a higher plane. There are two ideas—he has completed or 'filled up' the meaning of the Old Testament, and he is the final interpreter of Torah.[19]

The concept of fulfilment is further elaborated in Matthew's rich use of typology. Matthew's view of Jesus as the one who fulfils the whole fabric of scriptural revelation is most strikingly brought to light

14. Ibid., 113–14.

15. Ibid., 114. Cf. Hagner, *Matthew 1–13*, 105–6.

16. France, *Matthew*, 113–14. These equations are found in: 1:22–23; 2:15; 2:17–18; 2:23; 4:14–16; 8:17; 12:17–21; 21:4–5; 27:9–10 and also 2:5–6, although the format of the latter is slightly different from the rest. Cf. Carson, *Matthew*, 143–44.

17. France, *Matthew*, 39. The reference is to C. F. D. Moule, *The Origin of Christology*, chapter 5, "The Fulfilment Theme in the New Testament" (full reference not given).

18. Ibid., 39–40.

19. Osborne, *Hermeneutical Spiral*, 333.

in the large number of "typological" allusions to the Old Testament. Although elements of typology are not restricted to Matthew, being found in many of the New Testament books, typology is particularly pronounced in Matthew.[20] Typology amplifies the conviction that as God worked in the Old Testament, so he has worked in the ministry of Jesus "and yet with a 'something greater' which makes Jesus the 'fulfilment' of the whole warp and woof of the Old Testament, not just the explicit predictions of the prophets."[21] Matthew clearly sets up a Jesus-Israel correspondence by taking texts that refer to Israel and applying them to Jesus.[22] Nowhere in the New Testament is there any attempt to establish similar correspondences with other traditions, as would be expected if the fulfilment approach to other religions is valid.

Chapter 7 of this book has shown that Paul and Luke view the Christ-event as the turning point of history. So too does Matthew. For Matthew, Christ announces the arrival of the "kingdom of heaven"[23] in which the law and prophets are fulfilled. France rightly observes that Matthew had a strong sense of the importance of history, and Christ's work of fulfilment takes place in history. "Indeed it is not easy to see quite what 'fulfilment' might mean if there is no actual history in which the pattern is fulfilled."[24] Therefore, this particular history of salvation as recounted in Old and New Testaments must be respected in any analysis of fulfilment, but this is precisely what the fulfilment model fails to do when it extends the principle beyond the Judaeo-Christian tradition. As Francis Wright Beare concludes:

> [T]he use of Mt V:17 in fulfilment theology, takes it a long way from its original context. While there is a linkage in that it was part of Matthew's attempt to portray Jesus as a fulfiller, the passage itself appears to have been inserted as a defence against

---

20. France (*Matthew*, 40) defines *typology* as "The recognition of a correspondence between New and Old Testament events, based on a conviction of the unchanging character of the principles of God's working, and a consequent understanding and description of the New Testament events in terms of the Old Testament model." He notes that "events" is too narrow since Old Testament persons and institutions come in for the same treatment.

21. Ibid., 41.

22. For a detailed treatment of Matthew's use of Israel-Jesus and Israel-Church typology, see France, *Matthew: Evangelist & Teacher*, 206–12.

23. Matt 4:17; 10:7; cf. Mark 1:15.

24. France, *Matthew: Evangelist & Teacher*, 205.

charges that the scheme Matthew presented was violating the strong Jewish taboos about altering the law. The passage was, then, originally a response to the warning in Deuteronomy, where those within the early Church were aware of the antinomy situation engendered by the need to show that Jesus was truly was, not just in accord with the Mosaic law, but holding fast to it and, on the other side, the need to present Jesus' vision of what the law really entailed.[25]

In chapter 8 I argued that the New covenant fulfils the Old covenant, but that the nature of this fulfilment is different for the various biblical covenants that constitute the Old covenant. The Abrahamic covenant, while fulfilled still has a continuing place in Christ's ongoing work. However, the Mosaic covenant is completely fulfilled in the death of Christ and ceases to have an ongoing role in salvation-history. Yet, that does not mean that the law itself has no role in the life of the New Testament believer. However, the way in which the law applies to the Christian "is determined by the authority of Christ and the fulfillment that takes place in His work."[26] As Moo explains, even if Christ's followers "are no longer bound by the commandments of the law, they are still to read and profit from it . . . It is the law *as fulfilled by Jesus* that must be done, not the law in its original form."[27]

9.1.2. Fulfilment in John's Prologue (John 1:1–14)?

John's testimony to the universal enlightening ministry of the Word (*Logos*) is widely cited in support of the fulfilment model. For example Dupuis states:

> while the Christ-event is the universal sacrament of God's will to save humankind, it need not therefore be the only possible expression of that will . . . In terms of a Trinitarian Christology,

---

25. Francis Wright Beare, *The Gospel according to Matthew: A Commentary*, 138, quoted in Hedges, *Preparation and Fulfilment*, 18.

26. Poythress, *Shadow of Christ*, 268. Cf. Carson, *Matthew*, 146 'The entire Law and the Prophets are not scrapped by Jesus' coming, but fulfilled. Therefore the commandments of these Scriptures . . . must be practiced. But the nature of the practicing has already been affected by vv.17–18. The law pointed forward to Jesus and his teaching; so it is properly obeyed by conforming to his word. As it points to him, so he, in fulfilling it, established what continuity it has, the true direction to which it points and the way it is to be obeyed.'

27. Moo, "Law of Christ as the Law of Moses," 353.

this means that the saving action of God through the nonincarnate Logos (Logos *asarkos*), of whom the Prologue of John's gospel states that he 'was the light that enlightens every human being by coming into the world' (Jn 1:9), endures after the incarnation of the Logos (Jn 1:14) . . . The mystery of the incarnation is unique; only the individual human existence of Jesus is assumed by the Son of God. But while he alone is thus constituted the 'image of God,' other 'saving figures' may be . . . 'enlightened' by the Word or 'inspired' by the Spirit, to become pointers to salvation for their followers.[28]

Such is the prominence of the *Logos* in fulfilment theology that Hedges suggests fulfilment theology cannot be fully developed in its absence.[29]

The *Logos* concept has a complex background, and its English rendering is not straightforward. F. F. Bruce states that the term "Word" is perhaps an inadequate rendering of the Greek (λόγος), but it would be difficult to find a word less inadequate.[30] The term was in common usage in some first century Greek philosophical schools, where it meant the "the principle of reason or order immanent in the universe, the principle which imposes form on the material world and constitutes the rational soul in man."[31] Kraemer describes the ancient Greek concept of *Logos* as "an expression for the cosmos as an ordered intelligible and rational whole, which was identical with God. The Logos is, therefore, at the same time the creative, constitutive principle of the world . . . and the immanent power which penetrates matter and organizes it."[32]

The background to John's usage of *Logos*, however, is not primarily the Greek concept. According to F. F. Bruce, John relies on the Old

---

28. Dupuis, *Toward a Christian Theology of Religious Pluralism*, 298. Cf. 164. Dupuis, commenting on *Nostra Aetate* writes: "Though no explicit reference is made in the official text to Jn 1:9, the allusion is unmistakable. It is the incomplete but real presence of 'that Truth' in the other religions which guides the Church's attitude of respect toward them and its wish to promote their spiritual and cultural values" (Dupuis is commenting on NA 1 and 2). Cf. 319, 328. Other examples of the use of the Logos to support fulfilment theology include Braaten, *No Other Gospel!* 69–70; and Farquhar, *Crown of Hinduism*, 27.

29. Hedges, *Preparation and Fulfilment*, 37.

30. Bruce, *Gospel of John*, 29. Bruce notes that it is wrong to equate logos with "reason," as is often done, as this is even more misleading.

31. Ibid., 29. Carson, *Gospel according to John*, 114–16.

32. Kraemer, *Religion and the Christian Faith*, 278.

A Biblical, Historical, and Theological Critique of the Fulfilment Model

Testament to provide the background for this term. Here it denotes God in action, especially in creation, revelation, and deliverance.[33] Kraemer has made the same point, suggesting that Genesis 1 and Proverbs 8, are particularly important in providing the background meaning for this concept.[34] Therefore, to equate John's use of *Logos* with Greek thought results in a misunderstanding of his Prologue.[35] This misunderstanding is, I suggest, apparent in much fulfilment theology. In John's prologue, *Logos* is Word not Reason.[36] This points to the Old Testament and is "the argument par excellence against a too simplistic use of the Johannine Logos for a *mesure commune* or formula of synthesis for philosophy and religion on one side, and revelation on the other. An adequate understanding of the New Testament Logos-idea leads to the conclusion that it is the most inappropriate *Anknüpfungspunkt* (point of contact) for Christian doctrine with Greek philosophy."[37]

This understanding of the background to the *Logos* in the prologue is reinforced by John's use of the concept in the rest of the Gospel which implies that the *Logos* he is speaking about "is that prophetic word which goes forth from God's mouth to accomplish creation, judgement, redemption and renewal. John uses *logos* because it is the natural word for expressing the meaning of the Hebrew word *dabar* when that word was used in the context of God's revelation."[38]

Bruce rightly highlights the link between the opening statement of the prologue and the start of Genesis 1, for both commence with the same phrase. In Genesis 1, "in the beginning" introduces the story of the creation; in John 1 it introduces the story of the new creation.[39] Christ

---

33. Bruce, *John*, 29 Cf. Carson, *John*, 115–17.

34. Kraemer, *Religion and the Christian Faith*, 279.

35. Ibid., 277.

36. According to A. F. Walls, the source of John's doctrine of the *Logos* "differs radically from philosophic usage. For the Greeks, Log*os* was essentially reason; for John, essentially word. Language common to Philo and the NT has led many to see John as Philo's debtor. But one refers naturally to Philo's Logos as 'It,' to John's as 'He.' Philo came no nearer than Plato to a Logos who might be incarnate, and he does not identify Logos as Messiah. John's Logos is not only God's agent in creation; He is *God*, and becomes incarnate, revealing, redeeming" (Walls, "Logos," 646).

37. Kraemer, *Religion and the Christian Faith*, 278.

38. Johnson, "Logos," 484.

39. Bruce, *John*, 28–29. Cf. Carson, *John*, 113.

is mediator of both creation and redemption.[40] The prologue focuses on the nature and function of this *Logos*, and it is clear throughout that John is making a direct connection between the pre-incarnate *Logos* and the historical Jesus. The incarnate Son of God was part of the divine reality before the incarnation (vv. 1b–2). The *Logos* is the mediating instrument of creation (v. 3), he is the source of Life and Light (v. 4).[41]

Verse 9, "The true light, which enlightens everyone, was coming into the world," is particularly important for fulfilment theology, where it is interpreted to suggest that Christ enlightens *all people without exception*. However, rather than referring to the illumination of all humankind without exception, I suggest the reference is to the illuminating work of the *Logos*, who is now coming into the world, i.e. "it is the Word, the light that is coming into the world, in some act distinct from creation."[42] Thus, John is referring here to the incarnation (cf. v.14).[43] Therefore, John is declaring that Christ is the one source of true light and "every person who finds light must find it in Christ (1:9)."[44] As C. J. H. Wright points out, the interpretation "'He was the true light who enlightens every man who comes into the world' . . . seems tautologous as a description of every man (what man doesn't)."[45]

With regard to the nature of this enlightenment, those adopting a fulfilment model take this enlightenment to refer to salvation. However, as Wright shows, this is contrary to the immediate context—and to the rest of the gospel: "If the enlightening of all humanity in verse 9 means that all already have *saving* knowledge of God, then what was the necessity or purpose of the light becoming incarnate? . . . And if all human beings are redemptively enlightened by the 'non-incarnate' Christ, why

---

40. See this volume, section 7.1.2 for elaboration.

41. Kraemer, *Religion and the Christian Faith*, 273–74.

42. Carson, *John*, 122.

43. Bruce writes "The participial phrase 'coming into the world' might be attached grammatically either to 'light' or to 'human being.' But 'coming into the world' is repeatedly predicated in this Gospel of him who is the eternal Word and the true light. It is from this true light that all genuine illumination proceeds. Whatever measure of truth men and women in all ages have apprehended has been derived from this source." Bruce, *John*, 35.

44. Ladd, *Theology of the New Testament*, 252. Ladd adds, "'Every person' is potential, not actual" (252 n. 1).

45. C. J. H. Wright, "The Christian and Other Religions," 12 n. 24.

do some reject the light of the incarnate Christ, preferring darkness, and therefore expose themselves to God's judgement (Jn 1:10f; 3:19f)?"[46]

Indeed, even among "his own"—Jesus' Jewish contemporaries—who had been recipients of God's light of special covenantal revelation—many rejected him (v. 11). As Kraemer states: "The consequence of the Fall is that man (contrary to his assertions and assumptions) does not recognize God when he meets God, but on the contrary ignores or rejects Him."[47] The prologue testifies to the enlightening ministry of the *Logos*, but this enlightenment is knowledge of God available universally through general revelation. All genuine illumination proceeds from this *Logos* and whatever measure of truth men and women in all ages have apprehended has been derived from this source.[48] The fact that Christ is the agent of this enlightenment does not mean it is redemptive.[49] In his commentary on John, Calvin offers a helpful assessment of the nature and function of this universal light: "For we know that men have this particular excellence which raises them above other animals, that they are endued with reason and intelligence, and that they carry the distinction between right and wrong engraven on their conscience. There is no man, therefore, whom some perception of the eternal *light* does not reach."[50]

I have stated that the fulfilment model misunderstands the *function* of the *Logos*. The model also misrepresents the *medium* of its operation by presenting it as operative in other religions. Paul Hedges' study of fulfilment theology argues that "From this symbolism of light [in John's Prologue], with Jesus as the Light of the World, came the commonly used expression of 'broken lights' to refer to non-Christian religions."[51] The Anglican Board of Mission and Unity report, *Towards a Theology for Inter-Faith Dialogue* presents other religions as manifestations of the *Logos*:

> While 'Logos Theology' understands the unique expression of God as being in Jesus Christ (there can be no surrendering of that

---

46. C. J. H. Wright, *Thinking Clearly about the Uniqueness of Jesus*, 127. Cf. Shenk, *Who Do You Say That I Am?* 100.
47. Kraemer, *Religion and the Christian Faith*, 274.
48. Bruce, *John*, 35
49. C. J. H. Wright, "The Christian and Other Religions," 12.
50. Calvin, *Calvin, Commentary on the Gospel of John*, 38.
51. Hedges, *Preparation and Fulfilment*, 20.

belief), at the same time it takes seriously other manifestations of the *logos* in other places and at other times. This suggests that in relations with those of other faiths, Christians have to hold to that unique self-expressive activity of God in Jesus Christ, self-guarded and passed down within the Christian Church. But equally Christians need to be open to recognise and respond to all manifestations of the *logos*. The decisive revelation of God in Jesus has to be safe-guarded, for that is the canon by which we are enabled to recognise all other manifestations. Furthermore, in the encountering of those other revelations, new depths are discovered in that fullest revelation of God in Jesus Christ. Such reflection on the mystery of the person of Jesus in the Bible and Tradition points in the direction of an inclusivism in relation to those of other faiths, but with an unswerving loyalty to Jesus Christ.[52]

With Wright, I suggest that such use of *Logos* theology goes far beyond what John says in his prologue and is incompatible with it:

> There is so much in this paragraph about "other manifestations of the Logos in other places and at other times" that a reader might take this as the self-evident gist of John's Logos theme. But it is decidedly not so. Two assertions are made about the universal role of the Logos in John's Prologue. One is his part in the creation of all things and all people . . . The other aspect is that, as Light, the Logos enlightens every human being (v 9) . . . Then, against this background of the universal creating and universal enlightening roles of the Logos, John moves on to speak of the one and only actual manifestation proper of the Logos—namely the incarnation of the "one and only" Son of God: "The Logos became flesh" (v 14). A unique, historical, particular, personally witnessed incarnation is the only mode of "manifestation of the Logos" to be found in John's prologue, so unless we are willing to postulate other alleged incarnations as parallels or analogous to Jesus, we should not use John to accredit the idea of "other manifestations of the Logos," or "other revelations." Such ideas are simply not present here, still less that in being open to such "revelations" we might discover new depths in the fulness of Christ's revelation of the Father. This constitutes such a radical modification (if not logical contradiction) of the uniqueness of the Incarnation.[53]

---

52. Church of England General Synod Board for Mission and Unity, *Theology for Inter-Faith Dialogue*, 18–19.

53. C. J. H. Wright, "Inter Faith Dialogue," 244.

A Biblical, Historical, and Theological Critique of the Fulfilment Model

Kraemer makes the important observation that in the Bible the primary purpose of the *Logos* concept is *not* an endeavor to deal with the question of the relationship of Christianity to other religions. It is rather "an attempt to allude to the ultimate, divine background of life, history and the universe, and to express Christ's cosmic significance, his place in the Godhead, or, to say it in classical, post-biblical terms, in the *oikonomia* (household) of the Trinity, as turned to the world."[54]

Kraemer contends that a misuse of the *Logos* theology has contributed to false notions of continuity between other religions and Christianity, such that the religions are seen as preparation for Christianity. However, John's Prologue "is peculiarly unfit to have put upon it the constructions which have been used in relation to it, since Justin Martyr . . . In other words, the age-long recourse to this classical passage as the scriptural basis or justification to interpret all non-Christian religion and philosophy as *praeparatio evangelica*, to evaluate them accordingly and to take their so-called 'best and highest elements' as indications that they are well on the road to Christ, needs drastic revision."[55]

I maintain therefore that John is writing here about the enlightening of people—as people, *not* about the possibility of light within non-Christian religions. Thus, the suggestion that the light has shone through other religious leaders or founders is not supported by this text. "It is not talking about special light of a religious nature to be found in special people, but about universal light that every human being everywhere shares simply by being human."[56] To speak of the *Logos* as a kind of cosmic and somewhat abstract "Christ principle" which is present in other great religious traditions is therefore not supported by John's

---

54. Kraemer, *Religion and the Christian Faith*, 260. Newbigin similarly cautions against viewing religions as manifestations of the *Logos*: "[T]his assumption has to be questioned. When the New Testament affirms that God has nowhere left himself without witness, there is no suggestion that this witness is necessarily to be found in the sphere of what we call religion . . . When the Fourth Gospel affirms that the light of the Logos who came into the world in Jesus shines on every human being, there is no suggestion that this light is identified with human religion" (Newbigin, *Gospel in a Pluralist Society*, 172–73).

55. Kraemer, *Religion and the Christian Faith*, 276. He adds here "Perhaps one is even forced to say that this classical interpretation of the Logos-idea is an error, a misinterpretation of the Biblical data." In section 9.2 I consider Justin Martyr's understanding of the *Logos*.

56. C. J. H. Wright, *Thinking Clearly about the Uniqueness of Jesus*, 128.

Prologue.[57] The narrative sections in the Prologue serve as a reminder that John is not simply stating abstract timeless truths, but is concerned to show how these truths are anchored in human history.[58] Therefore, a *Logos* separated from the incarnate Christ becomes an abstraction.[59] To avoid abstraction, the incarnate Jesus must more fully define and illuminate the *Logos*.[60] However, the formulation of *Logos* theology in the fulfilment model undermines the connection between salvation and the historical revelation of Jesus Christ.

9.1.3. Fulfilment in Acts (10:34–35; 14:16–17; 17:30–31)

I have dealt extensively with the texts from Acts 14 and Acts 17 in section 7.2 of this work and will not rehearse the arguments again here. The conclusions I presented regarding the nature of the former religions and their relationship to Christianity, apply to Acts 10 also, and due to space constraints I will not elaborate in detail here. Suffice it to state that the conclusion reached in these earlier accounts is that that these passages should not be used as evidence of a positive assessment of non-Christian religions, nor should these religions be presented as preparations awaiting fulfilment in Christ. In chapter 9, I will consider whether non-Christian religions can act as "preparations" and "points of contact."

9.1.4. Fulfilment in Galatians 3:24[61]

Paul's statement in Galatians 3:24: "So the law was put in charge to lead us to Christ" (Gal 3:24 NIV) is interpreted by the fulfilment model as an indication that other religions act as various preparations that lead their followers to Christ.[62] Together with Matthew 5:17 this is, suggests

---

57. Ibid., 131.

58. Bruce, *John*, 34.

59. Indeed, this is one of the concerns raised in the Vatican's "Notification" on Dupuis' *Toward a Christian Theology of Religious Pluralism*. See section 2.1.5 of the current volume for elaboration.

60. Shenk, *Who Do You Say That I Am?* 100. Cf. Bardley, "Logos Christology and Religious Pluralism," 202. Here Bradley challenges Pinnock's use of Logos theology to support his inclusivist paradigm.

61. The reader should refer to section 8.3.2 of this volume for further discussion of this passage.

62. While proponents of fulfilment do not always explicitly state this verse as the source of the concept of pedagogy is almost certainly borrowed from this text. The

A Biblical, Historical, and Theological Critique of the Fulfilment Model

Hedges, the most important text used to justify fulfilment theology.[63] A key term here is παιδαγωγός, often taken to mean "schoolmaster" or "teacher," but more properly understood as a slave of the ancient world who prepared his master's son for adulthood by teaching him all the skills considered to be customarily necessary. When the son was proficient, he was ready to be officially adopted into his birth family.[64]

The fulfilment model misconstrues this text in two important ways. First, it treats the "preparation" or *paidagōgos* in existential terms, suggesting that individual followers of other religions may be being directed to Christ through their religion. However, such an interpretation does not sit well with the salvation-historical orientation of Paul's theology (see section 7.2.2). Douglas Moo identifies the weakness of an existential interpretation. He notes how the verse is often translated and interpreted (as in the NIV) to infer that the law was given to show people their need of God and so lead them to Christ. This interpretation cannot account for the full meaning of the text, firstly because a salvation-historical perspective dominates Galatians 3–4, and especially 3:15—4:7. The context is the *historia salutis,* not the *ordo salutis*: "Paul is not speaking of the experience of individuals with the law, but of the purpose of the law in the history of the people of Israel. Consequently, the first person plural ('us') probably refers to Paul and his fellow Jews, not Paul and his fellow Christians."[65]

Secondly, the telic interpretation "to lead us to Christ," (as in the NIV) is, judges Moo, not justified, because temporal statements provide the context for Verse 24 ("before faith came" v.23; "now that faith has come" v.25). This temporal context makes it likely that *eis* in v.24 also has a temporal meaning: "the law was our custodian *until* Christ came." Furthermore, *paidagōgos* does not suggest the notion of instruction that leads to Christ (as in the KJV). As I have already noted, *paidagōgos* denotes a person, usually a servant, who had charge over young children. It was, judges Moo, a babysitter rather than a teacher. Thus, Galatians 3:24 is asserting that the Mosaic law functioned among the people of

---

only other usage of the term in the New Testament is in 1 Cor 4:15, where it is applied to the Mosaic law, "as dealing with men as in a state of mere childhood and tutelage" (Mounce, *Analytical Lexicon to the Greek New Testament*, 348).

63. Hedges, *Preparation and Fulfilment*, 19.
64. Corduan, *Tapestry of Faiths*, 87–88.
65. Moo, "Law of Christ as the Law of Moses," 338.

Israel to direct their behavior until the time of their maturity when the promised messiah would be revealed.[66] This is important, for there is nothing in this text to suggest a wider pedagogy principle is warranted beyond Old Testament Judaism.

A further weakness of the fulfilment model's use of this verse is the potential it affords to non-Christian religions in the economy of salvation. However, this verse does not credit even the Old Testament law with this function. "It is not possible" contends Richard Longenecker, "to interpret Gal 3:24-25 as assigning a positive or preparatory role to the Law. The point of the analogy for Paul is not that the Law was a preparation for Christ. Rather, the focus is on the inferior status of one who is under a pedagogue and the temporary nature of such a situation."[67]

This interpretation is reinforced by Paul's teaching in Galatians 4:1–7, where he again presents his argument in salvation-historical terms. Paul is teaching that the guardianship of the Mosaic Law was for a period only, "but now with the coming of Christ the time set by the Father has been fulfilled and Christians are to live freely as mature sons apart from the Law's supervision."[68] Thus, "until Christ came" (3:24) emphasizes that Paul is speaking here of the temporal sense of the law: "For the immediate context makes it clear that Paul is speaking of successive periods in salvation history, first that of the reign of the law and then that associated with the coming of Christ—with the first being displaced by the second (cf. vv 23 and 25)."[69]

Thus this verse refers explicitly and exclusively to the place of Old Testament law in the economy of salvation, and it is not possible to extend the principle of pedagogy established here to other religions or to any period after the Christ-event as the fulfilment model does.

9.2. The Early Church Fathers and Fulfilment Theology

Proponents of the fulfilment model suggest the early Church had a much more open-minded view of non-Christian religions than has been the

---

66. Ibid., 338. Cf. Guthrie, *Galatians*, 114.
67. Longenecker, "Pedagogical Nature of the Law," 55–56.
68. Ibid., 57.
69. Longenecker, *Galatians*, 149. Cf. Bruce, *Epistle to the Galatians*, 183.

A Biblical, Historical, and Theological Critique of the Fulfilment Model

dominant view since.[70] This open-mindedness is attributed in part to the suggestion that the Church Fathers advocated an early form of the fulfilment model. However, interpretations of the Fathers on this issue vary considerably and the assertion that they represent forerunners of the fulfilment model, or had a more inclusive understanding of the relationship between Christianity and other religions will be disputed here. The focus of the following discussion will be on the work of Justin Martyr for he is most often cited in relation to the fulfilment model, and is arguably the most misunderstood or misused in this context and is arguable "the most important of the Greek apologists."[71]

The early Church developed in the context of two dominant ideologies—the Jewish and the Graeco-Roman worldviews. In this context, Christians had to defend both the novelty and exclusivity of their religion. This defense was no mere academic exercise but often became a matter of survival.[72] The early apologists were Gentiles writing primarily to fellow Gentiles (particularly the intelligentsia and officialdom) with the aim of persuading them of the reasonableness of Christianity.[73] While evidence of any success is scant, their success was more in the provision for the Church of "an intellectually respectable apologetic in the face of a dominant paganism."[74] This apologetic aim greatly influenced their method and should be borne in mind when drawing conclusions from their writings and applying them to the subject of a contemporary theology of religions.[75]

---

70. I have previously given examples of some of the writings of the Church Fathers which are commonly cited in support of the fulfilment model, and I refer the reader back to this section (section 1.3) for these details.

71. Dupuis, *Toward a Christian Theology of Religious Pluralism*, 56. Hedges' study of fulfilment theology concurs: 'Far and away the most significant figure in this regard is Justin Martyr.' Hedges, *Preparation and Fulfilment*, 21. Cf. Chadwick, *Early Christian Thought and the Classical Tradition*, 9. Chadwick suggests "of all the early Christian theologians Justin is the most optimistic about the harmony of Christianity and Greek philosophy" (Chadwick, *Early Christian Thought*, 10). Space prohibits a full assessment of the other Church Fathers cited in section 1.3.

72. Keith, "Justin Martyr and Religious Exclusivism," 162–63. Cf. Kraemer, *Religion and the Christian Faith*, 147–49.

73. Bray, "Explaining Christianity to Pagans," 10.

74. Ibid.

75. Price, "Are There 'Holy Pagans' in Justin Martyr?" 171. "[I]t is a fundamental error to seize on statements made in the context of a particular argument by Justin or the other Apologists and read them as dogmatic statements . . . What we have is a

The challenges that faced the early Christians are not identical to the challenges facing Christians today seeking to understand the relationship of Christianity to other religions. The Church Fathers did not write early "theologies of religions"—their writings are primarily the "writings of 'pastors' and preachers, and they addressed the questions of their own day."[76] An important difference between their theological context and that of the contemporary theological milieu concerns the vexed question of the "fate of the unevangelised." While it is clearly apparent today that a significant section of the world population (arguably the majority, if the entire history of humankind is under consideration) can be classed as "unevangelized," this was not apparent to the early Christians, who believed the Gospel had been propagated successfully to the entire known world.[77] With this qualification in mind I will proceed to examine the contribution of Justin Martyr and some of the other early apologists to the topic.

Contemporary scholars who wish to present Justin as an early proponent of fulfilment theology (or inclusivism generally), typically highlight Justin's description of some people who did not know Christ, but who were nevertheless described by him as "Christians." They also refer to his grouping of some Old Testament saints along with pagans, who Justin said, "lived according to the *Logos*." The text most often cited in this regard reads: "We have been taught that Christ is the first-born of God, and we have declared above that He is the Word of whom every race of men were partakers; and those who lived reasonably are Christians, even though they have been thought atheists; as, among the Greeks, Socrates and Heraclitus, and men like them; and among the

---

group of apologetic texts that need to be interpreted according to the conventions of the genre, which was less philosophical than forensic, and aimed less at sincerity than plausibility. It is to the history of Christian rhetoric rather than of Christian doctrine that Justin and the other Greek Apologists belong."

76. Saldanha, *Divine Pedagogy*, 33. Cf. Netland, *Encountering Religious Pluralism*, 252.

77. Justin thought every nation had heard the gospel: "For there is not one single race of men, whether barbarians, or Greeks, or whatever they may be called, nomads, or vagrants, or herdsmen living in tents, among whom prayers and giving of thanks are not offered through the name of the crucified Jesus" (*Dialogue with Trypho*, 117). Similarly, according to Tiessen, Irenaeus "had no concept of the unreached, who loom so large in our own attempts to understand the prospect of salvation for people today. Irenaeus believed that the world had been evangelized in the time of the apostles. (AH IV, 36,5; cf. IV,39,3)" ("Tiessen, "Irenaeus on the Salvation of the Unevangelized," 2).

barbarians, Abraham, and Ananias, and Azarias, and Misael, and Elias, and many others whose actions and names we now decline to recount, because we know it would be tedious."[78]

This text is taken by proponents of the fulfilment model as an indication of Justin's openness to, and positive assessment of other religions and ideologies. However, this interpretation seriously misrepresents Justin's views for the following reasons.

First, the title "atheist" was in the prevailing Graeco-Roman worldview given to all who did not acknowledge the existence of the customary deities and thus the title applied to *Christians* as well as the philosophers referred to by Justin, such as Socrates.[79] Justin offers a nuanced use of the title:

> Hence are we called atheists. And we confess that we are atheists, so far as gods of this sort are concerned, but not with respect to the most true God, the Father of righteousness and temperance and the other virtues, who is free from all impurity. But both Him, and the Son (who came forth from Him and taught us these things, and the host of the other good angels who follow and are made like to Him), and the prophetic Spirit, we worship and adore, knowing them in reason and truth, and declaring without grudging to every one who wishes to learn, as we have been taught.[80]

Thus, in referring to Socrates and others as "atheists" Justin is merely stating they had something significant in common with Christians. Justin viewed pagan religions as demonic in origin and was very critical of idol worship.[81] Socrates and others were commended by Justin for recognizing the true nature of the pagan religions—namely, they were evil superstitions.[82] Indeed, Socrates was executed because he attempted to expose the true nature of pagan religion.[83] According

---

78. Justin Martyr *1 Apology* 46: "Lived reasonably" is a translation of μετα λογου, "with reason," or "with the Word."

79. Sigountos, "Did Early Christians Believe Pagan Religions Could Save?" 234. Cf. Saldanha, *Divine Pedagogy*, 45. The reasons for the Philosophers rejection of the customary deities will be discussed below.

80. *1 Apology* 6.

81. *1 Apology* 5. Saldanha notes that Justin's criticism was rooted in his understanding of Scripture even if he did not always quote it. Saldanha, *Divine Pedagogy*, 46.

82. *2 Apology* 10.

83. Price, "Are There 'Holy Pagans' in Justin Martyr?" 168. Here Price cites Xenophon *Memorabilia*, 1.1.1, which reports that Socrates was convicted by his fellow

to Sigountos, the early Christian apologists were "unremittingly negative" in their attacks on pagan religion.[84] They attacked these beliefs and practices in lengthy treatises which were often vitriolic and mocking in character, but which "reflect a deeper and more philosophical rejection of all existing non-Christian religions, one that Christians took over from their past."[85] Early Christians inherited the attitude of Second Temple Judaism towards other religions, namely that worship of any other God than the God of Scripture constituted idolatry.[86]

While Justin recognized certain parallels or analogies between some Christian and Pagan beliefs, this recognition should not be seen primarily as an affirmation of the truth of the latter, rather, it was an apologetic device to support Justin's assertion that Christians should be treated fairly by the authorities, as the pagans were. Justin writes

> If, therefore, on some points we teach the same things as the poets and philosophers whom you honour, and on other points are fuller and more divine in our teaching, and if we alone afford proof of what we assert, why are we unjustly hated more than all others? For while we say that all things have been produced and arranged into a world by God, we shall seem to utter the doctrine of Plato; and while we say that there will be a burning up of all, we shall seem to utter the doctrine of the Stoics: and while we affirm that the souls of the wicked, being endowed with sensation even after death, are punished, and that those of the good being delivered from punishment spend a blessed existence, we shall seem to say the same things as the poets and philosophers; and while we maintain that men ought not to worship the works of their hands, we say the very things which have been said by the comic poet Menander, and other similar writers, for they have declared that the workman is greater than the work.[87]

Thus, drawing parallels between Christian truth and truths found in pagan culture was a way to assert the supremacy of Christian truth. Kraemer explains that the Apologists' method of arguing for the intellectual and spiritual respectability and superiority of Christianity was to

---

Athenians for "refusing to recognize the gods the city recognizes and introducing new divinities."

84. Sigountos, "Did Early Christians Believe Pagan Religions Could Save?" 231.
85. Ibid.
86. Ibid.
87. *1 Apology* 20.

try to demonstrate that this new religion was not contrary to "the highest ideals of the existing culture, but confirmed, transformed and perfected the most precious conquests of philosophy, as then understood."[88] Similarly, Timothy Tennent suggests that for Justin "Greek philosophy became a tool to turn people away from the worship of false gods and to prepare them to receive the gospel of Jesus Christ, who alone is the fullness of *logos*."[89]

Justin's recognition of some partial truths in non-Christian religions is based partly on his understanding of the *Logos* (see below for discussion of the *Logos* in Justin's theology) but also on the conviction that some of the truths within Greek philosophy had been plagiarized from the Old Testament. Justin writes:

> And so, too, Plato, when he says, 'The blame is his who chooses, and God is blameless,' took this from the prophet Moses and uttered it. For Moses is more ancient than all the Greek writers. And whatever both philosophers and poets have said concerning the immortality of the soul, or punishments after death, or contemplation of things heavenly, or doctrines of the like kind, they have received such suggestions from the prophets as have enabled them to understand and interpret these things. And hence there seem to be seeds of truth among all men; but they are charged with not accurately understanding [the truth] when they assert contradictories.[90]

Justin also ascribes some of the scriptural parallels identified in Greek philosophy to demonic forces, who had created these parallels to confuse those seeking the truth.[91]

---

88. Kraemer, *Religion and the Christian Faith*, 147–48.

89. Tennent, *Christianity at the Religious Roundtable*, 202. Cf. Keith, "Justin Martyr and Religious Exclusivism," 172. Keith writes: "Effectively Justin has adopted a positive attitude to pagan glimmerings of the truth, not so much to praise aspects of Hellenistic culture as to boost the status of Christian revelation. He wanted to encourage those who already highly prized the pearl of Greek culture to discover a pearl of considerably greater worth elsewhere."

90. Justin Martyr, *1 Apology*, 44. This claim is also made by other Church Fathers such as Eusebius (see *Preparation for the Gospel*, 14.1.1–3). Eusebius suggests anything of value in Greek philosophy has been borrowed from the Bible. He suggests a number of times that Plato all but directly translated sections of the Hebrew Scriptures. See *Preparation for the Gospel*, 11–14.

91. Keith, "Justin Martyr and Religious Exclusivism," 173–74.

"Though there were some myths that doubtlessly showed some similarity with the tenor of the Biblical teaching, yet this could not entice them to milder judgement. On the contrary, they were convinced that in these cases the devil had patterned them after the beliefs of Israel for immunizing people against the influence of Christian faith."[92]

A second reason why Justin is misrepresented by the fulfilment model concerns his use of the title "Christian" in referring to Socrates and Heraclitus along with Abraham and other Old Testament characters. Justin uses this title for two main reasons. The first reason is related to the previous point—that is, it is because Justin sees the situations of these characters as in some way parallel to that of Christians in his own day. The philosophers listed had opposed idolatry, and suffered as a consequence. This is clear from the reasons Justin offers for listing Socrates as a Christian—namely he has taught others to reject the demonic deception of the customary deities and to become acquainted with the God who was unknown to them.[93] Justin is innovative in seeking common ground between Christianity and the culture in which he lived.[94] He claimed that "Whatever things were rightly said among all men, are the property of us Christians."[95] Keith highlights two possible interpretations of this claim: First, Justin could be interpreted as being very generous in his appraisal of non-Christian culture and philosophy. Second, Justin is "attempting to place Christianity on the intellectual map without much real interest in a theological assessment of other cultures."[96] Keith favors the second interpretation, and I believe he is right to do so given the apologetic thrust to Justin's writings, which must be recognized if they are to be interpreted correctly. The apologist's task was to rebut objections from different, even mutually opposed sources, and therefore, states Eric Osborn, "We must expect what Justin says to one of his audiences might conflict with what he says elsewhere. In face of pagan polytheism, he will identify the Christian position with that of the philosopher and the Jew who have denied the popular gods and followed reason. In face of philosophers and Jews, he will insist on the

---

92. Bavinck, "General Revelation and the Non-Christian Religions," 43.
93. *2 Apology*, 10.
94. Keith, "Justin Martyr and Religious Exclusivism," 164.
95. *2 Apology*, 13.
96. Keith, "Justin Martyr and Religious Exclusivism," 165.

difference between the logos they have known and the whole divine logos which is Christ."⁹⁷

Therefore Justin was not attempting a comprehensive theological assessment of non-Christian ideologies. Keith concedes that even if Justin did consider Socrates and others to be Christians in the full sense of the title, Justin failed to provide the sort of evidence necessary to prove that they were righteous in any biblical sense.⁹⁸

Henry Chadwick argues that Justin considered Socrates to be a Christian on the ground that "all rational beings share in the universal Logos or Reason who is Christ."⁹⁹ However, I believe Chadwick is wrong here, and concur with Gerald Bray who explains that while it is true that Justin considered that all could partake of the *Logos*, that is *not* the reason why Socrates could be called a Christian.¹⁰⁰ A Christian was one who lived by reason, but this is not the same thing as being a rational creature. Bray points out that Chadwick has made an important omission here—he has not taken into account the reality of sin in Justin's thought, "which entails humankind's enslavement to demonic forces that prevent them from realizing the goal of their creation."¹⁰¹ Justin was well aware of this reality and "lamented the fact that the ideal of a truly rational existence was unattainable after the fall."¹⁰² Justin suggested that Socrates had some knowledge of the *Logos*—but this was only a limited knowledge—this being all the innate *Logos* could reveal to a person without the revelation of the gospel. Thus, Socrates and Heraclitus "were honorary Christians, not because they were philosophers, but because they were persecuted for their lack of belief in the

---

97. Osborn, "Justin Martyr and the *Logos Spermatikos*," 146–47.

98. Keith, "Justin Martyr and Religious Exclusivism," 173. While seeking "evidence" to "prove" the righteousness of anyone is perhaps misdirected, the point is established that far too much is made of Justin's description of these characters as "Christians."

99. Chadwick, *Early Christian Thought*, 16.

100. Bray, "Explaining Christianity," 19.

101. Ibid.

102. Ibid. See *1 Apology*, 10: "For as in the beginning He created us when we were not, so do we consider that, in like manner, those who choose what is pleasing to Him are, on account of their choice, deemed worthy of incorruption and of fellowship with Him. For the coming into being at first was not in our own power; and in order that we may follow those things which please Him, choosing them by means of the rational faculties He has Himself endowed us with, He both persuades us and leads us to faith."

pagan theological system."[103] Furthermore, as Wright observes, it was not the Greek religion that was a manifestation of the *Logos*—but on the contrary, it was those who saw its inadequacy and rejected it that lived according to the *Logos*: "This is not properly acknowledged by those who want to make Justin the patron saint of modern inclusivism."[104] Therefore, Justin did *not* suggest that sincere worshippers of non-Christian deities are Christians or are saved. He merely affirms that some throughout human history have exposed the demonic deception of pagan religion.[105]

The second reason for Justin describing Abraham, Socrates and others as "Christians" is as a way of demonstrating that Christianity was not completely novel. This was vital to Justin's apologetic because the Christian faith was opposed or rejected partly because it was seen to be such a recent novelty.[106] However, on the contrary, Justin considered the *Logos* of the Christian faith to be ancient. Although Justin believed the *Logos* was only fully manifested in the historical incarnation, he also maintained this same *Logos* was active before the incarnation, throughout history.[107] In naming Abraham and others from the Old Testament, Justin is keen to establish the link between Christianity and Judaism. Bray explains: "The first and most fundamental line of attack that the Apologists used was their conviction that Christianity, which was directly dependent on its Jewish predecessor, was a more ancient religion that anything known to the Greeks, whose best ideas had all been cribbed from the Old Testament."[108]

Kraemer asserts that in his *Apologia* and his *Dialogue with Trypho* Justin presented Christianity as the true philosophy.[109] His assertion is based on the conviction that the facts of Christ's life and work were predicted by the prophets and the fulfilment of the prophecies guarantees the validity of Christ's claims.[110] His *Dialogue with Trypho* makes

---

103. Ibid.19–20. Cf. 2 *Apology* 10.
104. C. J. H. Wright, *Thinking Clearly about the Uniqueness of Jesus*, 130.
105. Sigountos, "Did Early Christians Believe Pagan Religions Could Save?" 233.
106. Tennent, *Christianity at the Religious Roundtable*, 202.
107. Ibid.
108. Bray, "Explaining Christianity," 11.
109. Kraemer, *Religion and the Christian Faith*, 148.
110. Ibid. Cf. Tennent, *Christianity at the Religious Roundtable*, 199. Tennent notes that after his conversion Justin was fascinated by the Hebrew prophets and how they

A Biblical, Historical, and Theological Critique of the Fulfilment Model

the case that Judaism is inferior to Christianity and had been intended solely as a preparation for Christianity, which had now supplanted Judaism.[111]

A third reason for suggesting Justin is misinterpreted by the fulfilment model concerns the applicability of some of Justin's arguments to the current age. Even if it is conceded that "living according to the *Logos*" can be interpreted as representing true Christian faith (and I have argued it should not be), the figures cited by Justin (such as Socrates, Heraclitus, Abraham and others) lived *before* Christ and Justin nowhere suggests that anyone living "according to the *Logos*" in his own day (and by extension in the current age) could be saved on this basis. Indeed, Justin considered that even the Jews of his day needed to believe that Jesus was the Messiah to be saved.[112] Keith rightly states: "He [Justin] was never seriously suggesting that anyone of his own day should look into Plato's teaching in order to attain salvation. He may have been prepared to say that Socrates and others from the past who lived with *logos* would be saved. But they were all figures from past history. Justin gave no hint that his broader hope was to be extended to people of his own day who were not professing Christians. It did not apply to unbelieving Jews, however carefully they observed the Mosaic Law."[113]

Saldanha recognizes the problem of chronology here and concedes that the Fathers considered divine pedagogy to operate in the *pre-Advent* dispensation, and with the dawning of the Advent the goal of the educative process was now fully present and complete. However, Saldanha does not believe that post-Advent the religions have lost their educative role in the economy of salvation. He considers it valid to view modern day religions as (he alleges) the fathers saw Greek philosophy—that is, as a providential pedagogy. He refers to Heinz Schlette, who argues that

---

prepared for and were fulfilled by Christ. Justin addresses this subject particularly in *1 Apology* 53–59.

111. Saldanha, *Divine Pedagogy*, 44.

112. Keith, "Justin Martyr and Religious Exclusivism," 171. See *Dialogue With Trypho*, 45–47. Keith points out that Justin considers that Jews in Old Testament times who were faithful to the law would be saved, but in New Testament times those who were faithful to the law would not be saved unless they believed Jesus was the Christ. Keith identifies a weakness in Justin's argument here, namely, that this implies that obedience of the law is sufficient for salvation in one period but not in another. He suggests Justin has not sufficiently grasped the link between law and gospel.

113. Ibid., 172.

the educative action to Christ in Greek philosophy was recognized only *post factum*—after its actual fulfilment in Christianity.[114] On this basis Saldanha suggests the fulfilment of other religions may only be realized in the future.

> It is not from a *material* point of view that the attempt is made to apply the patristic concept of 'pedagogy to Christ' to today's religions of the world, for while the latter bear certain similarities to Greek philosophy . . . there are also real and enormous differences as well. The viewpoint is rather of a *formal* kind. In a vision of the world and its history centred on Christ, all religions stand in some kind of relationship to Him; consequently, what is predicated of the relationship of Greek philosophy to Christ or Christianity can likewise be admitted, in principle, in the case of all other religions.[115]

For Saldanha the key is in understanding the nature of the *parousia* ("coming of the Lord"), which although referring to the coming of Christ in the flesh is according to Saldanha, not limited to this fleshly incarnation. Saldanha argues that the fathers saw the Church as the continuation of Christ's presence in history and it is now through the Church that Jesus Christ calls people to salvation.[116] Thus, until an existential encounter with the gospel occurs, other religions retain their divine educative role. "For the non-Christian religions of today . . . Christ has not yet come, and therefore, the term 'pedagogy to Christ' best describes their position within the economy of salvation insofar as it brings out their pre-Christian and pro-Christian character."[117]

However, such a view fails to recognize the universal significance of the Christ-event for all space and time and for all people living both before and after this event. The Christ-event constitutes the centre of salvation-history, and it marks a radical turn, a crisis point rendering the "BC period" complete and fulfilled. A new situation has been created objectively in history independent of the circumstances of indi-

---

114. Saldanha, *Divine Pedagogy*, 168. The reference is to Schlette, *Towards a Theology of Religions*, 100–104.

115. Saldanha, *Divine Pedagogy*, 168.

116. Ibid., 169. I have earlier argued that the extension of the incarnation to the Church is due to a failure in Roman Catholic theology to sufficiently distinguish between *hapax* and *mallon*. See section 7.1.3 of the current volume.

117. Ibid., 170.

A Biblical, Historical, and Theological Critique of the Fulfilment Model

viduals. (I have argued this at length in chapter 7, and refer to the reader to that chapter.)

My fourth reason for suggesting Justin is misinterpreted by the fulfilment model is the observation that many who use Justin in support of this model fail to distinguish between how Justin views *religion* and how he views *philosophy*. Proponents of the fulfilment model (and critics of exclusivism in general), in their attempt to demonstrate the open-mindedness of the early Church towards other *religions*, often refer to sections of the work of the Church Fathers dealing *not* with religion, but with *philosophy*. These insights are then applied, without due qualification, to contemporary religions. Justin and the other early apologists were much more positive about Greek philosophy than pagan religion.[118] As already noted, Justin viewed other religions as idolatrous, and of demonic origin. He did not recognize them as being of any salvific value.[119] Rather, they resulted in evil in the present world and punishment in the next.[120] Justin dismisses pagan religions parallels to Christianity as demonic,[121] but is more positive about parallels to the truth in other spheres of culture.[122] The validity of the distinction drawn between religion and philosophy was questioned by some of Justin's contemporaries, such as Celsus and it continues to provoke debate.[123] Keith questions whether the distinction is facile, but concedes that "Justin was surely justified in making some distinction between the specifically religious and the purely cultural."[124]

Moreover, although Justin was more positive about Greek philosophy than Greek religion, this philosophy was not accepted *en bloc*,

---

118. Ibid., 51.

119. Sigountos, "Did Early Christians Believe Pagan Religions Could Save?" 234.

120. Ibid., 233–34.

121. According to Saldanha, Justin did not discern truth in the heathen analogies to Christianity: "they were all concoctions of the demons . . . There could not possibly be any divine educative activity here, leading people to Christ, but only the power of evil, holding them in the bonds of slavery" (ibid., 50).

122. Keith, "Justin Martyr and Religious Exclusivism," 174.

123. Keith writes "In Celsus' mind pagan religion and Greek philosophy formed and indissoluble whole which could not be put asunder. To state otherwise was to reveal a gross misunderstanding of the Greek tradition, and Celsus was at heart convinced that Christians were extreme simpletons" ("Justin Martyr and Exclusivism," 175; original references to Celsus are not given by Keith).

124. Ibid., 174–77, 182.

but is carefully sifted by him.[125] Bray accepts that Justin is the most positive of the apologists towards Greek philosophy, but he argues that Chadwick—along with majority of modern scholars "has reconstructed a picture of Justin's relationship to pagan philosophy that is altogether too positive and encouraging. What he and others have ignored is Justin's strong insistence on the reality of corruption, induced as often as not by demonic forces, which has obscured the light of natural reason, and rendered the attempts of pagan intellectuals to recover it null and void."[126]

A fifth reason Justin is misconstrued by the fulfilment model is due to the erroneous assessment of the role of the *Logos* in Justin's theology by this model. The general concept of the *Logos* was well known in the ancient world, being used in a variety of ways in the writings of Platonists, Stoics and Hellenistic Jews. The background to Justin's use of the concept is the subject of much debate, and has resulted in diverse assessments of Justin's appraisal of the potential of the *Logos*. D. M. Johnson argues Justin was the earliest proponent of a developed *Logos* doctrine and generally followed the platonic model in which *Logos* denoted all-pervading Reason which gives form to and governs the universe. This view is based partially on Johnson's observation that in his extant writings Justin quotes the Fourth Gospel just once (in *1 Apology*, 61), and on the basis of this Johnson judges that "It seems likely that he interprets the Logos of John 1:1, 14 in the Platonic or neo-Platonic sense of Reason."[127] However, Tennent suggests that "Jesus' parable of the sower depicts the Word (*logos*) being sown broadly in the world, leading many to argue that this theological usage, rather than the more philosophical orientation of the Stoics and Platonists, is the primary reference for Justin. Indeed, Justin even uses the expression 'sowing of the implanted word [*logos*]' in his Second Apology."[128]

---

125. *2 Apology* 13. Sigountos notes that Justin commends every philosophical school for something but also criticizes them all too (Sigountos, "Did Early Christians Believe Pagan Religions Could Save?" 235).

126. Bray, "Explaining Christianity," 22.

127. Johnson, "Logos," 481.

128. Tennent, *Christianity at the Religious Roundtable*, 200 Cf. Justin, *2 Apology*, 13. Saldanha also argues that Justin's use of the Logos points to a Johannine source of inspiration. Sigountos, "Did Early Christians Believe Pagan Religions Could Save?" 61. Similarly, M. J. Edwards convincingly contends that "The search for pagan elements in his [Justin's] concept of the Logos has all but blinded us to the numerous occurrences

A Biblical, Historical, and Theological Critique of the Fulfilment Model

Saldanha argues that key to understanding Justin's use of the *Logos spermatikos* is an appreciation of the significance of his conversion—which too often is overlooked. His conversion was prompted by a search for truth he did not find in the philosophers:

> The change in Justin is obvious—and profound. No doubt he wears the philosopher's cloak after his conversion, but in doing this his only objective is that of indicating that he has found in Christianity the true philosophy and that he is eager to defend its truth by argument. No doubt, too, he calls Christianity a 'philosophy', but the word now has a new and richer significance for him: *philô-* retains the meaning it had for the Greek philosophers, namely, a desire and love for wisdom; but, *-sophia* becomes the revealed Wisdom, Jesus Christ. In Holte's words, 'Justin is in the first place a theological traditionalist, fast in the conviction that the whole truth is only to be found in the Church.' And therefore . . . all attempts to establish the basis of Justin's *Logos spermatikos* teaching on one philosophical system or another are vitiated from the start.[129]

Similarly, Tennent acknowledges the various possible backgrounds for Justin's *Logos*, but suggests most scholars "agree that even if he were influenced by others, he developed the concept in his own way."[130] Carson gives priority to the Old Testament background to the concept but also adds that the range of possible backgrounds for the term *Logos* "suggests that the determining factor is not this or that background but the Church's experience of Jesus Christ. This is not to say the background is irrelevant. It is to say, rather, that when Christians looked around for suitable categories to express what they had come to know

---

of the same term in his *Dialogue with Trypho*, whose important contribution to the problem of Christian thought is thus severely underrated." Edwards continues "even the *Apologies* cannot be elucidated from the pagan schools alone, and that the womb of his Logos-doctrine was the *Dialogue*, where the term is used to confer on Christ the powers that were already attributed in Jewish literature to the spoken and written utterance of God." Edwards, "Justin's Logos and the Word of God," 262. Cf. Edwards, "Justin's Logos and the Word of God," 266–67. "We cannot prove that Justin was acquainted with rabbinic thought, or even with the Fourth Gospel, but the Johannine terms for Christ were in his own vocabulary, and he shared with John a desire to trace the thread from Judaism to Christianity."

129. Sigountos, "Did Early Christians Believe Pagan Religions Could Save?" 59. The internal reference is to Ragner Holte, "Logos Spermatikos: Christianity and Ancient Philosophy according to St. Justin's Apologies," *Studia Theologica* 12 (1958), 147.

130. Tennent, *Christianity at the Religious Roundtable*, 200.

of Jesus Christ, many that applied to him necessarily enjoyed a plethora of antecedent associations."[131]

This allowed the early Christians to shape these terms to make them convey in the contexts in which they lived what they knew to be true of Jesus Christ.[132] Justin's belief in the universal enlightening of the *Logos* partially explains his acceptance of elements of truth outside Christianity. However his estimation of the potential of this *Logos* is often exaggerated. In his critique of Chadwick's analysis of Justin's view on the *Logos* Sigountos writes:

> If one assumes that the Logos was as seriously active among pagans as he was among Jews and Christians, then one might agree with scholars who say that Justin thought Christianity and Greek philosophy were 'almost identical ways of apprehending the same truth.' [As Chadwick alleges] But there is a price to pay for this assertion. It is difficult, if not impossible, to reconcile the *logos spermatikos* explanation with either the theft theory or the idea of demonic inspiration. How could a serious thinker like Justin one minute claim the Greeks were both demonically inspired and plagiarists, and the next that Jesus Christ, the Logos, gave them a system comparable to Christianity? Surely Justin was not confused about an idea of such central importance to him. 'Is it not more likely,' as Ragner Holte puts it, 'that modern scholars have tried to see Justin as an exponent of their own modern theological viewpoint?'[133]

Sigountos highlights here the importance of an accurate assessment of the *Logos* in Justin's theology. It is apparent that Justin does *not* consider the *Logos* to be as active among pagans as he was among Jews and Christians, and neither does he suggest the *Logos* has given the Greeks a system comparable to Christianity. These claims are made or implied by much fulfilment theology but they are unsubstantiated.[134]

---

131. Carson, *John*, 116.

132. Ibid., 116.

133. Sigountos, "Did Early Christians Believe Pagan Religions Could Save?" 239. The internal references are to Chadwick, *Early Christian Thought*, 11; and Holte, "Logos Spermatikos," 113.

134. Price, "Are There 'Holy Pagans' in Justin Martyr?" 169. Here, Price commenting on 1 *Apology*, 46.3 and 2 *Apology*, 8.1–3 states, "the reference to a universal participation in the Logos may mislead . . . Justin's concern is not with Greeks, or even philosophers, generally, but with those who could be represented as Christian fellow travellers and as fellow victims of demonic malice."

A Biblical, Historical, and Theological Critique of the Fulfilment Model

The following extract from Justin's Second Apology offers a more cautious view of the potential of the *Logos:*

> For I myself, when I discovered the wicked disguise which the evil spirits had thrown around the divine doctrines of the Christians, to turn aside others from joining them, laughed both at those who framed these falsehoods, and at the disguise itself, and at popular opinion; and I confess that I both boast and with all my strength strive to be found a Christian; not because the teachings of Plato are different from those of Christ, but because they are not in all respects similar, as neither are those of the others, Stoics, and poets, and historians. For each man spoke well in proportion to the share he had of the spermatic word, seeing what was related to it. But they who contradict themselves on the more important points appear not to have possessed the heavenly wisdom, and the knowledge which cannot be spoken against. Whatever things were rightly said among all men, are the property of us Christians. For next to God, we worship and love the Word who is from the unbegotten and ineffable God, since also He became man for our sakes, that, becoming a partaker of our sufferings, He might also bring us healing. For all the writers were able to see realities darkly through the sowing of the implanted word that was in them. For the seed and imitation imparted according to capacity is one thing, and quite another is the thing itself, of which there is the participation and imitation according to the grace which is from Him.[135]

So, while Justin understands the innate *Logos* to have a revelatory function for non-Christians, he qualifies this, referring to the limited truths (the seeds) available to these individuals and the full revelation Christians possess.[136] Greek philosophy has only a fragmentary and vague knowledge of the truth and the seeds of the Word have only a limited capacity for growth in the pagan, but the Christian participates in the *Logos* itself which is shared and imitated according to his grace. This difference is crucial, as N. Pycke explains: "Knowledge of Christ and participation in his grace are therefore for Justin the constitutive elements of a direct and personal contact between Christ and Christians.

---

135. *2 Apology*, 13.

136. Sigountos, "Did Early Christians Believe Pagan Religions Could Save?" 239. Cf. Saldanha, *Divine Pedagogy*, 53; Tennent, *Christianity at the Religious Roundtable*, 202.

This contact is essentially superior to the contact between the *logos* and pagans for the latter is both indirect and impersonal."[137]

Justin argued that one consequence of this limited, partial participation in the *Logos*, was that the philosophers contradicted one another at crucial points, and he saw in this evidence of their error. Only Christianity was true because it was consistent.[138] Keith explains the apologetic value of this insight: "These tensions made a helpful springboard for Christian apologetic—and sometimes polemic for that matter. They did not adequately demonstrate the existence of true believers within that tradition. They can be explained in terms of the argument of Romans 1. The Hellenist tradition did provide evidence against itself that it knew something of the true God but failed to acknowledge him as such."[139]

I suggest therefore that Justin offered a cautious appraisal of the work of the *Logos* in his assessment of pagan religion and philosophy. However, even with this qualification some theologians believe the early apologists overestimated the value of the *Logos*. For example, J. H. Bavinck argues the apologists did not sufficiently understand that the *Logos* of John's Gospel is "quite different from the logos experienced by Socrates."[140] Bavinck contends that the course taken by the early apologists did much harm by overestimating the value of reason in attaining a right knowledge of God.[141] Similarly, Kraemer argues that Origen and Clement made Greek philosophical categories too dominant in their thought. "[T]he synthesis of Christianity and culture, in this case Greek culture, is brought about too easily at the cost of ignoring or devaluating central elements of the Biblical revelation."[142] Kraemer states, "There is a tendency inherent in this *logos spermatikos* theory to obscure the central point in the Christian revelation, i.e. that it means entering in and through Christ into a new *life*-relationship with God. Instead the emphasis is shifted towards attaining a fuller rational knowledge of God."[143]

---

137 Pycke, "Connaissance rationnelle et connaissance de grâce chez saint Justin" *Ephemerides Theologicae Lovanienses*, 37 (1961), 85, quoted in Keith, "Justin Martyr and Religious Exclusivism," 172.

138. Sigountos, "Did Early Christians Believe Pagan Religions Could Save?" 235.

139. Keith, "Justin Martyr and Religious Exclusivism," 167.

140. Bavinck, *Introduction to the Science of Missions*, 224–26.

141. Ibid., 224.

142. Kraemer, *Religion and the Christian Faith*, 152.

143. Ibid., 153.

Whether Justin overestimated the role of the *logos spermatikos* in his appraisal of pagan religion and philosophy or whether this has been exaggerated in recent assessments of Justin, I suggest it remains the case that he did *not* consider the *logos spermatikos* to have inspired entire theological systems (*contra* the fulfilment model), but to have only implanted a small number of basic theological and moral ideas and to render all humanity culpable, even those who lived before Christ.[144] All people have a knowledge of "universal and immutable standards of righteousness."[145] This, says Sigountos, reflects the Pauline teaching of Romans 1. All people are recipients of the light of general revelation but have largely rejected it.[146] Justin wrote: "In the beginning God made the human race with the power of thought and of choosing the truth and doing right, so that all men are without excuse before God; for they have been born rational and contemplative."[147]

Justin employed the concept of the *logos spermatikos* in order to justify his universal claims for the *Logos*, and to appeal to his hearers. In common with the other early apologists he stressed the fact that Jesus Christ was both revealer and revealed. Following the Johannine tradition, the Fathers identified Christian truth with the person of the incarnate Word.[148]

Proponents of the fulfilment model often suggest the early apologists viewed Greek philosophy as a pedagogy for the Gospel for the Greeks, alongside the Old Testament for the Jews. However, while it is the case that Clement for example, considered Greek philosophy to be "in a sense a work of divine Providence,"[149] the Fathers saw Old Testament Judaism as a special and unique divine intervention. According to Justin, The Old Testament prophets served a unique purpose:

> There existed, long before this time, certain men more ancient than all those who are esteemed philosophers, both righteous

---

144. Keith, "Justin Martyr and Religious Exclusivism," 168. Keith refers to *1 Apology* 28, which he suggests is an allusion to Rom 1:20.

145. Ibid., 167. Cf. Justin, *Dialogue with Trypho*, 93.

146. Sigountos, "Did Early Christians Believe Pagan Religions Could Save?" 240.

147. *1 Apology,* 28. According to Keith, *rational* here entails "an instinct for justice and truth, along with the wisdom to recognise these," rather than denoting a skill in reasoning (Keith, "Justin Martyr and Religious Exclusivism," 165).

148. Saldanha, *Divine Pedagogy,* 159.

149. Clement, *Stromata* I, 1.

and beloved by God, who spoke by the Divine Spirit, and foretold events which would take place, and which are now taking place. They are called prophets. These *alone* both saw and announced the truth to men, neither reverencing nor fearing any man, not influenced by a desire for glory, but speaking those things alone which they saw and which they heard, being filled with the Holy Spirit. Their writings are still extant, and he who has read them is very much helped in his knowledge of the beginning and end of things, and of those matters which the philosopher ought to know, provided he has believed them.[150]

Clement also emphasizes the difference between the role of the Old Testament prophets and the Greek philosophers arguing that the "philosophers among the Greeks, and the wise men among the Barbarians besides were ignorant of the future coming of the Lord," but that "the prophets . . . foretold the Lord's coming, and the holy mysteries accompanying it."[151]

In drawing parallels between the Old Testament and Greek philosophy the apologists were highlighting the pre-incarnate activity of the *Logos*, rather than suggesting they are equivalent as pedagogues. As Saldanha states, "Justin's 'seeds of the Word', Irenaeus's teaching about the education of the human race, and Clement's concept of the divine pedagogy in the Jewish and Greek religions—all three, in fact, bear on the same theme of the Word's activity in the world prior to, and leading up to, His Incarnation.'"[152]

Saldanha considers the contributions of Justin, Clement and Irenaeus to this subject and judges that their approach to the question of the relationship of non-Christian religions to Christianity was directed by their salvation-historical perspective. For them the "economy" of salvation was Christocentric and organic. All three consider the period preceding Christ to be a preparation for the gospel.[153] However, Greek philosophy was essentially different from Old Testament Judaism in that its pedagogy to Christ consisted in orientating its adherents first and foremost to the one God or to the Word; on the other hand Old Testament Judaism's role as pedagogy to Christ lay in directing the Jews

---

150. *Dialogue with Trypho*, 7 (italics added).

151. *Stromata*, VI,15, Cf. *Stromata*, VI 3, titled "Plagiarism by the Greeks of the Miracles Related in the Sacred Books of the Hebrews."

152. Saldanha, *Divine Pedagogy*, 32.

153. Ibid., 151–52.

towards the Word-to-become-man: "This is the Christological element that is missing in non-Christian religions, and it is because of this lack that it is hard, not to say impossible, to justify the use of the religious writings of non-Christian religions on a par with the Old Testament Scriptures in the Christian liturgy."[154]

According to Saldanha, Justin saw the Old Testament Scriptures as a privileged preparation and he stopped short of describing the God given "seeds" as a preparation or pedagogy to Christianity.[155]

In conclusion, I concur with Sigountos, who asserts that recent use of the early Fathers to support a more positive view of the salvific role of other religions may contain some truth, "but it has been grossly overstated. Even the most open-minded Christians in those early days never claimed that non-Christian religions were an alternative route to God."[156] Similarly, Keith maintains:

> Justin was not as generous as he appears at first sight. He may have confidently asserted that Socrates, Heraclitus and others were all Christians, and this was further than he needed to go if his prime concern was to affirm that previous Gentile civilizations possessed aspects of the truth. But, as has been shown, Justin failed even here to provide the sort of evidence necessary to prove that these men were righteous in any biblical sense. And if Justin is arguably one of the most sympathetic of early Christians to the Greek tradition, he gives some idea of the limits of the patristic appraisal of pagan culture.[157]

9.3. Biblical and Extra-Biblical Fulfilment

The preceding sections dealing with biblical and patristic material often cited in support of the fulfilment model have highlighted a number of wider theological issues that will now be considered. The central thesis of

154. Ibid., 180.

155. Ibid., 72–73.

156. Sigountos, "Did Early Christians Believe Pagan Religions Could Save?" 229.

157. Keith, "Justin Martyr and Religious Exclusivism," 173. Cf. Price, "Are There 'Holy Pagans' in Justin Martyr?" 170: "In all there is no reason to suppose that Justin though that pagans, before or after Christ, could be dear to God and capable of salvation. Contrary to the claim often made for him, he was, for better or worse, no more broad-minded than his Christian contemporaries."

this chapter is that the fulfilment model for understanding the relationship of other religions to Christianity is seriously flawed. However, the principle of fulfilment itself is essential to the Bible's portrayal of salvation history. Christ is indeed the fulfilment of the Old covenant, and the New Testament does fulfil the Old Testament. However, what distinguishes this biblical pattern is the continuity of salvation-history through both Testaments. This continuity was vital to the self-understanding of the Church from its inception. The fact that Christ fulfils the Old covenant was not recognized with hindsight from the vantage point of the post-Advent faith community. Rather, salvation history from its very start has a Christological and eschatological orientation.[158] The Old covenant itself is orientated to the future, a future when the demands of the covenant will finally be fulfilled from the human side.[159] Until that time the covenant is maintained by the faithfulness of God, despite Israel's failure to live within the terms of its obligations. The reality of Israel's life, according to the Old Testament, is "often an unholy mixture of recalcitrance, waywardness, disobedience, and bad faith."[160] However, God is faithful to his covenant, and out of Israel's continual chastisement and exile there begins to emerge her hope for the future:

"Chief among its themes is the expectation of a time when God's covenant with his people will be renewed and established for ever, when the law will be written in human hearts rather than tablets of stone, when the Spirit of God will be poured out and the demands of the covenant finally fulfilled from the human side. And in the midst of this hope there emerges a concomitant expectation that all this will be accompanied by the appearance of an anointed instrument of the covenant, a messianic mediator who will bear this salvation in his train."[161]

Therefore the Old covenant looked forward to the time of fulfilment. The new covenant looks back to the time of promise.[162] The redemptive significance of Jesus draws directly on the apostolic perception that in Christ's person and ministry are found a fulfilment of "this entire long history of foreshadowing and promise. In him the kingdom of God is brought near, and the new covenant inaugurated . . . In the

---

158. See section 6.4 of this work for elaboration of this point.
159. Hart, "Christ the Mediator," 74.
160. Ibid., 74.
161. Ibid.
162. This point is further developed in section 8.2.6.

apostolic perception the covenant between God and Israel (now revealed to be an open rather than a closed covenant, and one which embraces the gentiles also) has been fulfilled and established on a rock solid foundation by the self-substitution of God for sinful human beings."[163]

This dimension of future anticipation, and the orientation of the Old covenant toward its consummation in the New covenant sets the biblical portrayal of fulfilment apart from extra-biblical fulfilment.

9.3.1. The Status of Other Scriptures

The fulfilment model regards the Old Testament simply as one of many "preparations" or "propaedeutics" for the Christian faith, replaceable with the scriptures of other religions. However, treating other religions and their scriptures as parallels to the Old Testament is extremely problematic. Emil Brunner has described the idea that "for an Indian his Bhagavad-Gita, for a Chinese his Laotse or Confucius, for a Japanese his Buddhist literature could become the Old Testament," as "a quite fatal misunderstanding."[164]

"This is nothing other than what we heard from Schleiermacher: that Christianity has no closer relation to Judaism than to paganism. One can speak this way only if, in the most dubious manner, he has already smoothed away what is specifically biblical—the whole contrast between the biblical revelation and the extrabiblical, the contrasts between idealism or mysticism and the Christian faith."[165]

For Brunner "the content, the substance, the Word of God, of the New Testament can be understood only in connection with that of the Old. That holds for all times and for every individual in every time."[166] The Old Testament is the beginning of the New, "The criterion and the basis for understanding the New."[167] Brunner refers to Schleiermacher above, and I believe a parallel between the attitude of nineteenth century Protestant liberalism to the Old Testament, and the way in which the Old Testament is considered by proponents of the Israel analogy and fulfilment model is merited. Liberal Protestantism denied the Old

---

163. Hart, "Christ the Mediator," 76; see 75–76 for elaboration on how Christ fulfils the threefold office of prophet, priest, and king.

164. Brunner, "Significance of the Old Testament," 250.

165. Ibid.

166. Ibid., 247.

167. Ibid., 263–64.

Testament any unique role which it had played in the traditional conception of the communication of revelation. Rather, the Old Testament was seen as of historical interest for understanding Jesus' Jewish background and at best was just the propaedeutic to Christianity. Alan Richardson summarizes this view as follows:

> The Old Testament merely recorded man's evolution toward the true God-consciousness; its realization of human spiritual potentiality, however, was only partial, and when that which is perfect is come, that which is in part is done away. Besides, other religions also had their own remarkable spiritual achievements, and they also anticipated the new God-awareness that was perfected in Christ ... The OT revelation of God is bound to the history of a particular people, whose history is not our history. Our history is just as closely bound up with that of the Greeks as that of the Hebrews; Jerusalem is not a holier city for us than is Athens or Rome ... Israel's history is not for Christian faith the history of revelation; for the Christian faith the Old Testament is not in the true sense God's Word. The religion of the Old Testament is not intrinsically more closely related to Christ's revelation of God than is the religion of Confucius or of Mohammed, even though extrinsically the historical connection is closer.[168]

However, as Richardson rightly states:

> The Old Testament is not adequately described as the propaedeutic to Christian faith. Temporally, of course, the faith and history of the Old Testament come before the faith and history of the New Testament. But the Old Testament is not propaedeutic in the sense that it can be laid aside when the New Testament is written. The Old Testament is the kerygmatic record of God's saving action in that history which is completed in the New Testament. God's saving activity in history is the theme of both Testaments, and neither Testament alone contains the complete record of it. Each Testament, however, testifies to the whole of God's saving activity, not merely to a part of it. The Old Testament bears witness to the saving action of God which will be completed in Christ; the New Testament testifies that the events it records are the fulfilment of those saving acts of God about which we learn from the Old Testament. Thus the Old Testament is not merely propaedeutic to Christian faith, since Christian faith itself is faith in God's salvation of the world

---

168. Richardson, "Is the Old Testament the Propaedeutic to Christian Faith?" 37–38.

through his action in the history of his chosen people, which culminated in the historical death and resurrection of Jesus Christ and the coming of his Church.[169]

The fact that the Old Testament is the immediate precursor and preparation for the New Testament is broadly recognized by proponents of the Israel analogy and fulfilment model, but this important fact is then overlooked or qualified in such a way that empties this connection of its full meaning and significance. I have already noted (in chapter 2) that Rahner, Dupuis, Farquhar, and Tiessen all explicitly make reference to the unique relationship between Old and New covenants, but nevertheless believe the analogical extension of this relationship to other religions is valid. None specify in any detail why they believe this move to be valid. For example, Dupuis contends:

> Other religious traditions too may contain prophetic words interpreting historical happenings as divine interventions in the history of peoples . . . Such historically tangible saving deeds of God are analogous to those performed by God in favor of Israel according to the Old Testament record—*notwithstanding the fact that the Christian tradition ascribes to the history of Israel the singular distinctive character of being the immediate historical prologue to God's decisive saving intervention in the Christ-event* . . . *Israel and Christianity obviously represent a singular case, owing to the unique relationship existing between the two religions; however . . . it may furnish, mutatis mutandis, an emblematic model for the relationship between Christianity and other religions.*[170]

Similarly, Farquhar argues "Christ's own attitude to Judaism ought to be our own attitude to other faiths, *even if the gap be far greater and the historical connections absent.*"[171] However, this historical connection is *not* merely an insignificant historical detail but is of constitutive significance for *both* Testaments. Francis Watson recognizes the vital nature of this connection:

---

169. Ibid, 47–48.

170. Dupuis, *Toward a Christian Theology of Religious Pluralism*, 219–20, 229 (italics added).

171. Farquhar, Papers Submitted to Commission Four of the World Missionary Conference, Edinburgh, 1910, # 153, 17; quoted in Hedges, *Preparation and Fulfilment*, 286 n. 47 (italics added).

The Old Testament is old only in relation to the newness of the New; there would be no Old Testament without a New Testament, which can therefore be said to call the Old Testament into being, that is, to constitute an existing collection of writings as Old Testament. Conversely, the New Testament is new only in relation to the oldness of the Old. Neither collection is self-sufficient; both of them are what they are only in relation to the other. The traditional terminology indicates that the twofoldness of the Christian Bible consists not in an arbitrary yoking together of two independent collections of writings but in a mutually constitutive relationship.[172]

At the core of the Israel analogy and fulfilment model is the willingness to confer the New Testament with a normative status not given to the Old Testament. This is contrary to salvation history which demands a proper recognition of the historical unfolding of the redemptive process. Baker asserts that "The relationship between the two covenants is essentially historical, not doctrinal—a relationship between two complementary series of events in the plan of salvation-history, not between

---

172. Watson, *Text and Truth*, 180. Watson elaborates the constitutive relationship by explaining the relationship "Takes the form of a preceding and a following. Jewish scripture is construed as that which comes before. It does not contain its centre in itself; it points forward to the moment that will retrospectively establish that its reality consists in whatever is implied by 'oldness.'... The New Testament is separated from the Old by a chronological interval which is, however, not to be measured merely in years; for this interval is the time of the *kairos*, the moment that definitively establishes both newness and oldness." He argues further that the relationship is qualitative as well as chronological: "not merely that of an earlier to a later, a first to a second. If that were the case, then the Old Testament would be only relatively old and the New Testament only relatively new"; rather "the old/new polarity ascribes an absolute, qualitative oldness and newness to the two Testaments. That which is new is always new" (180). Watson rightly defends the traditional old/new terminology over against "first" and "second," or "Hebrew" and "Greek." He acknowledges the unpopularity of such a proposal in much recent biblical (esp. Old Testament) scholarship. However, he highlights the difficulty of interpreting the Old Testament as an autonomous collection of texts, namely, how the abyss that has now opened up between Old and New Testaments may then be bridged. He concludes, "it is impossible to reach an adequate solution to this problem where the relationship between old and new is understood as a secondary issue arising out of the prior reality of two relatively autonomous collections of texts, each with it's own interpretative community." Such approaches "must be rejected ... They fail to take into account the event that constitutes the oldness of the Old and the newness of the New. They find in the interval between Old and New an abyss which may be bridged, if at all, only with great difficulty and with many qualifications and reservations; and to find an abyss at precisely the point where Christian faith identifies the Word made flesh is simply to invalidate Christian faith" (181). Cf. ibid., 182–85.

two collections of timeless truths."[173] The content of Scripture cannot be separated from its form, as Lints explains:

> The Christian theological framework finds its uniqueness in its fundamental commitment not only to the redemption brought by Christ but also to the redemptive revelation of which Christ is the climax. The final authority for the theological framework resides not in our experience of the redemptive work of God but in his interpretation of that redemptive experience. Theology in its form and substance as well as its function in the church must be determined by God's authoritative Word . . . The revelation of redemption must be seen in its entirety. The theologian must not lose sight of either the beginning or the end of this process. God's redemptive history moves with a purpose, and the consummation of that history is fundamental to the proper interpretation of each of its original episodes. This serves to underscore the point that the Christian theological framework must be grounded in the *entire* canon of scripture. Theology must not lose sight of the whole book as it looks at the parts. This is true not only with respect to the content of theology but also with respect to its form.[174]

Thus, the Old and New Testaments are inseparable, and neither can be replaced or dismissed without rendering the entire scriptural revelation ineffective and implausible. Baker highlights the enormous implications of dismissing the Old Testament: "To separate the central event of history from the events which lead up to and follow on from it robs the centre and the context of their full significance for revelation and salvation."[175] Similarly, Wilhelm Vischer stresses that the Old Testament is essential for apprehending God's revelation in Jesus Christ. This cannot be known without the Old Testament, for it is the Old Testament that defines the concept of Christ. "The Old Testament tells us *what* the Christ is; the New, *who* he is."[176] Likewise, Gerhard von Rad

---

173. Baker, *Two Testaments, One Bible*, 166. Baker's point is valid, although I would prefer to say that the connection is both historical and doctrinal (or theological).

174 Lints, *Fabric of Theology*, 78–79.

175 Baker, *Two Testaments, One Bible*, 165.

176. Wilhelm Vischer, *Witness of the Old Testament to Christ I: The Pentateuch*, 7; quoted in Baker, *Two Testaments, One Bible*, 103. Cf. Brevard Childs' canonical approach, in which both Testaments are considered to be vital witnesses to God's redemptive activity: "The Old Testament within the context of the canon is not a witness to a primitive level of faith, nor does it need to be Christianized. Within its historical

states, "The way in which the Old Testament is absorbed into the New is the logical end of a process initiated by the Old Testament itself."[177] The Old Testament is orientated towards the future and "can only be read as a book of ever increasing anticipation."[178] The World Council of Churches *Loccum Report* (1978) rightly states that the Old Testament is "an integral and indispensable part of the one authoritative Scripture ... neither obsolete nor antiquated nor should it be regarded merely as preparation for Christ."[179] Therefore, the Old and New Testaments are together part of the same salvation history, and cannot be separated. Christians appropriate the Old Testament as Christian Scripture because the New Testament itself provides the grounds for doing so.[180]

"When one reads the New Testament—and this is especially true if one comes to it from the Old Testament—one encounters an unshakeable conviction on the part of its writers that in Jesus Christ the story of Israel has achieved a consummating fulfillment. All the writers of the New Testament are seized by this prodigious reality."[181]

---

context it is a witness to Jesus Christ" (Childs, *Biblical Theology in Crisis*, 111). Cf. Gerhard von Rad: "Our knowledge of Christ is incomplete without the witness of the Old Testament. Christ is given to us only through the witness of those who await and those who remember" (Rad, "Typological Interpretation of the Old Testament," 39). Cf. Edwards, *History of the Work of Redemption*, 285–88.

177. Von Rad, *Old Testament Theology*, 321. Cf. C. J. H. Wright, *Knowing Jesus through the Old Testament*, 35. "if we were to jettison the Old Testament, we would lose most of the meaning of Jesus himself. For his uniqueness was and is built upon the foundation of the uniqueness of the story that prepared for him. Unfortunately, this is a link which is not often preserved in the current debate about the relationship between Christianity and other faiths. Many discussions about the significance of Jesus Christ within the context of world religions virtually cut him off from his historical and scriptural roots and speak of him as the founder of a new religion. Now, of course , if by that is meant merely that Christianity has historically become a separate religion from Judaism, that may be superficially true. But certainly Jesus had no intention of launching another 'religion' as such. Who Jesus was and what he had come to do were both already long prepared for through God's dealings with the people he belonged to and through their scriptures . . . We must clearly face up to the distinctive claims of the Hebrew scriptures if we are to get our understanding of Christ's uniqueness straight also."

178. Rad, *Old Testament Theology*, 2:319.

179. Faith and Order Commission, *Loccum Report, The Bible* (Geneva: WCC, 1978) (full reference not given); quoted in Petersen, "Continuity and Discontinuity," 32.

180. Goldsworthy, "Relationship of Old Testament and New Testament," 86.

181. Edwards, *Is Jesus the Only Savior?* 164.

A Biblical, Historical, and Theological Critique of the Fulfilment Model

This fundamental point is a key strand in my critique of the Israel analogy and the fulfilment model. For, in considering Christ as the fulfilment not only of the Old Testament, but also of other sacred scriptures, the fulfilment model misunderstands the nature and function not only of the Old Testament—but also of the scriptures of other religions. An example of this error is found in the Church of England Report *Towards A Theology for Inter-Faith Dialogue*. In its discussion of inclusivism,[182] this report maintains the relationship between Christianity and the other religions is

> analogous to the traditional Christian judgement on its own Jewish heritage. As Judaism became interpreted as a preparation for the greater light of the Gospel, so the other religions are seen as forerunners of the Gospel. Some inclusivists would wish to underline more strongly than others the special place of Judaism among the forerunners of the Gospel as witnessing to a special divine disclosure and redemptive activity. The revelation of God in Christ is the concrete, historical form of what remains hidden in the depth of other religions . . . Inclusivist theory stresses how Christianity does in fact complete other forms of religion. As the New Testament writers searched the Jewish Scriptures (what we have come to call the Old Testament), for signs of Christ before his incarnation in the person of Jesus, so the same can be done in relation to other religions. They too have their teachers, prophets, holy people and scriptures.[183]

However, as Chris Wright has correctly pointed out, this report questions the normative nature of the canon of Scripture, "and the historical particularity of Jesus as the completion of *this* particular story and no other."[184] The approach is also fundamentally a-historical. "That is, it shifts the focus of salvation from God's redemptive activity in the particular biblical history, to abstractions like 'hidden depths' and 'spiritual truths' which are found in all religions:

"Because such issues are at stake, this procedure of accepting the traditions or scriptures of other religions as forerunners of the Gospel equivalent to the Old Testament has been a deeply divisive matter of

---

182. As noted above, fulfilment is an essential part of the inclusivist paradigm. See introduction.

183. Church of England General Synod Board for Mission and Unity, *Theology for Inter-Faith Dialogue*, 18–19.

184. C. J. H. Wright, "Inter Faith Dialogue," 235.

debate among theologians and missiologists in different continents. But here it is presented with little hint of its controversial implications, as though it were an obvious step."[185]

The Christian Church accepts the Scriptures of the Old and New Testaments as the uniquely inspired word of God. However, the fulfilment model extends the concept of inspiration beyond the Christian Scriptures. For Vempeny, "analogical inspiration" affirms that the ontological connection between the Old Testament religion and the New Testament religion is of a different degree of intensity than the ontological connection between the non-Christian religions and the New Testament religion; nevertheless it is true inspiration. He bases this proposal on the assertion that the inspiration of the Old Testament is also analogical in relation to that in the New Testament because "the causality of God with regard to the NT religion and with regard to the NT are incalculably more intense than that with regard to the OT religion and with regard to the OT."[186] I dispute this claim and maintain the Old and New Testaments are equally inspired, for they both recount the same salvation history. Vempeny's thesis is reliant on a number of major assumptions, but he does not attempt a biblical defense of any of these. The three following assumptions are particularly pertinent to our discussion: 1) All non-Christian religions are founded by God, through his historical interventions and are oriented towards Christ and his Church; 2) God willed the non-Christian religions, 3) God founded non-Christian religions through His historical interventions. They are directly the heirs to the pre-Mosaic covenants and indirectly to all the pre-Christian covenants.[187]

Vempeny recognizes parallel doctrines in non-biblical scriptures, and this leads him to suggest that if these are accepted as inspired when found in the Bible then they should also be accepted as such when found in the non-biblical scriptures.[188] However, I suggest that truths

---

185. Ibid., 235.

186. Vempeny, "Approach to the Problem of Inspiration in Non-Biblical Scriptures," 85. Similar views on the New Testament being more inspired than the Old Testament are held by Amalorpavadas, *Research Seminar on Non Biblical Scriptures*, 109–11; and Dupuis, "Cosmic Economy of the Spirit and the Sacred Scriptures of Religious Traditions," 130.

187. Vempeny, "Approach to the Problem of Inspiration in the Non-Biblical Scriptures," 173–75.

188. Vempeny asks, "on what ground can we say that these [parallel doctrines] . . . are not inspired by the Holy Spirit?" Vempeny, "Approach to the Problem of Inspiration in Non-Biblical Scriptures," 31.

in non-Christian scriptures can be affirmed without affording these truths inspired or revealed status. If truth is taken to be that which corresponds to reality—then other scriptures evidently do contain truth. The Koran's affirmation of monotheism, for example, can be accepted as truth by Christians. However, the presence of truths should not be interpreted as evidence of inspiration.[189] A statement cannot be isolated from the broader context in which it fits and which gives the individual statement meaning. David Clark rightly states that when religions are taken as wholes the "the issue is not individually true statements, but the referent or object of the religious belief system's hard core."[190] Therefore, when other scriptures are being considered as possible parallels to the Old Testament, the religious worldview in which they function must be given due attention. Once a statement is detached from its larger biblical context and linked to other propositions one cannot attribute inspiration to it.

Thus, while truths undoubtedly exist in non-Christian scriptures, these truths are not evidence of special revelation or inspiration, but can be attributed, according to Clark, to general revelation "mixed with echoes of special revelation."[191] In his discussion of the Vatican II documents concerning Christianity's relationship with other religions, D'Costa identifies an issue that is of particular importance to this

---

189. An explanation for such truths is proposed below.

190. Clark, *To Know and Love God*, 325. See also D'Costa's critique of inclusivism in D'Costa, *Meeting of the Religions*, 22–24. D'Costa writes 'If religious traditions are properly to be considered in their unity of practice and theory, and in their organic interrelatedness, then such "totalities" cannot simply be dismembered into parts . . . which are then taken up and "affirmed" by inclusivists, for the parts will always relate to the whole and will only take their meaning in this organic context" (22–23). Cf. Corduan, *Tapestry of Faiths*, 75.

191 Clark, *To Know and Love God*, 325. These "echoes" may include, for example, remnants of "original monotheism." This form of revelation comprises the preserved remnants of original/primeval revelation. See Schmidt, *Origin of Religion*. For a more recent proponent of original monotheism, see Corduan, *Tapestry of Faiths*, 31–33. Corduan writes: "Christian theologians traditionally recognize two types of revelation: general revelation, according to which God is known through nature in such a way that all human beings have access to knowledge of him, and special revelation, which is limited to God's more direct self-disclosure in history and Scripture. Provisionally at least, I wish to stipulate an additional way in which people come to know of God. This is not a new revelation, but it is a way of acquiring knowledge about God that does not rely directly on either special or general revelation. I am referring to the knowledge of God that has persisted throughout the history of humankind." This point is elaborated further below, see section 9.3.2.

discussion. He notes that in *Nostra Aetate* the term "revelation" is used exclusively of the Old Testament, and he states. "This is highly significant, for the term "revelation" is not used in any of the sections dealing with other religions. This also highlights the *sui generis* relationship with Judaism."[192] The fulfilment model, however, requires a relegation of the unique nature of this relationship.

Therefore, the proposition that other religious scriptures can be considered as parallels to the Old Testament is seriously flawed from the perspective of the Christian faith. However, it is also flawed from the perspective of the religions themselves. Other scriptures may be viewed in their own settings in a way that makes then incompatible with the Christian context. As Corduan suggests "This makes for a strong incompatibility between the Bible and other world scriptures."[193] Corduan argues that to maintain that the essence of another religion can be gleaned from its scriptures in the same way as the essence of Christianity can be gleaned from the Bible is a flawed idea.[194] This is even true for that religion closest to Christianity—Judaism. It is a mistake to suggest that study of the Old Testament will lead one to a correct understanding of contemporary Judaism, for most forms of Judaism interpret the Hebrew Scriptures through the lens of subsequent writings, particularly the Talmud.[195] The scriptures of other religions play a different function in these religions than the Bible does in Christianity and therefore to suggest other scriptures can perform the function of the Old Testament does violence to both the Christian understanding of Scripture and the understanding of the other scripture in its own context.[196]

A further significant difference between the Old Testament and other scriptures concerns the question of historical continuity (or lack thereof) with Christianity. Rahner recognizes the unique historical

---

192. D'Costa, *Meeting of the Religions*, 102–3.

193. Corduan, *Tapestry of Faiths*, 56.

194. Ibid., 58. I recognize the diversity that exists between different Christian confessional communities regarding the role Scripture plays in their religion (for example, with Roman Catholics relying on Scripture *and* tradition to inform their faith). However, the central thrust of my argument is not altered by this observation.

195. Ibid., 59–60.

196. See ibid., 55–106 for a helpful discussion of these issues. Corduan cautions against what he describes as the "Protestant Fallacy," that is, viewing the Scriptures of other religions as Protestant Christians view their Bible. He highlights the flawed assumption that to understand Judaism one must study the "Old Testament" (59).

A Biblical, Historical, and Theological Critique of the Fulfilment Model

connection between Old and New Testaments: "Of course, it remains the privilege of Israel that its tangible and to some extent distinct salvation-history was the immediate historical prelude to the Incarnation of the divine Word, and that this history of Israel alone was interpreted authoritatively by the word of God in Scripture in such a way that it was thereby distinguished from any other profane history."[197]

However, Rahner considers that God made arrangements for the salvation of other peoples, arrangements that he argues are analogous to the Old Testament.[198] He bases this proposal on his notion of "general salvation history" which he distinguishes from special salvation history. He contends that the main difference between these histories "will presumably lie in the fact that the historical, factual nature of the New Testament has *its* immediate pre-history in the *Old Testament*."[199]

Dupuis concurs, suggesting that the way Judaism relates to Christian is an important clue as to how the "Divergent Paths" relate to Christianity:

> What applies in the first instance holds good, analogically, in the other . . . Even as the Mosaic covenant has not been suppressed by the coming to its fullness in Jesus Christ, neither has the cosmic covenant in Noah with the nations been obliterated by reaching in the Christ-event the goal for which it was ordained by God. The implication is that the distinction between the general and special history of salvation must not be taken too rigidly: extrabiblical traditions . . . cannot be excluded a priori from belonging to special salvation history. To include them in it would presuppose . . . events in the history of peoples which, in function of a prophetic charism, are interpreted as divine interventions.[200]

Similarly, Vempeny contends that the non-Christian religions are oriented towards Christ and his Church but not in the same way as the Old Testament is. For "The OT religion was oriented towards the historical Christ, who was born in Bethlehem, brought up in Nazareth, listened to by the Palestinians and crucified on Mount Calvary at

---

197. Rahner, "History of the Word and Salvation-History," 109.

198. Ibid., 109

199. Rahner, "Christianity and the Non-Christian Religions," 131. Cf. Legrand, "Letter and Spirit: The Role of the Book in the Christian Economy," 72–73.

200 Dupuis, *Toward a Christian Theology of Religious Pluralism*, 233.

a definite time in history."[201] However, "the non-Christian religions cannot make such a claim."[202] Despite this major difference, Vempeny asserts that there is a "mysterious" connection between other religions and Christianity which cannot be denied, on the basis of the doctrine of faith that there has been and there is one and only one plan of salvation.[203] However, Vempeny concedes that "it escapes our mental categories as to how the non-Christian religions can be truly oriented towards Christ, since the incarnation has taken place one and for all."[204] I suggest Rahner, Dupuis and Vempeny all have an erroneous understanding of the relationship between non-Christian religions and Christianity, and this is due in large part to their belief in universal salvation history.[205] Scripture is the record of the history of salvation. That history is particularistic and unique, and therefore the scriptural record of it is necessarily unique also.

9.3.2. Continuity, Discontinuity, Preparation, and Points of Contact

The fulfilment model presupposes a significant degree of continuity between other religions and Christianity. For example, the Conciliar document *Ad Gentes* describes other religions as ways in which people "search for God, groping for Him that they may by chance find Him," and as initiatives which "need to be enlightened and purified" by the gospel. They can sometimes "serve as pedagogy toward the true God or as preparation for the gospel" finding their fulfilment there.[206] However, as Peter Cotterrell rightly cautions, an emphasis on continuity tends to idealize religions:

"The fact is that religions do not prepare their adherents for the revelation of Christ. Paradoxically, the closer any religion stands to Christianity, so higher is the barrier erected between its own adherents and the Christian revelation. If salvation is to be found by the adherents

---

201. Vempeny, "Approach to the Problem of Inspiration in Non-Biblical Scriptures," 148.

202. Ibid.

203. Ibid.

204. Ibid., 149.

205. This point is developed in chapter 8, where I consider the nature and relationship of the biblical covenants. (See especially 8.2.2 and 8.3.1.)

206. *Ad Gentes*, 3, Cf. *Lumen Gentium*, 23.

A Biblical, Historical, and Theological Critique of the Fulfilment Model

of these religions, it may well be found while they are still in them, but it will not be found because of them, but in spite of them."[207]

The lack of continuity between other religions and Christianity is due in part to the historical nature of the Christian faith. The Christian gospel is, as Chris Wright notes, good *news*—not a good *idea*. It is "the declaration of historical events by which God has intervened to save us from our sin."[208] Those traditions that do not recount these historical events do not stand in continuity with Christianity. Some elements of continuity between other religions and Christianity can be expected, but should not be taken as evidence that the religion itself stands in continuity with Christianity. The elements of continuity are due to the universal religious consciousness of all who are created in the image of God, and to God's providential governance of history.[209]

Furthermore, the fact that a convert to Christianity recognizes or can identify elements of continuity with their former religion does not necessarily mean their former religion prepared them for the gospel. For these "points of contact" are often recognized only with hindsight. Bray notes that among all the early apologists Aristides was the only one to argue that it was possible to find Christ by pursuing an intellectual path, and Aristides argues this on the basis of his own experience. However, he was speaking from hindsight. "The good elements in Greek philosophy fell into place once Christianity was understood and adopted; they were not sufficient on their own to lead people in the way of truth."[210]

Fulfilment theology is flawed because, as Kraemer maintained, it implies that the non-Christian religions, left to their own devices would naturally reach Christ.[211] However, on the contrary: "The cross and its real meaning—reconciliation as God's initiative and act—is antagonistic to all human religious aspirations and ends, for the tendency of all human religious striving is to conquer God, to realize our divine nature

---

207. Cotterell, *Mission and Meaninglessness*, 51. Overestimation of the continuity between other religions and Christianity is a criticism Rowan Williams levels at Rahner. Williams comments: "Faith in Christ is not straightforwardly a recognition of the satisfaction of my needs; the form of Christ is always a revelation of our untruth (and thus unreality and unloveliness)" (Williams, "Rahner and Balthasar," 32).

208. C. J. H. Wright, *Thinking Clearly about the Uniqueness of Jesus*, 64.

209. Shenk, *Who Do You Say That I Am?* 150.

210. Bray, "Explaining Christianity," 24.

211. Kraemer, *Christian Message in a Non-Christian World*, 123.

(theosis). Christ is not the fulfilment of this but the uncovering of its self-assertive nature."[212]

Furthermore, the nature of the fulfilment sought in other religions is not the same as the fulfilment found in Christ. Often they ask different questions.[213] "The supreme longing of the Hindu after escape from *samsara* is not satisfied by Christ. The gift of Rebirth as offered by Christ does not appeal to the Hindu. On the contrary, Jesus kindles new hopes not felt before and kills some of the deepest and most persistent longings of man."[214]

Therefore, there is no direct continuity from the religions to Christ, such that they can be seen as the "beginnings or foundations of which Christ is the superstructure . . . As Lesslie Newbigin has observed, non-Christian religions represent goals and methods too foreign to Christ for there to be any direct line of continuity. They face in different directions, ask different questions and look for different kinds of religious fulfilments."[215]

However, while Christ should not be seen as the fulfilment of non-Christian religions themselves, I concur with Kraemer who affirms that "in the religions of mankind there stir deep aspirations, longings and intuitions which find their fulfilment in Christ."[216] Fulfilment theology misunderstands the nature of revelation outside of the Judaeo-Christian tradition. Carson rightly accepts the reality of revelation in

---

212. Ibid.

213. D'Costa, *Theology and Religious Pluralism*, 109.

214. Kraemer, *Religion and the Christian Faith*, 215–16. Cf. Fredericks, *Buddhists and Christians: Through Comparative Theology to Solidarity*, 16. Here Fredericks states "fulfillment theologies . . . distort the teachings of other religious traditions. This puts Christians in the unhelpful position of claiming to known more about the religious lives of other believers than they know about themselves . . . fulfillment theologies require Christians to make statements about other religious believers that those 'others' find puzzling, mistaken, or even offensive."

215. McDermott, *Can Evangelicals Learn from World Religions?* 91. Cf. Newbigin, *Finality of Christ*, 43–44. More recently, S. Mark Heim has proposed that the different religions should not be seen as different paths to the same goal, but represent completely different goals. See Heim, *Salvations*; and Heim, *Depth of the Riches*.

216. Kraemer, *Christian Message in a Non-Christian World*, 123. D. A. Carson concurs: "Although the Bible as a whole can sometimes speak of the gospel and of Jesus as bringing to fruition the aspirations of pagans who surround the covenant community, it does not speak of the gospel or of Christ as fulfilling their religion" (Carson, *Gagging of God*, 31). See also Bavinck, "General Revelation and the Non-Christian Religions," 52; Shenk, *Who Do You Say That I Am?* 154–55.

A Biblical, Historical, and Theological Critique of the Fulfilment Model

all religions, (based on the concepts of the *Imago Dei*, general revelation, and primeval revelation). However, fulfilment theology moves beyond this "weak" sense of revelation to a much stronger sense—that of special revelation."[217]

It follows then, that if Christianity should not be understood as the fulfilment of other religions, then other religions should not be construed as alternative preparations or pedagogues for Christianity. It is significant that Paul contrasts the pre-Christian situation of Christians converted from Jewish and from pagan backgrounds (Gal 4:1–11), and while he is positive about the role of the Old covenant—for it led to Christ, he is not positive about the role the pagan religions played for the Gentiles. Indeed, Paul judges that the Gentiles formerly "did not know God" but "were enslaved to those that by nature are not gods" (Gal 4:8b).

In chapter 2 I observed that many of the theologians who employ the Israel analogy consider it necessary for all religions to act as preparations for the Gospel. For example, Braaten writes: "Every religion has prophets who are similar to John the Baptist preparing the way for the coming of Christ. If this were not so, the gospel of Christ would drop like a stone from heaven and could not be translated into other religio-cultural settings."[218]

However, I dispute this assertion for the Old Testament is the story of all people, not just the Jews.[219] Godfrey Phillips rightly states that the Old Testament is not replaceable with other national stories or scriptures. It is the "story of 'Everyman,' which is part of the story of how God has won for Himself a people, which when Christ comes into the world becomes the Church, the body through which He functions in the world. So *no* race or nation, however gifted, can do without it, just

---

217. Carson, *Gagging of God*, 31.

218. Braaten, *No Other Gospel!* 69. The same view is expressed by Timothy Tennent, who proposes it is valid to extend the concept of *praeparatio evangelica* from Judaism to other cultural and historical movements because "A declaration that the Messiah has finally arrived and that Jesus has fulfilled the hope of the prophets is largely unintelligible to someone who has not previously been schooled in the expectations of Judaism prior to the coming of Christ" (Tennent, *Christianity at the Religious Roundtable*, 203).

219. In stating this, I am not proposing Old Testament universalism but rather acknowledging that the Old Testament's metanarrative (creation, fall, etc.) is universally applicable.

as no person, however brilliant, can makes sense of a sentence of which the first half is omitted."[220]

A study of Paul's communication with non-Jewish audiences reveals a substantial reliance on the Old Testament. In Paul's conversation with God-fearing Gentiles at Lystra (Acts 14) the Old Testament plays a very significant role. Although Paul does not quote from it directly, Phillips comments,

"No one can read this brief summary without perceiving that it consists of the concentrated essence of the O.T. message concerning the living God Who made heaven and earth, beside Whom all other objects of worship are vanities . . . The summary probably represents the introduction to a missionary speech rather than the speech itself, but it is significant that the teaching of the Old Testament has to be laid as a foundation for the introduction of these pagans to Christ."[221]

Similarly, Paul's speech in Athens (Acts 17) makes abundant use of the Old Testament. Greg Bahnsen states that in this speech, "Paul's utilization of Old Testament materials is rather conspicuous. For example, we can see Isaiah 42:5 coming to expression in Acts 17:24–25."[222] Bahnsen observes that although Paul is "addressing an audience which is not committed or even predisposed to the revealed Scriptures, namely educated Gentiles, his speech is nevertheless a *typically* Jewish polemic regarding God, idolatry, and judgement!"[223] Phillips states that "throughout the New Testament knowledge of the Old is presupposed among Churches where probably the majority of members were Gentile in origin."[224] The missiologist Charles Kraft makes the interesting point that among the Africans with whom he worked the Old Testament was actually more understandable than some New Testament books, such as Romans.[225] Thus, Braaten's premise (see above) that each religion must have its own preparation for Christ "otherwise the gospel of

---

220. Phillips, *Old Testament in the World Church*, 128–29.

221. Ibid., 70. "O.T" and "Old Testament" are given as such in the original.

222. Bahnsen, "Encounter of Jerusalem with Athens."

223. Ibid.

224. Phillips, *Old Testament in the World Church*, 71.

225. Kraft, *Christianity in Culture*, 178, 182–83. Similarly, Peter Nyende argues that Hebrews, with its strong Old Testament background, is a very fruitful way of communicating the gospel in an African culture (Nyende, "Why Bother with Hebrews? An African Perspective," 514–15).

A Biblical, Historical, and Theological Critique of the Fulfilment Model

Christ would drop like a stone from heaven and could not be translated into other religiocultural settings"[226] does not follow.

Bavinck is critical of the search for anticipations of the gospel that are sometimes suggested as existing in non-Christian religions.[227] He notes "The conviction that redemption is due solely to the 'grace of God' which sometimes is found in non-Christian religions, has been regarded as constituting a tremendous point of contact."[228] However, Bavinck judges "It is understandable that such efforts have been made, but from the point of view of Scripture, to seek such a point of contact is erroneous."[229] Such points of contact, argues Bavinck, conflict with the unique character of the gospel.[230] However, he accepts that mission does not occur in a void, and recognizes that there is a point of contact, quite different from the ones usually presupposed. General revelation is affirmed by Bavinck as "the great and sole point of contact which the church possesses in its work of evangelization . . . We are to speak to the heathen as to those with whom God has already been concerned for a long time, as to those who have already done many things with God and have tried to wrest free from his grip, by changing his truth into a lie (Rom 1:18)."[231]

Bavinck suggests that communicating the gospel should start with the Old Testament—particularly the early chapters of Genesis. He disputes the idea that each nation must have its own religion, for there is only one God and one human race, and all humans are in the same situation—that is fallen and needing a redeemer.[232] Similarly, Kraemer is critical of the points of contact theory. He judged that religions should be seen as totalities rather that attempting to identify isolated aspects that can be points of contact.[233] For Kraemer, the only point of

---

226. Braaten, *No Other Gospel!* 69.

227. Bavinck, *Introduction to the Science of Missions*, 135. He lists a number of such anticipations including the feeling of awe for the majesty of Allah in Islam, the assertion that each nation has its own Old Testament, and the notion of grace found in some religions.

228. Ibid.

229. Ibid.

230. Ibid.

231. Ibid., 136.

232. Ibid., 144.

233. Kraemer, *Christian Message in a Non-Christian World*, 135.

ONE OF A KIND

contact is "the disposition and attitude of the missionary."[234] Revelation in Christ is not the fulfilment of all religious aspirations but is God's judgment on these religions.[235]

Bavinck makes a distinction between "substantive" and "formal" contact between Christianity and other religions: formal engagement is unavoidable but substantive engagement, impossible.[236] The rejection of this substantive or material point of contact is based on Bavinck's theological starting point that non-Christian religion taken as a whole constitutes a turning away from God. If there are things in other religions that are compatible with Christianity, in the end they are always just apparent similarities.[237] With regard to the formal point of contact there are three aspects to this. The first is theological and the other two practical.

First, in every non-Christian religion "vague and general intuitions" are encountered that have their origin in the revelation of God. Mission does not take place "in a void." God has not left himself without witness, and this fact constitutes the great point of contact. Paul

---

234. Ibid., 140. Cf. Bavinck, *Introduction to the Science of Missions*, 230. Here Bavinck cites Abraham Kuyper, *Encyclopaedie der H. Godgeleerdheid III*, 449: "As soon as you, as a man, encounter a person as a man, whether he be a pagan or a Mohammedan, you possess with him a common starting point, and this is first of all, the sin you both have committed, and, secondly, the grace which saved you and which alone can save him when the light from Christ penetrates into the darkness, and the sinner is gripped by the mercy of God. Thus, there arises on the one hand a feeling of a common tie with the pagan, a common human heart, and in that heart, there is the same *sensus divinitatis*; that heart is disturbed by the same sin; you are by nature as heathen as he, the sole difference is the grace which has been given to you, and that he too can share in."

235. Visser, *Heart for the Gospel, Heart for the World*, 114. Kraemer writes: "'Because the revelation of God in Christ transcends and contradicts all human wisdom by its divine folly, and all human aspiration and expectation by its entirely unexpected way of fulfilling them, it is wrong to use the term fulfilment. Conversion and regeneration would be truer to reality. At any rate, the term fulfilment, in the customary sense of bringing to perfection what has already naturally grown to a more or less successful approximation to the life and the truth revealed in Christ, is not applicable to the relation of the non-Christian religions to the revelation in Christ" (Kraemer, *Christian Message in a Non-Christian World*, 124).

236. Visser, *Heart for the Gospel, Heart for the World*, 251. Visser does not state how Bavinck defines these terms. However, the context would indicate that "substantive" is used to denote essential essence or substance, whereas "formal" is used in reference to appearance or form as distinguished from substance.

237. Ibid., 251.

Visser suggests that here Bavinck resembles Kraemer who considered that "points of contact in other religions can be established only by way of antithesis, which 'is not meant as a negative way of condemnation, but as a deeply positive way of dealing realistically with the dialectical reality' of human religion."[238] For Bavinck, "religious awareness may be understood as a point of contact only to the extent that it is an answer to earlier revelation of God: 'the only thing revelation fastens onto is revelation.'"[239]

Second, the missionary cannot avoid adopting existing words and expressions in order to communicate effectively.[240] "'Paul and the other apostles did not hesitate to use numerous highly specific words and expressions from Hellenistic culture' such as *logos* and *soteria*, 'which were, of course, loaded with wrong connotations, in the preaching of the gospel.'"[241] Thirdly, the missionary must seek a "very thorough adaptation to the nature and possibilities of the peoples to whom we preach."[242]

Francis Watson's approach to the point of contact theory resembles that of Bavinck. In considering Paul's address to the Athenians, Watson maintains it is evident that there exists a point of contact between Paul and his audience in the form of the Greek language that offers Paul a vocabulary that is religious as well as secular. Furthermore, even if what he says is genuinely new (v.19–21), the newness cannot be absolute "for his message would then be unintelligible and incommunicable, an instance of *glossolalia*."[243] Indeed, the universal claim of the Christian gospel presupposes its universal intelligibility.[244] Therefore, "the altar 'to an unknown God' serves as a point of contact between Paul and his audience, but not in such a way as to establish a common ground on which both parties can agree. On the contrary, this small fragment

---

238. Ibid., 251, quoting Kraemer, *The Christian Message in a Non-Christian World*, 139.

239. Visser, *Heart for the Gospel, Heart for the World*, 251, citing J. H. Bavinck, "Het probleem der 'Anknüpfung' bij de evangelieverkondiging' in R. van Woudenberg (ed.), *J. H. Bavinck: Een keuze uit zijn werk*, (Kampen, 1991), 67.

240. Ibid., 252

241. Ibid., citing J. H. Bavinck, "Het probleem der 'Anknüpfung' bij de evangelieverkondiging," 67.

242. Ibid., citing J. H. Bavinck, "Het probleem der 'Anknüpfung' bij de evangelieverkondiging," 66.

243. Watson, *Text and Truth*, 248–49.

244. Ibid., 250.

of Athenian religious life is identified as the weak point which makes it possible to destroy the entire edifice . . . An obscure altar is the point at which the deconstruction of the Athenian sacred canopy can begin; and that is the only sense in which it constitutes a 'point of contact' between Paul and his audience."[245]

In chapter 2 I outlined various approaches to the fulfilment concept and suggested that Daniélou, Rahner, Dupuis, Farquhar, and Braaten and Pinnock all consider other religions to be preparations for the gospel.[246] A more nuanced and qualified approach is adopted by Tiessen, who rejects the notion that other religions themselves are preparations for the gospel, but suggests non-Christian religions represent "providential preparations" by virtue of the hypothesis that God has placed "types" in them.[247] I have argued thus far that other religions do not represent preparations for the gospel. However, with Tiessen, I accept that there may be aspects of non-Christian religions which can act as points of contact with the gospel. But I wish to qualify this assertion in two important ways. First, these points of contact do not lead the adherent of the non-Christian religion to Christianity unassisted by the proclamation of the gospel.[248] Second, affirming that positive values or truths may exist in non-Christian religions should not be interpreted as suggesting God is actively working in these religions. So, for example, I see no need to hypothesize (with Tiessen) that God has "placed types" in other religions.[249] Such truths or values can, as I have noted above

---

245. Ibid., 252

246. That is not to say all approach the concept in the same way. Refer to chapter 2 of this volume for a fuller exposition.

247. Tiessen, *Who Can Be Saved?* 379–82. See this volume, section 2.3.2 for elaboration on how Tiessen employs the category of "types."

248. I do not suggest however that such proclamation needs to be by a human messenger. Other modalities of extraordinary special revelation are possible. See also chapter 10, 287 n. 5.

249. McDermott also supports the hypothesis that God has placed "types" in other religions. McDermott attempts to show that Jonathan Edwards was a forerunner of this hypothesis. However, I consider McDermott's case to be unconvincing. The Edwards material that McDermott surveys does indicate that Edwards allowed that God, in his providence, could use elements of non-Christian religions to point to Christian truths. However, he stops short of showing that Edwards believed God had "placed types" in non-Christian religions. See McDermott, *Jonathan Edwards Confronts the Gods*, 110–29. Cf. McDermott, "What If Paul Had Been from China? Reflections on the Possibility of Revelation in Non-Christian Religions," 27–29; McDermott, *Can Evangelicals Learn from World Religions?* 91–93.

(9.3.1), be explained by the reality of general revelation and original monotheism. As Calvin Shenk notes "Because people are in the image of God and share the same background through creation, there will be parallel insights between biblical faith and other religious traditions."[250]

The work of Jonathan Edwards is instrumental in this regard. Recently, revisionist readings of Edwards have proposed he was a proponent of soteriological inclusivism.[251] However this claim is disputed.[252] The proposal for Edwards' inclusivism is based on two concepts. The first is his utilization of the concept of *prisca theologia* (ancient theology).[253] The second concept which is instrumental in Edwards' alleged inclusivism is his "dispositional soteriology"—namely, the suggestion that Edwards understood salvation in terms of an individual's disposition rather than the possession of conscious faith.[254] This second

250. Shenk, *Who Do You Say That I Am?* 77.

251. Morimoto, *Jonathan Edwards and the Catholic Vision of Salvation*; Morimoto, "Salvation as the Fulfillment of Being: The Soteriology of Jonathan Edwards and Its Implications for Christian Mission"; McDermott, "Jonathan Edwards, John Henry Newman, and Non-Christian Religions,"; McDermott, *Jonathan Edwards Confronts the Gods*.

252. See, e.g., Gilbert, "Nations Will Worship"; Bombaro, "Jonathan Edward's Vision of Salvation"; Holmes, "Does Jonathan Edwards Use a Dispositional Ontology? A Response to Sang Hyun Lee." According to Bombaro, "There is no indication in either Edwards's private or public records that he favored or was developing a non-particularistic salvation scheme. In fact, the evidence holds the opposite true. To be sure, he believed that pre-Israelite characters such as Melchizedek enjoyed salvation, as well as the 'Old Testament church'—God effectually working through the Word-based protoevangelium revelation first given to their antediluvian fathers and then to them. Nevertheless, the same could not be said about Greco-Roman thinkers, Chinese philosophers, or (prior to the New Testament dispensation) non-Jewish religions and (subsequent to the First Advent) non-Christian religions. Though Edwards held that the sages of Athens and Rome were 'eminent for many moral virtues' derived from ancient revelation, yet without 'true virtue' obtained from the God of the Hebrew religion and the 'means' pertaining thereto, their morality was but splendida peccata and their theological insights 'almost' and only 'seemingly' divine truths" (Bombaro, "Dispositional Peculiarity History," 137). Bombaro cites Edwards, "Scripture" Nos. 138a, 232, and 236 in *Yale-Works*, vol. 15; and his MS sermon on Isa 27:13 (1741) and *Charity and Its Fruits*, in *Yale-Works*, 8:310; and "Miscellanies" Nos. 965 and 979, in *Yale-Works*, 20:249, 291–96 to support his argument.

253. Gilbert suggests the concept of *prisca theologia* was first introduced by Clement, Origen, and Eusebius to show that the religious knowledge of the heathen philosophers had been passed down to them from earlier generations (Gilbert, "Nations Will Worship," 55).

254. See, for example, Lee, *Philosophical Theology of Jonathan Edwards*, 47–115, 170–211.

aspect is not directly related to the matter in hand, and therefore I will not elaborate further here.[255]

Edwards used the concept of *prisca theologia* in order to show (contrary to the Deists) that "nearly all humans have received revelation, and therefore all knowledge of true religion among the heathen is from revelation rather than the light of natural reason."[256] Greg Gilbert suggests McDermott interprets Edwards as therefore maintaining God would use *prisca theologia* to reveal sufficient truth to pagan peoples to bring about their salvation.[257] However, this claim is contested by many Edwards' scholars. For example, Gilbert judges that "a closer look at Edwards's use of the *prisca theologia* . . . will show that he never intended it to provide the means of salvation in this way, but only to prepare the nations for the preaching of the gospel."[258] Therefore, Edwards does not credit the *prisca theologia* with a salvific function.

---

255. For some recent assessments of dispositional soteriology see: Bombaro, "Jonathan Edward's Vision of Salvation"; Bombaro, "Dispositional Peculiarity History"; Holmes, "Does Jonathan Edwards Use a Dispositional Ontology? A Response to Sang Hyun Lee"; Hunsinger, "Dispositional Soteriology: Jonathan Edwards on Justification by Faith Alone." Oliver Crisp notes that all the examples which McDermott cites in order to support his case for dispositional soteriology are "standard Reformed examples: Old Testaments saints and holy pagans (Melchizedek), and infants." He concludes that despite McDermott's attempts to depict a "new Edwards," he is unsuccessful. Edwards "is not an inclusivist, nor is he a proto-Rahner" (Crisp, "Book Review: Gerald R. McDermott, *Jonathan Edwards Confronts the Gods*," 83).

256. McDermott, *Jonathan Edwards Confronts the Gods*, 94.

257. Gilbert, "Nations Will Worship." Gilbert highlights McDermott's observation that "Edwards made a series of important theological moves beyond his Reformed predecessors that could have opened the door for a more hopeful view of the salvation of the heathen. The advances he made in typology, the extensive use he made of the *prisca theologia*, and his development of a dispositional soteriology prepared the theological way for a more expansive view of salvation" (McDermott, *Jonathan Edwards Confronts the Gods*, 143). It should be noted, however, that Gilbert's interpretation of McDermott appears to be going beyond what McDermott actually states. McDermott says "On the question of salvation, [Edwards] usually only conceded the possibility that heathen could be saved, and never spoke in the expansively hopeful terms of a Watts, Ramsay or Skelton, or even a Baxter or Wesley. So while he built the theological foundations upon which a more hopeful soteriology could quite naturally have been erected, *he himself never chose to do so*" (McDermott, *Jonathan Edwards Confronts the Gods*, 144; italics added).

258. Gilbert, "Nations Will Worship," 56. Bombaro concurs, stating that the "oral tradition of the prisca theologia (a) was never intended to redeem, that is, it was not an "ends" but a "means"; (b) was superseded by special revelation in a covenantal context; and (c) was contextualized within the history of redemption as being merely prepara-

Furthermore, and of particular relevance for the current issue, is the origin of the *prisca theologia*. According to Bombaro,

> Edwards was concerned to substantiate the two-pronged point that 'HEATHENS had what they had of truth in divine things by TRADITION from the first fathers of nations, or from the Jews' and that this divine 'truth' or revelation trickled down through non-Jewish cultures to ancient Greece and Rome, India and Africa, and even to China and the Americas. The idea was to demonstrate that every major thinker from Socrates to Plato to every leading religion from Islam to Confucianism to the animism of the Iroquois and Delaware Indians were indebted to God's special oral (and sometimes transcribed) revelation to Adam, the line of Seth, the Patriarchs, and, particularly, Moses' Pentateuch.²⁵⁹

Therefore, while Edwards certainly acknowledges truths in other religions, these he suggests have their origin in the Christian Scriptures or have "trickled down" from the covenant community. They are not evidence of other religions *themselves* preparing for the gospel. Bavinck's position is similar to that of Edwards', for he adopts a form of *prisca theologia* which he refers to as proto-word revelation.²⁶⁰ He adds what he calls the radiation or inflow of special revelation into another religious tradition; for example, Plato being influenced by the Old Testament prophets, St. Thomas preaching in India and Nestorian influence in China.²⁶¹

---

tory for that which does facilitate regenerative salvation—the gospel means of Christ" (Bombaro, "Jonathan Edward's Vision of Salvation," 48).

259. Bombaro, "Dispositional Peculiarity History," 130, quoting Jonathan Edwards "Miscellanies" no. 959, in *Miscellanies: Entry Nos. 833–1152*, 239 (capitals are Edwards'). Cf. Edwards, *History of the Work of Redemption*, 399: "And hence it is that all that part of the world that now does own one only true God, Christians, Jews, Mohammedans, and even Deists too, originally came by the knowledge of him. 'Tis owing to this [they] ben't in general at this day left in heathenish darkness. They have it all, first of all either immediately from the Scriptures or by tradition from their fathers, who had it first from the Scriptures. And doubtless those that now despises the Scriptures, and boast of the strength of their own reason as sufficient to bring them to knowledge of the one true God, if the gospel had never have come abroad in the world to enlighten their forefathers, would have been as sottish and brutish idolaters, as the world in general was before the gospel came abroad."

260. Bavinck, "General Revelation and the Non-Christian Religions," 51.

261. Ibid., 52.

Therefore, I dispute the assertion that other religions act as alternative preparations for the gospel, and also dispute the premise that God is actively revealing himself through other religions. Rather, the elements of truth that do exist in non-Christian religions are remnants of original monotheism, in conjunction with general revelation. With Kraemer and Bavinck I adopt a cautious approach to the theory of points of contact and suggest it should not be assumed that any point of contact represents theological common ground. For, as I have already noted, a doctrine cannot be separated from the system in which it is found. The position I adopt follows Kraemer's dialectical approach. He emphasized "the dialectical relation in which Christianity, if true to its nature and mission, ought to stand to the world—the combination of a fierce 'yes' and at the same time a fierce 'no' to the world: the *human* and *broken* reflection of the divine 'no' and 'yes' of the holy God of reconciliation who held the world under His absolute judgement and at the same time claimed it for His love."[262]

Kraemer's dialectical approach to points of contact maintains "that there are no points of contact between revelation and the non-Christian systems of thought, but there may be many situational encounters between Christians and others."[263] He rejects any theory of points of contact that takes doctrines in isolation from their total context.[264] While Christ does not fulfil other religions Kraemer considers there to be "longings and apperceptions in the religious life of mankind outside the special sphere of the Christian revelation, of which Christ, what He is and has brought, may be termed *in a certain* sense the fulfilment. Yet, it is mistaken and misleading to describe the religious pilgrimage of mankind as a preparation or a leading up to a so-called consummation or fulfilment in Christ."[265]

---

262. Kraemer, *Christian Message in a Non-Christian World*, 104. (italics original).

263. Perry, *Radical Difference*, 61. Cf. Kraemer, *Christian Message in a Non-Christian World*, 300: "[A]lthough fundamentally speaking there is no point of contact, in practice the religious needs and aspirations that are embedded in these great religious systems often offer, of course, splendid opportunities of practical, *human* contact" (italics original).

264. Kraemer viewed the world religions as asking and answering different questions (Kraemer, "Continuity or Discontinuity," 5). "The claims of the various religions are clearly conflicting" (Cf. Kraemer, *Christian Message in a Non-Christian World*, 299–301).

265. Kraemer, "Continuity or Discontinuity," 3. Cf. Kraemer, *Christian Message in a Non-Christian World*, 135; Kraemer, *Religion and the Christian Faith*, 85. Kraemer's

Thus, I suggest if the term "fulfilment" is to be applied to the relationship between other religions and Christianity, then it must be used with appropriate nuance to indicate what Kraemer describes as "contradictive or subversive fulfilment."[266]

9.4. Summary

I have examined the biblical texts most commonly cited by proponents of the fulfilment model in support of their position, and have demonstrated that these are exegeted and applied erroneously. I have asserted that the biblical fulfilment concept involves a *sui generis* fulfilment of the Old covenant in the new covenant, and is never applied more widely in scripture. I have surveyed some of the patristic material (focusing on the contribution of Justin Martyr) often cited in support of the fulfilment model and have shown that the Fathers' approach was far more cautious and nuanced than is acknowledged by those who wish to present the Church Fathers as early proponents of the fulfilment approach. I have considered the status of other religious scriptures, and have argued that while there may be elements of truth in these scriptures, they should not be considered as alternative preparations for the

---

fulfilment "never represents a perfecting of what has gone before. In this fulfilment is contained a radical recasting of values, because these longings and apprehensions when exposed to the searching and revolutionary light of Christ, appear to be blind and misdirected" (Kraemer, "Continuity or Discontinuity," 3). Cf. ibid., 5: "to represent the religions of the world as *somehow,* however imperfect and crude it may be, a παιδαγωγός, a schoolmaster to Christ, is a distorted presentation of these religions and their fundamental structure and tendencies, and a misunderstanding of the Christian revelation."

266. Kraemer, "Continuity or Discontinuity," 5. Newbigin adopts this term, according to Mike Goheen, from Kraemer. See Goheen, *"As the Father Has Sent Me, So I Am Sending You,"* 42, 208, 344, and passim. J. H. Bavinck prefers the term *possessio*: "We would ... prefer to use the term *possessio*, to take possession ... Within the framework of the non-Christian life, customs and practices serve idolatrous tendencies and drive a person away from God. The Christian life takes them in hand and turns them in an entirely different direction; they acquire an entirely different content. Even though in external form there is much that resembles past practices, in reality everything has become new, the old has in essence passed away and the new has come ... [Christ] fills each thing, each word, and each practice with a new meaning and gives it new direction. Such is neither 'adaptation,' nor accommodation; it is in essence the legitimate taking possession of something by him to whom all power is given in heaven and on earth" (Bavinck, *Introduction to the Science of Missions*, 178–79).

gospel, or as potential replacements for the Old Testament. Finally, after assessing the elements of continuity and discontinuity between other religions and Christianity, I have proposed a model of this relationship, which maintains a cautious approach to the points of contact theory, and which (after Kraemer), I have described as subversive fulfilment.

10

CONCLUSIONS AND RECOMMENDATIONS

In considering the relationship between other religions and Christianity, the inclusivist paradigm relies on an analogy with the relationship between the Old and New covenants. I have submitted this analogy, and the concomitant fulfilment paradigm to a biblical and theological critique, and have established that these approaches are fundamentally flawed. I have argued that the errors inherent in these concepts have at root a misunderstanding of the relationship between Old and New covenants and between Israel and the church. The root of this misconstrued relationship, I have suggested, is in a faulty understanding of the nature of the Old covenant and of Israel. I have also demonstrated that the Israel analogy and fulfilment model do not adequately recognize the varied nature of the biblical covenants that together constitute the Old covenant, and the form of their fulfilment in the New covenant. Any truly *Christian* theology of religions must start with a correct understanding of the nature of the Christian faith, that is, a proper self-understanding, and an accurate understanding of that religion that is closest to Christianity, namely, Judaism. For this reason I have considered the relationship between Israel and the church, and between the Old and New covenants as a prerequisite to the consideration of the relationship between other religions and Christianity.

This study has highlighted the *sui generis* nature of the relationship between the Old and New covenants, and the organic, progressive nature of salvation history. Salvation history has been a key strand throughout the study, and I have shown that the Israel analogy and fulfilment model have not adequately grasped the nature of this history as portrayed in Scripture. I have further argued that the exegetical and patristic data are misinterpreted in support of the Israel analogy and fulfilment model.

These approaches to the relationship between other religions and Christianity rely on a correspondence between the chronologically pre-messianic (Israel) and the epistemologically pre-messianic (other religions), and in so doing consider the "BC condition" to continue today. In so doing, they undermine the significance of the Christ-event in the unfolding plan of redemption by failing to appreciate the decisive effect of this event on history and the nature of existence. The Christ-event is the midpoint of salvation history and is of universal significance for all space and time and for all people. It marks a radical turn in salvation history, a crisis point, rendering the BC period complete and fulfilled. The effect of the atonement cannot be limited to one strand of subsequent history, namely, that which is coextensive with the church or knowledge of the Gospel. Therefore, the concept of a continuing "pre-Messianic" condition or state is seriously flawed. An aspect of this understanding of the atonement that has not been pursued in any detail in this study is the affect (if any) of the atonement on the unevangelised, and I propose this would be a fruitful avenue of further enquiry. Such a study should, I suggest, consider the relationship between the *historia salutis* and the *ordo salutis*.[1]

I have concluded that the Israel analogy and fulfilment model are fundamentally defective and should not be employed in a Christian theology of religions. The Israel analogy is what Juthe defines as a "bad analogy,"[2] because the "elements that determine the Assigned-Predicate of the Analogue do not correspond one-to-one with a counterpart element in the Target-Subject."[3] In this instance, the elements that do not correspond are the Old covenant and non-Christian religions. As the inclusivist paradigm is reliant on these faulty concepts this paradigm itself is substantially weakened and this presents a challenge to inclusivists who need to re-examine the basis of their approach to the rela-

---

1. Here, as earlier in this volume, I am using the term *ordo salutis* in its general sense to refer to "the ongoing application of salvation, in distinction from its once-for-all accomplishment." Cf. Gaffin, *By Faith, Not By Sight*, 18. See chapter 7 n. 108, for elaboration.

2. See the introduction to this book for Juthe's full definition of analogy.

3. Juthe, "Argument by Analogy," 2–5.

tionship between other religions and Christianity. In particular, I have noted how the inclusivist model regularly employs the Israel analogy without offering any significant defense for doing so. Indeed, it often appears to be "assumed." Inclusivists who wish to continue using the analogy now need to provide a substantial defense for this approach.

I have noted that the inclusivist paradigm employs the Israel analogy and fulfilment model to provide evidence of the accessibility of salvation outside of the knowledge of Christ. This study has not dealt in detail with soteriological issues, and my assertion that the Israel analogy and fulfilment model are erroneous concepts, as is the inclusivist paradigm which relies on them, should *not* be interpreted as necessarily indicating that people without knowledge of Christ are without hope of salvation. I have noted how Kraemer firmly denied the fulfilment approach; however, he correctly asserts that such a denial "does not, however, *include* denying that God has been working in the minds of men outside the sphere of Christian revelation and that there have been, and may be now, acceptable men of faith who live under the sway of non-Christian religions—products, however, not of these non-Christian religions but of the mysterious workings of God's spirit. God forbid that we mortal men should be so irreverent as to dispose of how and where the Sovereign God of grace and love has to act."[4]

Kraemer's caution is entirely appropriate. This is an area of theology requiring further research, and I suggest profitable avenues of exploration include the origin, nature and function of truth and general revelation in non-Christian religions. The relationship between general and special revelation, and the possibility of other "modalities" of special revelation also warrants further research.[5]

This study has dealt with an aspect of the relationship between other religions and Christianity—and specifically, it has considered how this relationship should *not* be understood, namely, it should not be understood as analogous to the relationship between Old and New covenants. While I believe this "negative" thesis is entirely warranted,

---

4. Kraemer, "Continuity or Discontinuity," 4–5.

5. Here I am referring to the possibility of modalities of special revelation in addition to the proclamation of the Gospel by a human messenger or the reading of the Scriptures. Christopher Little's book *Revelation of God among the Unevangelized* is a useful introduction to this topic, and his proposal that other modalities of special revelation exist warrants more detailed consideration. Among the modalities proposed by Little are oral tradition, miraculous events, dreams, visions, and angels.

the "positive" dimension merits more research—how should the relationship between other religions and Christianity be conceived? and what is the purpose, in God's economy, of non-Christian religions?[6]

Last, this study has highlighted a wider issue concerning the methodology of a Christian theology of religions. It is apparent from this study that the Israel analogy and fulfilment model have been developed with insufficient interface with central tenets of Christian theology, such as Israel, covenant, salvation history, and atonement, and that it is this isolation that has permitted these erroneous concepts to subsist. Therefore, any consistently Christian theology of religions must be developed with systematic attention to the entire compass of Christian theology, rather than as a separate sub-discipline as has tended to be the case to date, and as is evidenced in the use of the Israel analogy and fulfilment model.

---

6. This issue is the subject of a recent book by Gerald R. McDermott: *God's Rivals: Why Has God Allowed Different Religions?* This book is, according to Veli-Matti Kärkkäinen, "the first major work on the topic" (Kärkkäinen, writing on the back cover).

BIBLIOGRAPHY

Abraham, William J. *The Logic of Evangelism*. London: Hodder & Stoughton, 1989.
Alexander, T. D. "Abraham Reassessed Theologically: The Abraham Narrative and the New Testament Understanding of Justification by Faith." Online: http://www.beginningwithmoses.org/articles/abrahamreassessed.htm/.
Amalorpavadas, D. S., editor. *Research Seminar on Non-Biblical Scriptures*. Bangalore: National Biblical, Catechetical and Liturgical Centre, 1974.
Amerding, Carl Edwin. "The Meaning of Israel in Evangelical Thought." In *Evangelicals and Jews in Conversation on Scripture, Theology and History*, edited by Marc Tanenbaum et al., 119–41. Grand Rapids: Baker, 1978.
———. *The Old Testament and Criticism*. Carlisle, UK: Paternoster, 1997.
Anderson, Bernhard, editor. *The Old Testament and the Christian Faith*. London: SCM, 1964.
———. "The Old Testament as a Christian Problem." In *The Old Testament and Christian Faith*, edited by Bernhard Anderson, 1–7. London: SCM, 1964.
Anderson, Gerald, editor. *The Theology of the Christian Mission*. London: SCM, 1961.
Anderson, Norman. *Christianity and World Religions: The Challenge of Pluralism*. Leicester, UK: InterVarsity, 1984.
Aquinas, Thomas Saint. *The Summa Theologica of St. Thomas Aquinas*. Translated by the Fathers of the English Dominican Province. Online: http://www.newadvent.org/summa/.
Armerding, Carl E. Augustine. *St. Aurelius Augustin's City of God and Christian Doctrine*. Edited by Philip Schaff. Edinburgh: T. & T. Clark, 1886.
Avis, Paul. editor. *Divine Revelation*. Grand Rapids: Eerdmans, 1997. Reprint, Eugene OR: Wipf & Stock Publishers, 2004.
Bahnsen, Greg. "The Encounter of Jerusalem with Athens." 1980. Online: http://www.cmfnow.com/articles/pa045.htm/.
Baillie, D. M. *God Was in Christ*. 1947. Reprint, Eugene, OR: Wipf & Stock, 2001.
Baker, David L. "Covenant: An Old Testament Study." In *The God of Covenant: Biblical, Theological and Contemporary Perspectives*, edited by Jamie A. Grant and Alistair I. Wilson, 21–53. Leicester, UK: InterVarsity, 2005.
———. *Two Testaments, One Bible*. Downers Grove, IL: InterVarsity, 1991.
Barnes, Michael. *Christian Identity & Religious Pluralism*. London: SPCK, 1989.
Barrett, C. K. *Acts*. 2 vols. International Critical Commentary. Edinburgh: T. & T. Clark, 1994.
Barth, Karl. *Dogmatics in Outline*. Translated by G. T. Thompson. London: SCM, 1949.
Baugh, S. M. "Galatians 3:20 and the Covenant of Redemption." *WTJ* 66 (2004) 49–70.
Baumann, Arnulf. "The Two Ways/Two Covenants Theory." *Mishkan* 11 (1989) 36–43.
Bavinck, Herman. *Reformed Dogmatics*. Vol. 1, *Prolegomena*. Translated by John Vriend. Edited by John Bolt. 4 vols. Grand Rapids: Baker, 2003.

———. *Reformed Dogmatics*. Vol. 3, *Sin and Salvation in Christ*. Translated by John Vriend. Edited by John Bolt. Grand Rapids: Baker, 2006.
Bavinck, J. H. *The Church between Temple and Mosque*. Grand Rapids: Eerdmans, 1966.
———. "General Revelation and the Non-Christian Religions." *Free University Quarterly* 4 (1955) 43–55.
———. *An Introduction to the Science of Missions*. Translated by David Freeman. Philadelphia: Presbyterian and Reformed, 1960.
———. "Theology and Mission." *Free University Quarterly* 8 (1961) 59–66.
Bea, Augustin. *The Church and the Jewish People*. Translated by Philip Loretz. New York: Harper & Row, 1966.
Begbie, Jeremy. "Rediscovering and Re-Imagining the Atonement." *Anvil* 11 (1994) 193–202.
Berkhof, Hendrikus. "Israel as a Theological Problem in the Christian Church." *JES* 6 (1969) 329–47.
Berkhof, Louis. *Systematic Theology*. London: Banner of Truth, 1941.
Berkouwer, G. C. *General Revelation*. Grand Rapids: Eerdmans, 1955.
Blacketer, Raymond. "Definite Atonement in Historical Perspective." In *The Glory of the Atonement*, edited by Charles Hill and Frank James, 304–23. Downers Grove, IL: InterVarsity, 2004.
Blackham, Paul. "Faith in Christ in the Old Testament." Online: http://www.theologian.org.uk/bible/blackham.html/.
Blackham, Paul, and Graeme Goldsworthy. "The Blackham-Goldsworthy Debate: Question Time." Online: http://www.theologian.org.uk/bible/blackham-golsdworthy-questions.html/.
Blaising, Craig. "The Future of Israel as a Theological Question." *JETS* 44 (2001) 435–51.
Blaising, Craig A., and Darrell L. Bock. *Progressive Dispensationalism*. Wheaton, IL: 1993.
Blewett, David. "Must Jews Become Christians?" Online: http://www.j-cinstitute.org/Articles/Blewett_Must_Jews_become_Christians.htm/.
Blocher, Henri. "The Scope of Redemption and Modern Theology." *Scottish Bulletin of Evangelical Theology* 9 (1991) 80–103.
Bloesch, Donald G. *Jesus Christ: Saviour & Lord*. Carlisle, UK: Paternoster, 1997.
———. *Jesus Is Victor! Karl Barth's Doctrine of Salvation*. Nashville: Abingdon, 1976.
———. *A Theology of Word and Spirit*. Carlisle, UK: Paternoster, 1992.
Bock, Darrell L. "Athenians Who Have Never Heard." In *Through No Fault of Their Own? The Fate of Those Who Have Never Heard*, edited by William Crockett and James Sigountos, 117–24. Grand Rapids: Baker, 1991.
Bombaro, John J. "Dispositional Peculiarity, History, and Edwards's Evangelistic Appeal to Self-Love." *WTJ* 66 (2004) 121–57.
———. "Jonathan Edwards's Vision of Salvation." *WTJ* 65 (2003) 45–67.
Bonnington, Mark. "Is the Old Covenant Renewed in the New? A Response to James D. G. Dunn." In *Covenant Theology: Contemporary Approaches*, edited by Mark J. Cartledge and David Mills, 57–84. Carlisle, UK: Paternoster, 2001.
Borland, James A. *Christ in the Old Testament*. Rev. & exp. ed. Fearn: Christian Focus, 1999.
Bosch, David. *Theology of Religions—Study Guide*. Msr303. Pretoria: UNISA, 1977.
———. *Transforming Mission*. Maryknoll: Orbis, 1991.
Bowler, Maurice. "Rosenzweig on Judaism and Christianity." *Mishkan* 11 (1989) 1–8.

Bibliography

Braaten, Carl. *No Other Gospel!* Minneapolis: Fortress, 1992.
Braaten, Carl, and Robert Jenson, editors. *Jews and Christians: People of God.* Grand Rapids: Eerdmans, 2003.
Bradley, James. "Logos Christology and Religious Pluralism: A New Evangelical Proposal." In *The Challenge of Religious Pluralism: An Evangelical Analysis and Response*, edited by David K. Clark, et al., 190–215. Wheaton: Wheaton College and Graduate School, 1992.
Bray, Gerald. "Explaining Christianity to Pagans." In *The Trinity in a Pluralistic Age*, edited by Kevin J. Vanhoozer, 9–25. Papers of the Fifth Edinburgh Dogmatics Conference held in Edinburgh August 31–September 3, 1993. Grand Rapids: Eerdmans, 1997.
Braybrooke, Marcus. *Christian-Jewish Dialogue: The Next Steps.* London: SCM, 2000.
Brown, Harold O. J. *Heresies: Heresy and Orthodoxy in the History of the Church.* Peabody, MA: Hendrickson, 1984.
Bruce, F. F. *The Book of the Acts.* NICNT. Grand Rapids: Eerdmans, 1998.
———. *The Epistle to the Galatians.* Exeter, UK: Paternoster, 1982.
———. "Eschatology." In *Evangelical Dictionary of Theology*, edited by Walter A. Elwell, 362–65. Baker Reference Library 1. Grand Rapids: Baker, 1984.
———. *The Gospel of John.* Basingstoke, UK: Pickering, 1983.
———. "Salvation History in the New Testament." In *Man and His Salvation*, edited by Eric Sharpe and John Hinnells, 75–90. Manchester: Manchester University Press, 1973.
———. *The Time Is Fulfilled: Five Aspects of the Fulfillment of the Old Testament in the New.* Exeter, UK: Paternoster, 1978.
Brunner, Emil. "The Significance of the Old Testament for Our Faith." In *The Old Testament and Christian Faith: A Theological Discussion*, edited by Bernhard Anderson, 243–64. London: SCM, 1963.
Bühlmann, Walbert. *The Chosen Peoples.* Translated by Robert Barr. Slough, UK: St Paul Publications, 1982.
Bultmann, Rudolf. "Ignorance." In *Theological Dictionary of the New Testament Abridged in One Volume*, edited by Geoffrey Bromiley, 18. Grand Rapids: Eerdmans, 1986.
Calvin, John. *Acts 14–28.* Translated by John W. Fraser. Calvin's New Testament Commentaries 7. Grand Rapids: Eerdmans, 1995.
———. *Commentary on the Gospel according to John.* Translated by William Pringle. 2 vols. Calvin Translation Society Publications 33–34. Edinburgh: Calvin Translation Society, 1847.
———. *Institutes of the Christian Religion.* Translated by Henry Beveridge. Grand Rapids: Eerdmans, 1989.
Cameron, Nigel M. De S., editor. *Universalism and the Doctrine of Hell.* Scottish Bulletin of Evangelical Theology Special Study 5. Grand Rapids: Baker, 1992.
Caragounis, Chrys. "Divine Revelation." *Evangelical Review of Theology* 12 (1988) 226–39.
Carey, Patrick, and Joseph Lienhard, editors. *Biographical Dictionary of Christian Theologians.* Westport, CT: Greenwood, 2000.
Carson, D. A. "Atonement in Romans 3:21–26." In *The Glory of the Atonement: Biblical, Historical & Practical Perspectives*, edited by Charles Hill and Frank James, 119–39. Downers Grove, IL: InterVarsity, 2004.
———. *The Gagging of God.* Leicester, UK: Apollos, 1996.

Bibliography

———. *The Gospel according to John*. Leicester, UK: InterVarstiy, 1991.

———. *Matthew*. In *The Expositor's Bible Commentary*, Vol. 8, edited by Frank E. Gaebelein, 3–603. Grand Rapids: Zondervan, 1984.

———. "Mystery and Fulfillment: Toward a More Comprehensive Paradigm of Paul's Understanding of the Old and New." In *Justification and Variegated Nomism: The Paradoxes of Paul*, edited by D. A. Carson, et al., 393–436. Grand Rapids: Baker, 2004.

Carson, D. A., et al. *Justification and Variegated Nomism*. Vol. 2, *The Paradoxes of Paul*. Tübingen: Mohr Siebeck, 2004.

Carson, D. A., and John D. Woodbridge, editors. *Hermeneutics, Authority and Canon*. 1986. Reprinted, Eugene, OR: Wipf & Stock Publishers, 2005.

Chadwick, Henry. *Early Christian Thought and the Classical Tradition: Studies in Justin, Clement, and Origen*. Oxford: Clarendon, 1966.

———. *The Early Church*. Rev. ed. London: Penguin, 1993.

Chapman, Colin. "'Israel and Palestine: Where Is God in the Conflict?'" *Redcliffe College Encounters Mission E-zine* 5 (2005). Online: http://www.redcliffe.org/uploads/documents/israel_palestine1_05.pdf.

Charleston, Steve. "The Old Testament of Native America: Constructing Christian Theologies from the Underside." In *Lift Every Voice: Constructing Christian Theologies from the Underside*, edited by Susan Brooks Thistlethwaite and Mary Potter Engel, 69–81. Rev. and exp. ed. Maryknoll, NY: Orbis, 1998.

Childs, Brevard. *Biblical Theology in Crisis*. Philadelphia: Westminster, 1970.

———. *Old Testament Theology in a Canonical Context*. London: SCM, 1985.

Christian Scholars Group on Christian-Jewish Relations. "A Sacred Obligation." Online: http://www.bc.edu/research/cjl/meta-elements/sites/partners/csg/Sacred_Obligation.htm/.

Church of England Doctrine Commission. *The Mystery of Salvation: The Story of God's Gift; A Report by the Doctrine Commission of the General Synod of the Church of England*. GS 1155. London: Church House, 1995.

Church of England General Synod Board for Mission and Unity. *Towards a Theology for InterFaith Dialogue*. London: Church House, 1984.

Clark, David. *To Know and Love God*. Wheaton, IL: Crossway, 2003.

Clark, R. Scott. "A Brief History of Covenant Theology." Online: http://public.csusm.edu/guests/rsclark/History_Covenant_Theology.htm/.

———, editor. *Covenant, Justification, and Pastoral Ministry: Essays by the Faculty of Westminster Seminary California*. Phillipsburg, NJ: P & R, 2007.

Clarke, Andrew D. and Bruce W. Winter, editors. *One God, One Lord: Christianity in a World of Religious Pluralism*. 2nd ed. Exeter, UK: Paternoster, 1992.

Clement of Alexandria. *The Miscellanies; Or Stromata, Book I*. In *The Ante-Nicene Fathers: Translations of the Writings of the Fathers down to AD 325*, edited by Alexander Roberts and James Donaldson et al. Vol. 2, *The Writings of Clement of Alexandria*, 349–470. Grand Rapids: Eerdmans, 1988.

Clendenin, Daniel. *Many Gods, Many Lords: Christianity Encounters World Religions*. Grand Rapids: Baker, 1995.

Clowney, Edmund P. *Preaching and Biblical Theology*. Grand Rapids: Eerdmans, 1961.

———. *The Unfolding Mystery: Discovering Christ in the Old Testament*. Leicester, UK: InterVarsity, 1998.

Cohn-Sherbock, Dan. *Judaism and Other Faiths*. London: Macmillan, 1994.

Bibliography

Collins English Dictionary. Online: http://www.collinslanguage.com/Default.aspx/.
Congregation for the Doctrine of the Faith. *Dominus Iesus: Declaration on the Unicity and Salvific Universality of Jesus Christ and the Church.* Vatican: 2000. Online: http://www.vatican.va/roman_curia/congregations/cfaith/documents/rc_con_cfaith_doc_20000806_dominus-iesus_en.html/.

———. "Notification on the Book *Toward a Christian Theology of Religious Pluralism.*" Online http//www.vatican.va/roman_curia/congregations/cfaith/documents/rc_con_cfaith_doc_20010124_dupuis_en.html/.

Conn, Harvie M. "Do Other Religions Save?" In *Through No Fault of Their Own? The Fate of Those Who Have Never Heard,* edited by William Crockett and James Sigountos, 195–208. Grand Rapids: Baker, 1991.

Conzelman, Hans. *The Theology of St. Luke.* Translated by Geoffrey Buswell. New York: Harper & Row, 1961.

Corduan, Winfried. *A Tapestry of Faiths: The Common Threads between Christianity & World Religions.* Downers Grove, IL: InterVarsity, 2002.

Cotterell, Peter. *Mission and Meaninglessness: The Good News in a World of Suffering and Disorder.* London: SPCK, 1990.

Cousins, Ewert. "Judaism-Christianity-Islam: Facing Modernity Together." *JES* 30 (1993) 417–25.

Cracknell, Kenneth. *Justice, Courtesy and Love: Theologians and Missionaries Encountering World Religions, 1846–1914.* London: Epworth, 1995.

Cragg, Kenneth. *The Christ and the Faiths: Theology in Cross-Reference.* London: SPCK, 1986.

Craig, William Lane. "Politically Incorrect Salvation." In *Christian Apologetics in the Postmodern World,* edited by Timothy Phillips and Dennis Okholm. Downers Grove, IL: InterVarsity, 1995.

Cranfield, C. E. B. *A Critical and Exegetical Commentary on the Epistle to the Romans.* 2 vols. International Critical Commentary. Edinburgh: T. & T. Clark, 1979.

———. *A Critical and Exegetical Commentary on the Epistle to the Romans.* 2 vols. Vol. 1. Edinburgh: T. & T. Clark, 1975.

———. "Light from St. Paul on Christian-Jewish Relations." In *The Witness of the Jews to God,* edited by David Torrance, 22–31. Edinburgh: Handsel, 1982.

———. *Romans: A Shorter Commentary.* Edinburgh: T. & T. Clark, 1985.

Crisp, Oliver. "Augustinian Universalism." *International Journal for Philosophy of Religion* 53 (2003) 127–45.

———. Review of *Jonathan Edwards Confronts the Gods,* by Gerald R. McDermott. *International Journal of Systematic Theology* 4 (2002) 82–83.

Crockett, William V., and James G. Sigountos, editors. *Through No Fault of Their Own?: The Fate of Those Who Have Never Heard.* Grand Rapids: Baker, 1991.

Cullmann, Oscar. *Christ and Time.* London: SCM, 1962.

———. *Salvation in History.* London: SCM, 1967.

Daniélou, Jean. "Christianity and Non-Christian Religions." In *The Word in History,* edited by T. Patrick Burke, 86–101. London: Sheed and Ward, 1966.

———. *Holy Pagans of the Old Testament.* Translated by Felix Faber. London: Longmans, 1957.

———. *The Lord of History.* London: Longmans, 1958.

———. *The Salvation of the Nations.* London: Sheed and Ward, 1949.

Das, A. Andrew. *Paul and the Jews.* Peabody, NJ: Hendrickson, 2003.

Bibliography

Davies, Alan, editor. *Antisemitism and the Foundations of Christianity*. New York: Paulist, 1979.

Davies, Glenn. *Faith and Obedience in Romans: A Study of Romans 1-4*. Sheffield: JSOT, 1990.

Davies, Margaret. *Matthew*. Sheffield: JSOT Press, 1993.

D'Costa, Gavin. "Karl Rahner's Anonymous Christian: A Reappraisal." *Modern Theology* (1985) 131–48.

———. *The Meeting of Religions and the Trinity*. Maryknoll: Orbis, 2000.

———. "One Covenant or Many Covenants?" *JES* 27 (1990) 441–52.

———. *Theology and Religious Pluralism*. Signposts in Theology. Oxford: Blackwell, 1986.

———. "Theology of Religions." In *The Modern Theologians: An Introduction to Christian Theology in the Twentieth Century*, edited by David F. Ford, 626–44. 2nd ed. Cambridge: Blackwell, 1997.

De Chirico, Leonardo. "The Blurring of Time Distinctions in Roman Catholicism." *Themelios* 29 (2004) 40–46.

Demerest, Bruce A. "Analogy of Faith." In *Evangelical Dictionary of Theology*, edited by Walter A. Elwell, 43–44. Baker Reference Library 1. Grand Rapids: Baker, 1984.

———. *The Cross and Salvation: The Doctrine of Salvation*. Foundations of Evangelical Theology 1. Wheaton: Crossway, 1997.

———. *General Revelation: Historical Views and Contemporary Issues*. Grand Rapids: Zondervan, 1982.

Dewick, Edward Chisholm. *The Christian Attitude to Other Religions*. Hulsean Lectures, 1949. Cambridge: Cambridge University Press, 1953.

Dhavamony, Mariasusai. *Christian Theology of Religions: A Systematic Reflection on the Christian Understanding of World Religions*. Studies in the Intercultural History of Christianity 108. Bern: Lang, 1998.

Diprose, Ronald. "Israel and Christian Theology: Some Effects of the New Majority View." *Emmaus Journal* 10 (2001) 59–74.

———. *Israel and the Church: The Origin and Effects of Replacement Theology*. Waynesboro, GA: Authentic Media, 2000.

———. *Israel in the Development of Christian Thought*. Rome: Instituto Biblico Evangelico Italiano, 2000.

———. "The Jewish-Christian Dialogue and Soteriology." *Trinity Journal* 20 (1999) 23–38.

Donaldson, Terence. "Jewish Christianity, Israel's Stumbling and the *Sonderweg* Reading or Paul." *JSNT* 29 (2006) 27–54.

Drummond, Richard H. *Toward a New Age in Christian Theology*. American Society of Missiology Series 8. Maryknoll: Orbis, 1985.

Dulles, Avery. *Models of Revelation*. New York: Image, 1985.

Dumbrell, William. *Covenant and Creation*. Carlisle, UK: Paternoster, 1997.

Dunn, James D. G. *The Parting of the Ways: Between Christianity and Judaism and Their Significance for the Character of Christianity*. London: SCM, 1991.

———. "Judaism and Christianity: One Covenant or Two?" In *Covenant Theology: Contemporary Approaches*, edited by Mark J. Cartledge and David Mills, 33–56. Carlisle, UK: Paternoster, 2001.

Dupuis, Jacques. *Christianity and the Religions: From Confrontation to Dialogue*. Maryknoll: Orbis, 2001.

Bibliography

———. "The Cosmic Economy of the Spirit and the Sacred Scriptures of Religious Traditions." In *Research Seminar on Non Biblical Scriptures*, edited by D. S. Amalorpavadass, 117–35. Bangalore: National Biblical, Catechetical and Liturgical Centre, 1974.

———. "Inclusivist Pluralism as a Paradigm for the Theology of Religions." Paper prepared for Leuven Conference, 2003. Online: http://www.theo.kuleuven.ac.be/.

———. *Toward a Christian Theology of Religious Pluralism*. Maryknoll: Orbis, 1997.

Edwards, James R. *Is Jesus the Only Savior?* Grand Rapids: Eerdmans, 2005.

———. *Romans*. NIBC. Peabody: Hendrickson, 1992.

Edwards, Jonathan. *A History of the Work of Redemption*. Transcribed and edited by John F. Wilson. The Works of Jonathan Edwards 9. New Haven: Yale University Press, 1989.

———. *The Works of Jonathan Edwards*. Vol. 1. Peabody, MA: Hendrickson, 1998.

Edwards, M. J. "Justin's Logos and the Word of God." *Journal of Early Christian Studies* 3 (1995) 261–80.

Eichrodt, Walther. *Theology of the Old Testament*. 2 vols. London, 1970.

Erickson, Millard J. "The Fate of Those Who Never Hear." *Bibliotheca Sacra* 152 (1995) 3–15.

Estelle, Bryan. "The Covenant of Works in Moses and Paul." In *Covenant, Justification, and Pastoral Ministry*, edited by R. Scott Clark, 89–136. Phillipsburg, NJ: P & R, 2007.

Eusebius of Caesarea. *Preparation for the Gospel*. Translated by Edwin Hamilton Gifford. 2 vols. Twin Book Series. Grand Rapids: Baker, 1981.

Evans, Tony. *Totally Saved*. Chicago: Moody, 2004.

Fackre, Gabriel. *The Doctrine of Revelation*. Grand Rapids: Eerdmans, 1997.

———, editor. *Ecumenical Faith in Evangelical Perspective*. Grand Rapids: Eerdmans, 1993.

———. "Israel's Continuing Covenant and God's Deed in Christ." *New Conversations* 12 (1990) 25–27.

———. "Perspectives on the Place of Israel in Christian Faith." *Andover Newton Review* 1 (1990) 7–17.

———. "The Place of Israel in Christian Thought." In *Ecumenical Faith in Evangelical Perspective*, edited by Gabriel Fackre, 147–67. Grand Rapids: Eerdmans, 1993.

Falaturi, Abdoldjavad, et al., editors. *Three Ways to the One God: The Faith Experience in Judaism, Christianity and Islam*. Translated by John Griffiths, et al. New York: Crossroad, 1987.

Farquhar, John N. *The Crown of Hinduism*. London: Oxford University Press, 1913.

Farris, T. V. *Mighty to Save: A Study in Old Testament Soteriology*. Nashville: Broadman, 1993.

Feinberg, John S. *No One Like Him: The Doctrine of God*. The Foundations of Evangelical Theology. Wheaton: Crossway, 2001.

———. "Systems of Discontinuity." In *Continuity and Discontinuity: Perspectives on the Relationship between the Old and New Testaments*, edited by John Feinberg, 63–88. Westchester, IL: Crossway, 1988.

Feinberg, John S., editor. *Continuity and Discontinuity: Perspectives on the Relationship between the Old and New Testaments*. Westchester, IL: Crossway, 1988.

Feinberg, John S., and Paul D. Feinberg, editors. *Tradition and Testament: Essays in Honor of Charles Lee Feinberg*. Chicago: Moody, 1981.

Bibliography

Fiddes, Paul S. *Past Event and Present Salvation: The Christian Idea of Atonement.* London: Darton Longman Todd, 1989.
Fleischner, Eva, editor. *Auschwitz: Beginning of a New Era?: Reflections on the Holocaust; Papers Given at the International Symposium on the Holocaust, Held at the Cathedral of Saint John the Divine, New York City, June 3 to 6, 1974.* New York: Ktav, 1979.
Flender, Helmut. *St. Luke: Theologian of Redemptive History.* Translated by Reginald Fuller and Ilse Fuller. London: SPCK, 1967.
Forsyth, P. T. *The Cruciality of the Cross.* Carlisle, UK: Paternoster, 1997.
———. *The Work of Christ.* London: Collins, 1948.
Frame, John. "The Doctrine of the Christian Life." *Reformed Perspectives Magazine* 7 (2005) 256–81.
———. *The Doctrine of the Knowledge of God.* Phillipsburg: P & R, 1987.
———. "Westminster Confession." In *Evangelical Dictionary of Theology*, edited by Walter A. Elwell, 1168–69. Baker Reference Library 1. Grand Rapids: Baker, 1984.
France, R. T. *Matthew: Evangelist and Teacher.* Exeter: Paternoster, 1989.
———. *Matthew: An Introduction and Commentary.* TNTC. Leicester, UK: InterVarsity, 1985.
Fredericks, James L. *Buddhists and Christians: Through Comparative Theology to Solidarity.* Faith Meets Faith Series. Maryknoll: Orbis, 2004.
———. "The Catholic Church and the Other Religious Paths: Rejecting Nothing That Is True and Holy." *Theological Studies* 64 (2003) 225–54.
———. *Faith among Faiths: Christian Theology and Non-Christian Religions.* New York: Paulist, 1999.
Fruchtenbaum, Arnold. *Israelology: The Missing Link in Systematic Theology.* Revised edition. Tustin, CA: Ariel Ministries, 1994.
Frymer-Kensky, Tikva, et al., editors. *Christianity in Jewish Terms.* Radical Traditions. Boulder: Westview, 2000.
———, editors. "Dabru Emet." Online: http: //www.icjs.org/what/njsp/dabruemet.html/.
Fuller, Daniel P. *The Unity of the Bible: Unfolding God's Plan for Humanity.* Grand Rapids: Zondervan, 1992.
Gaffin, Richard B. Jr. *By Faith, Not by Sight: Paul and the Order of Salvation.* Carlisle, UK: Paternoster, 2006.
———. *Resurrection and Redemption: A Study in Paul's Soteriology.* 2nd ed. Phillipsburg, NJ: P & R, 1987.
———. "Review Essay: Paul the Theologian." *WTJ* 62 (2000) 121–41.
———, editor. *The Shorter Writings of Geerhardus Vos: Redemptive History and Biblical Interpretation.* Phillipsburg: P & R, 1980.
———. "Systematic Theology and Biblical Theology." *WTJ* 38 (1976) 281–99.
Garvey, John. *Seeds of the Word: Orthodox Thinking on Other Religions.* Crestwood: St Vladimir's Seminary Press, 2005.
Geisler, Norman L., and Winfried Corduan. *Philosophy of Religion.* 2nd ed. Grand Rapids: Baker, 1988.
Gilbert, Greg D. "The Nations Will Worship: Jonathan Edwards and the Salvation of the Heathen." *Trinity Journal* 23 (2002) 53–80.
Glaser, Mitch. "Critique of the Two-Covenant Theory." *Miskan* 11 (1989) 44–70.
Glatzer, Nahum. *Franz Rosenzweig: His Life and Thought.* New York: Schocken, 1961.
Goheen, Michael W. *"As the Father Has Sent Me, I Am Sending You": J. E. Lesslie Newbigin's Missionary Ecclesiology.* Zoetermeer, Netherlands: Boekencentrum, 2000.

Goldberg, Louis. "Are There Two Ways of Atonement?" *Mishkan* 11 (1989) 9–30.

Golding, Peter. *Covenant Theology: The Key of Theology in Reformed Thought and Tradition*. Fearn: Christian Focus, 2004.

Goldingay, John. *Approaches to Old Testament Interpretation*. Leicester, UK: InterVarsity, 1981.

———. *Theological Diversity and the Authority of the Old Testament*. Carlisle, UK: Paternoster, 1995.

Goldingay, John E., and Christopher J. H. Wright. "'Yahweh Our God Yahweh One': The Oneness of God in the Old Testament." In *One God, One Lord: Christianity in a World of Religious Pluralism*, edited by Andrew D. Clarke and Bruce W. Winter, 43–62. 2nd ed. Exeter: Paternoster, 1993.

Goldsworthy, Graeme. *According to Plan: The Unfolding Revelation of God in the Bible*. Downers Grove, IL: InterVarsity, 1991.

———. "Relationship of Old Testament and New Testament." In *New Dictionary of Biblical Theology*, edited by Desmond Alexander, Brian Rosner, D. A. Carson and Graeme Goldsworthy, 81–88. Leicester, UK: InterVarsity, 2000.

———. "A Response to Paul Blackham." Online: http://www.theologian.org.uk/bible/goldsworthy.html/.

Grant, Jamie A., and Alistair I. Wilson, editors. *The God of Covenant: Biblical, Theological and Contemporary Perspectives*. Leicester, UK: Apollos, 2005.

Grudem, Wayne. *Systematic Theology: An Introduction to Biblical Doctrine*. Leicester, UK: InterVarsity, 1994.

Gudel, Joseph. "To the Jew First: A Biblical Analysis of the Two-Covenant Theory of the Atonement." *Christian Research Journal* 21:1 (1998) 36–42. Online: http://www.equip.org/articles/to-the-jew-first-a-biblical-analysis-of-the-two-covenant-theory-of-the-atonement/.

Gundry, Stanley, et al., editors. *Four Views on Salvation in a Pluralist World*. Grand Rapids: Zondervan, 1995.

Gunton, Colin. *The Actuality of the Atonement: A Study of Metaphor, Rationality and the Christian Tradition*. Edinburgh: T. & T. Clark, 1988.

———. "Universal and Particular Atonement." In *Readings in Modern Theology*, edited by Robin Gill, 147–62. Nashville: Abingdon, 1995.

Guthrie, Donald, editor. *Galatians*. London: Nelson, 1969.

Hagner, Donald. *Matthew 1–13* WBC 33a. Nashville: Nelson, 1993.

Hamilton, James M. *God's Indwelling Presence: The Holy Spirit in the Old and New Testaments*. NAC Studies in Bible & Theology. Nashville: B&H, 2006.

———. "The Skull Crushing Seed of the Woman: Inner-Biblical Interpretation of Genesis 3:15." *Southern Baptist Journal of Theology* 10 (2006) 15–33.

Harink, Douglas K. *Paul among the Postliberals: Pauline Theology beyond Christendom and Modernity*. Grand Rapids: Brazos, 2003.

Harper, Brad. "Recent Roman Catholic Statements on the Relationship of the Church to Other Religions." Paper presented at the 54th National Conference of the Evangelical Theological Society, Toronto, ON, November 20–22, 2002.

Harrelson, Walter, and Randall Falk. *Jews & Christians: A Troubled Family*. Nashville: Abingdon, 1990.

Harrison, Everett. *Acts: The Expanding Church*. Chicago: Moody, 1975.

Hart, Trevor. "Christ the Mediator." In *Reformed Theology in Contemporary Perspective*, edited by Lynn Quigley, 66–86. Edinburgh: Rutherford House, 2006.

Bibliography

Hedges, Paul. *Preparation and Fulfilment: A History and Study of Fulfilment Theology in Modern British Thought in the Indian Context*. Studies in the Intercultural History of Christianity 124. Oxford: Lang, 2001.

Heiler, Friedrich. *The Gospel of Sâdhu Sundar Singh*. Delhi: ISPCK, 1996.

Heim, S. Mark. *The Depth of Riches: A Trinitarian Theology of Religious Ends*. Grand Rapids: Eerdmans, 2001.

———. *Salvations: Truth and Difference in Religion*. Maryknoll, NY: Orbis, 2003.

Hellwig, Monika. "Christian Theology and the Covenant of Israel." *JES* 7 (1970) 37–51.

———. "From the Jesus of Story to the Christ of Dogma." In *Antisemitism and the Foundations of Christianity*, edited by Alan T Davies, 118–36. New York: Paulist, 1979.

Helm, Paul. "Calvin and the Covenant: Unity and Continuity." *Evangelical Quarterly* 55 (1981) 65–81.

———. "Of God's Eternal Decree." In *Reformed Theology in Contemporary Perspective*, edited by Lynn Quigley, 143–61. Edinburgh: Rutherford House, 2006.

Helm, Paul, and Oliver D. Crisp, editors. *Jonathan Edwards: Philosophical Theologian*. Aldershot: Ashgate, 2003.

Henry, Matthew. *Matthew Henry's Commentary on the Whole Bible in One Volume: Genesis to Revelation*. Edited by Leslie F. Church. Basingstoke: Marshall Morgan & Scott, 1960.

Herter, Theophilus. *The Abrahamic Covenant in the Gospels*. Cherry Hill: Mack, 1966.

Hick, John. *An Interpretation of Religion: Human Responses to the Transcendent*. New Haven: Yale University Press, 1989.

———. *A Rainbow of Faiths: Critical Dialogues in Religious Pluralism*. London: SCM, 1995.

Hillman, Eugene. *The Wider Ecumenism: Anonymous Christianity and the Church*. London: Burns & Oates, 1968.

Hodge, Charles. *Romans*. The Crossway Classic Commentaries. Wheaton: Crossway, 1994.

Hoekema, Anthony A. *The Bible and the Future*. Exeter, UK: Paternoster, 1978.

Holmes, Stephen R. "Does Jonathan Edwards Use a Dispositional Ontology? A Response to Sang Hyun Lee." In *Jonathan Edwards: Philosophical Theologian*, edited by Paul Helm and Oliver D. Crisp, 99–114. Aldershot: Ashgate, 2003.

Holwerda, David E. *Jesus and Israel: One Covenant or Two?* Leicester, UK: Apollos, 1995.

Horton, Michael S. *Covenant and Eschatology: The Divine Drama*. Louisville: Westminster John Knox, 2002.

———. *God of Promise: Introducing Covenant Theology*. Grand Rapids: Baker, 2006.

———. "Which Covenant Theology?" In *Covenant, Justification, and Pastoral Ministry*, edited by R. Scott Clarke, 197–228. Phillipsburg: P & R, 2007.

Hunsinger, George. "Dispositional Soteriology: Jonathan Edwards on Justification by Faith Alone." *Westminster Theological Journal* 66 (2004) 107–21.

Hvalvik, Reidar. "A 'Separate Way' for Israel?" *Mishkan* 16 (1992) 12–29.

Jocz, Jakob. *The Jewish People and Jesus Christ*. London: SPCK, 1949.

———. *A Theology of Election: Israel and the Church*. New York: Macmillan, 1958.

Johnson, Dennis E. *The Message of Acts in the History of Redemption*. Phillipsburg: P & R, 1997.

Johnson, D. H. "Logos." In *Dictionary of Jesus and the Gospels*, edited by Joel B. Green and Scot McKnight, 481–84. Leicester, UK: InterVarsity, 1992.

Bibliography

Johnson, John. "A New Testament Understanding of the Jewish Rejection of Jesus." *JETS* 43 (2000) 229–46.

Jones, Hywel R. *Only One Way: Do You Have to Believe in Christ to Be Saved?* Facing the Issue Series. Bromley, UK: Day One, 1996.

Justin Martyr. *1 Apology*. In *The Ante-Nicene Fathers: Translations of the Writings of the Fathers Down to AD 325*, edited by Alexander Roberts and James Donaldson et al., 1:159–88. Grand Rapids: Eerdmans, 1988.

———. *2 Apology*. In *The Ante-Nicene Fathers: Translations of the Writings of the Fathers Down to AD 325*, edited by Alexander Roberts and James Donaldson et al., 1:198–93. Grand Rapids: Eerdmans, 1988.

———. *Dialogue with Trypho*. In *The Ante-Nicene Fathers: Translations of the Writings of the Fathers Down to AD 325* edited by Alexander Roberts and James Donaldson et al., 1:194–207. Grand Rapids: Eerdmans, 1988.

Juthe, A. "Argument by Analogy." *Argumentation* 19 (2005) 1–27.

Kaiser, Walter. "An Assessment of 'Replacement Theology.'" *Mishkan* 21 (1994) 9–20.

———. "The Law as God's Gracious Guidance for the Promotion of Holiness." In *Five Views on Law and Gospel*, edited by Wayne G. Strickland, 177–228. Grand Rapids: Zondervan, 1993.

Kärkkäinen, Veli-Matti. *An Introduction to the Theology of Religions: Biblical, Historical, and Contemporary Perspectives*. Downers Grove, IL: InterVarsity, 2003.

———. *Trinity and Religious Pluralism: The Doctrine of the Trinity in Christian Theology of Religions*. Aldershot, UK: Ashgate, 2004.

Karlberg, Mark W. *Covenant Theology in Reformed Perspective*. Eugene: Wipf & Stock, 2000.

Keith, Graham A. *Hated without a Cause? A History of Anti-Semitism*. Carlisle, UK: Paternoster, 1997.

———. "Justin Martyr and Religious Exclusivism." In *One God, One Lord: Christianity in a World of Religious Pluralism*, edited by Andrew D. Clarke and Bruce W. Winter, 161–85. 2nd ed. Exeter, UK: Paternoster, 1992.

Khodr, Georges. "The Economy of the Holy Spirit." In *Faith Meets Faith,* edited by Gerald H. Anderson and Thomas F. Stransky, 36–49. Mission Trends 5. New York: Paulist, 1981.

Kistemaker, Simon J. *New Testament Commentary*. Vol. 17, *Exposition of the Acts of the Apostles*. Grand Rapids: Baker, 1990.

Kjær-Hansen, Kai. "The Problem of the Two-Covenant Theology." *Mishkan* 21 (1994) 52–81.

Klett, Fred. "Not Replacement . . . Expansion!" Online: http://www.chaim.org/xpansion.htm/.

Kline, Meredith G. *By Oath Consigned: A Reinterpretation of the Covenant Signs of Circumcision and Baptism* Grand Rapids: Eerdmans, 1968.

———. *The Structure of Biblical Authority*. Revised ed. Reprint, Eugene: Wipf & Stock, 1989.

Klooster, Fred. "The Uniqueness of Reformed Theology." *Calvin Theological Journal* 14 (1979) 32–54.

Knitter, Paul. *Introducing Theologies of Religions*. Maryknoll, NY: Orbis, 2002.

———. *No Other Name? A Critical Survey of Christian Attitudes toward the World Religions*. American Society of Missiology Series 7. Maryknoll, NY: Orbis, 1985.

Bibliography

———. *Towards a Protestant Theology of Religions: A Case Study of Paul Althaus and Contemporary Attitudes.* Marburger theologische Studien 11. Marburg: Elwert, 1974.

Korn, Eugene B., and John T. Pawlikowski, editors. *Two Faiths, One Covenant? Jewish and Christian Identity in the Presence of the Other.* The Bernadin Center Series. Lanham, MD: Rowman & Littlefield, 2005.

Köstenberger, Andreas J., and Peter T. O'Brien. *Salvation to the Ends of the Earth: A Biblical Theology of Mission.* Leicester, UK: Apollos, 2001.

Kraemer, Hendrik. *The Christian Message in a Non-Christian World.* London: Edinburgh House Press, 1938.

———. "Continuity or Discontinuity." In *The Authority of the Faith*, edited by William Paton, 1–23. London: Oxford University Press, 1939.

———. *Religion and the Christian Faith.* London: Lutterworth, 1956.

———. *Why Christianity of All Religions?* London: Lutterworth, 1962.

———. *World Cultures and World Religions.* London: Lutterworth, 1960.

Kraft, Charles, with Marguerite G. Craft. *Christianity in Culture: A Study in Dynamic Biblical Theologizing in Cross Cultural Perspective.* Rev. 25th ann. ed. Maryknoll, NY: Orbis, 2005.

Ladd, G. E. *A Theology of the New Testament*, edited by Donald A. Hagner. 2nd rev. ed. Cambridge: Lutterworth, 1993.

———. *The Wycliffe Bible Commentary.* Edited by Charles F. Pfeiffer and Everett F. Harrison. Chicago: Moody, 1962.

Langer, Ruth. "Jewish Understandings of the Religious Other." *TS* 62 (2003) 255–77.

Lapide, Pinchas. "Christians and Jews—New Protestant Beginning." *JES* 12 (1975) 485–92.

Larkin, William J. *Acts.* The IVP New Testament Commentary Series 5. Downers Grove, IL: InterVarsity, 1995.

———. "The Contribution of the Gospels and Acts to a Biblical Theology of Religions." In *Christianity and the Religions: A Biblical Theology of World Religions*, edited by Edward Rommen and Harold Netland, 72–91. Evangelical Missiological Society Series 2. Pasadena, CA: William Carey Library, 1995.

Lee, Sang Hyun. *The Philosophical Theology of Jonathan Edwards.* Princeton: Princeton University Press, 1988.

Leer, Ellen Flesseman-van. "Aspects of Historical Reformed Theology Which Are Pertinent to the Relations between Reformed Church and the Jewish People." In *Reformed Theology and the Jewish People*, edited by Alan Sell, 3–29. Walsall: World Alliance of Reformed Churches, 1986.

Legrand, Lucien. "Letter and Spirit: The Role of the Book in the Christian Economy." In *Research Seminar on Non-Biblical Scriptures*, edited by D. S. Amalorpavadass, 53–77. Bangalore: National Biblical, Catechetical and Liturgical Centre, 1974.

Leithart, Peter J. *Did Plato Read Moses? Middle Grace and Moral Consensus.* Niceville: Biblical Horizons, 1995.

———."Paul on God's Righteousness." Leithart.com blog. Posted on January 22, 2004. Online: http://www.leithart.com/archives/000437.php/.

Letham, Robert. *Through Western Eyes: Eastern Orthodoxy, A Reformed Perspective.* Fearn: Mentor, 2007.

———. *The Work of Christ.* Contours of Christian Theology. Leicester, UK: InterVarsity, 1993.

Bibliography

Lewis, Gordon R., and Bruce A. Demerest. *Integrative Theology*. Grand Rapids: Zondervan, 1996.

Lillback, Peter A. *The Binding of God: Calvin's Role in the Development of Covenant Theology*. Texts and Studies in Reformation and Post-Reformation Thought. Grand Rapids: Baker, 2001.

Lints, Richard. *The Fabric of Theology: A Prolegomenon to Evangelical Theology*. Grand Rapids: Eerdmans, 1993.

Little, Christopher. *The Revelation of God among the Unevangelized*. Pasadena, CA: William Carey Library, 2000.

Lloyd, G. E. R. "Analogy in Early Greek Thought." In *Dictionary of the History of Ideas*. Online: http://etext.lib.virginia.edu/cgi-local/DHI/dhi.cgi?id=dv1-09/.

Lohfink, Norbert . *The Covenant Never Revoked: Biblical Reflections on Christian-Jewish Dialogue*. Translated by John J. Scullion. New York Paulist, 1991.

Lombardi, Riccardo. *The Salvation of the Unbeliever*. Translated by Dorothy M. White. London: Burns & Oates, 1956.

Longenecker, Richard N. *Galatians*. WBC 41. Dallas: Word, 1990.

———. "The Pedagogical Nature of the Law in Galatians." *JETS* 25 (1982) 53–61.

Luther, Martin. "On the Jews and Their Lies" (1543). Trans. Martin H. Bertram. In *The Christian in Society IV*, edited by Franklin Sherman, 121–306. Luther's Works 47. Philadelphia: Fortress, 1971.

Macleod, Murdo. "The Witness of the Church to the Jewish People." In *The Witness of the Jews to God*, edited by David Torrance, 71–80. Edinburgh: Handsel, 1982.

Magnum, Todd. "Is There a Reformed Way of Getting the Benefits of the Atonement to Those Who Have Never Heard?" *JETS* 47 (2004) 121–36.

Marshall, Bruce. "Christ and the Cultures: The Jewish People and Christian Theology." In *The Cambridge Companion to Christian Doctrine*, edited by Colin Gunton, 81–100. Cambridge Companions to Religion. Cambridge: Cambridge University Press, 1997.

———. *Christology in Conflict: The Identity of a Saviour in Rahner and Barth*. Oxford: Blackwell, 1987.

Marshall, I. Howard. *Acts: An Introduction and Commentary*. TNTC 5. Leicester, UK: InterVarsity, 1980.

Martensen, Daniel F. "Lutheranism and Interfaith Dialogue." In *Grounds for Understanding: Ecumenical Resources for Responses to Religious Pluralism*, edited by S. Mark Heim, 175–87. Grand Rapids: Eerdmans, 1998.

Masson, Robert. "Rahner, Karl." In *Biographical Dictionary of Christian Theologians*, edited by Patrick Carey and Joseph Lienhard, 427–31. Westport: Greenwood, 2000.

McCarthy, Dennis J. *Old Testament Covenant: A Survey of Current Opinions*. Richmond: John Knox, 1972.

McComiskey, Thomas Edward. *The Covenants of Promise*. Nottingham, UK: InterVarsity, 1985.

McDade, John. "Catholic Christianity and Judaism since Vatican II." *New Blackfriars* 88 (2007) 367–84.

———. "One, Two or More Covenants? Covenant in Christian Jewish Relations." Paper presented at the Council of Christians and Jews Conference on Superssionism. December 2001. Online: http://www.eauk.org/theology/key_papers/holy-land/loader.cfm?csModule=security/getfile&pageid=9093/.

McDermott, Gerald R. *Can Evangelicals Learn from World Religions?: Jesus, Revelation, and Religious Traditions*. Downers Grove, IL: InterVarsity, 2000.

Bibliography

———. *God's Rivals: Why Has God Allowed Different Religions?; Insights from the Bible and the Early Church*. Downers Grove, IL: IVP Academic, 2007.
———. *Jonathan Edwards Confronts the Gods: Christian Theology, Enlightenment Religion, and Non-Christian Faiths*. New York: Oxford University Press, 2000.
———. "Jonathan Edwards, John Henry Newman, and Non-Christian Religions." In *Jonathan Edwards: Philosophical Theologian*, edited by Paul Helm and Oliver D. Crisp, 127–37. Aldershot, UK: Ashgate, 2003.
———. "What If Paul Had Been from China? Reflections on the Possibility of Revelation in Non-Christian Religions." In *No Other Gods before Me?: Evangelicals and the Challenge of World Religions*, edited by John G. Stackhouse, 17–36. Grand Rapids: Baker Academic, 2001.
McGowan, A. T. B. "In Defence of 'Headship Theology.'" In *The God of Covenant: Biblical, Theological and Contemporary Perspectives.*, edited by Jamie A. Grant and Alistair I. Wilson, 178–99. Leicester, UK: Apollos, 2005.
Moberly, R. W. L. *The Old Testament of the Old Testament: Patriarchal Narratives and Mosaic Yahwism*. OBT. Minneapolis: Fortress, 1992.
Moo, Douglas J. *The Epistle to the Romans*, NICNT. Grand Rapids: Eerdmans, 1996.
———. "The Law of Christ as the Fulfillment of the Law of Moses: A Modified Lutheran View." In *Five Views on Law and Gospel*, edited by Wayne G. Strickland, 319–76. Grand Rapids: Zondervan, 1993.
Morimoto, Anri. *Jonathan Edwards and the Catholic Vision of Salvation*. University Park: Pennsylvania State University Press, 1995.
———. "Salvation as the Fulfillment of Being: The Soteriology of Jonathan Edwards and Its Implications for Christian Mission." *PSB* 20 (1999) 13–23.
Morris, Leon. *The Atonement: Its Meaning and Significance*. Leicester, UK: InterVarsity, 1983.
———. *The Gospel according to Matthew*. Grand Rapids: Eerdmans, 1992.
Motyer, Steve. "Israel in God's Plan." Paper for the Evangelical Alliance Holy Land Consultation, June 26, 2003. Online: http://www.eauk.org/theology/key_papers/holy-land/loader.cfm?csModule=security/getfile&pageid=9093/.
———. *Israel in the Plan of God*. Leicester, UK: InterVarsity, 1989.
Mounce, Robert H. *Romans*. NAC 27. Nashville: Broadman & Holman, 1995.
Mounce, William D. *The Analytical Lexicon to the Greek New Testament*. Grand Rapids: Zondervan, 1993.
Muck, Terry C. "Is There Common Ground among Religions?" *JETS* 40 (2002) 99–112.
Murray, John. "The Adamic Administration." In *The Collected Writings of John Murray*, edited by John Murray, 47–59. Edinburgh: Banner of Truth, 1977.
———. *The Covenant of Grace*. London: Tyndale, 1954.
———. *The Epistle to the Romans: The English Text with Introduction, Exposition, and Notes*, vol. 2. NICNT. Grand Rapids: Eerdmans, 1968.
———. *Redemption Accomplished and Applied*. Edinburgh: Banner of Truth, 1961.
Nash, Ronald H. "Restrictivism." In *What about Those Who Have Never Heard? Three Views on the Destiny of the Unevangelized*, by Gabriel Fackre, et al., 107–39. Edited by John Sanders. Downers Grove, IL: InterVarsity, 1995.
Netland, Harold A. *Dissonant Voices: Religious Pluralism and the Question of Truth*. Leicester, UK: Apollos, 1991.
———. *Encountering Religious Pluralism: The Challenge to Christian Faith & Mission*. Downers Grove, IL: InterVarsity, 2001.
Newbigin, Lesslie. *The Finality of Christ*. London: SCM, 1969.

Bibliography

———. *The Gospel in a Pluralist Society*. Grand Rapids: Eerdmans, 1989.

Novak, David. *The Image of the Non-Jew in Judaism: An Historical and Constructive Study of the Noahide Laws*. Toronto Studies in Theology 14. Lewiston, NY: Mellen, 1983.

Nyende, Peter. "Why Bother with Hebrews? An African Perspective." *HeyJ* 46 (2005) 512–24.

O'Brien, Peter. "Was Paul a Covenantal Nomist?" In *Justification and Variegated Nomism*. Vol. 2, *The Paradoxes of Paul*, edited by D. A. Carson, et al., 249–96. WUNT 2/181. Grand Rapids: Baker Academic, 2004.

———. "Was Paul Converted?" In *Justification and Variegated Nomism*. Vol. 2, *The Paradoxes of Paul*, edited by D. A. Carson, et al., 361–92. WUNT 2/181. Grand Rapids: Baker Academic, 2004.

O'Donovan, Oliver. *Resurrection and Moral Order: An Outline for Evangelical Ethics*. 2nd ed. Leicester, UK: Apollos, 1994.

Osborn, Eric. "Justin Martyr." In *The First Christian Theologians*, edited by G. R. Evans, 115–20. The Great Theologians. Oxford: Blackwell, 2004.

———. "Justin Martyr and the Logos Spermatikos." *Studia Missionalia* 42 (1993) 143–59.

Osborne, Grant R. *The Hermeneutical Spiral: A Comprehensive Introduction to Biblical Interpretation*. Revised and expanded. 2nd ed. Downers Grove, IL: InterVarsity, 2006.

———. *Romans*. IVP New Testament Commentary Series 6. Leicester, UK: InterVarsity, 2004.

Osten-Sacken, Peter van der. *Christian-Jewish Dialogue: Theological Foundations*. Translated by Margaret Kohl. Philadelphia: Fortress, 1986.

Owen, John. *The Death of Death in the Death of Christ*. Edinburgh: Banner of Truth, 1959.

Pannenberg, Wolfhart. "Redemptive Event and History." In *Essays on Old Testament Interpretation*, edited by Claus Westermann, 314–35. Translated by James Luther Mays. Preacher's Library. London: SCM, 1963.

Pannikkar, Raymon. *The Unknown Christ of Hinduism*. London: Darton, Longman & Todd, 1964.

Parkes, James W. *The Foundation of Judaism and Christianity*. London: Vallentine, Mitchell 1960.

———. *Judaism and Christianity*. London: Gollancz, 1948.

Pate, C. Marvin, et al., *The Story of Israel: A Biblical Theology*. Downers Grove, IL: InterVarsity, 2004.

Pawlikowski, John T. "Contemporary Jewish-Christian Theological Dialogue Agenda." *JES* 11 (1974) 599–616.

———. "Reflections on Covenant and Mission." In *Themes in Jewish-Christian Relations*, edited by Edward Kessler and Melanie Wright, 1–48. Prepublication manuscript provided by author, 2004.

———. "The Search for a New Paradigm for the Christian-Jewish Relationship: A Response to Michael Signer." In *Reinterpreting Revelation and Tradition: Jews and Christians in Conversation* edited by John Pawlikowski and Hayim Goren Perelmuter, 25–48. Bernadin Center Series. Franklin, WI: Sheed and Ward, 2000.

———. "Toward a Theology for Religious Diversity: Perspectives from the Christian-Jewish Dialogue." *JES* 26 (1989) 138–53.

Bibliography

———. "Vatican II's Theological About-Face on the Jews: Not yet Fully Recognized." *The Ecumenist* 37 (2000) 4–6.
———. *What Are They Saying about Jewish-Christian Relations?* New York: Paulist, 1980.
Pawlikowski, John, and Hayim Goren Perelmuter, editors. *Reinterpreting Revelation and Tradition: Jews and Christians in Conversation*. Franklin, WI: Sheed & Ward, 2000.
Perry, Tim S. *Radical Difference: A Defence of Hendrik Kraemer's Theology of Religions*. Editions SR 27. Waterloo, ON: Wilfrid Laurier University Press, 2001.
Petersen, Rodney. "Continuity and Discontinuity: The Debate throughout Church History." In *Continuity and Discontinuity: Perspectives on the Relationship between the Old and New Testaments*, edited by John Feinberg, 17–36. Westchester, IL: Crossway, 1988.
Petuchowski, Jakob. "The Christian-Jewish Dialog: A Jewish View." *Lutheran World* 10 (1963) 381–88.
Phillips, Godfrey. *The Old Testament in the World Church*. Cambridge: James Clarke, 2002.
Pinnock, Clark H. *Flame of Love: A Theology of the Holy Spirit*. Downers Grove, IL: InterVarsity, 1996.
———. "An Inclusivist View." In *More Than One Way?: Four Views on Salvation in a Pluralistic World*, by John Hick, et al., 93–123. Edited by Dennis L. Okholm and Timothy R. Phillips. Grand Rapids: Zondervan, 1995.
———. "Religious Pluralism: A Turn to the Holy Spirit." Paper presented at the 54th Annual National Conference of the Evangelical Theological Society, Toronto, ON, October 20–22, 2002.
———. *A Wideness in God's Mercy: The Finality of Jesus Christ in a World of Religions*. Grand Rapids: Zondervan, 1992.
Piper, John. *Let the Nations Be Glad! The Supremacy of God in Missions*. Leicester, UK: InterVarsity, 1994.
Pontifical Biblical Commission. "The Jewish People and Their Sacred Scriptures in the Christian Bible." Online: http://www.vatican.va/roman_curia/congregations/cfaith/pcb_documents/rc_con_cfaith_doc_20020212_popolo-ebraico_en.html/.
Poythress, Vern S. *The Shadow of Christ in the Law of Moses*. Phillipsburg, NJ: P & R, 1991.
———. *Understanding Dispensationalists*. 2nd ed. Phillipsburg, NJ: P & R, 1994.
Price, Robert. "An Evangelical Version of the Double Covenant." *JES* (1983) 33–42.
Price, R. M. "Are There 'Holy Pagans' in Justin Martyr?" StPatr 31 (1997) 167–71.
Punt, Neal. *What's Good about the Good News? The Plan of Salvation in a New Light*. Chicago: Northland, 1988.
Race, Alan. *Christians and Religious Pluralism*. London: SCM, 1983.
Rad, Gerhard von. *Old Testament Theology*. Vol. 2, *The Theology of Israel's Prophetic Traditions*. Translated by D. M. G. Stalker. Edinburgh: Oliver and Boyd, 1965.
———. "Typological Interpretation of the Old Testament." In *Essays in Old Testament Interpretation*, edited by Claus Westermann, 17–39. London: SCM, 1963.
Rahner, Karl. "Anonymous and Explicit Faith." In *Theological Investigations* 16:52–59. London: Darton, Longman & Todd, 1979.
———. "Anonymous Christianity and the Missionary Task of the Church." In *Theological Investigations* 12: 161–78. London: Darton, Longman & Todd, 1974.
———. "Anonymous Christians." *Theological Investigations* 6:390–98. London: Darton, Longman & Todd, 1969.

Bibliography

———. "Christianity and the Non-Christian Religions." In *Theological Investigations* 5:115–34. London: Darton, Longman & Todd, 1966.
———. "Church, Churches and Religions." In *Theological Investigations* 10:30–49. New York: Herder & Herder, 1973.
———. *Foundations of the Christian Faith*. London: Darton, Longman & Todd, 1978.
———. "History of the Word and Salvation-History." In *Theological Investigations* 5:97–114. London: Darton, Longman & Todd, 1966.
———. "Jesus Christ in the Non-Christian Religions." In *Theological Investigations* 20:39–50. London: Darton, Longman & Todd, 1981.
———. "Observations on the Problem of the Anonymous Christian." In *Theological Investigations* 14:280–94. London: Darton, Longman & Todd, 1976.
———. "On the Importance of the Non-Christian Religions for Salvation." In *Theological Investigations* 19:288–95. London: Darton, Longman & Todd, 1983.
Rajashekar, J. Paul, editor. *Religious Pluralism and Lutheran Theology: Papers and Report[s] from an LWF-Sponsored Working Group, Geneva, Switzerland, October/November 1986*. LWF Report 23/24. Geneva: Lutheran World Federation, 1988.
Ratzinger, Joseph. *Many Religions, One Covenant: Israel, the Church, and the World*. Translated by Graham Harrison. San Francisco: Ignatius, 1999.
Reymond, Robert L. *A New Systematic Theology of the Christian Faith*. Nashville: Nelson, 1998.
Richard, Ramesh P. *The Population of Heaven*. Chicago: Moody, 1994.
Richardson, Alan. "Is the Old Testament the Propaedeutic to Christian Faith?" In *The Old Testament and Christian Faith: Essays by Rudolf Bultmann and Others*, edited by Bernhard W. Anderson, 36–48. London: SCM, 1964.
Ridderbos, Herman N. *The Coming of the Kingdom*. Translated by H. de Jongst. Edited by Raymond O. Zorn. St. Catherines: Paideia Press, 1978.
———. *Paul and Jesus: Origin and General Character of Paul's Preaching of Christ*. Translated by David H. Freeman. Philadelphia: P & R, 1958.
———. *Paul: An Outline of His Theology*. Translated by John Richard De Witt. Grand Rapids: Eerdmans, 1975.
———. *When the Time Had Fully Come: Studies in New Testament Theology*. 1957. Reprint, Eugene: Wipf & Stock, 2001.
Roberts, Alexander, and James Donaldson, editors. *Ante-Nicene Fathers: Translations of the Writings of the Fathers Down to AD 325*. 10 vols. Grand Rapids: Eerdmans, 1988.
Robertson, O. Palmer. *The Christ of the Covenants*. Phillipsburg, NJ: P & R, 1980.
Rosenzweig, Franz. *The Star of Redemption*. Notre Dame: University of Notre Dame Press, 1985.
Rottenberg, Isaac. "Fulfillment Theology and the Future of Christian-Jewish Relations." *Christian Century*, January 23, 1980, 66–69.
Ruether, Rosemary Radford. *Faith and Fratricide: The Theological Roots of Anti-Semitism*. 1979. Reprint, Eugene: Wipf & Stock, 1996.
Ruler, A. A. van. *The Christian Church and the Old Testament*. Translated by Geoffrey Bromiley. Grand Rapids: Eerdmans, 1971.
Ruokanen, Miikka. *The Catholic Doctrine of Non-Christian Religions: According to the Second Vatican Council*. Studies in Christian Mission 7. Leiden: Brill, 1992.
Rust, Eric Charles. *Salvation History: A Biblical Interpretation*. Richmond: John Knox, 1961.

Bibliography

Saldanha, Chrys. *Divine Pedagogy: A Patristic View of Non-Christian Religions*. Biblioteca di scienze religiose 57. Rome: Libreria Ateneo Salesiano, 1984.

Sanders, E. P. *Paul and Palestinian Judaism: A Comparison of Patterns of Religion*. London: SCM, 1977.

Sanders, John, editor. *No Other Name: An Investigation into the Destiny of the Unevangelized*. 1994. Reprint, Eugene, OR: Wipf & Stock, 2001.

———, editor. *What about Those Who Have Never Heard? Three Views on the Destiny of the Unevangelized*. Downers Grove, IL: InterVarsity, 1995.

Satyavrata, Ivan. "God Has Not Left Himself without Witness." PhD diss. Open University, 2001.

Sauer, Erich. *The Dawn of World Redemption: A Survey of Historical Revelation in the Old Testament*. Translated by G. H. Lang. Exeter, UK: Paternoster, 1964.

Schaff, Philip, editor. *Augustin: "City of God." "Christian Doctrine."* 1886. NPNF1 2. Peabody, MA: Hendrickson, 1994.

Schleiermacher, Friedrich. *The Christian Faith*. Translated and edited by H. R Mackintosh and J. S. Stewart. Edinburgh: T. & T. Clark, 1928.

Schlette, Heinz. *Towards a Theology of Religions*. London: Burns & Oates, 1966.

Schmidt, Wilhelm. *The Origin and Growth of Religion: Facts and Theories*. Translated by H. J. Rose. London: Methuen, 1931.

Schreiner, Thomas R. *The Law and Its Fulfillment: A Pauline Theology of Law*. Grand Rapids: Baker, 1993.

———. *Romans*. Baker Exegetical Commentary on the New Testament 6. Grand Rapids: Baker, 1998.

Scott, J. Julius Jr. *Jewish Backgrounds of the New Testament*. Grand Rapids: Baker, 1995.

Seifrid, Mark A. "Righteousness Language in the Hebrew Scriptures and Early Judaism." In *Justification and Variegated Nomism*. Vol. 1, *The Complexities of Second Temple Judaism*, edited by D. A. Carson, et al., 415–42. WUNT 2/140. Grand Rapids: Baker, 2004.

Sell, Alan P. F, editor. *Reformed Theology and the Jewish People*. Studies from the World Alliance of Reformed Churches 9. Geneva: World Alliance of Reformed Churches, 1986.

Sharpe, Eric J. *Not to Destroy but to Fulfil: The Contribution of J. N. Farquhar to Protestant Missionary Thought in India before 1914*. Studia Missionalia Upsaliensia 5. Uppsala: Gleerup, 1965.

Shedd, W. G. T. *Calvinism Pure and Mixed: A Defence of the Westminster Standards*. Edinburgh: Banner of Truth, 1986.

———. *Dogmatic Theology*. Edited by Alan W. Gomes. 3rd ed. Phillipsburg, NJ: P & R, 2003.

Shenk, Calvin E. *Who Do You Say That I Am? Christians Encounter Other Religions*. Scottdale, PA: Herald, 1997.

Sigountos, James. "Did Early Christians Believe Pagan Religions Could Save?" In *Through No Fault of Their Own?: The Fate of Those Who Have Never Heard*, edited by William Crockett and James Sigountos, 229–44. Grand Rapids: Baker, 1991.

Skarsaune, Oskar. "Salvation in Judaism and Christianity." *Mishkan* 16 (1992) 1–9.

Soares-Prabhu, George. "The Inspiration of the Old Testament as Seen by the New and Its Implication for the Possible Inspiration of Non-Christian Scriptures." In *Research Seminar on Non-Biblical Scriptures*, edited by D. S. Amalorpavadass, 99–116. Bangalore: National Biblical, Catechetical and Liturgical Centre, 1974.

Bibliography

Soulen, R. Kendall. *The God of Israel and Christian Theology*. Minneapolis: Fortress, 1996.

———. "Israel's Eternal Covenant and the Universality of Christ." Online: http://www.bc.edu/research/cjl/meta-elements/sites/partners/ccjr/soulen03.htm/.

Sparks, Adam. "The Use of the Relationship between the Old and New Covenants as an Analogical Basis for the Relationship of Other Religions to Christianity." PhD diss., University of Bristol, 2007.

Spillman, Joann. "The Image of Covenant in Christian Understandings of Judaism." *JES* 63 (1998) 63–84. Online: http://www.questia.com/.

Stackhouse, John G., editor. *No Other Gods before Me? Evangelicals and the Challenge of World Religions*. Grand Rapids: Baker, 2001.

Stamn, Johann Jakob. "Jesus Christ and the Old Testament." In *Essays on Old Testament Interpretation*, edited by Claus Westermann, 200–10. London: SCM, 1963.

Stendahl, Krister. *Paul among Jews and Gentiles*. London: SCM, 1976.

Stibbs, Alan M. *The Finished Work of Christ*. Tyndale Biblical Theology Lecture. London: Tyndale, 1954.

Stott, John R. W. *The Message of Romans: God's Good News for the World*. The Bible Speaks Today Series. Leicester, UK: InterVarsity, 1994.

Strange, Daniel. *The Possibility of Salvation among the Unevangelized*. Paternoster Biblical and Theological Monographs. 2002. Reprint, Eugene, OR: Wipf & Stock, 2007.

Stravinskas, Peter M. J. *Salvation Outside the Church?* Huntington, IN: Our Sunday Visitor, 2002.

Strickland, Wayne G. "The Inauguration of the Law of Christ with the Gospel of Christ: A Dispensational View." In *The Law, The Gospel, and the Modern Christian*, by Willem A. VanGemeren, et al., 229–319. Grand Rapids: Zondervan, 1993.

Sullivan, Francis. *Salvation Outside the Church?: A History of Christian Thought about Salvation for Those "Outside."* London: Chapman, 1992.

Tanenbaum, Marc H., et al., editors. *Evangelicals and Jews in Conversation on Scripture, Theology and History*. Grand Rapids: Baker, 1978.

Tennent, Timothy C. *Christianity at the Religious Roundtable*. Grand Rapids: Baker, 2002.

The Christian Scholars Group on Christian-Jewish Relations. "A Sacred Obligation." (2002). Online: http://www.bc.edu/research/cjl/meta-elements/sites/partners/csg/Sacred_Obligation.htm/.

Thielman, Frank. *Paul & the Law: A Contextual Approach*. Downers Grove, IL: InterVarsity, 1994.

Tiessen, Terrance L. "Irenaeus on the Salvation of the Unevangelized " Paper presented at the Annual Meeting of the Evangelical Theological Society, Washington DC, November 18–20, 1993.

———. *Who Can Be Saved? Reassessing Salvation in Christ and World Religions*. Downers Grove, IL: InterVarsity, 2004.

Torrance, David W. "Two Covenant Theology." *Mishkan* 11 (1989) 31–35.

———, editor. *The Witness of the Jews to God*, by David H. S. Lyon, et al. Edinburgh: Handsel, 1982.

Torrance, James B. "The Incarnation and 'Limited Atonement." *EQ* 55 (1983) 83–94.

Torrance, Thomas F. "The Atonement, the Singularity of Christ, and the Finality of the Cross: The Atonement and the Moral Order." In *Universalism and the Doctrine of Hell*, edited by Nigel M. De S. Cameron, 223–54. Scottish Bulletin of Evangelical Theology Special Study 5. Grand Rapids: Baker, 1992.

———. *Divine and Contingent Order*. Oxford: Oxford University Press, 1981.
———. *The Mediation of Christ*. Exeter, UK: Paternoster, 1983.
———. *The School of Faith: The Catechisms of the Reformed Church*. London: James Clark, 1959.
———. *Space, Time and Incarnation*. London: Oxford University Press, 1969.
———. *Space, Time and Resurrection*. Edinburgh: Handsel, 1976.
Tuit, Pieter. "The Relationship between Church & Kingdom within the Missionary Theology of Johan H. Bavinck." *REC Focus* 4 (2001) 21–52.
Vance, Melvin. "Daniélou, Jean." In *Biographical Dictionary of Christian Theologians*, edited by Patrick Carey and Joseph Lienhard. Westport: Greenwood, 2000.
Van Buren, Paul. "Covenantal Pluralism?" *Common Ground* 3 (1990) 21–27.
———. "Discerning the Way to the Incarnation." *AThR* 63 (1981) 291–301.
Van Drunen, David, and R. Scott Clark. "The Covenant before the Covenants." In *Covenant, Justification and Pastoral Ministry: Essays by the Faculty of Westminster Seminary California*, edited by R. Scott Clark, 167–96. Phillipsburg, NJ: P & R, 2007.
Van Engen, John H. "Belgic Confession." In *Evangelical Dictionary of Theology*, edited by Walter A. Elwell, 132. Baker Reference Library 1. Grand Rapids: Baker, 1984.
VanGemeren, Willem. "Israel as the Hermeneutical Crux in the Interpretation of Prophecy (1)." *WTJ* 45 (1983) 132–45.
———. "Israel as the Hermeneutical Crux in the Interpretation of Prophecy (2)." *WTJ* 46 (1984) 254–97.
———. "The Law Is the Perfection of Righteousness in Jesus Christ: A Reformed Perspective." In *The Law, the Gospel, and the Modern Christian: Five Views*, by Willem VanGemeren, et al., 13–92. Grand Rapids: Zondervan, 1996.
———. *The Progress of Redemption: From Creation to the New Jerusalem*. Biblical and Theological Classics Library 8. Carlisle, UK: Paternoster, 1988.
———. "Systems of Continuity." In *Continuity and Discontinuity Perspectives on the Relationship between the Old and New Testaments*, edited by John Feinberg, 37–62. Westchester, IL: Crossway, 1988.
Vanlaningham, Michael G. "Christ, the Savior of Israel: The 'Sonderweg' and Bi-Covenantal Controversies in Relation to the Epistles of Paul." PhD diss., Trinity Evangelical Divinity School, 1997.
Vatican Council II. "Declaration on the Relation of the Church to Non-Christian Religions (*Nostra Aetate*)." Online: http:// www.vatican .va/ archive/hist _councils/ ii_vatican_council/documents/vat-ii_decl_19651028_nostra-aetate_en.html/.
———. "Decree on the Mission Activity of the Church (*Ad Gentes*)." Online: http://www.vatican.va/archive/hist_councils/ii_vatican_council/documents/vat-ii _decree_19651207_ad-gentes_en.html/.
———. "Dogmatic Constitution on the Church (*Lumen Gentium*)." Online: http://www.vatican.va/archive/hist_councils/ii_vatican_council/documents/vat-ii _const_19641121_lumen-gentium_en.html/.
Veliath, Dominic. *Theological Approach and Understanding of Religions: Jean Daniélou and Raimundo Panikkar; a Study in Contrast*. Bangalore: Kristu Jyoti College, 1988.
Vempeny, Ishanand. "An Approach to the Problem of Inspiration in the Non-Biblical Scriptures." In *Research Seminar on Non Biblical Scriptures*, edited by D. S. Amalorpavadass, 153–78. Bangalore: National Biblical, Catechetical and Liturgical Centre, 1974.

Bibliography

———. *Inspiration in the Non-Biblical Scriptures*. Bangalore: Theological Publications In India, 1973.

Visser, Paul J. *Heart for the Gospel, Heart for the World: The Life and Thought of a Reformed Pioneer Missiologist, Johan Herman Bavinck*. Eugene, OR: Wipf & Stock, 2003.

Vlach, Michael. "Has the Church Replaced Israel in God's Plan? A Historical and Theological Survey of Replacement Theology." *CTJ* 4 (2000) 6–33.

———. "Variations within Supersessionism." Online: http://www.pre-trib.org/pdf/Vlach-VariationsWithinSupersess.pdf/.

Vos, Geerhardus. *Biblical Theology: Old and New Testaments*. Edinburgh: Banner of Truth, 1975.

———. "The Doctrine of the Covenant in Reformed Theology." In *Redemptive History and Biblical Interpretation: The Shorter Writings of Geerhardus Vos*, edited by Richard B. Gaffin Jr., 234–67. Phillipsburg, NJ: P & R, 1980.

———. "The Eschatological Aspect of the Pauline Conception of the Spirit." In *Redemptive History and Biblical Interpretation: The Shorter Writings of Geerhardos Vos*, edited by Richard B. Gaffin Jr. Phillipsburg, NJ: P & R, 1980.

———. "Hebrews, the Epistle of the Diatheke." In *Redemptive History and Biblical Interpretation: The Shorter Writings of Geerhardus Vos*, edited by Richard B Gaffin Jr., 161–233. Phillipsburg, NJ: P & R, 1980.

———. "The Idea of Biblical Theology as a Science and as a Theological Discipline." In *Redemptive History and Biblical Interpretation: The Shorter Writings of Geerhardus Vos*, edited by Richard B. Gaffin Jr., 3–24. Phillipsburg, NJ: P & R, 1980.

Walls, A. F. "Logos." In *Evangelical Dictionary of Theology*, edited by Walter A. Elwell, 645–46. Baker Reference Library 1. Grand Rapids: Baker, 1984.

Warfield, Benjamin B. *Selected Shorter Writings of Benjamin B. Warfield*. Vol. 1. Edited by John E. Meeter. Nutley, NJ: P & R, 1970.

Waters, Guy Prentiss. *The Federal Vision and Covenant Theology: A Comparative Analysis*. Phillipsburg, NJ: P & R, 2006.

Watson, Francis. *Text and Truth: Redefining Biblical Theology*. Grand Rapids: Eerdmans, 1997.

Wells, David F. *God in the Wasteland: The Reality of Truth in a World of Fading Dreams*. Grand Rapids: Eerdmans, 1994.

Westerholm, Stephen. *Israel's Law and the Church's Faith: Paul and His Recent Interpreters*. Grand Rapids: Eerdmans, 1988.

Whaling, Frank. *Christian Theology and World Religions: A Global Approach*. Contemporary Christian Studies. Basingstoke: Pickering, 1986.

Williams, David John. *Acts*. NIBCNT 5. Peabody, NJ: Hendrickson, 1990.

Williams, Rowan. "Rahner and Balthasar." In *The Analogy of Beauty: The Theology of Hans Urs von Balthasar*, edited by John Riches, 11–34. Edinburgh: T. & T. Clark, 1986.

Williamson, Clark M. *A Guest in the House of Israel: Post-Holocaust Church Theology*. Louisville: Westminster John Knox, 1993.

Williamson, Paul R. *Sealed with an Oath: Covenant in God's Unfolding Purpose*. NSBT 23. Nottingham, UK: Apollos, 2007.

Wilson, Alistair I. "Luke and the New Covenant: Zechariah's Prophecy as a Test Case." In *The God of Covenant: Biblical, Theological and Contemporary Perspectives*, edited by Jamie A. Grant and Alistair I. Wilson, 156–77. Leicester, UK: Apollos, 2005.

Wilson, Marvin R. *Our Father Abraham: Jewish Roots of the Christian Faith*. Grand Rapids: Eerdmans, 1989.

Bibliography

Witherington, Ben III. *The Acts of the Apostles: A Socio-Rhetorical Commentary.* Grand Rapids: Eerdmans, 1998.

World Council of Churches. "The Second Assembly of the World Council of Churches." In *The Theology of the Churches and the Jewish People: Statements by the World Council of Churches and Its Member Churches*, 10–11. Geneva: WCC Publications, 1988.

———. *The Theology of the Churches and the Jewish People.* Geneva: WCC Publications 1988.

World Evangelical Fellowship. "Willowbank Declaration on the Christian Gospel and the Jewish People." *IBMR* 13 (1989) 161–64.

Woudstra, Marten. "Israel and the Church: A Case for Continuity." In *Continuity and Discontinuity: Perspectives on the Relationship between the Old and New Testaments; Essays in Honor of S. Lewis Johnson, Jr*, edited by John Feinberg, 221–38. Westchester, IL: Crossway, 1988.

Wright, Christopher J. H. "The Christian and Other Religions: The Biblical Evidence." *Themelios* 9:2 (1994) 4–15.

———. "InterFaith Dialogue." *Anvil* 1 (1984) 235–58.

———. *Knowing Jesus through the Old Testament: Rediscovering the Roots of Our Faith.* London: Pickering, 1992.

———. *Thinking Clearly about the Uniqueness of Jesus.* Thinking Clearly Series. Crowborough: Monarch, 1997.

Wright, David. "Protestantism." In *Evangelical Dictionary of Theology*, edited by Walter A. Elwell, 888–90. Baker Reference Library 1. Grand Rapids: Baker, 1984.

———. "The Watershed of Vatican II." In *One God, One Lord: Christianity in a World of Religious Pluralism*, edited by Andrew D. Clarke and Bruce W. Winter, 207–26. 2nd ed. Exeter, UK: Paternoster, 1992.

Wright, N. T. *The Climax of the Covenant: Christ and the Law in Pauline Theology.* Edinburgh: T & T Clark, 1991.

———. *The New Testament and the People of God.* Christian Origins and the Question of God 1. Minneapolis: Fortress, 1992.

Wyngaarden, M. J. "Testament." In *Evangelical Dictionary of Theology*, edited by Walter A. Elwell, 1079. Baker Reference Library 1. Grand Rapids: Baker, 1984.

Yarbrough, Robert. "Paul and Salvation History." In *Justification and Variegated Nomism.* Vol. 2, *The Paradoxes of Paul*, edited by D. A. Carson, et al., 297–342. WUNT 2/181. Grand Rapids: Baker, 2004.

Yoder, John Howard. *The Jewish-Christian Schism Revisited.* Edited by Michael G. Cartwright and Peter Ochs. London: SCM, 2003.

Yong, Amos. *Beyond the Impasse: Toward a Pneumatological Theology of Religions.* Grand Rapids: Baker Academic, 2003.

Zaretsky, Tuvya, editor. *Jewish Evangelism: A Call to the Church.* Lausanne Occasional Paper 60. Pattaya, Thailand: Issue Group on Reaching the Jews with the gospel (Issue Group No. 31), Lausanne Committee for World Evangelization, 2005.

Zimmerli, Walther. "Promise and Fulfillment." In *Essays on Old Testament Interpretation*, edited by Claus Westermann, 89–22. London: SCM, 1963.

INDEX

Abel, 26, 60, 207
Abimelech, 60
Abraham, 21, 22, 25, 27–29, 30, 32, 35, 37, 61, 65–67, 75, 81, 84, 86, 88, 96, 99, 103, 104, 106–8, 130, 169, 172, 182–84, 189–97, 199, 205–7, 208, 210–20, 221, 241, 244, 246, 247, 276, 289, 309
accessibilism, 9, 10, 63, 69, 70
Ad Gentes, xxv, 45, 50, 270, 308
Adam, iii, iv, ix, 65, 179–83, 184, 193, 194, 206–8, 210, 218, 281, 307
agnoia, 160
agnosticism, 9
aletheia, 5
Alexander, D., 297
Amalorpavadass, D. S., 266, 289, 295, 300, 306, 308
Amerding, C., 76, 289
analogy, vii, viii, ix, x, xiii, xviii, xix, xx, xxi, xxii, xxiv, 3, 6, 10, 12, 13, 18–20, 30–32, 36, 51, 52, 56, 58–62, 64–66, 67, 69, 70, 72, 81, 113, 119–21, 122, 129, 131, 135–37, 139–41, 142, 157, 163, 173, 176, 177, 179, 195, 197, 200, 201, 203–5, 210, 212, 220–22, 223, 238, 242, 249, 259, 261, 262, 265, 269, 273, 285–87, 288, 294, 299, 301, 309
analogia entis, xix
analogia fidei, xix, xx, 10, 12, 13, 38, 40, 66, 70, 72, 117, 131, 203, 222, 223, 261, 266, 307
Ananias, 241
Anderson, B., 121, 122, 289
Anderson, G., 289

Anderson, N., xvii, 66, 289
Anonymous Christians, 35, 205, 304
Apocrypha, xxii
apologetic, 239, 242, 244, 246, 250, 251, 254, 293
apologia, 246
apologists, 16, 239, 240, 242, 246, 249, 250, 254–56, 271
apophatic, 19
apostasy, 108
apostolic, 48, 113, 158, 164, 258, 259
Aquinas, Thomas, xix, 128, 289
Aristides, 271
Aristotle, 31
Arminian, 149
atheists, 240, 241
Athenian, 160–62, 174, 241, 277, 278, 290
atonement, x, xviii, 102, 108, 110, 127, 148, 149, 152–56, 157, 168, 170, 172, 175, 176, 192, 203, 215, 286, 288, 290, 291, 296, 297, 301, 302, 307
  cosmic, 11, 12, 16, 19, 21–25, 27, 28, 30, 31, 37, 43, 61, 65, 146–52, 157, 167, 185, 205–7, 209, 221, 222, 235, 266, 269, 295
  expiation, 148, 152, 192
  limited, 148, 152
  propitiation, 128, 148, 154
  substitutionary nature, 155, 194
Augustine, 148, 293
Auschwitz, 97, 296
Avis, P., 289
Azarias, 241

Index

Bahnsen, G., 160, 162, 163, 166, 274, 289
Baillie, D. M., 289
Baker, D., 80, 123, 124, 128, 131, 132, 138, 179, 190, 194, 262, 263, 289–95, 296, 298, 299, 301–3, 306–10
Balthasar, Hans Urs von, 22, 41, 271, 309
baptism, 26, 30, 46, 191, 299
Barnes, M., 24, 28, 29, 43, 46, 289
Barrett, C. K., 101, 159, 160, 289
Barr, J., 124
Barth, K., 55, 75, 86, 149, 289
Baugh, S. M., 180, 191, 214, 289
Baumann, A., 110, 111, 289
Bavinck, H., 148–50, 152, 178–80, 182–84, 186, 188–90, 191, 193, 197, 208, 219, 289
Bavinck, J., 244, 254, 272, 275–77, 281–83, 290, 308, 309
Baxter, R., 280
Begbie, J., 290
berith (*see* covenant)
Berkhof, H., 77, 290
Berkhof, L., 180, 290
Berkouwer, G., 290
Bianchi, E., 90
Blacketer, R., 148, 290
Blackham, P., 124, 290, 297
Blaising, C., 78, 81, 84, 90–92, 95, 103, 104, 116, 290
Blewett, D., 290
Blocher, H., 125, 148, 152, 290
Bloesch, D., 148, 153, 157, 290
Bombaro, J., 134, 279–81, 290
Bonnington, M., 199, 200, 220, 290
Borland, J., 290
Bosch, D., 102, 290
Bowler, M., 290
Braaten, C., 58–60, 80, 230, 273–75, 278, 291
Bradley, J., 236, 291
Bray, G., 239, 245, 246, 250, 271, 291
Braybrooke, M., 291
Bromiley, G., 291, 305

Brown, H., 123, 291
Bruce, F., 75, 86, 91, 103, 145, 146, 158, 165, 166, 168, 230–32, 233, 236, 238, 291, 292, 294, 297, 299, 301, 310
Brunner, E., 123, 259, 291
Buddhism, 28, 40, 68, 259, 272, 296
Bullinger, H., 178, 216
Bultmann, R., 131, 162, 291, 305
Buren, P. van, 98, 110, 114, 308

Cain, 183
Calvin, J., 78, 79, 84, 86, 87, 135–39, 154, 162, 168, 178, 216, 233, 279, 291, 298, 299, 301, 306
Calvinism, 51, 148, 149, 152, 306
Cameron, N. De S., 291, 307
Canaan, 191
canon, xxiii, 77, 80, 82, 123, 125, 127, 131, 135, 178, 214, 234, 263, 265, 292
canonical, 77, 135, 214, 263
Canons of Dort, 80
Caragounis, C., 161, 163, 291
Cardinal Bea, 290
Carey, P., 291, 300, 301, 308
Carson, D., 8, 145, 168, 170, 174, 217, 227, 229–31, 232, 251, 252, 272, 273, 291, 292, 297, 303, 306, 310
Celsus, 249
Chadwick, H., 239, 245, 250, 252, 292
Chapman, C., 90, 292, 307
Chardin, Pierre Teilhard de, 11
Charleston, S., 67, 68, 292
Childs, B., 263, 292
Christ
  crucifixion, 146, 152, 240, 292
  Incarnation, 3, 17, 34, 52, 64, 77, 110, 111, 127, 134, 138, 141, 142, 148–50, 151, 153–55, 156, 230, 232, 234, 246, 248, 256, 265, 269, 270, 307, 308
  Lordship, 122, 167
  Mediator, 5, 46, 47, 49, 96, 105, 133, 136, 137, 145, 152–54, 180, 184, 189, 192, 201, 216, 222, 232, 258, 259, 297, 308

Index

Messiah, xxii, 17, 19, 67, 73, 74, 81, 90, 95, 101, 103, 104, 106, 110, 116, 123, 144, 146, 147, 158, 173, 183, 187, 192, 216, 219, 225, 226, 231, 238, 247, 273

Redeemer, 123, 150, 192, 275

Resurrection, x, 28, 44, 102, 103, 110, 111, 121, 127, 128, 132, 134, 138, 141, 142, 144–52, 154, 155, 164, 165, 167, 168, 172, 173, 175, 261, 296, 303, 308

Christendom, 297

Christian, iii, iv, vii, viii, ix, x, xi, xiii, xvii, xviii, xix, xxi, xxii, xxiv, xxv, 1, 3–5, 7, 9–19, 21–29, 30, 32–50, 51, 54–56, 57, 62–64, 68–70, 72–78, 80–84, 85, 87–99, 100, 102, 103, 106, 108–16, 117, 120, 122, 123, 127, 130, 131, 135, 137, 140, 141, 147–49, 155, 158, 161, 163, 164, 172, 178, 191, 200, 203, 205–9, 210, 215, 216, 220, 221, 224, 228–36, 238, 239, 242–48, 250, 252–56, 257, 259–73, 275–79, 281–83, 285–309, 310

Christianity, iv, ix, x, xiii, xvii, xviii, xix, xxi, xxiv, 3–5, 7, 10–14, 15, 17, 19, 21–25, 27–31, 33–35, 36, 38–44, 46, 49, 51–57, 58, 63, 64, 66, 68–70, 72–74, 75, 80, 93–95, 97, 98, 100, 104, 106, 108, 110, 113–17, 121, 123, 131, 132, 141, 143, 154, 158, 161, 164, 171, 199, 204, 213, 219, 222, 223, 235, 236, 239, 240, 242–54, 256–60, 261, 264, 265, 267–71, 273, 274, 276, 278, 282–86, 287, 289–301, 303–7, 310

Christology, viii, 77, 95, 97, 111–13, 116, 138–40, 143, 149, 150, 153, 155, 227, 229, 236, 257, 258, 291, 301

chronology, viii, xiii, 10, 29, 101, 142–44, 147, 165, 176, 184, 197, 222, 247, 262, 286

church, vii, viii, ix, xvii, xix, xxiv, xxv, xxvi, 5, 9, 10, 12–14, 17–19, 24, 26–28, 29, 31, 35, 36, 38, 39, 43–51, 52, 58, 59, 70–86, 89–95, 96, 100–104, 109–15, 116, 120–22, 123, 129–31, 132, 138, 140, 149, 154–56, 164, 176, 178, 191, 204, 207, 209, 212, 215, 216, 220, 223, 228–30, 234, 238–40, 243, 248, 249, 251, 258, 261, 263, 265, 266, 269, 273–75, 279, 283, 285, 286, 290–94, 296–98, 300–302, 304, 305, 307–9, 310

Clarke, A., 292, 297–99, 304, 310

Clark, D., 5, 7, 267,

Clark, R., 178, 180, 193, 194,

Clendenin, D., 154, 292

Clowney, E., 125, 292

Confucius, 259, 260, 281

Conn, H., xviii, 293

Conzelman, H., 142, 166, 293

Corduan, W., xvii, xix, xxii, 237, 267, 268, 293, 296

Corinthians, 197, 202, 203, 213

Cornelius, 141

Cotterell, P., 270, 271, 293

Cousins, E., 293

covenant, iii, iv, vii, viii, x, xiii, xviii, xxi, xxii, xxiv, 7, 19, 21–31, 32, 34, 37, 43, 60, 61, 65–67, 70, 72–74, 76, 78–84, 85, 88–92, 94–112, 114–16, 122, 123, 128, 131, 132, 135–37, 141, 144, 147, 150, 159, 164–66, 168–72, 173, 177–213, 214, 216–22, 224, 226, 229, 258, 259, 262, 266, 269, 270, 272, 281, 283, 285, 288–90, 292, 294–304, 305, 307–10

Abrahamic, 43, 89, 92, 101, 137, 178, 183, 185, 189–97, 198, 200, 201, 203–5, 206, 210–14, 216–22, 226, 229, 298

Adamic, 181, 194, 210, 302

cosmic, 21–23, 28, 167, 205, 207

Davidic, 183, 185, 195, 196, 198, 204, 219

Index

covenant (*continued*)
  Edenic, 180
  Mosaic/Sinaitic, 31, 32, 34, 89, 92, 101, 170, 185, 190, 191, 193–95, 196, 198–204, 205, 210–14, 216–22, 229, 266, 269
  New, xiii, xviii, xix, xxi, xxii, xxiv, 10, 12, 13, 34, 36, 38, 40, 61, 66, 70, 72, 79, 80, 84, 89, 101, 103–5, 114, 117, 123, 131, 136, 137, 177, 178, 182, 183, 185, 190, 197–203, 211–13, 216, 219–23, 229, 261, 285, 287
  Noahic, 22, 30, 37, 137, 181, 185–89, 193, 204–8, 210, 221, 303
  Old, xiii, xxiv, 11, 30, 34, 35, 56, 59, 61, 65, 66, 103, 113, 114, 116, 132, 136, 142, 169, 173, 177, 195, 197–99, 200, 203, 204, 209, 211, 213, 218, 220, 221, 229, 258, 259, 273, 283, 285, 286
  pactum salutis, 180
Covenant Theology, 74, 79, 95, 122, 130, 150, 177–79, 181–83, 184, 193, 194, 202, 221, 290, 292, 294, 297–99, 301, 307, 309
covenantal nomism, 203, 292, 303, 306, 310
Cracknel, K., 52, 53, 293
Cragg, K., 293
Craig, W., 9, 78, 290, 293
Cranfield, C. E. B., 85, 101, 109, 159, 166, 168, 169, 293
creation, 16, 17, 21, 29, 43, 48, 58, 77, 82, 123, 124, 133, 134, 136, 138, 140, 144, 148–52, 158, 159, 166, 167, 183, 185–87, 193, 194, 197, 202, 205, 206, 231, 232, 234, 245, 273, 279, 294, 308
Crisp, O., xv, 148, 280, 293, 298, 302
Crockett, W., xvii, 290, 293, 306
Cullmann, O., 16, 123, 130–32, 138, 140–42, 155, 167, 293

D'Costa, G., iv, vii, ix, xi, xv, xvii, 5, 8, 34, 35, 47, 48, 50, 205, 267, 268, 272, 294

Dabru Emet, 93, 296
Davies, A., 294
Davies, G., 169, 294
Davies, M., 225, 294
De Chirico, L., 156, 294
Decalogue, 194
Deists, 281
Demarest, B., xix, 152, 159, 167, 294, 301
Dewick, E. C., 294
Dhavamony, M., 207, 294
Dialogue with Trypho, 240, 246, 247, 250, 255, 256, 299
diatheke, 184, 190, 197, 202, 213, 309
Diprose, R., 74, 76–78, 83, 84, 87, 90, 92–94, 102, 103, 109, 114–16, 294
dispensation, 9, 14–16, 17, 19, 134, 173, 190, 247, 279
Dispensationalism, 74, 81, 122, 167, 172, 180, 203, 290, 304, 307
  transdispensationalizing, 173
Dominus Iesus, 48, 49, 293
Donaldson, T., xxvi, 106, 292, 294, 299, 305
Dordrecht, The Canons of, xxiii
Drummond, R., 14, 294
Dulles, A., 14, 22, 294
Dumbrell, W., 202, 294
Dunn, J., 199, 204, 290, 294
Dupuis, J., xvii, 13–15, 16, 18, 20–22, 23, 25, 27, 28, 36–44, 46, 47, 49, 50, 57, 69, 70, 114, 156, 161, 200, 201, 206, 207, 209, 210, 220, 221, 229, 230, 236, 239, 261, 266, 269, 270, 278, 294

Eastern Orthodoxy, 19, 300
ecclesiocentrism, 9, 67, 172
ecclesiology, 74, 296
Eckardt, R., 94
Eden, Garden of, 125, 150, 185
Edwards, James, 160, 168, 169, 295
Edwards, Jonathan, 68, 134, 135, 151, 155, 216, 264, 278–80, 281, 290, 293, 295, 296, 298, 300, 302
Edwards, M., 250, 295

Index

Eichrodt, W., 137, 204, 295
election, 79, 83, 84, 86–88, 91, 94, 103, 104, 107, 192, 194, 200, 201, 210, 298
    corporate, 79, 87, 88, 91, 92, 107, 108
    individual, 87, 92, 107, 108
Eliade, M., 11
Elwell, W., 291, 294, 296, 308–10
Engen, J. Van, 80, 308
Enoch, 60, 65
Ephesians, 143
epistemology, xiii, 5, 6, 8, 10, 61, 63, 142, 176, 286
Erickson, M., xviii, 84, 295
eschatology, viii, 48, 59, 89, 90, 92, 103, 104, 106, 109, 123, 126, 127, 133, 138–40, 141, 143, 145–47, 148, 150, 165–67, 176, 199, 206, 222, 258, 309
    under-realized, 176
Estelle, B., 181, 295
Eusebius, 14, 243, 279, 295
evangelical, vii, xvii, xxv, 8, 60, 63, 66, 68, 76, 81, 93, 94, 109, 110, 122, 125, 272, 278, 289–91, 294–98, 300–304, 307–10
evangelism, 8, 65, 67, 69, 75, 77, 104, 110, 111, 134, 275, 289, 290, 310
exclusivism, ix, x, 3–9, 10, 14, 34, 44–46, 149, 239, 243–45, 247, 249, 254, 255, 257, 299
exegesis, 84, 91, 102, 106, 122, 129, 179, 180, 224
Exile, 199, 211
Exodus, the, 97, 127, 191, 192, 194, 196, 225
Ezekiel, 198, 201

Fackre, G., 77, 82, 94, 95, 186, 208, 295, 302
Farquhar, J., 41, 52–58, 70, 224, 230, 261, 278, 295, 306
Farris, T., 184, 295
Feinberg, J., 122, 143, 144, 295
Feinberg, P., 295
Fiddes, P., 296

Fleischner, E., 97, 296
Flender, H., 165, 296
Forsyth, P. T., 155, 296
Fraser, J., 291
Fratricide, 95, 97, 106, 305
Fredericks, J., 43, 47–49, 272, 296
Fruchtenbaum, A., 296
fulfil, 13, 29, 53, 81, 143, 150, 190, 218, 224, 226, 227, 258, 282, 306
fulfilment, vii, viii, xiii, xviii, xxi, xxii, xxiv, 3, 6, 10–14, 15, 18–20, 29, 31–33, 36, 39–43, 44, 46–48, 50–64, 67–69, 70, 72, 74, 81, 89–91, 100, 101, 103, 111, 113, 119–21, 122, 129–31, 132, 135–37, 139–43, 145, 146, 150, 157, 161, 163, 164, 170, 171, 176, 177, 179–81, 182, 184, 189, 191, 193, 195, 197–99, 202–4, 206, 208, 209, 211–13, 215, 217–33, 236–40, 241, 244, 246–50, 252, 255, 257–61, 262, 264–66, 268, 270–72, 273, 276, 278, 279, 282–88, 291, 292, 298, 302, 305, 306, 310
Fulgentius, 14

Gaebelein, F., 292
Gaffin, R., 125–27, 128, 144, 147, 157, 164, 165, 204, 286, 296, 309
Galatians, 13, 180, 191, 212–14, 217, 220, 224, 236–38, 289, 291, 297, 301
Gamaliel, 187
Garvey, J., 296
Geisler, N., xix, 296
Gentiles, 7, 17, 27, 59, 73, 81, 83, 84, 86, 89, 91, 95, 96, 98, 99, 101–5, 106, 108–10, 115, 145, 158–60, 168, 172, 206, 219, 239, 259, 273, 274, 307
Gilbert, G., 279, 280, 296
Glaser, M., 95, 96
Glatzer, N., 96, 296
Gnosticism, 123, 178
Goheen, M., 283, 296

Goldberg, L., 110, 297
Golding, P., 178, 297
Goldingay, J., 81, 123, 125, 208, 297
Goldsworthy, G., 124, 195, 196, 264, 290, 297
gospel, viii, ix, x, xvii, 5, 6, 8, 9, 11, 15, 22, 29, 30, 34, 35, 45, 46, 49, 52, 55, 58–60, 63–65, 68, 69, 80–82, 86–88, 96, 101–3, 105, 109–11, 113, 115, 116, 123, 126, 131, 132, 137, 151, 154, 163, 164, 167, 169, 171, 172, 174–76, 187, 191, 203, 212, 213, 215, 224, 225, 227, 229–33, 235, 240, 243, 245, 247, 248, 250, 251, 254–56, 265, 270–78, 280–82, 284, 286, 287, 291, 292, 295, 298, 299, 302, 303, 307–10
   ignorance of, 19, 158–60, 163, 168, 174
Greece, 281
Greeks, 15, 18, 56, 160, 161, 231, 240, 243, 246, 250, 252, 255, 256, 260, 277
Grudem, W., 84, 144, 206, 297
Gundry, S., 297
Gunton, C., 297, 301
Guthrie, D., 238, 297

Hagar, 213
Hagner, D., 227, 297, 300
Hallam, G., 19
Hamilton, J., 183, 215, 295, 297
hapax, 24, 156, 248
Harink, D., 115, 297
Harnack, A., 54, 80
Harper, B., 50, 297
Harrelson, W., 78, 297
Harrison, E., 159, 297, 300, 305
Hart, T., 189, 258, 259, 297
heathen, 216, 249, 276, 279, 280
heathens, 29, 80, 158, 216, 249, 275, 276, 279–81, 296
Hebrew Scriptures, 74, 75, 77, 82, 100, 108, 122, 123, 130–32, 197, 212, 219, 224, 243, 264, 268, 306

Hebrews, 24, 56, 114, 147, 184, 190, 197, 200, 202, 203, 213, 256, 260, 274, 303, 309
Hedges, P., 10, 11, 13, 40, 42, 54–56, 57, 224, 229, 230, 233, 237, 239, 261, 298
Hegel, G., 80
Heidelburg. Catechism, xxiii, 80
Heiler, F., 298
Heilsgeschichte, 122–24, 140, 165 (*see also* salvation history)
Heim, S. M., xvii, 4, 272, 298, 301
Hellwig, M., 98, 99, 298
Helm, P., 143, 178, 298, 302
Heraclitus, 15, 240, 244, 245, 247, 257
heresy, 17, 25, 123, 155, 178, 182, 212, 291
hermeneutics, iii, iv, xix, 36, 80, 86, 136, 137, 139, 164, 191, 227, 292, 303, 308
Herter, T., 226, 298
Hezekiah, 199
Hillman, E., 15, 28, 298
Hinduism, 40, 51, 53–55, 56, 68, 224, 230, 272, 295, 303
Hinnells, J., 291
Hodge, C., 101, 298
Hoekema. A. A., 146, 298
Holmes, S., 279, 280, 298
Holmgren, F. C., 199
Holocaust, 76, 94, 296, 309
Holte, R., 251, 252
Holwerda, D., 76, 78, 79, 81, 87–89, 91, 92, 94, 107, 298
Horton, M., 141, 147, 165, 166, 178–84, 187–89, 192–94, 197, 199, 200, 203, 208, 212, 218–20, 298
Hosea, 181
Humanae Vitae, 48
Hunsinger, G., 280, 298
Hvalvik, R., 106, 298

idolatry, 14, 158, 160, 241, 242, 244, 249, 274, 281, 283
inclusivism, ix, x, xi, xiii, xix, xxi, xxiv, 3–9, 10, 12, 13, 38, 39, 44, 52,

60–64, 69, 70, 149, 173, 223, 234, 236, 239, 240, 246, 265, 267, 279, 280, 285–87, 295, 304
inclusivist, 5, 6, 8, 173, 236, 265, 280
inclusivists, 4, 5, 64, 173, 267
infralapsarianism, 144
innocence, 22, 163, 194, 217
inspiration, 55, 198, 208, 209, 250, 252, 266, 267, 270, 306, 308, 309
interfaith, 52, 58, 199, 210, 301
Irenaeus, 14–18, 25, 80, 123, 138, 178, 182, 240, 256, 307
Isaiah, 107, 198, 274
Ishmael, 212
Islam, 19, 27–29, 32, 97, 114, 260, 275, 276, 281, 293, 295
Israel, vii, viii, ix, x, xiii, xviii, xix, xxi, xxii, xxiv, 1, 3, 6, 7, 9, 10, 12, 13, 17–21, 30–32, 36, 38, 51, 52, 55, 58–62, 64, 66–96, 98, 99, 101–17, 119–21, 122, 129–31, 132, 135–37, 139–41, 142, 157–59, 163, 176, 177, 179, 181, 183, 187–89, 191–97, 199–201, 203–5, 207–11, 212, 215, 216, 218–26, 228, 237, 238, 244, 258–62, 264, 265, 269, 273, 285–89, 290, 292, 294, 295, 298, 302–4, 305, 307–10
Israelocentrism, 67
Israelology, 296
Israel-Church relationship (*see* Jewish-Christian Theology)
Israelite, 21, 34, 76, 91, 103, 107, 108, 192, 193, 200, 203, 204, 207, 218, 224, 279

Jenson, R., 80, 291
Jeremiah, 99, 197–201, 202, 219
Jerusalem, 102, 160, 162, 163, 166, 184, 196, 212, 213, 260, 274, 289, 308
Jethro, 60
Jewish, vii, xi, xxii, xxiii, xxv, 17, 18, 21, 29–31, 37, 52, 59, 65, 73–75, 76, 78, 79, 81–83, 85–97, 99–115, 116, 131, 132, 137, 164, 191, 203–5, 210, 213, 214, 216, 219–21, 225, 229, 233, 239, 246, 250, 256, 260, 262, 265, 273, 274, 279, 281, 290–94, 296, 298–300, 301, 303–7, 309, 310
Jewish-Christian theology
dual/two-covenant theory, 95, 96, 99, 100, 103, 105, 106, 115, 297
single-covenant theory, 95, 98–100, 101, 116, 203, 220
multi-covenant theory, 97, 98, 114, 115, 203
Jews, viii, xxii, 19, 28, 31, 65–67, 73–75, 77–79, 80, 82–86, 91–99, 101–12, 114, 116, 136, 160, 168, 172, 173, 201, 212, 215, 216, 219, 237, 244, 247, 250, 252, 255, 256, 273, 281, 289–91, 293, 297, 300, 301, 303, 304, 307, 310
Jocz, J., 75, 90, 107–9, 110, 298
John, 155, 231, 250, 255
Johnson, D. E., 158, 164, 298
Johnson, D. H., 231, 250, 298
Johnson, J., 85, 106–8, 299
Jones, H., 207, 299
Joshua, 191, 199
Judaism, x, xi, xxii, xxiii, 25, 27, 28, 32, 38, 40, 44, 47, 52, 54, 64, 74, 78, 80, 93–95, 97, 98, 100, 104, 105, 108, 112, 113, 116, 178, 199, 203, 204, 213, 219, 238, 242, 246, 247, 251, 255, 256, 259, 261, 264, 265, 268, 269, 273, 285, 290, 292–94, 295, 301, 303, 306, 307
Palestinian, 105, 108, 203, 204, 306
Rabbinic, xxiii, 251
Judaizers, 212–14, 217
justification, 127, 154, 165, 169–71, 193, 203, 212, 214–16, 217, 235, 280, 289, 292, 295, 298, 303, 306, 308, 310
Justin Martyr, 14–16, 18, 78, 80, 123, 235, 239–47, 249–57, 283, 292, 295, 299, 303, 304
Juthe, A., xx, 286, 299

kairos, 155, 262
Kaiser, W., 86, 214–16, 299
Karlberg, M., 299
Keith, G., 239, 243–45, 247, 249, 254, 255, 257, 299
Kessler, E., 303
Khodr, G., 299
Kistemaker, S., 161, 162, 299
Klett, F., 90, 299
Kline, M., 125, 178, 179, 193, 194, 214, 299
Klooster, F., 122, 299
Knitter, P., xvii, 12–14, 29, 44, 47, 299
Koran, 267
Korn, E., 300
Kraemer, H., xviii, 5, 230–32, 233, 235, 239, 242, 243, 246, 254, 271, 272, 275–77, 282–84, 287, 300, 304
Kraft, C., 274, 300
Krishna, 51
Kuyper, A., 276

Ladd, G. E., 84, 123, 125, 130, 162, 232, 300
Langer, R., 300
Lapide, P., 300
Larkin, W., 161, 163, 175, 300
law, 80, 106, 113, 123, 137, 159, 160, 164, 170, 171, 182, 191, 199, 202, 203, 212, 215, 218, 224, 229, 236, 247
Leer, E., 300
Legrand, L., 269, 300
Leithart, P., 169, 300
Letham, R., xv, 19, 148, 300
Lewis, G., 159, 167, 301, 310
Lillback, P., 178, 216, 301
Lints, R., 122, 125, 129, 130, 133–35, 137, 263, 301
Lloyd, G., xx, 301
Logos, xx, xxi, 11, 13–17, 18, 50, 59, 229–35, 236, 240, 241, 243, 245–47, 250–56, 277, 291, 295, 298, 303, 309
  asarkos, 50, 230
  ensarkos, 50
  implanted, 250, 253, 255
  pre-incarnate, 232, 256
  spermatikos, 245, 251, 252, 254, 255, 303
Lohfink, N., 98, 99, 301
Lombardi, R., 301
Longenecker, R., 217, 238, 301
Lubac, H. de, 41
Lumen Gentium, xxv, 45, 46, 50, 270, 308
Luther, M., 78, 166, 301, 303
Lutheranism, xxiii, 51, 58, 59, 93, 122, 301, 302, 304, 305
Lystra, 161, 274

Macleod, M., 109, 301
Malachi, 127
mallon, 156, 248
Marcion, 80, 123, 131, 138, 139, 178
Marshall, B., 75, 86, 87, 91, 92, 95, 101, 103, 110, 153, 298
Marshall, I. H., 64, 158, 162, 171, 172, 298,
Martensen, D., 58, 301
Masson, R., 46, 301
Matthew, 13, 102, 142, 159, 174, 224–28, 229, 236, 292, 294, 296–98, 302
Melchizedek, 60, 206, 279, 280
Melito of Sardis, 28, 78
Meter, J., 309
Micah, 107
Midrashim, xxii
Mills, D., 290, 294
miracles, 256, 287
missiology, xviii, 52, 74, 102, 116, 211, 266, 274, 294, 299, 300, 309
missions, xviii, xxv, 21, 29, 45–47, 52–54, 55, 63, 77, 83, 94, 98–100, 102–4, 110, 112, 130, 140, 156, 210, 233, 234, 254, 261, 265, 271, 274–76, 277, 279, 282, 283, 289, 290, 292, 293, 296, 299, 300, 302–6, 308
Moberly, W., 302
Moltmann, J., 178

Index

monotheism, 27, 29, 115, 210, 267, 279, 282
Moo, D., 86, 88, 89, 91, 101, 105, 159, 166, 168–70, 171, 175, 215, 229, 237, 302
Morimoto, A., 279, 302
Morris, L., 224, 225, 302
Moses, 21, 35, 65, 173, 181, 192, 197, 199, 202, 205, 207, 208, 212, 215, 218, 225, 229, 237, 243, 281, 295, 300, 302, 304
Motyer, S., 83, 86, 103, 302
Moule, C., 227
Mounce, R., 159, 160, 168, 302
Mounce, W., 236, 302
Muck, T., 302
Murray, J., 79, 91, 92, 135, 152, 153, 155, 179, 181, 191, 193, 194, 302

Netland, H., xvii, 3–7, 19, 240, 300, 302
Newbigin, L., xvii, 5, 235, 272, 283, 296, 302
Newman, J. H., xix, 279, 302
Noah, 22, 29, 32, 37, 60, 61, 65, 183–89, 199, 204–8, 210, 218, 221, 222, 269
Nostra Aetate, xxv, 42, 44, 47, 48, 90, 94, 95, 230, 268, 308
Novak, D., 303
Nyende, P., 274, 303

Ochs, P., 310
Oikonomia, 235
Okholm, D., 293, 304
ontology, 5, 6, 82, 176, 279, 280, 298
ordo, 165, 286
ordo salutis, 165, 286
Origen, 14, 15, 28, 254, 279, 292
Osborn, E., 244, 245, 303
Osborne, G., 159, 168, 170, 171, 227, 303
Otto, R., 11
Owen, J., 303

pagan, 23, 25, 30, 163, 174, 243, 249, 250, 276

pagan saints, 22, 26, 30, 32, 63, 174, 207
paganism, 24, 29, 239, 259
pagans, xxi, 16, 21–23, 26–28, 30–32, 60, 66, 110, 173, 207, 239–41, 242, 252, 254, 257, 272, 274, 280, 291, 293, 304
paidagogos, 18, 218, 219, 237
Panikkar, R., 21, 42, 303, 308
Pannenberg, W., 303
Papademetriou, G., 19
Parkes, J., 95, 97, 303
parousia, 140, 248
particularism, 205, 210, 279
particularity, 188
Pate, C., 210, 303
Paton, W., 300
Patriarchs (Old Testament), 37, 86, 88, 90, 212, 281
patristic, xiii, 18, 25, 78, 223, 248, 257, 283, 286, 306
Paul, 83, 85, 88, 91, 102, 103, 105–9, 115, 121, 124, 130, 142, 145, 146, 148, 155, 160, 163, 165, 166, 168, 169, 174, 179, 181, 184, 191, 199, 202–4, 207, 213–17, 218, 255, 278, 297, 306, 309, 310
Pawlikowski, J. T., 94, 95, 97–99, 100, 111, 112, 300, 303, 304
pedagogy, 13, 14, 23, 25, 29, 33, 45, 51, 217, 236, 238, 240, 241, 247, 248, 253, 255–57, 270, 301, 306
Pelican, J., 94
Pentateuch, 185, 194, 224, 263, 281
Pentecost, 83, 140, 172
Perelmuter, H. G., 303, 304
Perry, T. S., 5, 6, 282, 304
Peter, 79, 95, 108, 131, 174, 214, 270, 274, 293, 297, 300, 301, 303, 307, 310
Petersen, R., 122, 123, 135, 264, 304
Petuchowski, J., 97, 304
Phillips, G., 273, 274, 293, 304
Philo, 231
Pinnock, C., xvii, 60–62, 63, 158, 161, 171, 173, 205, 206, 221, 236, 278, 304

Index

Piper, J., 175, 304
plagiarism, 243, 252, 256
Plato, 231, 242, 243, 247, 250, 253, 281, 300
pluralism, x, xvii, 3–5, 6, 9, 13, 14, 16, 18, 19, 21, 23, 25, 27, 28, 34–36, 38, 39, 41, 43, 44, 46, 47, 49–51, 57, 61, 94, 98, 112, 114–16, 161, 200, 206, 209, 210, 220, 230, 235, 236, 239, 240, 261, 269, 272, 289, 291–95, 297–99, 301–5, 308, 310
pneumatology, xvii, 310
point-of-contact, 68, 231, 275–82
polytheism, 244
possessio, 283
Poythress, V., 81, 125, 167, 225, 304
praeparatio, 273
prayer, 19, 49, 103, 240
preaching, 46, 74, 101, 155, 165, 171, 174, 175, 191, 213, 240, 277, 280, 281, 292, 305
pre-messianic, xiii, 60, 61, 142, 157, 176, 286
premillennialism, 74, 80, 81
preparatio, ix, 11, 14, 42, 48, 144, 235, 273
preparation, ix, 11, 13–15, 29, 31, 33, 40–44, 45, 49, 50, 52, 54, 55, 57, 60, 68, 69, 134, 138, 139, 150, 188, 209, 219, 224, 226, 229, 230, 233, 235–39, 243, 247, 256, 257, 259, 261, 264, 265, 270, 273, 274, 278, 282, 283, 295, 298
Presbyterian, xxiii, 51, 79, 93, 290
Price, R., 239, 241, 252, 257, 304
prisca theologia, 68, 279–81
promise-fulfilment, 57, 74, 189, 198, 199
propaedeutic, 259, 260, 305
prophecy, 26, 30, 81, 99, 121, 130, 136, 137, 139, 184, 190, 198, 199, 201, 226, 246, 308, 309
prophet, 114, 227, 243, 259
Protestant Reformation, xxiii, 51, 78–80, 178, 182, 212, 301
Protestantism, 51, 80, 122, 259, 310

protoevangelium, 182, 206, 279
Proverbs, 231
providence, 14, 17, 26, 33, 40, 41, 45, 68, 69, 144, 158, 160, 208, 210, 247, 255, 271, 278
Psalms, 181, 195, 227
Pseudepigrapha, xxii
Punt, N., 148, 304
Puritan Theology, 79, 134
Pycke, N., 253, 254

Quigley, L., 297, 298

Race, A., xvii, 3, 11, 15, 18, 19, 44, 46, 57, 107, 109, 115, 180, 188, 209, 219, 240, 255, 256, 273, 275, 304
Rahner, K., ix, x, 7, 15, 20, 33–35, 36, 38, 40–44, 46–48, 49, 51, 57, 60, 61, 63, 64, 69, 70, 113, 156, 161, 163, 164, 205–7, 209, 261, 268–70, 271, 278, 280, 294, 301, 304, 309
Rajashekar, J., 305
Ratzinger, J., 48, 305
reconciliation, 91, 107, 115, 136, 155, 271, 282
redemption, 22, 62, 74, 77, 82, 88, 90, 95, 96, 116, 121, 122, 124, 125, 127–29, 130, 133–35, 137, 139–45, 147–49, 150, 152–58, 159, 164, 165, 169, 175, 180, 182, 184, 186–92, 196, 205–7, 208, 210, 212, 214, 216, 218, 222, 231, 232, 263, 275, 280, 281, 286, 289, 290, 295, 296, 298, 302, 305, 306, 308
redemptive, 10, 22, 52, 84, 111, 121–31, 135, 137–39, 140, 142–46, 147, 154, 155, 157–59, 164–66, 167, 169, 175, 176, 178, 180, 183, 184, 186–90, 192, 206, 209, 217, 218, 222, 226, 232, 233, 258, 262, 263, 265, 296, 303, 309
redemption history (*see* salvation history)

Index

Reformed Theology (*see also* Covenant Theology), viii, xi, xxiii, xxiv, 51, 63, 68, 74, 79, 80, 93, 95, 121, 122, 124, 125, 127, 128, 144, 148–50, 152, 153, 156, 165, 174, 177–83, 184, 186, 188–90, 191, 193, 194, 197, 200, 203, 208, 219, 280, 289, 290, 296, 297, 298–300, 301, 306, 308, 309
Reidar, H., 298
relativism, 9, 115
religion, ix, x, xiii, xvii, xix, xxii, xxiii, 5, 8, 11, 12, 21, 23–25, 29–35, 36, 39, 40, 42, 43, 50, 52–62, 66, 68, 73, 80, 93, 100, 113–15, 143, 161, 163, 164, 204, 207, 208, 214, 216, 230–32, 233, 235, 237, 239, 241–43, 246, 249, 254, 255, 260, 264–82, 285, 291, 293, 296, 298, 300–302, 306
religions, iii, iv, vii, viii, ix, x, xi, xiii, xv, xvii, xviii, xix, xxi, xxii, xxiv, xxv, 1, 3–17, 19–69, 70, 72, 74, 76, 80, 97, 104, 111, 113–17, 120, 122, 124, 129, 131, 132, 136, 139, 141–43, 149, 154, 161, 163, 164, 177, 204–8, 210, 213, 220–24, 228, 230, 232, 233, 235–43, 244, 246–60, 261, 264–72, 273, 275–79, 281–89, 290, 292–96, 297, 299–301, 302, 304–10
   lawful, ix, x, 34, 36, 44, 61, 113, 114
religious instrumentalism, 9, 63, 64
replacement theology (*see also* supersessionism), vii, 12, 53, 78, 82–86, 88, 90, 92, 93, 115, 132, 200, 203, 222, 294, 299, 309
restrictivism, 6, 172, 173, 302
revelation, x, xiii, xvii, xviii, 4, 5, 8, 11, 14–18, 19, 21–33, 36, 37, 40, 42, 43, 47, 49–51, 52, 55–59, 60, 62, 64–66, 67, 69, 74, 75, 77, 82, 94, 95, 97, 107, 112, 114, 122–32, 133, 135, 140, 141, 143–45, 147, 158–62, 163, 168, 169, 171, 173–75, 179, 182, 185, 186, 188, 191, 200, 204, 205, 207, 208, 210, 218, 220, 226, 227, 231, 233, 234, 236, 243–45, 253, 254, 259, 260, 263, 265, 267, 268, 270–72, 273, 276–82, 283, 287, 289–91, 294, 295, 297, 298, 301–3, 304, 306
   general, 58, 68, 159, 161, 168, 175, 226, 233, 255, 267, 273, 275, 279, 282, 287
   history of, 147, 260
   ignorance, 19, 64, 157–63, 166, 168, 171, 172, 174–76, 291
   special, 18, 30, 38, 58, 67, 68, 125–27, 158, 162, 163, 171, 175, 206, 267, 273, 280, 281, 287
   special, modalities of, 287
   times of ignorance, 64, 69, 157, 163, 164, 166, 168, 171, 174–76
Reymond, R., 127, 128, 143, 144, 158, 178, 181, 183, 184, 189–91, 192, 216, 305
Richardson, A., 260, 305
Ridderbos, H., 83, 125, 142, 145–47, 148, 165, 167, 213, 216, 305
righteousness, 103, 108, 109, 168–70, 181, 188, 192, 193, 200, 214, 215, 217, 218, 241, 245, 255, 300, 306, 308
Roberts, A., xxvi, 292, 299, 305
Robertson, O. P., 150, 179, 183–89, 191, 193, 194, 197, 198, 201, 202, 212–14, 305
Roman Catholicism, vii, xi, xix, 13, 20, 25, 39, 43, 44, 46–50, 51, 64, 90, 94, 95, 108, 113, 156, 164, 212, 248, 268, 279, 294, 296, 297, 301, 302, 305
Romans, 19, 59, 78, 85–91, 92, 94, 101, 103, 105–9, 110, 116, 130, 155, 159, 160, 166, 168–70, 171, 175, 214, 215, 224, 254, 255, 274, 291, 293–95, 298, 302, 303, 306, 307
Rommen, E., 300
Rosenzweig, F., 95–97, 290, 296, 305
Rosner, B., 297
Rottenberg, I., 89, 305

321

Index

Ruether, R., 95, 97, 106, 111
Ruokanen, M., 47, 305
Rust, E., 144, 146, 147, 151, 152, 305
Ryrie, C., 173

sacrifice, 77, 152, 153, 155, 168, 193, 194, 201, 215
Saldanha, C., 23, 240, 241, 247–51, 253, 255–57, 306
salvation, viii, ix, xiii, xvii, xviii, xix, xxiv, 3–9, 12–14, 16, 17, 21, 22, 24–38, 40–48, 50, 57, 58, 60–64, 66–68, 70, 73, 77, 82, 83, 86–88, 89, 91, 92, 94, 96, 98–100, 103–11, 113–15, 116, 121–25, 129–33, 134, 136, 138–42, 144, 146–48, 149, 151, 152, 154–56, 163, 165–69, 170, 172–76, 177, 180, 182–90, 192, 195, 197, 204–18, 219, 221, 222, 228–30, 232, 236–38, 240, 247, 248, 256–58, 260, 262–66, 269, 270, 272, 279, 280, 285–87, 288, 290–94, 296–98, 300–302, 304–6, 307, 310
salvation history, xiii, xxiv, 12, 14, 21, 22, 25, 28, 32, 34–36, 37, 40, 41, 43, 57, 60, 61, 70, 77, 83, 88, 92, 99, 105, 115, 121, 123–25, 129–33, 134, 138–40, 141, 156, 168, 170, 176, 177, 180, 183, 185–87, 188, 190, 195, 197, 204–6, 208–12, 214–16, 221, 222, 229, 237, 238, 248, 256, 258, 262, 264, 266, 269, 270, 285, 286, 288
   as Christocentric, 103, 171, 256
   Christ-event, xiii, xxiv, 15, 34, 38, 42, 43, 50, 98, 99, 112, 114, 125, 138, 139, 141–45, 146, 152, 154, 157, 163, 164, 166, 167, 169–71, 173, 175, 176, 209, 215, 221, 228, 229, 238, 248, 261, 269, 286
   consummated, 77, 133, 139, 140, 145–47, 151, 152, 169, 196, 259, 263, 282
   epochal nature, 124, 127–29, 135, 140, 176, 183, 190
   horizontal dimension, 131, 138, 139, 141, 147
   Jesus Christ as the mid-point of, viii, 123, 138, 141–43, 144, 155, 156, 167, 176, 286
   organic character, 124, 126, 129, 137, 165
   particularity, 188, 209, 210, 222, 265, 270, 279
   prehistory of, 21, 28, 32, 35, 43, 125, 269
   vertical dimension, 131, 138, 139, 141, 147
salvific, xiii, 4, 7, 8, 10, 12, 16, 27, 33, 35, 38, 40, 47–49, 50, 57, 60, 62, 69, 77, 85, 94, 99, 103, 108, 112, 115, 188, 192, 207–9, 221, 249, 257, 280, 293
samsara, 272
sanctification, 26, 127, 165, 217
Sanders, E. P., 85, 105, 108, 203, 306
Sanders, J., xvii, 6, 8, 172, 173, 306
Sarah, 99, 212, 213
Satan, 78, 183, 185
Satyavrata, I., 51, 53, 54, 56, 306
Sauer, E., 121, 133, 306
Schaff, P., 135, 289, 306
Schleiermacher, F., 11, 80, 259, 306
Schlette, H., 247, 248, 306
Schmidt, W., 267, 306
Schreiner, T., 168, 181, 202, 215, 217, 219, 220, 306
Scott, J., xxii, xxiii, 191, 292, 295, 298, 306, 308
Scripture, xix, 9, 46, 60, 64, 65, 75, 84, 90, 92, 109, 116, 122, 123, 129, 133–35, 137, 138, 171, 174, 178–80, 181, 184, 189, 204, 207, 209, 211, 216, 224, 227, 241, 242, 262–64, 265, 267–69, 270, 275, 279, 283, 286, 289, 307
Scriptures, xiii, xxii, xxv, 7, 11, 13, 14, 50, 52, 56, 67, 73–75, 77, 82, 100, 108, 112, 123, 124, 127, 129, 132,

Index

134–36, 137, 139, 140, 158, 195, 197, 204, 205, 208, 209, 224, 229, 243, 257, 259, 264–68, 270, 273, 274, 281, 283, 287, 289, 295, 300, 304, 306, 308, 309
Seifrid, M., 108, 306
sensus divinitatis, 276
Seth, 188, 281
Sharpe, E., 53, 54, 224, 291, 306
Sheba, Queen of, 60
Shedd, W., 148, 306
Shem, 189
Shenk, C., 64, 208, 233, 236, 271, 272, 279, 306
Sigountos, J., xvii, 241, 242, 246, 249–55, 257, 290, 293, 306
sin, 63, 66, 77, 106, 108, 143, 144, 152, 155, 159, 160, 163, 165, 167–69, 175, 176, 181–87, 189, 190, 192, 194, 201, 210, 213, 245, 259, 271, 276, 290
Sinai, 96–98, 108, 114, 182, 191, 193, 194, 196, 197, 199, 200, 204, 212, 213, 218, 219
Singh, S. S., 51, 298
Skarsaune, O., 306
Sloyan, G., 81
Socrates, 15, 31, 240, 241, 244–46, 247, 254, 257, 281
Sonderweg, 105, 106, 294, 308
    Christusweg, 106
    sonderplatz, 106
    Toraweg, 106
soteria, 277
soteriology, xviii, xix, 5, 7, 58, 74, 93, 95, 102, 108, 111, 115, 116, 129, 136, 149, 169, 192, 208, 279, 280, 287, 294–96, 298, 302
    ontology and epistemology, *relationship between*, 5, 6, 8, 41, 62, 82, 154, 266
    ordo salutis, 165, 166, 169, 176, 237, 286
Soulen, K., 75–77, 82, 116, 307
Spillman, J., 94, 99, 100, 116, 307
spirituality, 68

Stackhouse, J., xvii, 302, 307
Stamn, J., 307
Stendahl, K., 105, 307
Stibbs, A., 155, 307
Stoeckle, B., 207
Stott, J., 110, 307
Stransky, T., 299
Stravinskas, P., 48, 307
Strickland, W., 215, 299, 302, 307
substitute, 77, 181
substitutionary, 155, 194
Sullivan, F., xvii, 13, 17, 24, 45, 47, 48, 307
supersedes, 197
supersessionism, vii, 76–78, 80–82, 84, 86, 87, 90, 92–94, 95, 98, 101, 103, 111, 112, 115, 116, 309
supersessionist, 82, 115
supralapsarianism, 144
syncretism, 140

Talbert, C., 107
Talmud, xxii, 268
Tanenbaum, M., 289, 307
Tannach, 104
telos, 150, 202
Tennent, T., 243, 246, 250, 251, 253, 273, 307
Tertullian, 14, 80, 123, 178
Testament
    New, iv, xxii, xxiii, xxv, 7, 16, 25, 34, 35, 38, 50, 52, 53, 56, 61, 64, 67, 74, 75, 83, 85, 86, 88–90, 96, 100, 102–4, 106–8, 111, 115, 121–25, 127, 130–32, 136, 138–40, 141, 143, 145, 146, 151, 153, 154, 162, 165, 166, 170, 171, 173, 175, 178, 184, 190–92, 197, 199–203, 204, 215, 216, 219, 223, 224, 226–28, 229, 231, 232, 235, 236, 247, 258–66, 269, 274, 279, 289, 291, 295, 297, 299, 300, 302–6, 308–10
    Old, ix, x, xiii, xxi, xxii, xxiii, 7, 10, 12, 15, 16, 18, 19, 21, 26–28, 30–32, 34, 35, 38, 47, 50, 52, 54,

Testament (*continued*)
  56, 60–68, 73, 74, 77–81, 84, 88,
  89, 103, 107, 108, 115, 121–25,
  128, 130–32, 135–37, 139, 142,
  146, 158, 159, 167, 169–73,
  175, 177, 179, 184, 189–91, 192,
  194–200, 203–5, 207, 209–11,
  215, 216, 218, 221–27, 228, 231,
  238, 240, 243, 244, 246, 247, 251,
  255–69, 273–75, 279–81, 284,
  289–93, 295, 297, 301–7, 310
theocracy, 194, 218
theonomy, 122
theosis, 272
Thielman, F., 202, 307
Thils, G., 42
Thomas Aquinas, 26
Tiessen, T., xvii, 8, 9, 18, 63–69, 70,
  157, 160, 161, 171–73, 240, 261,
  278, 307
Torah, 108, 191, 218, 227
Torrance, D., 307
Torrance, J., 307
Torrance, T., 140, 144, 150–54, 307
Trinitarian, xvii, 37, 39, 51, 178, 229,
  298
Trinity, xvii, 21, 68, 98, 149, 180, 187,
  207, 235, 291, 294, 296, 299, 308
typological, 5, 218, 228, 263, 304
typologies, 8

unbelief, 88, 103, 105, 130
unbelievers, 88, 110, 160, 216, 301
unevangelized, xvii, xviii, xix, 6, 7, 9,
  28, 30, 60, 66, 67, 136, 142, 149,
  158, 159, 162, 163, 172–74, 185,
  188, 206, 240, 286, 287, 301, 302,
  306, 307
universalism, 92, 148, 210, 273, 291,
  293, 307
universalist, 148
universalistic, 187, 206, 208, 210
universality, 205, 293, 307

Van Drunen, D., 180, 308
Vanhoozer, K., 291

Vanlaningham, M., 308
Vatican Council, xviii, 7, 44, 46–50, 62,
  64, 94, 108, 111, 236, 267, 293,
  301, 304, 305, 308, 310
Veliath, D., xv, 20, 21, 23, 25, 27, 29, 32,
  42, 47, 48, 308
Vempeny, I., 207–9, 266, 269, 270, 308
Vischer, W., 263
Visser, P., 276, 277, 309
Vlach, M., 84, 309
Vos, G., 125–29, 134, 137, 146, 178,
  181, 184–86, 188–90, 197, 202,
  213, 296, 309
Vriend, J., 289, 290

Warfield, B. B., 148, 309
Watson, F., 160, 166, 167, 201, 261,
  262, 277, 309
Wells, D., 125, 145, 309
Westerholm, S., 309
Westermann, C., 303, 304, 307, 310
Whaling, F., 11, 12, 14, 57, 309
Williams, D., 158, 309
Williams, R., 271, 309
Williamson, C., 98, 99, 178–82, 309
Williamson, P., 91, 178–82, 185, 187,
  195–99, 201–3, 212, 309
Willowbank Declaration, 109, 110, 310
Wilson, A., 201, 309
Wilson, M., 309
Witherington, B., 158, 162, 163, 168,
  310
Woodbridge, J., 292
Woudstra, M., 92, 310
Wright, C., 7, 8, 189, 191, 195, 196,
  198, 199, 208, 210, 211, 225,
  226, 232–34, 235, 246, 264, 265,
  271, 310
Wright, D., 44, 46, 51, 91, 310
Wright, N. T., 91, 96, 105, 111, 115,
  138, 204, 310

Yahweh, 172, 189, 193, 201, 208, 297
Yahwism, 302
Yarbrough, R., 121, 165, 216, 310

Index

Zaehner, R. C., 11
Zechariah, 127, 201, 309
Zimmerli, W., 310
Zoroaster, 24

www.ingramcontent.com/pod-product-compliance
Lightning Source LLC
Chambersburg PA
CBHW061425300426
44114CB00014B/1542